Gaelic Language Revitalization Concepts and Challenges

Collected Essays

Gaelic Language Revitalization Concepts and Challenges

Collected Essays

Emily McEwan-Fujita

bradan press

Halifax, Nova Scotia
Canada

Gaelic Language Revitalization Concepts and Challenges: Collected Essays was first published by Bradan Press in 2020.

Bradan Press, Halifax, Nova Scotia, Canada
info@bradanpress.com
www.bradanpress.com

Text copyright © 2020 Emily McEwan-Fujita

Cover design and "Anti-Gaelic Bingo" cards copyright © 2020 Emily McEwan-Fujita

Author photo copyright © 2020 Rebecca Clarke

Map of Scotland in Figure 8.1 based on an original image created by Eric Gaba, licensed under Creative Commons Attribution-Share Alike 4.0 International.

All rights reserved. No part of this publication may be reproduced, distributed, or transmitted in any form or by any means, including photocopying, recording, or other electronic or mechanical methods, without the prior written permission of the author and the publisher.

Library and Archives Canada Cataloguing in Publication

Title: Gaelic language revitalization concepts and challenges : collected essays / Emily McEwan-Fujita.
Names: McEwan, Emily, author.
Description: Includes bibliographical references and index.
Identifiers: Canadiana 20189067144 | ISBN 9781988747361 (hardcover) | ISBN 9781988747378 (softcover)
Subjects: LCSH: Scottish Gaelic language—Revival.
Classification: LCC PB1514 .M34 2018 | DDC 491.6/3—dc23

ABOUT THE COVER ILLUSTRATION: The "Anti-Gaelic Bingo" cards depicted on the cover were originally created by the author for posts on the blog Gaelic.co (see McEwan-Fujita 2015 and 2018). The Gaelic-language instructions in the bingo cards on the cover are similar to the English-language instructions on the original cards, which read: "Prejudice against Gaelic getting you down? Next time you read about Gaelic in the news, why not play 'spot the stereotype' with a light-hearted game of... ANTI-GAELIC BINGO." The free space in the middle of the centre card says "SAOR" ("free" in Gaelic). Contact Bradan Press for reprint permission at info@bradanpress.com.

Contents

List of Figures	vii
List of Tables	viii
Sources	ix
Introduction	xi

Part 1 Knowledge and Representation — 1

1. Sociolinguistic ethnography of Gaelic communities — 3
2. Research and representation: Gaelic and Uist — 43

Part 2 Discourses of Death and Revitalization — 59

3. Discourses of death and denigration: Ethnolinguistic differentiation and the ideology of contempt — 61
4. "Gaelic doomed as speakers die out"? The public discourse of Gaelic language death in Scotland — 95
5. Language revitalization discourses as metaculture: Gaelic in Scotland from the 18th to 20th centuries — 115

Part 3 Neoliberalism and Language Revitalization — 149

6. Neoliberal discourses of Gaelic language revitalization: The "Gaelic economy" and "rocketing spending" — 151
7. Neoliberalism and minority language planning in the Highlands of Scotland — 179

Part 4 Language Ideologies and Affect — 197

8. Ideology, affect, and socialization in language shift and revitalization: The experiences of adults learning Gaelic in the Western Isles of Scotland — 199

9   Ideologies and experiences of literacy in interactions between adult Gaelic learners and first-language Gaelic speakers in Scotland   245

10 Working at "9 to 5" Gaelic: Speakers, context, and ideologies of an emerging minority language register   267

Part 5:   New Speakers and Reversing Language Shift 285

11 Gaelic revitalization efforts in Nova Scotia: Reversing Language Shift (RLS) in the 21st century   287

12 "Ìle ga Bruidhinn": A community-based Gaelic dialect revitalization proposal   315

References   333

Index   365

List of Figures

Figure 4.1: The dissemination of the scientific "100,000 speakers" concept   103

Figure 7.1: The structure of public funding for the Gaelic in the Community Scheme   184

Figure 8.1: Map of Scotland   200

List of Tables

Table 8.1: Gaelic language abilities claimed by respondents in the 2001 Scottish census — 206

Table 8.2: Scottish census results: Number of Gaelic speakers living in the Uists and Benbecula — 210

Table 8.3: Jean's denial and disclosure of Gaelic speaking, Gaelic speaking ability, and availability of Gaelic speakers with whom to speak — 218

Table 9.1: Gaelic language abilities claimed by respondents in the 2001 Scottish census — 253

Table 9.2: Gaelic language abilities claimed by respondents in the 2001 Scottish census, broken down by age — 261

Table 11.1: A summary of Fishman's Graded Intergenerational Disruption Scale (GIDS) — 291

Table 11.2: Fishman's EGIDS – Expanded Graded Intergenerational Disruption Scale — 293

Table 11.3: Revitalization EGIDS Levels — 295

Table 11.4: The Nova Scotia Gaelic EGIDS — 298

Sources

The following chapters in this book have been previously published and are used with permission from the following sources:

Chapter 1, "Sociolinguistic Ethnography of Gaelic Communities" was published in *The Edinburgh Companion to the Gaelic Language*, ed. Moray Watson and Michelle Macleod, 172–217. Edinburgh: Edinburgh University Press, 2010.

Chapter 4, "'Gaelic Doomed as Speakers Die Out'?: The Public Discourse of Gaelic Language Death in Scotland" was published in *Revitalising Gaelic in Scotland: Policy, Planning and Public Discourse*, ed. Wilson McLeod, 279–293. Edinburgh: Dunedin Academic Press, 2006.

Chapter 5, "Language Revitalization Discourses as Metaculture: Gaelic in Scotland from the Eighteenth to Twentieth Centuries" was published in *Language & Communication* 31 (1), 48–62, 2011.

Chapter 7, "Neoliberalism and Minority Language Planning in the Highlands and Islands of Scotland" was published in *International Journal of the Sociology of Language*, 171, 155–171, 2005.

Chapter 8, "Ideology, Affect and Socialization in Language Shift and Revitalization: The Experiences of Adults Learning Gaelic in the Western Isles of Scotland" was published in *Language in Society* 39 (1), 27–64, 2010.

Chapter 9, "Ideologies and Experiences of Literacy in Interactions between Adult Gaelic Learners and First-Language Gaelic Speakers in Scotland" was published in *Scottish Gaelic Studies* 26, 87–114, 2010.

Chapter 10, "Working at '9 to 5' Gaelic: Speakers, Context, and Ideology of an Emerging Minority Language Register" was published in *Sustaining Linguistic Diversity: Endangered and Minority Languages and Language Varieties*. Georgetown University Round Table on Languages and Linguistics Series, ed. Kendall A. King et al., 81–93. Washington, DC: Georgetown University Press, 2008.

Chapter 11, "Gaelic Revitalization Efforts in Nova Scotia: Reversing Language Shift in the 21st Century" was published in *Celts in the Americas*, ed. Michael Newton, 159–185. Sydney, NS: Cape Breton University Press, 2013.

Chapter 12, "Ìle ga Bruidhinn: A Proposal for Gaelic Dialect Revitalization" will be published in *Proceedings of Rannsachadh na Gàidhlig 2014*, ed. Sheila M. Kidd, Thomas Owen Clancy and Roibeard Ó Maolalaigh. Glasgow: Celtic and Gaelic, University of Glasgow, forthcoming.

Introduction

The research that forms the basis for this book was once criticized by someone who claimed that Gaelic language revitalization "after all... isn't exactly rocket science." I didn't know whether to laugh or cry when I heard that, because although the claim was made for all the wrong reasons, it was technically right. Language revitalization isn't rocket science—it's far more difficult!

Rocket science, or any other type of engineering, formulates and solves problems. Get the math right, solve the problem, double-check your work, and move onto the next problem. Did the solution fail, or create another problem? Find the math or programming mistake and fix it. Human error is a factor, but math and physics are reliable.

Language revitalization, on the other hand, is not simply a matter of math. It is the effort to "save" a language that is gradually going out of daily use among a group of people. Defined in more precise terms, language revitalization is:

> the attempt to add new linguistic forms or social functions to a language which is threatened with language loss or death, with the aim of increasing its uses and users (King 2001, 4).

Kendall King's definition above is extremely useful. However, my favourite description of language revitalization tells us not only what it is, but what it's like. This description comes from the late Alexandra Jaffe's research on Corsican language revitalization in linguistic anthropology. Jaffe analyzed a television broadcast of a public Corsican language event, in which the Corsican comedian Teatru Mascone said that saving the Corsican language is:

> as difficult as castrating a grasshopper... In other words, something that we can't ever accomplish. But we can save the language if we want to, if Corsicans who speak it, do speak it (Jaffe 1996, 824).

Why is it so difficult to save a minority language? Why is it so impossible, yet still possible? Because it involves a deliberate effort to reshape people's opinions, ideas, feelings, and behaviours. In this regard, I would say that language revitalization research is more similar to public health research and policy in its complexity and difficulty, than it is to rocket science.

Some universities contain schools of public health, where numerous scientists are employed to research, teach, and train future policymakers in multiple areas including epidemiology and nutrition. Have these scientists solved all the problems of public health yet? Hardly; look at what is happening now with vaccines. Although some deadly diseases were nearly eradicated by public health programs of vaccination, we are now seeing a resurgence of preventable diseases like measles worldwide. Why? Because a significant number of people have come to fear vaccines themselves as dangerous, instead of recognizing them as a tool in the fight against deadly diseases. How did the idea take hold that vaccines were dangerous? It's complicated, but the process seems to have included alarmism and deliberate disinformation campaigns on the internet; a dishonest vaccine safety researcher who faked his results; growing distrust of doctors, pharmaceutical companies, and governments; and trust of unqualified charismatic celebrities rather than experts.

Parents and other caregivers who are responsible for taking their children to get immunized—a behaviour—have opinions, ideas, and feelings. Through a combination of fear, mistrust, and misplaced trust, some have decided that it is in their children's best interests not to immunize them against deadly diseases. The caregivers engage in other behaviours instead: avoiding immunization, eating certain foods which they mistakenly believe will provide protection against deadly diseases, applying for non-medically-necessary vaccine exemptions, homeschooling to avoid public health requirements for public school students, and advising other parents to do the same.

Unfortunately, their behaviour is now affecting a much larger group of people due to the weakening of "herd immunity." People whose vaccines didn't provide full immunity, and people who cannot be immunized for medical reasons, are now catching measles and other deadly yet preventable viruses again in increasing numbers.

How can we get more parents to vaccinate their children? Some try to present more accessible scientific explanations to parents. Some try to do it by changing the laws to eliminate more vaccine exemptions. Some try to shame anti-vaccine parents by publicly mocking them on social media. Whether any of these strategies can head off another deadly pandemic still remains to be seen.

In language revitalization, we also see how the opinions, ideas, feelings, and behaviours of parents and other caregivers can be influenced by a whole range of sources: other parents, friends and family members, educators, celebrities, the media, the internet. What Gaelic-speaking parents heard from authority figures for a very long time was that they ought to speak only English to their children. Many parents were told by educators, clergy, and others to fear for their children's economic future if the children were raised with Gaelic. Then, the presence of growing numbers of English-speaking children increased the pressure on other parents and children to conform. The result was that many parents stopped transmitting Gaelic to their children in Gaelic "heartland" areas.

Even when caregivers do speak Gaelic to their children in the 21st century, the metaphorical "herd immunity" to language shift is gone. There is almost nowhere that children or even adults can be in a totally Gaelic-speaking environment. They will hear English and encounter prejudice against Gaelic almost everywhere they go. The media still regularly repeat the stereotypes and lies that Gaelic is pointless, outdated, and inferior. We are still fighting lies and unfounded fears about Gaelic; see Ch. 3–6 of this volume for examples.

Because of this, it becomes an even greater challenge to ensure that children and adults get enough Gaelic interaction and input to build up their language skills to fluency, and just as importantly, to build a positive emotional connection to the language.

Fifteen nations built the International Space Station. That is literal rocket science. But can we cooperate to save minoritized languages like Gaelic from going out of daily use? It's not rocket science. It's a far trickier job. It's a matter of coordinating struggles for recognition, rights, and funding at the national and regional levels. It's a matter of combating misinformation online, of defending ourselves from trolls and attacks, while refraining from attacking, trolling, and discouraging others, including fellow Gaelic speakers. It's a matter of helping people to feel willing, happy, safe, and supported as they go about using the language in daily life. Along with wisdom, experience, and research-based planning, the positive emotions of safety, trust, and enjoyment are key to language revitalization.

I now live in Nova Scotia, Canada, where I work towards Gaelic language renewal every day in ways both personal and professional. My experiences over the past decade here have increased my conviction that Gaelic language revitalization research should be conducted with ethics, compassion, cooperation, and a view towards immediate practical application.

The chapters of this collection represent the themes of my research on Gaelic during my years as an academic in the field of linguistic anthropology. They include most of my published work, as well as three previously unpublished papers. The chapters are based on research conducted from 1998–2011, mainly in Scotland, and mainly relating to the period 1990–2000. Although subsequent events such as the passing and implementation of the Gaelic Language (Scotland) Act 2005 are not discussed for the most part, nevertheless the themes and issues in this collection hold continuing relevance for the situation of Gaelic and other minority languages.

The "Anti-Gaelic Bingo" cards depicted on the book's cover were originally created for posts which I wrote in 2015 and 2018 for my blog, Gaelic.co. The concept was inspired by my research in the Western Isles in 2000, when an interviewee described wanting to make bingo cards of regional development jargon to play with co-workers during meetings with funding agencies. The concept of using bingo cards this way was already out there: *The Guardian* newspaper had run a "Lingo Bingo" feature in 1999 with bingo cards making fun of neoliberal business jargon.

In the Anti-Gaelic Bingo cards, I collect, quote, and distill the various discourses of death and denigration which I labeled and analyzed in Chapters 3–6 of this book. I designed the cards to convey the tiresome repetition of these ugly stereotypes in the media in a visually engaging way, using humour to try to break out of the never-ending dialectic of denigration and redemption.

I wish to thank a number of organizations and individuals who supported my research in various ways from 1998 to 2011. Field research on which this book is based was financially supported by the generous assistance of a Columbia University Council for European

Studies/Society for the Anthropology of Europe Pre-Dissertation Field Research Grant in 1998, a Social Science Research Council/American Council of Learned Societies International Dissertation Research Fellowship in 1999–2000, National Science Foundation Dissertation Improvement Grant #9974337 in 1999–2000, and a Faculty European Grant, a Hewlett International Grant, and a Central Research Development Fund Grant from the University of Pittsburgh 2007–2009.

Writing was financially supported in 2002–2003 by the Markovitz Dissertation Fellowship from the Division of the Social Sciences, University of Chicago, for the dissertation best exploring an aspect of the linkages and influences between social and economic behaviour, and a National Endowment for the Humanities Summer Stipend in 2010. In 2011, the Foundation for Endangered Languages in the UK provided a grant to my nonprofit organization Dìleab for Gaelic-medium childcare training in Nova Scotia. Our experiences of organizing this training and other activities helped inform my writing of Chapter 11.

The late Robert Storey opened doors in Scotland and made the research possible on which the majority of these chapters are based. He supported Gaelic language and culture, and he believed in the power of anthropology to do some good for Gaelic, and for that I will always be grateful. Chapter 3 is dedicated to his memory.

Nancy Dorian has been a mentor and an inspiration to me in so many ways, ever since agreeing to be a member of my dissertation committee in 1998. Without her support this book would not exist, and I dedicate it to her.

Emily McEwan-Fujita
Halifax, Nova Scotia
March 2019

PART ONE

Knowledge and Representation

CHAPTER 1

Sociolinguistic Ethnography of Gaelic Communities

1   Introduction

The sociolinguistic ethnography of Gaelic speakers in various settings, from crofting communities to language planning institutions, has contributed significantly to knowledge about the structures, uses, and meanings of Gaelic in the 20th and 21st centuries.[1] Such studies have also made contributions to the theoretical understanding of language shift and ethnolinguistic revitalization processes. Sociolinguistic ethnography, which involves "a close look at language practices in a specific setting" (Heller 2007, 13), has been conducted on Gaelic from a range of allied and overlapping disciplinary perspectives, including social and cultural anthropology, linguistic anthropology, education, linguistics, sociolinguistics, sociology, and the sociology of language. The term "sociolinguistic" indicates a basic research focus on language in its social context, while the term "ethnography" refers to the methodological orientation of these studies toward largely qualitative field research on the linguistic, social and cultural aspects of people's lives.

The reliance of these studies on ethnographic fieldwork to collect data distinguishes them from historical and literary research on Gaelic, and from policy-oriented surveys. Surveys and questionnaires are essential research tools, but researchers who conduct both surveys and ethnographic observations of the same population report difficulties with administering the surveys and disparities between responses and observed behaviour (Coleman 1975, 184–205; Dorian 1981a, 157–178; Pollock 2006, 189).[2] The advantage of fieldwork is that it lets local interests and categories emerge from the data (e.g., MacKinnon 1977, 7); it also helps the analyst to understand and convey the feel of everyday life in a particular place. Ethnographic fieldwork in the anthropological tradition requires long-term residence in an area and is therefore time-consuming, demanding, and potentially expensive:

the informal standard is to spend at least one full year "in the field," often with shorter follow-up visits. The most common methodologies of ethnographic fieldwork are participant observation and ethnographic interviewing. Participant observation involves active participation in local activities, while making fieldnotes with analytical observations about these activities, with the aim of combining both insider and outsider perspectives on the culture. Ethnographic interviewing is more loosely structured than other forms of interviewing, but aims to systematically elicit people's views and information on particular topics of cultural relevance. Other methodologies such as household censuses, language attitude and usage surveys, proficiency tests, elicitation, and matched guise experiments may also be used, but they are administered by the researcher in the field, and participant-observation fieldwork informs their design and interpretation. The fieldwork also may inform various modes of discourse analysis on media and other texts gathered in the field and archives.

This chapter will consider the theoretical contributions that sociolinguistic ethnographies of Gaelic have made to the study of two main areas: processes of Gaelic language shift in traditional Gaelic communities, and Gaelic language revitalization efforts in traditional and new Gaelic communities. Finally, the chapter considers issues of power and representation, disciplinary boundaries, and continuity in research on Gaelic-speaking communities, and future directions in the sociolinguistic ethnography of Gaelic speakers.

2 Processes of Gaelic Language Shift in Traditional Gaelic Communities

National boundaries, disciplinary interests, and institutional configurations have contributed to the temporal and conceptual gaps in academic approaches to Gaelic. Since the 19th century, Scottish folklore collecting (which later became ethnology) has focused on documenting the oral traditions of Gaelic speakers before they vanish, while Celtic studies developed around history, literature, and philology (MacKinnon 1977, 4). Although 20th-century ethnologists, geographers, and dialectologists conducted field research in the Highlands, ironically Scottish anthropologists preferred to focus on more "exotic" peoples, and mostly non-Scottish anthropologists and linguists pioneered the study of Gaelic speakers in sociolinguistic context.

MacKinnon was the first to undertake a sociolinguistic ethnography of Gaelic speakers in the early 1970s, though he describes some sociologically-aware approaches predating his own in Scotland (J.L. Campbell 1950) and Canada (Dunn 1953; D. Campbell and MacLean 1974), which have been followed by others in history and historical geography (Durkacz 1983; Withers 1984; Withers 1988). MacKinnon also points out that polymath scholars in the field of Celtic have produced valuable work describing changes in structures, uses, and ideologies of Gaelic in sociocultural context (including Black 1994; Gillies 1980, 1989; Macaulay 1976–78, 1978, 1979; 1982a, 1982b, 1986; Meek 1996, 2001; Thomson 1979, 1994; Thomson and Grimble 1968). In these cases, the authors' personal experiences of Gaelic-speaking communities, combined with their linguistic competence and interest in sociolinguistic matters, allow them to closely approximate the combined outsider-insider perspective of the ethnographer.

Overall, ethnographies in the traditions of anthropology and sociology of language have described and analysed the cultural meanings and practices of Scottish Gaelic in the context of ongoing processes of language shift from Gaelic to English from the 1950s to the 2000s (with a gap in the 1960s). Most studies have focused on the meanings and uses of Gaelic in traditional geographically-bounded community contexts: Hebridean crofting communities (Coleman 1975; Ducey 1956; Ennew 1980; Macdonald 1987, 1997b; MacKinnon 1977; Parman 1972, 2005; Vallee 1954), East Sutherland fishing communities (Dorian 1981a; Constantinidou 1992), and Canadian Cape Breton mining and fishing communities (Mertz 1982a). This focus is characteristic of the early orientation of the anthropology of Europe toward "community studies" of traditional, bounded rural localities (Cole 1977).

However, in the 1970s, anthropologists began to take a broader perspective, grounding their fieldwork in one or several crofting townships while insisting on analyzing wider processes of sociocultural change. These studies have explored the relatively recent 19th- and 20th-century historical construction of the "crofting community" and its cultural and social legitimation by community residents through the ongoing construction of history and local identity (Parman 1972;

Parman 1990, 2005; Ennew 1978, 1980; Macdonald 1987, 1997a). Rather than seeing the situation as modernity overtaking static tradition, anthropologists have chosen to highlight the intensive and longstanding economic relationships of crofting communities with mainland Scotland, the United Kingdom, the European Union, and the global capitalist economy. The most comprehensive ethnographies of this kind focused on the industries of Harris Tweed, fishing, and oil on the Isle of Lewis (Ennew 1980; Parman 1990, 1993).[3]

As Condry points out, however, the study of language in Scotland from a social perspective was severely lacking (1983, 89). Many of the ethnographic studies of Gaelic-speaking communities from the 1950s through the 1980s omit detailed information about the Gaelic linguistic practices and ideologies of their subjects, taking them for granted as a backdrop to the dramas of croft succession or underdevelopment. Nonetheless, such studies do provide a valuable and consistent picture of the local cultural, social, and economic practices of kinship, childrearing, social hierarchies, land ownership, agriculture, and religion that have formed the fabric of life in Hebridean crofting communities where Gaelic was or is still spoken by half or more of residents. The studies by and large focused on the institutions of crofting and Presbyterianism on Lewis and Skye; with the exception of Vallee (1954), Catholic Gaelic-speaking Hebridean communities have not been studied ethnographically, which constitutes a major oversight.

The sociolinguistic studies that treat Gaelic-speaking practices in detail have found that most Gaelic speakers assign very local meanings to Gaelic in crofting communities. Participant observation of daily life on Barra in the 1950s (Vallee 1954), Lewis in the 1970s (Coleman 1975), Harris in the 1970s (MacKinnon 1977), Skye in the 1980s (Macdonald 1997b), and South Uist and Benbecula in 2000 (McEwan-Fujita 2010a; see Ch. 8, this volume) all reveal remarkably consistent conceptions of Gaelic speaking as a local practice in the nexus of home, family, and crofting community. As a result of ongoing language shift, Gaelic has been conceptualised by these speakers as most suitable for interactions with kin and neighbours, and has been ideologized as egalitarian. For example, in the 1970s MacKinnon found in questionnaires with adults (1977, 167) and secondary pupils, and group interviews with secondary pupils from Harris (1977, 125), that "The significance of Gaelic within community life is seen essentially as being bound up with everyday behaviour patterns" (1977, 167) and not with, for example, political institutions.[4]

The local significance assigned to Gaelic is the result of speakers noticing and interpreting the replacement of Gaelic with English in non-domestic, non-locally-oriented domains. Domains may be defined as "distinct spheres of activity" (Dorian 1981a, 75) or "major clusters of interaction situations that occur in particular multilingual settings"; these tend to be organized around either "institutional contexts" or "socio-ecological co-occurrences" (Fishman 1965, 231). Identifying changes over time in the pattern of language usage in different domains is one way of conceptualizing and tracking language shift. Two other complementary ways of conceptualizing and measuring shift are assessing changes over time in the number of speakers in particular geographical areas, and testing for changes in linguistic proficiency across different generations of speakers.[5]

Ethnographies of Gaelic-speaking communities describe similar patterns of distribution of Gaelic & English use across various domains in the latter half of the 20th century. Domains are not universal, but specific to various cultural contexts and must be defined through the use of ethnographic observation (Dorian 1981a, 75). Some domains can be clearly associated with particular times, places, and settings, while others are more dispersed (Coleman 1975, 171). Due to the relative cultural and geographical homogeneity of the Highlands and Islands, analysts have identified similar types of domains in various Gaelic-speaking communities. In early 20th-century East Sutherland, for example, the domains of Gaelic use identified by Dorian were home, work (mainly fishing-related), and religion (Presbyterian), while the domains of English were the national secular institutions (school, political parties, military, police, the courts), local public life, and print media (Dorian 1981a, 75). Dorian reported that in some domains Gaelic and English linguistic compartmentalization was complete, while in others, such as the work domain, it was only partial. Factors such as setting and interlocutor could also determine or constrain language choice in various domains (1981, 76–77).

In the early 1970s on Harris, Gaelic represented solidarity and was used predominantly in the home and in local locations such as the post office, local shop, traveling grocery van, church, and village entertainment, while as in East Sutherland, "The domains within which English predominates are those where a power dimension is conspicuously to the fore" (MacKinnon 1977, 28). However, MacKinnon (1977, 145–149) points out the weaknesses of the domain concept, which cannot adequately explain the nuances of such activities as counting in English in an otherwise Gaelic conversation with a friend, or "the [recent] shift in favour of Gaelic in the usage with local councillors" (1977, 147). The relative nature of the domain concept is also apparent in the fact that Gaelic might be used at clubs or society meetings, "where solidary group values are encouraged" (MacKinnon 1977, 28) despite the expectation that English might be used in such a "public" domain. Moreover, because Gaelic actually had a temporarily stable legitimate place in the community, with some locally-prestigious uses such as the use of an elaborated code in religious worship (Dorian 1978e), MacKinnon proposed "demesne extension" as a supplementary concept to Weinreich's "dominance configuration," in order to "associate together the situations which predominantly call for one particular language and distinguish those other situations predominantly calling for the other language" (1977, 148).[6] His aim was to show how language use points up clusters of culturally-significant social behaviours, without focusing exclusively on the symbolic dominance of one language over another, which indeed cannot explain why Gaelic-speaking communities have continued to maintain and reproduce themselves for as long as they have.

Coleman's findings complement MacKinnon's critique of over-reliance on the analytical concept of domain to document or explain language shift. On the basis of participant observation and interviewing Coleman identified six domains for the 1970s crofting community of Carloway: household (both nuclear and extended), neighbourhood and peer group, religion, education, official and administrative, and speech to animals. He used these domains as the basis for a language usage survey conducted at the end of his fieldwork. On the basis of casual observation, Coleman had hypothesised that in his survey results, these domains would be arrayed in sequence such that "household" would be the domain where the most Gaelic and least English was spoken in Carloway, while the "official and administrative" domain would be the least Gaelic and most English, and that the older the respondent, the more domains in which they would report speaking Gaelic and the younger the respondent, the more domains in which they would report speaking English. However, the results of his survey did not completely or even strongly uphold this hypothesis (1975, 189). He speculated inconclusively on the various reasons why, including the fact that other factors such as personal affect (positive personal relationship, hostility, fear), topic, style of speech, and setting could affect code choice, that the survey was flawed,[7] and that men aged 20–29 who stayed in the village underwent a social transition from "student" to "adult worker" which may have caused them to over-estimate their usage of Gaelic at the time they were surveyed (Coleman 1975, 189–201).

Mertz (1993) made a further critique of the application of domains, based on a retrospective critique of her research methodology in Cape Breton. In examining and attempting to code her data, she found that interviewees responded to questions from a very different perspective than her own. For them, Gaelic or English "language preference is not an attribute of an individual approaching situations in the abstract, but is embedded in the complex social life of the community, a life that is not primarily understood as a series of segmented 'domains'" (Mertz 1993, 168). She therefore recommended that researchers not lose sight of the "focus on the unexpected, creative, contingent, and socially dependent character" of language choice in particular settings (Mertz 1993, 170). Such an approach would stay centered, in anthropological fashion, on the concerns of the people themselves who are under scrutiny.

For the sake of convenience, both Gaelic-English bilinguals and researchers often refer to the verbal repertoire of Gaelic-English bilinguals as composed simply of "Gaelic" and "English." However, analysts have identified multiple varieties of both Gaelic and English in 20th-century Gaelic-speaking communities based on observation and subjects' metalinguistic descriptions (Dorian 1981a, 84). Coleman identified three main varieties of Gaelic in 1973 in Carloway, providing transcripts of examples in an appendix. The first is "Casual Gaelic," sometimes called by the Carlowegians *"Gàidhlig taobh an teine"* ["fireside Gaelic"] or "tinker Gaelic" due to "the unusual intonational contours and stress patterns on the island [...], the ellipsis and often very fast and blurred pronunciation, and the very large amount of lexical borrowing from English that is found in rural Lewis" (Coleman 1975, 152). The second variety is "Careful Gaelic," characterized by far fewer English borrowings, which was almost never spoken and not very often encountered in Carloway except in the media, and which was "most closely associated with secular Gaelic literacy, language loyalism or public speech before socially heterogeneous audiences" (1975, 154).[8] The third was "Church Gaelic," a formal variety used for prayer and Presbyterian worship, "distinguishable by its archaic lexicon, its often distinctive intonational contours, the formality of settings in which it is used, and the near total lack of English loan words" (1975, 158).[9] Coleman also identified two varieties of English: "Island English" influenced by Gaelic syntax, semantics, and the distinctive prosody of Lewis Gaelic (1975, 166); and a regional "Standard English" which was spread by secondary education, the media, and English-speaking incomers (1975, 168).

Dorian likewise identified four varieties of Gaelic and at least four varieties of English spoken and heard in the east-coast fishing villages of Brora, Golspie, and Embo. The varieties of Gaelic included: (1) the local East Sutherland Gaelic (ESG), (2) other regional dialects, (3) a standard she called "textbook Gaelic" (analogous to Coleman's "Careful Gaelic"), and (4) "church Gaelic" which had a "higher prestige among ESG speakers than other regional dialects or textbook Gaelic" (1981a, 90).[10] Both Coleman and Dorian noted that the varieties can be described linguistically, but their relative prestige among speakers must also be considered from a sociolinguistic perspective.

Intra-situational codeswitching patterns, or patterns of switching between Gaelic and English in a single interaction, also received consideration from Coleman (1975) and Dorian (1981).[11] Coleman identified three types of switching, which he labeled instrumental, metaphorical, and macaronic. Instrumental switching from English to Gaelic could be done to "create temporary relations of solidarity for some specific purpose," particularly by a superordinate person to a subordinate person, while instrumental switching from Gaelic to English could be done to "establish or maintain social distance between interlocutors" (Coleman 1975, 210). Metaphorical switching "involves the use of a second code in the context of the first for purposes of emphasis, humour, exaggeration, ridicule, etc." which in Coleman's account, nearly always involved the incorporation of English phrases into Gaelic speech (1975, 211–212). Macaronic switching "involves the apparently unconscious, sometimes very rapid, alternation between English and Gaelic within the context of a single speech event, act or utterance." Coleman speculated that this seemed to be a partial blending of the codes of Gaelic and English into a single macaronic code. It was found when the interlocutors were "coordinate bilinguals of similar social status and background, and are very well known to each other"; when "participants in the speech situation are deeply engrossed in a task-oriented activity (as opposed to a speech-oriented activity)," "most often when topics of conversation are highly concrete, local, with a minimum of abstraction or esoterica," and often in the speech of people who were aged 25–55 at the time of the study (in other words, in the speech of people born in 1918–1948), but never, he noted, in the speech of people over 55 (born before 1918). Coleman also noted that certain individuals were known for macaronic switching, a point that Dorian also mentioned (1981, 98–99). In fact, in East Sutherland, Dorian observed that codeswitching was mostly done by individuals who were known for the behaviour, rather than on a community-wide basis, and also that the majority of codeswitching behaviour in the community was precipitated by a change in interlocutor (1981, 99).

Mertz described different codeswitching patterns related to the more advanced state of language shift in late 1970s Cape Breton. After intergenerational transmission had largely ceased in the 1930s and '40s, the status and popularity of Gaelic increased in Mabou and the North Shore, in part through the influence of urban revival efforts. Although English remained dominant, once again it became socially acceptable to use Gaelic in public domains; this took the form of a Gaelic "greeting routine" followed by a shift to English, and a "peppering" of Gaelic words, phrases, and sentences in English conversations (1982a, 245–59), which served the functions of marking boundaries (the beginnings and endings of conversations, or boundaries between insiders and outsiders) and expressing strong emotion or humour. Thus even though Gaelic was not being used in great quantity, its use was symbolically significant to the community (Mertz 1989, 113–4).

One notable aspect of both intra- and inter-situational codeswitching in Gaelic-speaking communities is a set of rules dictating the choice of Gaelic or English with particular interlocutors. This "ethic of politeness" or "ethic of accommodation" is similar to that found in other European situations of minority language shift (Gal 1979, 165–166; Woolard 1989, 68–82; Trosset 1986, 169). This pattern of behaviour is both an indicator and perpetuating mechanism of language shift, since it works to reduce the number of situations in which Gaelic may be spoken. Coleman, who has described the phenomenon most thoroughly, terms it the "Courtesy Rule" and sums it up as "English to strangers, Gaelic to locals" (Coleman 1975, 74–94). "English to strangers" means that "To speak Gaelic in Carloway in the presence of a non-Gaelic speaking stranger is widely and unequivocably considered to be extremely bad manners, even if the stranger is situationally peripheral" (1975, 80). The corollary to this is that for local Gaelic-English bilinguals, Gaelic must be used with other locals in informal situations; to use English would be negatively evaluated as "snobbish." Dorian also described such norms for East Sutherland (1981, 79), and McEwan-Fujita identified them in Uist in 1999–2000 (2010a; see Ch. 8, this volume). Coleman believed such behaviour to be a result of the defensive position of Gaelic speakers vis-à-vis English and English speakers in Scotland. He theorized that such behaviour helps Gaelic-English bilinguals to enact cultural norms of politeness and hospitality while simultaneously maintaining a sociolinguistic boundary between themselves and non-Gaelic speakers, whether consciously or unconsciously (Coleman 1975, 84).

Naming and kinship are areas of classic anthropological interest, and distinctive local Gaelic naming practices and orientations toward kinship, as well as the changes apparent in such practices with the process of language shift, are described in nearly every ethnography of a crofting community, sociolinguistic or otherwise.[12] The two main kinds of practices described are patronymics (*sloinnidhean*) and by-naming or nicknaming, which are generally used together (MacKinnon 1977, 23) to designate individuals in areas where many people have traditionally shared a relatively small number of surnames and given names. MacKinnon (1977, 22–24), who reports having documented naming practices and collected patronymics from three villages in Harris during his fieldwork, gives the example of a patronymic: "*Rachag Dhòmhnaill Iain Raghnaill* ("Little Rachel (daughter) of Donald (son) of John (son) of Ronald)," whose "official" English name might be Rachel MacLennan (1977, 22–23). MacKinnon observed that "Widespread knowledge of people's *sloinnidhean* acts as a constraint upon behaviour—and a form of social control. The *sloinneadh* places a person immediately upon a network of kin-relationships, as the form of the *sloinneadh* is a skeletal pedigree" (MacKinnon 1977, 23).[13] Ethnographic descriptions indicate that across the mid- to late-20th century the practice was incorporated or modified into a more general cultural practice of nicknaming or by-naming in both Gaelic and English (Dorian 1970; Ennew 1980, 77–79; Mertz 1982b).

Such abbreviated usage is also apparent in Dorian's thorough and detailed description of the Gaelic nicknaming and by-naming system of the East Sutherland coastal villages of Brora, Golspie, and Embo (Dorian 1970).[14] Dorian described five basic types of nicknames in great detail: (1) basic genealogical, which were like traditional Gaelic patronymics, but only included two generations, ego and first ascending, which could refer to the father or the mother (but could be different even for siblings); (2) descriptive; (3) derisive; (4) nonsense; and (5) secondary genealogical patterns built on the second, third, and fourth groups (Dorian 1970, 306). With reference to the first type, MacKinnon noted that typical usage in Harris in the 1970s would also consist of the brief two-generation *sloinneadh*, often in combination with other kinds of nicknames. Ennew noted that in Lewis, nicknames of the second, third, and fourth types could come from either family context in early childhood, or from the peer group, and might be English or Gaelic (1980, 77–79).

The nicknames circumscribed and enacted kinship and friendship networks at the local level, even encompassing the "exiles" who were away from the village or island (Mewett 1982b, 234–239). In day-to-day interaction, licence to use an offensive nickname to a person's face marked in-group status or intimacy (Dorian 1970; MacKinnon 1977). However, Dorian noted that there were social hazards for the outside researcher and even for residents of the community who did not speak Gaelic: the inability to determine which non-genealogical nicknames were offensive and which were not, and to determine to which kinship and friendship networks the nicknamed person belonged, meant that the outside researcher and even community residents who did not speak Gaelic ran the risk of inadvertently using a derogatory nickname to the person's face. In East Sutherland, this represented a hazard in varying degrees depending on English-speaking residents' kinship connections with the village and whether they were raised there or recent arrivals (Dorian 1970, 305–6, 315).[15]

Anthropologists have also noted the semantic re-calibration of Gaelic terms to English ones in the context of language shift. Ardener (1989, 134–154) presented an account of traditional Gaelic calendrical terms as non-linear and non-fixed: "the Scottish Gaelic year consisted of overlapping categories of weather and agricultural epochs, into which three or four ancient ritual seasons intruded." Such a system was incompatible with the modern Gregorian calendar. By tracing dictionary definitions over time, Ardener demonstrates how dictionary makers created standardized meanings for the context-dependent Gaelic calendrical terms, with the result that now every "English" month and season has its exact equivalent in modern Scottish Gaelic (Ardener 1989, 142).[16] Macdonald also discussed how the semantic domain of colour terminology in Gaelic may be shifting from a different cultural system to a code for English-language categories (Macdonald 1997b, 249–250; Macdonald 1999). Using examples from her research in Skye, Macdonald noted how this phenomenon seemed to be accompanied, or perhaps caused, by a shift on the part of native Gaelic speakers towards viewing written sources as prior and superior to oral ones, and English as the yardstick against which Gaelic should be measured (Macdonald 1999, 187–188, 190–191).[17]

Academically, Scottish Gaelic is best known outwith Scotland as a relatively well-documented case study of Celtic and Western European language shift. Scholars have taken multiple approaches in their theoretical contributions to our understanding of the sociolinguistic processes of Scottish Gaelic language shift. Coleman (1975) focused on the way that rapid social change, speech networks, and language acquisition patterns were contributing to the shift from Gaelic to English in 1970s Lewis. MacKinnon (1977) focused on the institution of the schools, and assessing changes in linguistic practices over time, in the context of local community life in 1970s Harris. Mertz

(1982a; 1989) focused on how people's views about the social meaning of language use acted as a "filter" through which they interpreted the significance of macro-level economic and social change, in the process of shift from Gaelic to English in 1970s Cape Breton Island, Nova Scotia. Dorian's work from the 1960s to the 2010s focused on structural, social, and ideological aspects of shift from the isolated east-coast dialect of East Sutherland Gaelic to English among the formerly stigmatized fisherfolk and their descendants. Dorian has made substantial contributions to the theorization of structural change in an obsolescing dialect (1972, 1973, 1978b, 1978c, 1978d, 1986, 1989), social, cultural, and ideological aspects of language shift (1977, 1978a, 1980a, 1980b, 1981a, 1981b, 1982b, 1987, 1993a, 1994a, 1998, 2009),[18] and micro-level linguistic variation (1982a, 1993b, 1994b, 2001, 2010).

Coleman (1975) describes how a variety of factors in 1970s Carloway contributed to the process of language shift from Gaelic to English. The most basic factor was rapid social and economic change in the village beginning around the time of World War I, which had increased in pace since World War II, bringing radical changes in the standard of living in the 1950s and 1960s, greater integration into the rest of the UK and the corresponding self-consciousness of the villagers as marginal, isolated, and backward (Coleman 1975, 69–70). After World War II, changes in subsistence and employment patterns contributed to the development of social networks along lines of sex, age, and religion, with deep cleavages that severely reduced the amount of verbal interaction across network lines, including interaction in Gaelic. Men became isolated in their working lives (in croft work or weaving tweed), and women were even more isolated in their homes, since at that time women had few opportunities for employment or a social role outside the home (Ennew 1980, 80–81). According to Coleman's observations, relations between the sexes, between the generations (1975, 65–67), and between the so-called "Bible" and "bottle" networks could be antagonistic, sometimes greatly so (also see Parman 1972, Ennew 1980). He visualized the village of Carloway as "consisting of a number of partially discrete speech networks based upon age, sex and religion." Although kin, neighbours, and communal work groups could help overcome the boundaries between these networks, the kinds of social situations in which people would cross network boundaries to speak to one another were declining in number due to a variety of interrelated factors, including outmigration, the decline of the village center, television, patterns of solitary labour, and the disappearance of local weddings. Thus,

> speech has tended to run more and more into isolated pockets. Differences of age, sex and religion, which once might have been largely overlarded by the sheer quantity and intricacy of social interaction, have taken on the nature of barriers inhibiting communication. Behind these barriers, and particularly among the young, changes in the quantity and quality of Gaelic spoken are rapidly taking place (Coleman 1975, 108).

Local cultural patterns of language acquisition in household, village, and school settings also contributed to language shift: in the household with mockery and inconsistent treatment of children by adults (see also Parman 1990) and the devaluation of children's speech, in the village with peer group interactions in English, and in the school which was an "essentially English domain." All interacted to produce processes of language shift from Gaelic to English on the west side of Lewis. These changes were accompanied by an entrenched pattern of sociolinguistic boundary maintenance of locals versus strangers through the "ethic of accommodation" as previously described.

Kenneth MacKinnon's (1977) study focused on the schools as an institution, within the context of Gaelic-speaking crofting communities in Harris. His field research included extensive participant observation which informed his main focus on questionnaires, surveys, interviews, a matched guise test, and group interviews with children. MacKinnon found that language shift from Gaelic to English was ongoing, both in real diachronic comparison (re-administering a survey of Harris school children in 1972–73 which he directly compared with the results of a 1957–58 survey conducted by the Scottish Council for Research in Education), and in virtual diachronic comparison of different age groups in the adult population in a language attitudes and usage survey.

One of MacKinnon's most important conclusions was about the role of the secondary education system in the Western Isles in the process of language shift. Secondary education was structured so that the most academically able girls and boys (and the girls in greater proportion), who also tend to be the most loyal to Gaelic and the most literate in Gaelic (MacKinnon 1977, 134, 169), were selected to be sent away from Harris (either to Portree or Stornoway). This became an "anticipatory socialization" for them eventually migrating away altogether to seek work (MacKinnon 1977, 104). In contrast, the young women who stayed in their Harris communities showed lower language loyalty to Gaelic on MacKinnon's survey (MacKinnon 1977, 161). Thus, summing up, "The individuals who might possibly change the situation are the ones most likely to leave the island" (MacKinnon 1977, 169).[19]

Based on his community- and island-level research, MacKinnon theorized about the macrosociological process of Gaelic language shift (MacKinnon 1977, 32–36). He proposed the "'cultural retreat' or *Gàidhealtachd* model" of shift, which is not so much a model as a description of the process, represented by the "ever-shrinking area" of the *Gàidhealtachd* in histories, maps, and census reports. MacKinnon pointed out that reality is not so neat, since Gaelic-English contact also occurs *within* Gaelic-speaking areas. To the extent that language shift is a function of language contact and culture clash, MacKinnon saw the "cultural retreat" as a result of the combination of four different factors or mechanisms which have been "differentially operative" in Gaelic-speaking areas: (1) "Clearance": large numbers of the native population are removed from an area, leaving it relatively depopulated; (2) "Economic Development": new forms of economic organization bring about cultural changes requiring language-shift; (3) "Changeover": new people migrate into an area while local people leave or die; and (4) "Social Morale": in which the power relationship changes between social groups identified with the local and the national language, such that "the local community loses confidence in its system of values" through the local influence of national institutions such as education and the church (1977, 35). No single factor among these can completely account for Gaelic language shift, and different combinations may account for shift in different areas.

While MacKinnon's work on Gaelic language shift on Harris and in national perspective is best known among Gaelic scholars in

Scotland, Nancy Dorian's work on the isolated east-coast dialect of East Sutherland Gaelic (henceforth ESG) is best known among scholars working on issues of language shift, obsolescence, and revitalization outside of Scotland. Dorian conducted field research in Scotland periodically from 1963–1978; her research by telephone began in 1991 and ended in the late 2010s (personal communication). Her 1981 book *Language Death* describes the history of Gaelic in Sutherland, the sociolinguistic situation of ESG in the latter half of the 20th century, and the linguistic changes to ESG in the final phases of obsolescence (Dorian 1981a, 4). Even in examining some of the most detailed and technical linguistic aspects of structural change and variation in an obsolescing variety of Gaelic, she has related these phenomena to the social conditions experienced by Gaelic-speaking individuals in communities undergoing language shift.

Dorian (1981a) details the historical formation of the east coast fishing communities of Brora, Golspie, and Embo, and the way in which their poverty, segregation in particular villages or neighbourhoods, occupational distinctiveness, and "linguistic lag" relative to the surrounding populations of agriculturalists and townspeople (Dorian 1980b, 38–39) led to their stigmatisation as a separate ethnic group from the early 19th to the mid-20th centuries. By the time Dorian worked with the population, her adult research participants had been raised in fisherfolk households but had found other occupations, since the fishing declined around the turn of the 20th century and even more around the time of World War I (Dorian 1981a, 46–47).

Dorian also explored and introduced several other important sociolinguistic aspects of language shift: "tip," "semi-speakers," and the variations among speakers' usage in a relatively homogeneous speech community. "Tip," Dorian theorized (1981, 51), might occur after several centuries of stable bilingualism or monolingualism; although the tip might have been "several centuries in the making," it would take a certain push in the form of an economic or social event to turn the tide. For example, Coleman (1975) identified a stable boundary between English-speaking Stornoway and the Gaelic-speaking rural crofting townships in Lewis in the description of Smith (1948) and located a "tip" to English in the rural areas by the time of his own research in the early 1970s. Mertz (1989) located a "tip" in Cape Breton, Nova Scotia during the 1930s–40s.

Semi-speakers are bilinguals who control the majority language well, and the minoritized language imperfectly, but who nonetheless choose to use the minoritized language frequently with others (1980a). Dorian found that ESG semi-speakers were characterized by two or more of the following factors: late birth order in a family with many children, having been linguistically socialized by an older relative outside the nuclear family, having a strong sense of community identity, particularly if they had been in exile, and/or an inquisitive and gregarious personality (1981, 107; also see 1980a for further discussion of the last three factors). Dorian also noted that semi-speakers have no conversation partners with whom Gaelic is the preferred language (2009).

Elizabeth Mertz's 1982 dissertation makes a theoretical contribution to the study of language shift based on the case of Gaelic in Cape Breton Island, Nova Scotia, Canada. She conducted research in the late 1970s in the communities of Mabou and the North Shore, chosen for their contrasting characteristics: Mabou was more affluent, more diverse in religious backgrounds though with a strong Catholic presence, settled relatively early (beginning in the 1790s), and had easier access to the outside world; the North Shore was settled later (beginning in 1843) by poorer, predominantly Presbyterian emigrants, and was a more geographically-isolated area with less access to natural resources.

These two communities, despite their contrasting situations, underwent a relatively rapid shift from Gaelic to English as the language of socialization of their children at about the same time, in the 1930s and 1940s. Mertz concludes that since they both underwent the shift at about the same time, despite being so different, ideological factors common to both areas, which she terms "metapragmatic views" (people's views about the social meaning of language use) must have been significant factors in parents' shift from Gaelic to English as the language of socialization for their children. Mertz argues that although factors like migration to industrial centers, economic dominance of majority language speakers, state boundaries, political events, and ecological and demographic factors have been significant in Cape Breton and other cases of language shift (1982a, 17–18), simply identifying various external "factors" and imputing a direct causal relationship does not help explain the relatively sudden tip from Gaelic to English in Cape Breton. Instead, speakers who observe and experience these "external" factors interpret them through an "internal" filter of cultural conceptions about the social nature of language, which Mertz terms a "metapragmatic filter." The particular filter that Mertz describes for Cape Breton consists of two main elements: (1) a view of Gaelic and English as incompatible (1982a, 175–8) and (2) a dichotomy between English and Gaelic such that English is seen as the language of the mainstream, the new, and progress, and Gaelic is seen as the language of rural areas, the old, and backwardness (1982a, 178–185). The former "provided the link between parents' desire for their children to learn English and their move away from Gaelic" (1982a, 178), while the latter took on "an economic focus" with the arrival of the Great Depression in the 1930s (1982a, 182). Specific evidence to support Mertz's hypothesis includes contemporary reports from the 1930s, oral histories, economic and general histories, archival records, and data from age proficiency profiles based on Gaelic language proficiency tests which she conducted.

3   Language Revitalization Efforts and New Gaelic Communities

Together with the focus on language shift, sociolinguistic researchers since the 1970s have increasingly turned their attention to Gaelic language revitalization efforts. These efforts create new kinds of social and linguistic identities, communities, and institutions, which in turn help dialectically shape the efforts themselves. Research on revitalization efforts focuses on the diversity and multiplicity of positions in, for, and against the revitalization of Gaelic, including conflict and accommodation between new and traditional cultural meanings of Gaelic, and new and emerging contexts and forms of use. Conflict arises because some people have difficulty accepting the legitimacy of new and diverse ways of conceptualizing Gaelic as a language, culture, or community (Oliver 2010, 18), especially when they have been socialized into conceptions of Gaelic as a "language of the local" in the crofting communities where concentrations of speakers are found (Oliver 2002, 160–161; Ch. 8, this volume). The paradox is that Gaelic-speaking areas are experiencing ongoing shift, even as Gaelic has been undergoing revitalization since the 1980s (or since the 19th century, if earlier efforts are included). How could Gaelic be experiencing a revitalization and a decline at the same time (Oliver 2002, 176)? Oliver has called the current revitalization efforts a "culturally imagined revival" rather than a "successful linguistic one" (Oliver 2002, 4). Lack of a successful linguistic revival to date may be attributed to: (1) the fact that the macro-level conditions contributing to language shift are extremely difficult for small groups to alter (see the discussion of Mertz 1982a below); and (2) the fact that once a revitalization effort is instituted, it generates a paradox of its own: in the process of garnering political support for a minoritized language and creating a standardized form to serve as the basis for education, such a movement further marginalizes the people who live in economically marginal rural areas and speak dialectal forms (Eckert 1983).

One of the biggest problems of Gaelic revitalization is why some native Gaelic speakers in Gaelic-speaking communities oppose or do not cooperate with revitalization efforts in their own communities. Various researchers have located the problem in the conflicts in cultural and sociolinguistic values between rural, crofting native speakers and urban, middle-class, university-educated activists. Coleman had noted of revitalization attempts in the 1960s and 1970s that they were based on either scholarly and "literary/antiquarian" orientations, or expatriate nostalgic romanticization of traditional Highland and island life. Both sets of values were meaningless to most of the Carloway crofters with whom he worked (Coleman 1975, 226–227).

Social anthropologist Sharon Macdonald engaged with this problem by focusing in part on the diversity and contestation emerging from Gaelic revitalization efforts on Skye. Her ethnography of a crofting community in Skye, based on Ph.D. thesis research conducted 1983–6, is about the ways that people who lived in a Gaelic-speaking area constructed their local identities out of a "repertoire" of available cultural meanings (1997a). Its major point is that identity, often conceptualized as fixed and inherent, is actually fluid and constructed or produced through ongoing social relationships, subject to ambivalence, diversity, and contestation.

As a precursor to her analysis of local Gaelic revitalization efforts, Macdonald presented ethnographic descriptions of everyday social relations and analyses of local cultural values in the crofting township.

She looked at the economic and symbolic roles of crofting in defining members of the community as "locals," and the way that crofters defined themselves as "classless" in contrast with "away" (1997, 117) while still being keenly aware of local differences in social status and power. She explored how nostalgia, exile, and emigration fed back into locals' understandings of place, and incomers' and locals' conflicting understandings of their own identity, belonging, and what it meant to be local.

Finally, Macdonald analyzed local-level disagreements and controversies over community-oriented Gaelic-related developments in the early to mid-1980s, including the village hall and the community cooperative (*co-chomunn*), which the Highlands and Islands Development Board intended to strengthen Gaelic as well as economic development in communities. Macdonald also described the competing English and Gaelic playgroups, and local parents' doubt and ambivalence over the Bilingual Education Project which was introduced on Skye in 1978. Macdonald showed how people constructed their opposing positions on these developments with reference to local cultural values and social relations (1997, 220). For example, in 1986 there was an existing playgroup in the crofting township. Two women helped to start a new *cròileagan* with newly-available HIDB funding, to provide a more intentionally Gaelic-medium and structured learning environment for their own children and others in the community. The women, who were both native Gaelic speakers (one raised in the township and the other elsewhere on Skye) articulated a number of reasons for wanting the playgroup. One criticized other local parents for "not bothering" with Gaelic (1997, 228). The other, concerned that her three-year old refused to speak Gaelic to her, worried that as a Gaelic teacher she would be judged negatively for trying to be "fancy" and teaching her son English (1997, 230). Local mothers who opposed the new playgroup (whose children could not speak Gaelic for the most part) criticized it on the grounds that they should not be made to feel excluded from the playgroup just because their children did not speak Gaelic and that language should not be used to divide people into different categories, and felt that the *cròileagan* would force the children to speak Gaelic (Macdonald 1997, 231). Macdonald identified a cultural repertoire of shared ideas among mothers on both sides about egalitarianism in local social relations (the avoidance of seeming "fancy"), the autonomy of children (in which education would provide the chance for their natural abilities to emerge), and disapproval of "pushing" and "forcing" children or adults to do anything (1997, 223–225, 232). Later, some mothers who initially opposed it ended up joining the Gaelic playgroup (1997, 243).[20]

There is also apparent conflict between attitudes and actions in support of Gaelic. Public support for Gaelic is now seen as a positive thing, and many people will make verbal expressions of support for Gaelic—but decline to speak it regularly themselves. Some will even teach it to others, or conduct other paid employment through the medium of Gaelic, while not speaking it regularly to their children or sending them to a Gaelic-medium playgroup or school (Coleman 1975, 229–230; McEwan-Fujita 2003, 116–118). As already discussed in the previous section, Mertz explains this conflict through the concept of "metapragmatic beliefs." Using the theories of Silverstein (1977, 1979) about the differing levels of awareness that speakers have about the structures and sociolinguistic functions of the languages they speak, Mertz theorizes that some beliefs about language are so deeply ingrained that speakers simply do not have conscious access to them (1982a, 261–272). They may deny holding such beliefs even if they are explicitly confronted with them. Local cultural concerns may also simply not include a need to explain language shift in the community, or culturally-relevant explanations may have been developed that do not match the ethnographic observations—for example, attributing to children themselves the choice not to speak Gaelic (Macdonald 1997, 223–225), even though children are linguistically socialized by their caregivers (Kulick 1992). Therefore, although Fishman (1991) included "prior ideological clarification" as a precursor to undertaking ethnolinguistic revitalization efforts, paradoxes and ideological conflict are in fact endemic to the process and it seems likely that such clarification may not be possible (Dauenhauer and Dauenhauer 1998).

Another problem of Gaelic revitalization efforts noted in sociolinguistic ethnographies (Coleman 1975, 225; Mertz 1982a) is a lack of coordination between various efforts across geographical space and across time. This fragmentation and lack of coordination may be a function of several issues, including the fact that due to historical prejudices and the unwillingness to commit financial resources, few regional or national-level governments give full, coordinated funding, legal, and logistical support to minority language movements (for the example of education, see critiques in Pollock 2006). The diversity in attitudes and experiences among Gaelic speakers also contributes to the fragmentation, as Coleman noted (1975, 225); in both Scotland and Nova Scotia, there has tended to be an ideological gap between urban and rural priorities, approaches, and concepts. Mertz's study of Gaelic-speaking communities in Cape Breton documented the scattered and uncoordinated local-level revitalization efforts in Nova Scotia from the 19th century to the late 1970s (1982a, 187–227). An additional factor in Cape Breton was a split between the Catholic west and south areas of Cape Breton, oriented toward Gaelic media from Antigonish, and the Protestant North Shore oriented toward the Sydney and Baddeck media and the Gaelic College (1982a, 210; Campbell and MacLean 1975, 222).

The role of "outsiders" of various kinds in ethnolinguistic revitalization presents us with another layer of complexity. Non-Gaelic speakers may be the ones to have denigrated the language in the first place, but other outsiders can help to restore social (and economic) value to the language, both to the outside world and in the eyes of speakers themselves. Mertz noted the contribution to the Cape Breton Gaelic revival of the urban and even international "outsiders," including hippies, "USers," and folklorists who visited and moved to Cape Breton, learned Gaelic and collected folklore, and demonstrated that some people outside of Cape Breton saw Gaelic as worthwhile (Mertz 1982a, 199). However, research in anthropology and ethnomusicology (Dembling 2005; Sparling 2003) reveals that the cultural orientations and priorities of native Gaelic speakers can be quite different from those of non-native speakers and non-Gaelic speakers. The latter groups, who are usually stronger in numbers or influence, may ironically end up imposing their own conceptions of "authentic" Gaelic culture onto the native Gaelic speakers, despite holding them up as paragons of authenticity, for example in regard to what constitutes the best or most authentic traditional Gaelic music and song. This is the paradox of minority language revitalization efforts: the more they proceed, the more they run the risk of marginalizing the cultural practices, views, and experiences of the very people whose language and culture they are meant to help (Eckert 1983).

According to a Corsican saying, saving the minoritized Corsican language is "as difficult as castrating a grasshopper" (Jaffe 1996, 824). Nonetheless, based on the cases of Scottish Gaelic and Irish, Dorian (1987) takes the view that language revitalization efforts are culturally useful, valuable, and laudable, even if they are not succeeding in reversing language shift. She has even advocated in the face of some opposition within her discipline that linguists who study minority languages and language shift could usefully take a position of advocacy, following the lead of speakers themselves, because when a researcher is working directly with speakers (or indeed collaborating with governments), there is no such thing as a neutral position (Dorian 1993a, 1994a).

On the whole, sociolinguistic ethnographies of Gaelic are descriptive of speakers, practices, and contexts, rather than normative or prescriptive (though some make recommendations for best practice in revitalization). But the disagreement in Gaelic-speaking communities that is documented by academics is sometimes interpreted by the national media, other outsiders, or community members themselves as pathological, rather than as a sign of a healthy, vigorous diversity (Macdonald 1997b).[21] Sometimes, "the Gaelic community" is held to an unrealistic standard, expected to show a united public face to the rest of the world (Macdonald 1997a). However, as Macdonald points out, it would only be logical for all Gaelic speakers to support all revitalization efforts if one assumes that Gaelic determines one's identity to the exclusion of everything else—a 19th-century romantic nationalist model of ethnolinguistic identity (Macdonald 1997a, 50–51, 219–220, 240–242).

In addition to studying the reception of revitalization efforts in traditional communities, sociolinguistic ethnographies of Gaelic revitalization have explored the new and changing contexts of use for Gaelic in institutions of education, the media, development, and language planning, with a focus on workplaces, classrooms, and the new and changing ideologies of participants. This represents a shift away from the traditional village study paradigm, to the study of new and emerging Gaelic "communities of practice" (Eckert and

McConnell-Ginet 1992; Wenger 1998; Oliver 2010) bound together by a shared workplace, a shared status as students on a course, or shared interests, values, or goals defined around the Gaelic language, and not necessarily by co-residence in a geographically-bounded community— or even a shared level of Gaelic language proficiency. Several recent studies of Gaelic-language and Gaelic medium educational practices, which are by definition oriented towards revitalization of the language, have focused on institutions, classroom practices, and students using a sociolinguistic ethnographic approach or survey informed by field experience (Gossen 2001; Oliver 2002; Pollock 2006). Other studies have focused on the attributes and experiences of adult Gaelic learners outside of institutional contexts (MacCaluim 2007; McEwan-Fujita 2010a; see Ch. 8, this volume).

Pollock (2006) conducted ethnographic research on the acquisition of Gaelic literacy in seven Gaelic-medium classrooms ranging from Primary 1 to 3 located in six local authority areas, together with interviews and questionnaires of parents, teachers, and education authorities.[22] She described and analyzed the available resources, the teaching techniques used to teach literacy, the behaviour of pupils, and the physical and sociolinguistic environment of the classrooms and the schools. While the Gaelic medium education (GME) system appeared to be "largely successful" in its goals stated in the National Guidelines for Gaelic 5–14 (Pollock 2006, 218), and literacy teaching in GME had made "significant progress," Pollock concluded that there were still a number of issues for concern. The first was uneven teacher training, which resulted in a wide range of teacher practices and competencies in the classroom. The second was a shortage of classroom resources, including Gaelic storybooks and reference books such as dictionaries (2006, 240). The third was not enough reading aloud in Gaelic taking place outside the school environment (2006, 243). Pollock cautioned that due to the limitations of her study, it was not possible to determine more than tentatively whether GME was successful in revitalizing Gaelic, but due to a range of factors and since the P1–P3 students were not reading Gaelic independently outside the school, "The children's academic success cannot […] be equated with the level of language use needed for Gaelic to be reinstated as a community language" (Pollock 2006, 239).

The research of James Oliver focused on the contextual and contingent nature of identities and the Gaelic language and culture (Oliver 2002, 2005, 2006, 2010).[23] His work aims to challenge the traditional bounded ideas about Gaelic and identity, showing instead how "multiple communities of practice... overlap with and extend beyond any bounded notion of Gaelic (as language, culture or community)" (2010, 4). In other words, there is not a single Gaelic community, but Gaelic communities, and even the most structured language planning efforts must take account of the multiplicity and constant change (2010, 5).

Oliver's dissertation research on Gaelic and young people's negotiations of identity was based on qualitative interviews and focus groups in the field with secondary pupils in Skye and Glasgow in 2000 (Oliver 2002). He found that the young people he interviewed felt themselves to be Scottish, and thought of Gaelic as Scottish, but this in itself did not motivate them to learn Gaelic or actually speak it outside of school. The Glasgow interviewees were more likely to identify themselves or others as "Gaels" purely on the basis of linguistic proficiency, while Skye interviewees were more likely to take family heritage and place into account, but again, this did not imply any increase in Gaelic usage. Gaelic medium education had not made these young people fluent in Gaelic, which supports Pollock's conclusions above, and the learners were not really keen to become Gaelic speakers in the future. There were differences between how young people in Skye and Glasgow viewed Gaelic, but overall, for the fluent speakers, Gaelic was "not used greatly" at home, and "sparsely used," if at all, at school (2002, 164).[24] In Skye, the local community networks of Gaelic and the social meaning of place were important in the definition of a "Gaelic identity." By contrast, in Glasgow, "a supra-community of dispersed Gaelic speakers and Gaelic learners" (2002, 167) rather than a traditional crofting community, linguistic ability was most important in the definition of a "Gaelic identity," with a distinct focus on the Gaelic media (and the possibility of getting a job).

The sociolinguistic bottom line, and "the dilemma for assessing Gaelic revival, then, is this: increasing the number of young people able to speak Gaelic does not directly equate with the reversal of language shift" (Oliver 2002, 169). Oliver concludes that while GME can be highly supportive of Gaelic in families, nevertheless a

Gaelic-speaking family unit and a Gaelic-speaking geographically-bounded local community giving a "local sense of relevance" are essential to intergenerational transmission of the language (2002, 171).

Anthropologist Andrew Gossen's (2001) Ph.D. dissertation was an ethnography of Sabhal Mòr Ostaig, the Gaelic college on the Isle of Skye (hereafter SMO), based on archival research, interviews, and nine months of participant observation on the *Cùrsa Comais* in 1998–1999. This was also the first year of the new Gaelic and Related Studies Scheme BA degree courses[25] of which the Cùrsa Comais had newly become a part. Gossen's study focused on "student response to the new degree courses and the problems that surfaced at the college during a period of dramatic institutional change," setting students' experiences in the context of the history of the "maverick" institution and its relatively recent and ongoing integration into the University of the Highlands and Islands Millennium Project as it was known at the time of his fieldwork (Gossen 2001, iii). Gossen concluded that SMO as an institution was so internally diverse, that it could not be approached and analyzed through a single theoretical approach (2001, 290).

Gossen described the structure of the new four-year degree courses, the first ever to be offered entirely through the medium of Gaelic, and their role in the larger curriculum of an institution "devoted to revitalization." The aim of the degree course was to "cultivate a particular worldview that is centered on the Highlands and Islands instead of the traditional foci of Edinburgh or London," and to train future leaders of the Highlands and Islands "to define and address local problems" in order to "bring about the social, cultural, and economic revival of the area" (Gossen 2001, 296). On the basis of his study of this strategy, Gossen pointed out that although revitalization is a social movement, analysts must focus not only on mass participation, but also on "strategic positioning" (and, I would add, on the efforts of key individuals doing the positioning) in order to understand how Gaelic language revitalization efforts work (Gossen 2001, 298).

Gossen's ethnography described the staff, faculty, and students of that academic year, a group that shared a commitment to Gaelic language and culture and to SMO, but who also held quite different understandings of what the mission and goals of SMO were. The views varied from rigid and essentializing to open and constructivist, and caused interpersonal conflict to erupt at times over contradictions between SMO's various missions and constituencies.

Gossen also explored the dilemmas of tertiary-level education through the medium of a minority language, which included in this case problems with using Gaelic in tertiary-education courses in which the bulk of course readings were in English, issues of coining new academic terminology for areas like social science, students' difficulty writing research papers in Gaelic based on reading materials in English, and the difficulty of finding instructors with both the necessary academic background and linguistic skills to teach university-level courses in Gaelic (2001, 128–129). Students were also not happy about being used as test subjects for the new degree course, as they felt was the case.

All of these ethnographies of Gaelic education note one crucial point: that pupils and students for the most part were not speaking Gaelic outside of the school, and at the school for the most part were only speaking Gaelic to the teacher in the classroom. Gossen (2001, 149) describes how the patterns of language choice among students at SMO were impacted by the presence or absence of the "institutional gaze"—in other words, when college staff were within earshot, Cùrsa Comais students tended to converse in Gaelic, but in private, all but a few habitually spoke English with one another (Gossen 2001, 149). These findings underline a number of points about language revitalization: (1) how difficult it is to engineer an all-encompassing sociolinguistic environment, even in the "bubble" of a residential college, when surrounded by a dominant language and culture; (2) how difficult it is to linguistically socialize, or re-socialize, people when there is no single compelling ideological motivation to unify them; and (3) the fact that one cannot rely on a single institution or "fix" to "save" a language.

Alasdair MacCaluim's (2007) study of adults learning Gaelic generates a detailed demographic description of Gaelic learners inside and outside Scotland, with the large number of open-ended comments by respondents providing a particularly interesting window on the learners' experiences.[26] MacCaluim analyzed the social identity of Gaelic learners as such, describing how the categories of "learner" and "native speaker" are culturally constructed (2007, 102). He explored the difficulty of acquiring Gaelic as an adult; this is due to several factors, among them fragmented provision in Scotland, the challenges of acquiring a language after the "critical period" of childhood, and a lack of interaction between learners and native speakers. A number of open-ended survey responses mentioned tension between learners and native speakers, which manifests in learners' complaints that native speakers do not always support their efforts. Indeed, learners challenge popular and traditional views of the contexts where Gaelic is appropriate (MacCaluim 2007, 89), namely the home-family-crofting community nexus and the Hebridean islands. MacCaluim discusses how learners could contribute to reversal of language shift and act as "consciousness raisers" for the language (2007, 93), in the process finding their own social identities evolving as their linguistic proficiency increases (2007, 97). While MacCaluim treats adult Gaelic learners as a national and even international group, those who live in traditional crofting communities seem to face greater barriers in their efforts to construct their own meanings for Gaelic. McEwan-Fujita identifies emotional stances of wariness, blame, and shame in adult learners' descriptions of their community-based Gaelic learning experiences in the Western Isles (2010a; see Ch. 8, this volume). These adult learners are socialized by Gaelic-speaking family members and community members into the etiquette of accommodation, in ways that make it difficult for them to speak Gaelic regularly and thus contribute to language revitalization in traditional Gaelic-speaking communities.

Glaser's (2007) comparison of Gaelic and Sorbian minority language revitalization efforts takes a broad ideological perspective on issues of cultural and linguistic distinctiveness as perceived by members of linguistic minorities. The Gaelic portion of her study was based on interviews with 53 Gaelic "elites" (defined as members of Gaelic-oriented societies, journalists, academics, artists, teachers, school and nursery staff, parents, and students of the language) across Scotland, together with a survey of teachers and parents involved in Gaelic medium education, collection of relevant media materials, and nonsystematic participant observation, with similar research performed on Sorbian in the former East Germany (Glaser 2007, 7–10). Glaser collated and presented the views of minority cultural "elites" on the relationship of the minority language to thought, culture, and self, the relative importance of linguistic and cultural continuity, and the role of language as a source of social and cultural boundaries. Echoing the insights of Macdonald (1997) and Oliver (2002), Glaser concluded that two conflicting paradigms, (1) essentializing and (2) dynamic/situationalist, characterize minority language community leaders' views about the role of language in identity. The former requires a cultural purism and "heartlandism" (305–306) that focus on "Gaelic or Sorbian culture as clearly delineated sets of traditional practices" (6), while the latter encourages hybridity, openness, and language-focused views that may be less respectful of ethnocultural unity, but may be of more help in ensuring that "some kind of 'Gaelic' and 'Sorbian' will still be spoken several generations down the line" (Glaser 2007, 6). Despite the continued popularity of essentialism (2007, 308), Glaser identifies a move towards the latter paradigm among minority language "campaigners and agencies," which she says they view as a "pragmatic compromise"; this is the difficult tightrope that minority language advocates must walk in the 21st century.

Based on field research in Uist crofting communities and a language planning organization in the Western Isles, Inverness, and Glasgow, McEwan-Fujita (2003) explored the impact of neoliberalism on Gaelic language revitalization in connection with local and regional economic development (see Ch. 6–7, this volume). Neoliberalism, broadly defined, is a mode of governance that "involves extending and disseminating market values to all institutions and social action" (W. Brown 2003). McEwan-Fujita traced the incorporation of Gaelic as a priority into the Highlands and Islands Development Board's mission of economic development, the founding of Comunn na Gàidhlig, and the roles of CNAG and HIDB (later Highlands and Islands Enterprise) in conceptualizing the "Gaelic economy" according to the quantifiable measures of neoliberalism promoted under Thatcher, Major, and Blair, such as the number of full-time equivalent jobs created (2003; 2005). Since the 1980s language planners have commonly promoted Gaelic as a skill, asset, or commodity that can aid in the economic development of Scotland (and conversely detractors have portrayed it as a waste of public money). Oliver found that secondary pupils in Glasgow perceived Gaelic "largely... as a skill and an opportunity provider" (2002, 172), and this is consonant with changes in the approach to minority languages elsewhere (Heller 2006). Unfortunately, the neoliberal approach has resulted in revitalization efforts that are successful in obtaining EU funding, but due to restrictions on the kinds of programmes that can be funded, they are not always able to take into account sociolinguistic aspects of actual Gaelic use. Consequently, some programmes can contribute little to the reversal of language shift. Oliver concurs, concluding that revitalization is not "dependent on a technical or structural intervention" (2009, 18–19).

McEwan-Fujita set her study against the backdrop of public media discourse about Gaelic in Scotland, finding that negative stereotypes of Gaelic, some of which originated as early as the 16th century, continued to circulate in the Scottish media even into the 21st century (see Ch. 3–5, this volume). For example, journalists have taken linguists' well-meaning warnings about the loss of endangered languages and transformed them into spurious "scientific" evidence of the death of Gaelic (McEwan-Fujita 2006; see Ch. 4, this volume). Revitalization efforts have portrayed Gaelic in rejoinder as natural, ancient, more expressive than English, Scotland's national language, and more recently as a precious natural resource akin to an endangered species. This discourse analysis of the media representations of Gaelic follows in the tradition of textual analyses by Malcolm Chapman (1978, 1993), Parman (1990, 2005, 32–47), and Macdonald (1997, 33–66) which have explored the historical and cultural construction of the Gael and the Celt as symbols of otherness and tokenistic national essence in Scotland.

Within the revitalization-focused institutions of the media, education, and development, new linguistic forms and new contexts of use emerge, which may coalesce into new registers of Gaelic. A register may be defined as "a variety of a language associated with situation and purpose" (Lamb 1999). Using interviews, recordings and original news scripts, Lamb (1999) traced the historical development of the register of Gaelic radio "news-speak" and the relationship between its changing institutional context and content, including professionalization, the strong influence of the BBC, and changes in linguistic forms including the lexicon, the genitive case, syntax, dialect and accent, and prosodic features. McEwan-Fujita (2008) described the speakers, context, and ideology of the register of white-collar workplace Gaelic as it was emerging through the daily experiences of workers in the offices of a Gaelic language planning organization. The workers had developed a variety of strategies for negotiating between constructing a new "professional Gaelic" and remaining true to their own linguistic socialization, which for many of them was in Hebridean island-based domains of family and village-level community (McEwan-Fujita 2008, 86–7; see Ch. 10, this volume).

More recently, Lamb conducted a comprehensive study of late 20th-century register variation in spoken and written Gaelic, based on the collection of examples of naturally-occurring discourse in the field (2008). Lamb identified spoken registers of conversation, radio interviews, radio sports reporting, and traditional narrative, and written registers of fiction, formal prose, radio news scripts, and popular writing, and described these based on a quantitative tabulation of linguistic features such as clause types and information structure, morphosyntax, lexicon, and noun phrase grammar and complexity, drawn from naturally-occurring examples. Lamb's study found that despite the endangerment of Gaelic, its register variation was comparable in level to major languages such as English, and it shared with English universal patterns of variation. These findings contribute to linguistic knowledge and also serve the social purpose of countering denigrating views of Gaelic.

4 Representation, Disciplinary Boundaries, and Continuity

Issues of power and representation are key in the sociolinguistic ethnography of Gaelic communities. Research always creates an unequal power relationship between the researcher and his or her "subjects" or "informants," because the researcher holds the power to represent the community and its members to a wider audience (Clifford and Marcus 1986). Contemporary social scientists tend to focus on the diversity of opinions and practices in a community, and the processes of contestation (that is, power struggles) through which language and culture are enacted. Subjects of a study may disagree with the author's analysis and/or be unhappy with the portrayal of themselves, others, or their community or institution (e.g., Black 1998; MacCaluim 1998; MacLeod 2005).

Dishearteningly, the researcher's promise to protect subjects through anonymity may be almost meaningless in such a densely interconnected social network of institutions and rural communities that are also well-informed by the media and connected to the internet. Even when the author gives pseudonyms and changes identifying details, readers familiar with *saoghal na Gàidhlig* will probably scan the text closely for clues to the true identity of subjects. Some researchers delay or abandon the effort to write up their research on Gaelic language shift partially out of reluctance to offend their subjects or a fear of compromising the goals of Gaelic revitalization. They so do in the agonizing awareness that delay or failure to complete the thesis or publish a book can spell the end of their academic career.[27]

Research techniques are ubiquitous in 21st-century Gaelic-speaking communities, and community members may also feel "research fatigue." Research is carried out not only by academics, but also by journalists, management consultants, and even by school pupils doing local investigation projects. Ordinary people are increasingly using research as a tool to constitute their own understanding of themselves as Gaelic speakers, and as members of a community, whether they want to or not. But outside researchers are still the focus of grievances over the unequal power relationship of research (see Ch. 2, this volume).[28]

The diversity of audiences for research on Gaelic, and the diversity of disciplinary perspectives from which is it conducted, also constitute major challenges for researchers. Sociolinguistic perspectives have been increasingly acknowledged and included in Celtic and Gaelic departments over the past two decades, and the biennial Rannsachadh na Gàidhlig conference has been making increasing contributions in this area since its inception in 2000.[29] However, the difficulty of cross-disciplinary communication remains, made all the more difficult by the obligation of social science researchers to use specialized terminology, engage with the latest theories, publish in the journals of their own field, and contribute to general theoretical knowledge in their discipline, knowledge that may be of little interest or practical use to Gaelic speakers in general, or language planners in particular.

Finally, continuity has been a major problem in studies of Gaelic communities. Although Dorian and MacKinnon have each sustained their focus on Gaelic-related research for decades, they are the exception rather than the rule. Several individuals have changed career paths before or after completing a Ph.D. thesis, many have stayed within academia but substantially changed their research focus, and most have never published a great deal beyond the dissertation or thesis and perhaps an article or two. Some of the reasons why may be apparent in the topics already discussed. Certainly, ethnographic fieldwork makes great demands on the researcher, to say nothing of his—or particularly her—family: "Ethnography is surely one of the most personally difficult, as well as one of the most ambitious, forms of intellectual enquiry…" (MacDonald 2005, 159). Whatever the reasons, this lack of continuity represents a shortcoming in the sociolinguistic ethnography of Gaelic communities.

5   Conclusions and Future Directions

A number of recommendations can be made for future studies. More research is needed on the proficiencies, usage patterns and ideologies of Gaelic speakers in residential community contexts, since language shift is so much further underway than in the early 1980s when the last "community studies" were conducted. Overall, more of the ethnography of communication in everyday life is needed for the 21st century. For example, how do people use Gaelic on the job, in both Gaelic-essential and Gaelic non-essential occupations? How are children linguistically socialized and educated in Gaelic?[30] For that matter, how are adults? (McEwan-Fujita 2010a; see Ch. 8, this volume). Following Pollock's (2006) line of inquiry, how is Gaelic literacy taught, learned, used and conceptualized? Gaelic language standardization, an ideological as well as technological process (Milroy and Milroy 1999), should be explored ethnographically as well as from historical and language planning perspectives.

We should also be examining differences within, and interconnections between, Gaelic communities. Lines of division such as rural and urban, Presbyterian and Catholic, "learner" and "native speaker," homeland and diaspora, should be acknowledged, questioned, and analyzed, for we may find that the flows of people, ideas, and practices across these historically and socially constructed boundaries make them as interesting and illuminating to study as the boundary construction process itself. In order to understand the complex, simultaneous processes of language shift and revitalization, we must maintain and refine the classic methodologies, concepts, and concerns of sociolinguistic ethnography, while incorporating rigorous contemporary social theory from a range of disciplines concerned with language in sociocultural context. Care should be taken not to utilize "identity" as a unit of analysis or an explanatory concept; if people are making language-based claims and ascriptions of identity, then that is an ethnographic fact that must be analyzed, not used in circular fashion as an explanation for linguistic behaviour (see Bucholtz and Hall 2006; Kiesling 2006).

Greater coordination and language training support is also needed for researchers to attain higher levels of proficiency in spoken Gaelic prior to undertaking field research. The fragmented provision for adult learners described by MacCaluim (2007) impacts would-be researchers from the US and elsewhere, as does the difficulty and expense of obtaining funding for Celtic language training outside of university Celtic and Gaelic departments. Support for language training of sociolinguistic researchers would not only enhance the quality of research, but also help to further normalize the idea that in order to do research on Gaelic speakers past and present, one should acquire linguistic proficiency in Gaelic—an idea that has been marginalized in Scottish popular opinion and academia, but seems only logical to sociolinguistic researchers.[31]

This chapter can be no more than a snapshot in time of studies of Gaelic speakers and communities in 2010. It is hoped that ten or twenty years after its publication, such studies will be even more abundant, even better integrated into Gaelic and Celtic studies, and given even stronger consideration in language planning efforts. At the same time, researchers also need to maintain a place in the academy outside the realm of policymaking, so that they may provide an independent perspective on Gaelic revitalization efforts.

Sociolinguistic ethnography is challenging to research and write, and the participants do not always agree with its findings. But the value of ethnographic field research on Gaelic speakers has been well established and should have a secure place in 21st-century Gaelic studies. Students and scholars of Celtic and the social sciences have much to offer one another through mutual understanding, cooperation, and collaboration.

Notes

1   Many thanks to the editors and to Andrew Carnie, Jonathan Dembling, Nancy Dorian, Fraser MacDonald, Nicholas Malaspina, and James Oliver for critical readings of the manuscript. Any remaining mistakes or omissions are entirely the responsibility of the author. Thank you also to the people who facilitated and agreed to participate in my own and others' research on Gaelic language revitalization and development; without their patience and generosity there would be no sociolinguistic ethnography of Gaelic. Finally, I wish to thank Meg Bateman, Colm Ó Baoill, Seumas Grannd, and Janet Hunter, who were the first to formally teach me about Gaelic language and culture at Aberdeen University. This chapter is dedicated to the memory of Angus Spence (2006–2009).

2   Dorian felt that responses to her survey were so problematic, she relegated them to an appendix in her book, together with a discussion of the methodological difficulties of administering the survey and interpreting the results (1981a, 157–160). In a classic article focusing on language shift from Hungarian to German in an Austrian village, Susan Gal (1978, 6) achieved 86% agreement for men and 90% agreement for women between observed behaviour and survey responses of the situations in which people habitually spoke German or Hungarian—and she considered this to be a very high level of agreement.

3   The influence of Edwin Ardener (1927–1987) is key to understanding how UK social anthropologists finally began to study Gaelic-speaking communities and other areas of the "Celtic fringe." Ardener had carried out studies in Nigeria and Cameroon, in British West Africa, from 1949 to 1969 (MacGaffey 1991). From 1963 until his death in 1987, he was a lecturer in social anthropology at the University of Oxford. Later in his career at Oxford, he developed an interest in minority language issues in Europe, specifically in the United Kingdom. While spending summers in the Cameroons, he studied modern Welsh with a native Welsh-speaking colonial officer, and by the early 1980s, Ardener had started making regular trips to the Outer Hebrides and making a comparative study of Gaelic dialects (Chapman 1989, xii). However, the work was still incomplete when he died (Callan 2004, 366). Ardener's published work on Gaelic speakers is brief, ethnographically and linguistically informed, and theoretical in nature. His most lasting contribution in this area was to train a generation of British social anthropologists of Europe, many of whom did their Ph.D. thesis research on the so-called "Celtic fringe": Malcom Chapman (Breton in Brittany), Edward Condry (Arnol, Isle of Lewis), Evi Constantinidou

(East Sutherland), Tamara Kohn (Inner Hebrides), Sharon Macdonald (Isle of Skye and Gaelic), and Maryon McDonald (Breton-medium education and cultural revival in Brittany). Ardener also trained Robert Storey in social anthropology at the undergraduate level at Oxford. Storey remained a keen proponent of cultural approaches to the Highlands and Islands in his work with the Highlands and Islands Development Board, and together with his wife Lisa encouraged and significantly assisted a number of anthropologists working in the region (including Susan Parman, Andrew Gossen, Gillian Munro, and the author).

4 Macdonald described her older interviewees as "rather amused that I should ask them about what language they used at home, so inevitable did it seem" (1997b, 219). This local, taken-for-granted meaning for Gaelic was also found by Dorian in former fishing villages in East Sutherland, in their case made even stronger by speakers' awareness that their dialect was divergent from dominant west coast forms (1981a, 75).

5 Dorian (1981a, 114–156) was the first to conduct these for Scottish Gaelic speakers. See Mertz (1982a, 85–144) for analysis of Cape Breton Gaelic combining proficiency and domain-based data; the appendices in Mertz (1982a, 362–370) reproduce the proficiency tests administered by Mertz and Dorian. See Smakman and Smith-Christmas (2008) and Smith-Christmas and Smakman (2009) for analysis of proficiency tests conducted by Smith-Christmas on three generations of a single family in Skye in 2007.

6 MacKinnon defines "demesne extension" as a situation of language "'occupying' or 'owning' particular 'hereditaments'" within social life and extending its ownership to link these together into an integrated "estate'" (1977, 148) to "associate together the situations which predominantly call for one particular language and distinguish those other situations predominantly calling for the other language. In such an exercise language becomes the index distinguishing the significances of one cluster of social behaviours from another with regard to the integration of social institutions with group life" (1977, 148).

7 Coleman describes how the survey design forced respondents to respond to a highly unlikely hypothetical situation in which they would speak first to a higher-ranking person who represented a particular domain.

8 Coleman borrowed the terms "Casual" and "Careful" from the sociolinguist William Labov (1972); they were not native terms (Coleman 1975, 151).

9 Ennew (1980, 107) corroborated Coleman's observations in the later 1970s for Lewis, noting a difference between the dialects in everyday use in the villages, the Gaelic used in broadcasting, and the Gaelic of the church.

10 Dorian also identified four varieties of English spoken in East Sutherland: RP or received pronunciation English, standard Highland English, Scots-influenced East Sutherland English, and Gaelic-influenced Highland English and East Sutherland English (Dorian 1981a, 84–85).

11   Since this review chapter was originally published, Smith-Christmas (2012) has completed a newer study of Gaelic-English codeswitching by speakers in an extended family on Skye. Smith-Christmas has subsequently published numerous other articles on the sociolinguistics of Gaelic.

12   Perhaps due to the intellectual division of labor between anthropologists and folklorists, oral traditions are barely mentioned at all in the ethnographic literature, except to say that they have vanished due to the influence of the Presbyterian church and changes to the way of life brought by modernisation. However, the former role of the *taigh-cèilidh* [cèilidh house] is described from memories of informants (Coleman 1975, 97; Ennew 1980, 86). Coleman describes the traditional *cèilidh* going extinct in Carloway in the early 1960s and discusses the reasons why (Coleman 1975, 97–98).

13   MacKinnon also notes that Dunn (1953) and Campbell and MacLean (1974) described the practice as continued by descendants of Scottish immigrants in Nova Scotia.

14   The nicknaming and by-naming system arose in concert with traditional Gaelic patronymic practices and the fact that there was a great deal of endogamy (in-group marriage) in the area, resulting in only three surnames accounting for the vast majority of surnames in each village (Dorian 1970, 304). There were also a relatively small number of Christian names used frequently (Dorian 1970, 305), and people had large families, so every family had children with at least one popular boy's and girl's name; this is likely related to the Hebridean practice in which people were obligated to name children after grandparents (Walker 1973, Chapter 4; Parman 1976, 103), thereby perpetuating a relatively small number of names.

15   Several crofting township ethnographies include brief descriptions of Gaelic kinship terminology, which is "descriptive" rather than "classificatory," meaning that collateral "blood" relations are described by an augmentation or combination of the primary terms of relationship (for example, "mother's brother" and "father's brother" instead of the more general classificatory term "uncle") (Ducey 1956, 259–261). Walker lists Gaelic kinship terms she collected from elderly informants (1973, 233–238), which she claims give an account of late 19th-century usage but were not in daily use by the early 1970s. Otherwise, however, most of Walker's descriptions of kinship are in English, with use of the term *teaghlach* (family) throughout her thesis being the only tantalizing hint of the Gaelic linguistic practices she must have observed.

16   Ardener believed that the original cultural meanings and references of the Gaelic terms were only preserved in older Gaelic dictionaries and texts (1989, 142). However, I speculate that the ongoing preference for the English month names in daily Gaelic conversation by older speakers may actually indicate avoidance of or resistance to repurposing the Gaelic lexicon.

17   Ennew (1980, 76) speculated (but offered no evidence) about the cognitive and behavioural implications of the "disappearance of the conceptual distinction between maternal and paternal kin" in Gaelic culture "as children reared in an increasingly English environment now translate the English 'my uncle' back into Gaelic as '*m'uncaill*,'" rather than *brathair mo mhàthair* (my mother's brother) or *brathair m'athair* (my father's brother), which "corresponds to a difference in attitude to maternal and paternal kin."
18   Sasse (1992) constructed his "Gaelic-Arvanítika Model" of language death partially upon Dorian's (1981a) description and analysis of East Sutherland Gaelic.
19   MacKinnon's insight provides a nuanced explanation of one way in which gender might play a factor in Gaelic language shift. Constantinidou (1994) argued that women played a significant role in Gaelic language shift in East Sutherland. However, Dorian (2010) contests this interpretation, finding that among the Gaelic speakers of Brora and Embo, more women than men continued to use Gaelic "despite imperfect speaker skill." For a classic and detailed discussion of how gender and social networks may influence language shift see Gal (1978).
20   Coleman had also noted that in Carloway, Lewis, a "Gaelic Infants Play School" set up in 1973 with external funding was subject to differing interpretations: "the function of the school, as envisaged by the financial backer and by the people whose children used it, was apparently rather different" (1975, 228). Unfortunately he did not go into any further detail about the situation.
21   Ironically, Macdonald's book itself was criticised in this very way. These ethnographies have also been criticised for portraying Presbyterian Gaelic-speaking communities in a negative light by frankly describing the alcohol-drinking habits of some of their members (Black 1998). Reviews of Macdonald's book tended to fixate on her brief, contextualized descriptions of local people drinking on Sunday morning and at the fank, a crofting township event where sheep are dipped (treated with pesticides), sheared, and earmarked (MacKinnon 1977, 40). Parman also received criticism for her analysis of social networks based on "the Bible and the Bottle" on the west side of Lewis.
22   The pupils in the observed classrooms totaled 104, or about 11% of the total number of P1–P3 Gaelic-medium pupils in Scotland for that year (Pollock 2006, 122).
23   Oliver is Sharon Macdonald's former student and thus constitutes a third intellectual generation in the British sociolinguistic ethnography of Gaelic speakers, since Edwin Ardener supervised Macdonald's research.
24   The fluent speakers in Skye reported that they spoke Gaelic in the home, with family members, and with older people, and very rarely used Gaelic with their peers, either in school or out (Oliver 2002, 159). The young people who had no opportunity to speak Gaelic in the home did not speak it

at all (2002, 163–4). Fluent Gaelic speakers in Glasgow also just "sometimes" used it with parents or other older family members, never with friends, and would not even think to initiate a conversation in Gaelic (2002, 165–6).

25   BA in Gaelic Language and Culture (BA *Cànan is Cultar*), and BA in Gaelic and North Atlantic Studies (BA *Gàidhlig is Iomall a' Chuain Shiar*).

26   Although MacCaluim's work is based on a survey and does not contain a fieldwork component, it was conducted from the perspective of the sociology of language.

27   A long gap between fieldwork and publication of research results on Gaelic-speaking communities has also been noted. This can happen for a number of reasons besides the difficulty of writing up ethnographic research. The length of time it may take to secure a tenure-track academic position after obtaining the Ph.D., the relative demand of different institutions of higher education for one to publish a monograph, and the challenge of finding a publisher are all possible factors, as is the fact that for female academics, the childbearing years often coincide with the period intervening between fieldwork and publication of a monograph. The gap between fieldwork and book has been highlighted by the unfortunate tendency of anthropologists to write in the "ethnographic present," phrasing in the present tense their descriptions of matters as they found them at the time of their fieldwork (e.g., Parman 1990, though this has been corrected to some extent in the 2005 edition). A book title like *The Western Isles Today*—which describes the world of Lewis in the 1970s—may give the misleading and unintended impression that Gaelic-speaking communities are frozen in time.

28   Ronnie Black quoted one resident of the crofting township where Macdonald (1997a) conducted her research: "*Daoine tighinn bhon taobh a-muigh 's a' sgrìobhadh leabhraichean mar gum biodh eòlas acasan air an àite! Bidh a' chaothaich air daoine gu bheil iad mar ann an test tube 's iad a' sealltainn orra.*" [Folk coming from the outside and writing books as if they knew the place! People hate feeling they're in a test tube being looked at.] (translation supplied in Black 1998).

29   The proceedings of Rannsachadh na Gàidhlig 4 (2006) at Sabhal Mòr Ostaig (Munro and Mac an Tàilleir 2010) contain a number of ethnographically-oriented papers, including Oliver (2010).

30   Will (2012) examines the Gaelic language socialization of children on the Isle of Lewis. Will has now left research academia.

31   Well does the author remember defending this position on the Highland Research Network email list some years ago against indignant historians of the Highlands, and being called a "fanatic" by a Scottish sociologist studying Highland communities for trying to speak to him in Gaelic at the first Scottish Gaelic Studies conference in 2000.

CHAPTER 2

Research and Representation: Gaelic and Uist

1   Introduction

In 1999, during my first month of linguistic anthropology field research at the Gaelic language revitalization organization Comunn na Gàidhlig (CNAG), I was discussing my research project with an employee during our initial interview. She told me, "We get regular letters from students like yourself who think they're the first to do a study on Gaelic language in primary schools." She allowed that "It's unusual you've got that far, that you're actually here, in this office. But the fact that you're writing a thesis is not unusual" (G1, #31).[1] For the several years she had been working at CNAG, she said they had received a regular stream of letters from throughout the UK, mainland Europe, and the US, asking for information about Gaelic in order to do a research project. Many of the letters came from primary and secondary pupils as well as university students and postgraduates (graduate students). The employee may well have intended to take me down a peg—she was known for her mischievous humour—but what she said about the general research interest in Gaelic was true. She herself was already versed in the conventions of social research; she had written an undergraduate university honors thesis in sociology on an aspect of culture in the Hebridean island of her origin. From her perspective, there was probably little to distinguish my doctoral research project from any other school or university project, apart from the fact that the head of her organization had graciously allowed me to conduct participant observation in their office for several months.

CNAG itself, and other Gaelic organizations, commissioned researchers to carry out studies of various Gaelic-speaking constituencies for their own purposes. For example, CNAG's emphasis in the 1990s on the "economics of Gaelic development" was based on the commissioning of research projects from an economist and his colleagues (Sproull and Ashcroft 1993; Sproull and Chalmers 1998).

These projects involved postal surveys and interviews of Gaelic-related businesses, organizations and individuals in the Western Isles (including the islands of North Uist, Benbecula, South Uist, and Eriskay, known collectively as "Uist" in English and "Uibhist" in Gaelic) and the Skye & Lochalsh area. In effect, the necessity for social research, in the form of surveys and evaluations, was built into the structure of the neoliberal system of which Gaelic development had become a part.

"Research" had a similar set of implications for the residents of Uist as it did among the employees of CNAG and other organizations concerned with Gaelic "development." Many people felt that there was a profusion of researchers in Uist who were not necessarily doing any good. There was a sense of betrayal among many about the stereotyped representations of Uist people in the media, and by researchers. And finally, despite these perceived shortcomings of research and researchers, people in Uist were also increasingly turning to research themselves, as a means of constituting and understanding their community.

My research agenda in Uist focused on the Gaelic dimension of community development groups, not on local Gaelic folklore or traditions. In focusing my research on Gaelic development, I had essentially chosen my main social network in Uist—the professionalized world of development. I gradually realized that I was not being invited to participate in the cooperative agricultural tasks of potato-planting, peat-cutting, and the fank,[2] where I knew that the participants would be speaking Gaelic. I felt oddly disappointed that as an anthropologist I had missed out on the chance to witness this traditional labour and record conversational Gaelic use, which always seemed so brief in other contexts. My disappointment reached new heights one day when I learned about an annual informal procession of a statue of the Virgin Mary around all the houses in a particular locale in South Uist with the recitation of prayers in Gaelic—that had just taken place the previous week. That I could miss these quintessentially Hebridean Gaelic cultural events probably attested to the existence of the two separate social networks observed by my friend, or at least two distinct spheres of activity connected to the language. That I could feel so disappointed about missing these events, however, attested to the power of ideas about what it meant to do "research" in Uist.

2   The Meaning of Gaelic Research in Uist

For such a relatively small area, Uist seemed saturated with research. The types of research being conducted in Uist included projects originating outside of Uist that were conducted for the interest or benefit of people outside the islands, and projects that were ostensibly performed for the interest or benefit of people living in Uist themselves (which originated both outwith and from within the islands). Research projects in Uist originating outwith Uist began in the late 19th century and focused for many years on Gaelic folklore collection.

A team from Cambridge University's Museum of Archaeology and Ethnology made one of the earliest "contributions to the anthropology of the Outer Hebrides" with the anthropometry—or scientific measurement of head size—of a sample population on Benbecula (Searight, Bathurts, and Noone 1944). In the 1950s and 1960s, folklore collection (e.g., MacLean 1956-1957), archaeological excavations (e.g., Lethbridge 1952), and ethnographically-focused geographical research on crofting carried out by a team of University of Glasgow honors students (Caird and Moisley 1961) was conducted in Uist, in relation to the campaign of opposition to the new rocket range proposed by the Ministry of Defense.[3] Later, doctoral students in sociology and cultural geography conducted research there (Burnett 1997; MacDonald 2003).

I met or heard about a range of other researchers working in various locations in Uist while I was conducting my own research in 1999-2000. Summer 2000 was an active period: there was a Sheffield University archaeological dig, and a Boston University archaeological dig, both in South Uist. In early summer 2000 I met two film students from Strathclyde University in Glasgow who were scouting North Uist as a location for a short film, based on their preconceived ideas about a "shortage of women" on the island (see 54).

In late summer I encountered a small group of US undergraduate students from Oklahoma Baptist University on the Isle of Lewis; they were headed to Uist as part of a research assignment to perform a census of Gaelic speakers in the Hebrides. The assignment had been given to them, they said, by a professor at the Welsh university where they were studying abroad for a semester. The project seemed too casual to me: they had arrived in the Hebrides with no research plan, and they were too young to rent a car to get around the islands easily. When I met them, they were searching for information on Gaelic in Scotland in the Stornoway Public Library.[4]

The first externally-planned research project I encountered in Uist surprised me the most, however. One spring day I was sitting in the kitchen of "Catriona," an older woman in South Uist. We were having tea and scones, a usual prelude to my series of interviews with her. Catriona asked me if I knew "Stephanie," another American woman who she said also did research on Gaelic in Uist. I was surprised I hadn't heard of her, so Catriona pulled out an old letter from Stephanie to give me her contact address in America. She said Stephanie was a teacher from New England who had often come to South Uist to do research on Gaelic. I searched the internet later that week and found the website for Stephanie's one-woman folklore collecting project.

On the website, Stephanie solicited private donations for her efforts to preserve the Gaelic oral tradition of Uist. The mission of her US-based project, "a non-profit 501(c)3 organization, run by committed volunteers," was:

> TO KEEP SCOTTISH FOLKLORE
> ALIVE AND ACCESSIBLE,
> RELATING SCOTTISH CULTURE
> AROUND THE WORLD.

On an information page, she described the activities of her organization, "to help preserve and continue the endangered oral traditions and folklore of the Outer Hebrides" by traveling to the Western Isles and making audio recordings from Harris to Barra:

> Many hours have been spent beside a peat fire with ears a'glow, listening to the Elders share generations of stories in their native language Gaelic.

Other pages on the site featured three days of a journal of Stephanie's 1998 folklore collection trip for the benefit of potential donors. The journal entries contained romanticized English-language descriptions of her activities in South Uist, Harris, and Inverness, signed "*Le mise meas*" (the correct wording would be "*Mise le meas*" ["I am respectfully"]). Included was a description of her journey to Catriona's house, including her real name and the real location:

> Monday I set off down the road in beautiful weather. Laundry laughed on the wash lines and the Lapwings flashed black and white in the Sun. I made my way to [Catriona's] house in [township name]. [Township name] is out along the eastern side of South Uist. Here on the haunches of [hill name] a cluster of crofts exists. Folk living here know a peace that is hard to find elsewhere on the island. [Catriona] and I had a good visit. She has a wealth of genealogical information and is so very helpful. She is quite a tradition bearer in this community and makes the best scones I've tasted yet!

As I read these lines, I thought about all the scones Catriona had baked for Stephanie... and for me. I recalled Catriona telling me about the painful loss of a neighbour; riding his bicycle down the road past her house, he had a heart attack, fell off his bicycle, and died. His body was later found by the roadside.

Another page of the website contained links to transcripts of five short English-language tales Stephanie had collected from a named woman in North Uist. These were presented as samples of the folkloric riches one could enjoy in exchange for financial support of the Project. Except for a decontextualized "Gaelic blessing" quoted in English from Alexander Carmichael's *Carmina Gadelica*, none of the materials on the website made any mention of, or indicated any familiarity with, the long history of folklore collecting in Uist (e.g., Bruford 1978; Campbell 1969 [1890]; Campbell and MacCormick 1969; Carmichael 1972 [1900]; MacLean 1956–1957; Shaw 1999 [1977]), or the critical theoretical turn in US folklore studies that I had studied in pre-dissertation coursework (e.g., Bauman 1984 [1977]; Bauman 1986; Bendix 1997; Briggs 1988; Paredes and Bauman 1972).

Later in the summer, I heard from Catriona that Stephanie was coming to visit Uist again. In the meantime several other people had also asked if I knew Stephanie after I told them I was conducting research on Gaelic. I was very curious to meet her. As it happened, I met Stephanie for the first time at a cancer charity cèilidh in a church hall on Benbecula. As we spoke in American English, she repeatedly used the Gaelic expression "*seadh*" ("yes" or "yes, indeed") in backchannel affirmation, so I assumed that she had some Gaelic-language competence. I arranged to meet her again the following day to ask her more about her activities. During our conversation, a Gaelic-speaking friend came by and asked Stephanie a series of simple questions in Gaelic including "Where are you from?" and "How long are you staying in Uist?" Her hesitations and incongruous answers made it clear that she could not understand even the most basic questions, let alone formulate replies in Gaelic. Her lack of Gaelic language competence was all the more surprising since she later mailed me a cassette recording of twelve tales that she had recorded entirely in Gaelic from seven different people in North Uist, Barra, and Harris in 1996–1999.[5]

Stephanie had obviously invested considerable time, energy, and personal resources in her independent five-year Gaelic folklore collecting project. She had completely bypassed existing local and national institutional channels in Scotland with her own American "vision to help preserve and continue the endangered oral traditions and folklore of the Outer Hebrides." She did not explicitly articulate for whom she thought she was saving Uist folklore—or how—but her approach appears to have sprung independently from the same "salvage paradigm" (Macdonald 2011) as earlier collectors, based on a prediction of decay and disappearance of Gaelic tradition (MacLean 1956–1957, 25).

However, as a self-funded private individual, not tied to any institution, and probably traveling on a tourist visa, Stephanie had not coordinated her efforts with any of the local or academic institutions already concerned with the tradition of collecting and preserving Hebridean oral traditions, including the venerable School of Scottish Studies at University of Edinburgh[6] and the Comuinn Eachdraidh, the local historical associations of South Uist and North Uist, both of which had their own active, ambitious local history projects. Instead she, like so many collectors and researchers before her, had perpetuated a set of powerful, enduring romantic stereotypes about the people of Uist, as existing in the past and in need of outside assistance to preserve their endangered traditions.

Thinking of the long training period I had to go through, and the long process of proposing and gaining my educational institution's approval for my research plan, gaining approval for working face-to-face with living individuals, institutional permission in Scotland, and a student visa, I was somewhat chagrined to realize that Catriona and the others who had told me about Stephanie made no distinction between her activities and mine. Both were simply "research" in their eyes. My institutional affiliations, future degree, hard-won research grants, research ethics training, and carefully-written and pre-approved informed consent agreements, explaining where interviewees could complain about my activities if they didn't like them, probably meant nothing at the end of the day. Indeed, I glumly realized, there was probably no intrinsic reason why these things should mean anything to them. Stephanie's and my sudden appearances in the community, our common identities as American, and our lack of prior connections to the community, together with our interests in Gaelic, our wishes to tape record local people speaking, and our potential abilities to publish our findings (whether on the internet or in print), would provide no basis for judgement of the different motivations of our projects. If anything, Stephanie's project could be considered more valid in a local frame of reference, since she was engaged in an altruistic effort to "preserve" a traditional aspect of life in Uist, not poking around in the workings of local development groups and asking awkward questions about how people used Gaelic in their daily lives or made a living working with the language.

The idea that all researchers are the same could even be seen as part of a general suspicion and research fatigue in Uist that had already developed out of island residents' cumulative negative experiences with previous researchers. In 2000, one resident concerned with the problem noted to me of Uist: "The place is studied to death. Living culture, natural flora and fauna, it's like an academic research centre." Virtually everyone I met was kind and hospitable to me, as indeed they had been to Stephanie and countless others who made their way to Uist. But I heard several people express the opinion that many of the researchers and writers who had come to Uist had betrayed Uist people, by publicly portraying them in an unflattering light or revealing confidential information.

One example cited was the author Alasdair Alpin MacGregor, who after writing several glowing accounts of the Hebrides and enjoying hospitality during many years of island visits, produced an "exposé" book called *The Western Isles*. In this book, MacGregor characterized Hebridean islanders as: "dilatory and totally unskilled labor," "unproductive and largely indolent," greedy, spoiled by money, inclined to give poor service in hotels, unmusical (in fact devoid of true musical appreciation), feudal and obsequious in manner, alcoholic, of poor personal hygiene, sexually promiscuous (predisposed to "early and indiscriminate mating" due in part to poor housing), given to bearing illegitimate children, generally "indifferent to sanitary standards," inclined to see illegal poaching as their right, cruel to animals, given to loafing and lounging at crossroads, pubs, and post-offices, tending towards a herd instinct ("only in a very narrow sense can they be said to be individualists"), given to vandalism and public drunkenness, given to staying up late and sleeping until noon, expecting to be paid for services they previously rendered to strangers for free, treating their women as beasts of burden, unwilling to observe postwar rationing properly, and "capable of being vindictive in a degree unbelievable to those strangers who, arriving amongst them for the first time, are impressed by their charm and naïvety" (MacGregor 1952).

Another example cited by Uist residents was Philip Coxon's account *A Curlew in the Foreground* (1988). Coxon had been a warden at a North Uist nature reserve owned by the Royal Society for the Protection of Birds, and he portrayed his neighbours in the book in a somewhat unflattering light as a set of idiosyncratic "characters," and the crofting townships as "squalid." Like MacGregor, he was writing in the English imperialist tradition about "the natives." Judging by the continued mention of these accounts to me in 2000, they appear to have hurt local people deeply, as did other more ephemeral yet equally denigrating portrayals of them in the Scottish and British press.

Along with the ongoing presence of externally-conceived research projects, other social research projects in Uist were initiated by institutions and individuals within Uist, or by institutions based elsewhere in Scotland that had claimed or been assigned responsibility for serving the area of Uist or administering it as a constituency. From the invention of statistics onward, the state has used the data obtained through surveys of the population as a mode of governmentality (Hacking 1991).[7] But as the author of another recent dissertation about a Gaelic-speaking institution in the Hebrides has pointed out, "There is a long history in the Highlands and Islands of bad experiences with researchers and with policies enacted on the basis of their research" (Gossen 2001, 308).

Marginal communities such as the ones in the Outer Hebrides have not fared well in interaction with the state and social science researchers (Gossen 2001, 310; citing Herzfeld 1987; Said 1978). Western social science research shares a common origin with European imperialism and nation-building, a common origin in an expansionist, objectifying, controlling ethos. One project worker in Uist, speaking about a particular area that was the target of a special economic development program (which also had its own locally-employed project worker), commented:

> There is no money going in, the whole population is getting consulted to death. People keep asking them, "What would you like? What would you like?" And people are saying they want real jobs, and one thing they can't deliver is real jobs. And there's not hellish much else being delivered either. And they just keep asking them, "What would you like? What would you like? What would you like?" (C4, #354).

With the neoliberal turn, the research project became a major mode of intervention for regional and state governments, and unelected quasi-NGOs and other organizations. It also became a mode through which Uist residents developed an understanding about their own locale and culture. In fact, the whole of civil society in Uist, including Gaelic, became enmeshed in a web of research. Research is now a mode through which the community understands itself to be a community. "Community consultation" is now a standard feature of local development projects, and local research has even been incorporated into the school curriculum. The optional sixth year of secondary education in Scotland ("Sixth Year Studies") includes a "Local Investigation" project in which the pupil has to design a research project about some feature of the local area in which he or she lives. On two different occasions in my year of field research, I even found Sixth Year Studies doppelgangers investigating the same organizations that I was.

3   Research, Media and the Violence of (Mis)representation

The Scottish media have formed an important adjunct to "research," both in the representation of the Gaelic language, Gaelic speakers, and Uist, as well as in the enterprise of linguistic, social, cultural, and economic development in the islands. The Hebrides, including Uist, are consistently represented in the Scottish media (and indeed in the wider British media) as remote and inaccessible, distant in both time and space.

As Chapters 3–6 in this volume make clear, the Scottish national media has tended to repeatedly portray Gaelic, Gaelic speakers, and Gaelic language revitalization efforts according to a limited set of negative stereotypes, stereotypes which implicitly compared Gaelic with English on the basis of an ideology of the superiority of standard language, and found it wanting on multiple dimensions. The CNAG employee who told me I was just the latest in a long line of researchers studying Gaelic explained that her organization had become wary about the motivations of researchers, due to the misrepresentation of both CNAG and the general situation of Gaelic in the Scottish press.

One particular example illustrates CNAG's point. In the mid-1990s a Strathclyde University postgraduate student in cultural geography conducted a research project on the current situation of Gaelic in Scotland. Her advisor co-authored an article with her about the results of the research which appeared in the *Scottish Geographical Magazine* (Rogerson and Gloyer 1995). However, after the publication of this academic journal article, Gloyer's research results appeared to have been brought to the attention of the media in a press release.

The *Times Higher Education* supplement ran an article about her research conclusions titled "Gaelic Revival Myth Scotched by Student":

> A Strathclyde University student research student has thrown cold water over the recent outpouring of enthusiasm about a Gaelic revival. The Scottish Office Education Department says Gaelic language and culture has been enjoying a period of growth, while the brochure from Comunn Na Gàidhlig, the Gaelic development agency extends a "welcome to Scotland's Gaelic renaissance".
>
> But Mandy Gloyer said the latest census figures on people who spoke, read or wrote Gaelic showed a continuing decline to 1.4

per cent of the Scottish population, compared to 5.2 per cent a century ago ("Gaelic revival myth scotched by student," 1996).

The "continuing decline" in census figures was already well-known, but the article attributed the observation to the researcher as though she had discovered it. In the remainder of the article, and even in her co-authored peer-reviewed journal article, Gloyer made it clear that she considered language shift and language revival to be mutually exclusive phenomena, which is not the case in reality. She also offered the not particularly original observation that language was not always the key element in group identity. Indeed, she said, it would be possible for people to consider themselves Gaels or Highlanders without speaking Gaelic, and for people to learn Gaelic without considering themselves Gaels. In the context of social science, these points were valid observations (see Ch. 1, this volume, pp. 21, 25). However, the researchers and the press took them out of context and utilized them to claim that Gaelic language revitalization efforts had no benefits at all, were a waste of money, and ought to be stopped.

Disseminating academic research about Gaelic in a press release is still risky, given the longstanding media biases against Gaelic. If negative framing of research findings by the researcher or the media causes distress to the research participants, and misrepresents the situation of Gaelic to the detriment of revitalization efforts, then the ethical dimensions of releasing research this way should be carefully examined and questioned.[8]

The problems of misrepresentation plague the Western Isles as a geographical and culture area, not only Gaelic speakers. In late 1999, BBC One premiered the new "reality" television show "Castaway 2000": "the story of a cross-section of the British population cast away on a remote island"—a formerly inhabited island in the Outer Hebrides.

The UK version of the "Big Brother" reality series was extremely popular at the time, as was the first "Survivor" series in the US. This program was to be in the same vein, albeit without the weekly eliminations. The production company commissioned by the BBC selected a group of 30 individuals and their families to participate in this "social experiment," which featured regular on-screen commentaries from a Glasgow Caledonian University psychologist.[9] On 31

December 1999, the group was transported to the Hebridean island of Taransay, moved into prefabricated housing, and provided with food supplies. On this small, long-uninhabited island off the coast of the Isle of Harris, the Castaways' struggles with the weather, the flu, the livestock, the production company, and one another were filmed 24 hours a day for six months.

I found it ironic to watch the likes of a stockbroker's assistant from Surrey on television competing for a place on a "remote Hebridean island" in a Robinson Crusoe-esque reality series, while I was living on the "remote" Hebridean island of South Uist myself. From a Hebridean vantage point, it was clear that landowners and administrative powers controlling the area had themselves created the perceived remoteness of the island of Taransay. The Highland Clearances of the late 19th century and further population loss throughout the 20th century had resulted in the total depopulation of the island by the 1980s, but prior to that the island had been inhabited at least since 300 CE (Lawson 1997). Little if any mention was ever made in the media of the social history of the island—its crofter population, its school (Duncan n.d.), or its former thoroughly Gaelic culture.

Even in its depopulated state, however, Taransay was not as remote or isolated a place as the rest of Britain had been led to believe. Throughout the run of the program, newspaper reporters found the "castaways" in situations compromising their isolation: staying in hotels on Harris, being visited on weekends by local fishing boat parties, and entering their vegetable garden produce into the Harris agricultural show. Even the program's own television cameras filmed them going on alcohol runs to the Co-op supermarket in the town of Stornoway.

"Castaway 2000" was only the latest in a long series of systematically skewed media representations depicting the Hebrides as remote, isolated, and essentially unfit for human habitation. As we were marveling over "Castaway," an academic colleague alerted me to a recent set of egregious misrepresentations concerning Uist in particular. In February 1999, the British media "picked up," or rather created, a story on a European Union regional economic development grant awarded to the North Uist section of the Dùthchas Project, a pilot sustainable development program funded by EU LIFE (the EU Financial Instrument for the Environment).[10] These particular funds from LIFE were to be used in North Uist to help create new opportunities for young people, to keep them from permanently emigrating to the mainland. However, journalists framed the news as a different kind of story:

> Lovelorn Hebridean bachelors hope Euro cash will help woo more women to their windswept islands. From the northern tip of North Uist to the tail of Benbecula, there are 2,064 men…and just 1,386 women. Outer Hebridean communities are seeking aid from a £711,000 European LIFE programme to attract women who will, hopefully, one day become wives of the islands' unmarried men. The European money could create jobs for women which encourage them to settle into a way of life that would break all but the most resilient (Fullterton 1999).

The goal of the stories in the press (including "Women's Rock: A chance to meet the Casanovas of the crofts" 1999, Barrowclough 1999, Fullerton 1999, Harris 1999, Mallon 1999, and Shields 1999) seemed to be to represent the Hebrides as the ends of the earth, to marvel in faint outrage at the amount of "Euro cash" being given to their inhabitants to maintain a remote, exotic lifestyle, and most of all, to entertain and have a laugh at their expense. Life in Uist was rural, but hardly as punishing as the newspapers gleefully depicted it. The articles were replete with stereotypes about the bad weather, primitive living conditions, and lack of amenities in Uist. These negative qualities of Uist were formulated explicitly with reference to the standards of mainland urban Scotland—no shopping, no cinema, no nightclubs.

Many of the indicators of global modernity were clearly visible in this rural area at the start of the 21st century; the media just chose to ignore them. In 2000, one could buy a cappuccino from the café in Balivanich. The latest UK pop chart songs of Craig David, Destiny's Child, Eminem, Britney Spears, and the Spice Girls' solo projects formed an everpresent soundtrack on radio, television, and in the pub that year. However, life in Uist was also characterized by the ironies of deliberate underdevelopment (cf., Carter 1974), which residents were attempting to address in part through the EU economic development funding.

As savage as the deliberate underdevelopment, though, and inextricably intertwined with it, was the ongoing, deliberate, even obstinate misrepresentation of the rural, the remote, and the Gaelic language and culture. This power to represent is intertwined with the multiple meanings of "research," both locally in Uist and in terms of academic disciplines. These activities, together with the language ideologies and discourses discussed in this volume, produce the paradoxes of Gaelic language revitalization in the era of neoliberalism.

Notes

1   The letter-number combinations and numbers in parentheses after quotations from individuals in this chapter are codes referring to entries in the author's fieldnotes.
2   The fank is a crofting township event where sheep are treated with pesticides, sheared, and earmarked (MacKinnon 1977,40).
3   For considerations of space, I will not discuss the early social research in Uist here; it is skillfully described and analyzed in a doctoral thesis in cultural geography (MacDonald 2003). I thank its author for bringing these studies to my attention.
4   It was an overly ambitious and irresponsible assignment to give to a group of undergraduate students for a number of reasons. First, the students were unprepared and unequipped to undertake the project. Second, the Scottish census already includes data on the number of Gaelic speakers in the Western Isles. Third, the research was not coordinated with any institutions in Scotland that might potentially have been interested in the more fine-grained results of a door-to-door survey, including the Celtic Departments of the universities and Comhairle nan Eilean Siar, the Western Isles regional government.
5   She would send me the cassette only in return for a donation of several dollars to the project. She had apparently recorded the narratives on an ordinary hand-held cassette tape recorder with a built-in microphone, and the sound was of poor quality.
6   Merged with the Department of Celtic in 2002, the School holds extensive archives of sound recordings of Hebridean folklore. They were difficult to access for non-academic researchers and family members of invidiuals who were recorded. Since 2010, many of the School's recordings have been made available online through the website of the project Tobar an Dualchais/ Kist o Riches (http://www.tobarandualchais.co.uk/).
7   Interestingly, the very concept of social research as a mode of knowing seems to have originated at least partially in the Highlands of Scotland. In the 18th century Sir John Sinclair (1754–1835), a supporter of Gaelic (Sinclair 1804) was the architect of the very first Statistical Account of Scotland and "introduced the word 'statistics' to the English language" (Black 1986, 5).

8   In addition to a number of other articles in the Scottish press during the same week, the *Daily Mail* tabloid ran a pair of opinion pieces about Gaelic designed so that one was apparently more supportive of Gaelic and one less (MacLeod 1996; Morrison 1996). Both articles are discussed in Chapter 3 of this volume for the descriptions they give of the Gaelic language, and the Morrison article is discussed in Chapter 6 for its position opposing public funding for Gaelic language planning.

9   All but two of the participants selected as "castaways" were English, and all but two of the English adult participants were white. The two non-English participants were from Ireland and the Isle of Man respectively; none were from Scotland or Wales. The only people residing in Scotland who were featured on the show were the psychologist and the architect who designed the houses (the people living within close proximity of Taransay were rarely shown).

10   According to the website, "The Dùthchas Project was a demonstration project funded by the EU Life Environment Programme from 1998–2001. Focused on the Scottish Highlands and Islands, the Project worked with 3 communities and 22 public agencies to explore ways of sustaining fragile rural areas—the natural heritage, the people and the economy. North Sutherland, North Uist and Skye's Trotternish peninsula were chosen as the 3 Pilot Areas." Quoted from http://www.duthchas.org.uk.

PART TWO

Discourses of Death and Revitalization

CHAPTER 3

Discourses of Death and Denigration: Ethnolinguistic Differentiation and the Ideology of Contempt

1   Prologue: "Newsnight Scotland"

On Thursday, 7 September 2000, at 10:40 p.m., BBC Two Scotland abruptly switched over from the London-based late-night news program "Newsnight" to the Glasgow-based "Newsnight Scotland." This customary practice cuts off the London-based program in midstream; on this particular night, a "Newsnight" report on the poverty and oppression of Aboriginal peoples in Australia was interrupted without warning by the "Newsnight Scotland" opening credits.

Following a summary of the day's Scottish news, presenter Gordon Brewer introduced the program's main story, the release of a new report issued by the Taskforce on Public Funding of Gaelic, a committee appointed to re-evaluate the structure of Scottish public spending on Gaelic language planning efforts:

> Now, Gaelic appears to be dying, but is it worth resuscitating the patient? Tomorrow an official report will call for yet more government money to be spent to keep it going for another few years at least, I'll be talking to the author in a moment. But first, Isabel Fraser examines why an ancient language once spoken by half or more of Scotland's population, is now spoken by only one percent.

A pre-recorded segment followed, beginning with the scene of a teacher and pupils engaged in a lesson in a Gaelic-medium primary school classroom. Reporter Isabel Fraser's voiceover described the scene:

> The face and sound of a vibrant and beautiful language in a Gaelic medium school in Glasgow, where the children are thriving academically. But these schools are points of light in a progressively darkening hinterland. The new millennium finds Gaelic at the edge of extinction. The number of Gaelic speakers keeps falling.

At the end of the last century, more than two hundred ten thousand people spoke the language. Ten years ago, that had fallen to fewer than seventy thousand. The projected figure for next year could be as low as fifty thousand.

While Fraser said, "the number of Gaelic speakers keeps falling," the camera panned upward from the children, and a computer-generated school blackboard appeared with a table of the census figures mentioned. In the remainder of Fraser's report, a series of soundbites from the Minister for Gaelic, the chief executive of Comunn na Gàidhlig, and a Gaelic-speaking journalist were interspersed with Fraser's voiceovers over Gaelic singing, and scenes of a loch, island ferries, a Gaelic children's choir, a beach, and Gaelic signs at the Scottish Parliament.

After the segment ended, the program went back to the studio, and the main presenter introduced his three guests. The first was John Alick Macpherson, the assistant director of Comataidh Craolaidh Gàidhlig (the Gaelic Broadcasting Committee). Macpherson appeared on the program as the head of the taskforce appointed to make recommendations on national public funding for Gaelic. The second guest was Mike Russell, the Scottish National Party MSP (Member of Scottish Parliament) for South of Scotland, and a self-appointed Gaelic advocate. The third guest was Allan Brown, a Scottish columnist for the "Ecosse" section of the conservative *Sunday Times* newspaper and a self-appointed Gaelic detractor.

Brewer started by briefly discussing the recommendations of the forthcoming "Macpherson report" for official recognition and increase in funding for Gaelic with Macpherson and Russell. Brewer then turned to Brown and asked his opinion of the recommendations. Brown answered with a small smile:

> 'S insane isn't it? It's wonderfully insane. It's like a, a, a kind of Swift novel, I mean if you stand back from it, and look at what's actually happening, this—you know, fifty thousand people dictating, and being chippy, and sort of edging their way into the agenda, I mean, it's a, it's a home crowd at Ibrox—[1]

After a sharp protest by Macpherson ("That's outrageous!") and a further short comment by Brown, Brewer broke in again:

> All right, but it's not unreasonable for a language which is in danger of dying out to say that um the government or the new Scottish Parliament ought to subvent some funds in order to keep it going, is it?

Brown, still smiling, replied:

> Well we're doing it such a profound courtesy by describing it as a language, and it isn't, it's an idiolect. It consists of fourteen thousand fifteen hundred words. [sic] The English language adds twenty thousand words every year. It [Gaelic] isn't a language, it's a form of code, it's a form of um, patois or argot.

Brown's comments provoked immediate and outraged responses again from Russell and Macpherson. The presenter turned to the sputtering Russell first: "Mike Russell's about to explode, so we'd better hear from him then." Russell called Brown's comment "the stupid and offensive type of remark that was made in the 19th century. It's a colonial approach." Russell then asserted, "Gaelic is a living thing," and ignoring a sigh and a muttered comment from Brown, as well as repeated attempts by the presenter to interrupt, he continued on this theme with vigour:

> We spend an awful lot of time and our money saving living things. We save the whale, we save the corncrake.[2] The way in which a people sa– see the world is being dismissed by this ludicrous commentator… absolutely ludicrously and offensively. And I think if we can't have a debate about how to save something of vital importance to our nation, our culture, and indeed our souls, then we shouldn't be having a debate at all, we might as well just give up.

After Russell's statement, the presenter did not comment on the validity of Brown's remarks, but implicitly acknowledged their inflammatory nature by adopting a neutralistic stance for himself (Clayman 2002; Greatbatch 1998). However, like Brown, he questioned Russell's assertion that Gaelic was living:

> But the point, Mike Russell, is, is—is—putting this, or trying to put this in a very neutral way, the point would be that, um, I mean that you say this is a living thing, but the point is the

numbers of Gaelic speakers are going down, and presumably the numbers of Gaelic speakers are going down because Gaelic-speaking families are choosing to have their children educated in English rather than Gaelic.

Russell rebutted this statement, but Brewer cut him off and turned to Macpherson to reiterate his claim that Gaelic families were deliberately choosing or willing Gaelic to die. Macpherson replied with his own vigorous rebuttal:

It's not true that Gaelic parents, Gaelic-speaking parents, are choosing the option of education in English! More and more of them are choosing the option of education through the medium of Gaelic. And one of the reasons that they haven't been choosing it in greater numbers is the– the– the– the pressures of a dominant language on their society. But you don't have to be a rocket scientist to understand that, bilingualism is an advantage. And this has been proven in studies, not only here with Gaelic medium education, but in various countries around the world.

Macpherson overrode the presenter's attempts to interrupt, to add his condemnation of Brown's earlier comments attacking Gaelic.

After Macpherson finished speaking, the presenter turned to Russell for a final comment: "Mike Russell, I just want to hear from you, what do you think. If nothing is done to stop the decline of Gaelic, I mean do you seriously think the language—very briefly, we're running out of time—could die out, and if so how long has it got." Russell responded:

Well figures clearly show the number of speakers has halved in about twenty-five to thirty years, eh the– the– the age range of speakers is getting older all the time. We have to act and act now. We must do so both with money, and with organizational and management tools that Seonaidh Alec is talking about, but most of all with passion to get this right… and that requires legislation.

After Russell finished talking, Brewer swiftly brought the interview and the entire segment to a close: "All right, John Alick Macpherson, Mike Russell, Allan Brown, thank you all very much indeed. Time for a quick look at tomorrow's papers…"

2 Introduction: Language Ideologies and Linguistic Differentiation in Scotland

The utterances of the participants in the thirteen-minute "Newsnight Scotland" television segment illustrate some of the multiple and conflicting ideologies of language (Gal 1992) that structured late 20th-century representations of Gaelic in Scottish media and politics. The television segment in its richness provides a useful starting point for the aim of this chapter: to describe and analyze ideologies of Gaelic in the Scottish public sphere in terms of the indexical relationships they create between language use and other forms of social action (Irvine and Gal 2000; Silverstein 1996). The national scope and applicability of these representations to Gaelic speakers in general, and the Gaelic language as a whole, distinguish them from the locally-based perspectives on Gaelic language use in community contexts.

Characterizations of Gaelic and Gaelic speakers in the Scottish public sphere have served as a site for the indexical reproduction of anxieties about ethnic boundaries in Scotland (cf., Hill 1995b). Although politicians and the English-language media reject the idea of Gaelic speakers as an ethnic group, their public characterizations of Gaelic and its speakers systematically place Gaelic speakers into an othered, marginalized, and primitivized position. The construction and deployment of these representations constitutes a semiotic process through which participants create and underline, even as some of them attempt to undermine, forms of anglophone Scottish cultural and economic domination over Gaelic speakers. This is possible because many Scots still interpret linguistic differences between Gaelic speakers and non-Gaelic speakers as markers of membership in different categories of race, ethnicity, and class, so that the policing of linguistic boundaries is also a covert policing of the boundaries of racial, ethnic, and class categories (Urciuoli 1998). The conscious and unconscious distancing and erasure of Gaelic and Gaelic speakers in the Scottish media is an example of this kind of policing.

The discourses utilized by participants in the language revitalization debate may be divided into two categories: discourses of language death and denigration, and discourses of language revitalization and redemption. I define discourses of death and denigration as a set of predications about Gaelic and its speakers that participants utilize in order to declare, explain, justify, or advocate for the death and/or disappearance of Gaelic, or to disparage the language and/or its speakers. I define discourses of revitalization and redemption as responses to the first category of discourses, a generally parallel set of predications about Gaelic and its speakers focused on proclaiming the virtues of Gaelic as justification for its preservation, salvation or revitalization (see Ch. 5, this volume). Although the denigrating discourses probably predated the redemptive responses initially, both types of discourse have existed in a dialectical relationship for centuries, and are of equal importance for understanding semiotically-mediated processes of Gaelic language shift.

Separating the ideologies into two categories facilitates their analysis, but in practice there are no absolute boundaries between them. Both sets of discourses predicate stereotypical characteristics of Gaelic on the basis of an ideology of standard language (Lippi-Green 1997; Milroy and Milroy 1999), while erasing (Irvine and Gal 2000) other aspects of the language that do not fit these stereotypes.

These discourses are produced by participants who observe indexical relationships between language and social groups: primary indexicalities which they explain and rationalize with second-order indexicalities in a dense dialectical process over time (Silverstein 1996). This dialectic is what constitutes the semiotic process of forming stereotypes:

> Participants' ideologies about language locate linguistic phenomena as part of, and evidence for, what they believe to be systematic behavioral, aesthetic, affective, and moral contrasts among the social groups indexed (Irvine and Gal 2000, 37).

The stereotypes rehearsed in the late 20th century are dialogical (Bakhtin 1981a) in the sense that they voice longstanding Scottish stereotypes about Gaelic, Highlanders, Celts, and the Highlands (described in detail in Chapman 1982; Clyde 1995; Donaldson 1988; Fenyö 2000; Pittock 1999; Womack 1989). Written examples of these stereotypes date back as far as the 14th century (Withers 1984, 22–24). One 18th-century observer noted that

> "...notwithstanding the Lowland Scots complain of the English for ridiculing other nations, yet they themselves have a great

number of standing jokes upon the Highlanders" (Burt 1876 [1754], 124; cited in Fenyö 2000, 43, note 32).

These stereotypes constitute the "systematic behavioral, aesthetic, affective, and moral contrasts" (Irvine and Gal 2000) between Highlanders and Lowlanders.

The cultural divide between inhabitants of the Lowlands and Highlands began to emerge in the 12th century, and Lowland Scottish denigration of Highlanders in royal decrees, travel accounts, and popular song formed a distinct pattern by the 15th and early 16th centuries in which

> the lines of opposition [were] already defined: Highlandmen are proud, obstinate, boastful, treacherous, violent, fickle, cowardly, and ragged; they speak very loudly in a barbarous language that nobody can understand, and there are altogether too many of them (Donaldson 1988, 49).

In this characterization, English-speaking Lowlanders made Gaelic-speaking Highlanders represent the negative pole of a set of contrasts: self/other, civilized/barbarous, honorable/dishonorable, human/animal (Chapman 1982).

The romantic era ushered in a reversal of the polarities in the late 18th century, such that the previously negative attributes of the Celts were transformed into positive attributes, although the basic set of terms remained intact (Chapman 1992, 212–5). Thus, "animal" or "barbarous" was positively re-evaluated as "natural," while the negative qualities of "violent" and "fickle" became the desirable qualities of "impetuous" or "emotional," and "impractical and disorganized" became "dreamy and fun" (Chapman 1978, 18). Redemptive praise for Gaelic, a set of reactions to the centuries of denigration that arose out of a situation of sustained Gaelic-English contact, made use of these romantic terms from the 19th century onward. However, the pre-romantic negative set of connotations also continue to be utilized for denigration, suggesting that the problematic terms of Gaelic's relationship to Scotland are still being negotiated.

In the following section of this chapter, I will first consider the problem of defining Gaelic ethnicity in Scotland, set in the context of the historical relationship of England to Scotland and Scotland to its formerly predominantly Gaelic-speaking Highlands. I will then discuss the significance of the increased public visibility of Gaelic in Scotland in the 1990s to the contested role of Gaelic in Scottish ethnicity. In the remainder of the chapter I will discuss the most prominent characteristics shared by both denigrating and redemptive discourses. These characteristics indicate that these discourses express ideologies of linguistic differentiation, which were used to negotiate the relationship between language and ethnicity in late 20th-century Scotland.

3   The Problem of Gaelic Ethnicity

The "Newsnight Scotland" segment described in the prologue highlights a problem.   Why would a news organization provide a platform for the racist denigration of Gaelic? The presenters of "Newsnight Scotland" represented themselves as neutral commentators, drawing their authority from the venerable British Broadcasting Corporation, an organization that cultivates an international reputation for impartial, high quality news reportage. British news interviewers almost always adopt neutralistic stances, though of course an apparently neutral stance may conceal bias against interviewees (Greatbatch 1998). Moreover, the late 20th-century Scottish public sphere, of which BBC broadcasts formed a significant portion, was an arena where overt denigration of ethnic minority groups was discouraged and punished (cf., Hill 1995a; e.g., Dinwoodie 2000, Boztas 2003).[3] In particular, the BBC Scotland division of the BBC would seem to be an organization that supports Gaelic language planning, since BBC Scotland contains a Gaelic Department, which produced Gaelic-medium radio and television programming in the same Glasgow office where "Newsnight Scotland" was produced.

Considering these factors, we must ask why representatives of the BBC, and other mainstream Scottish media institutions as we shall see, enabled and presided over over explicit public expressions of contempt for Gaelic on "Newsnight Scotland."

BBC Scotland's customary scheduling of "Newsnight Scotland" over the last one-third of "Newsnight" gives us a clue to the answer, as well as an example of the recursive reproduction of cultural and linguistic subordination in the Scottish public sphere. The title of the program itself is the marked "Newsnight Scotland," which contrasts with the unmarked "Newsnight" based in England and aimed at the entire UK viewing audience.[4]

Since the Union of 1707, Scottish politics, media, culture and language use have been marked categories subordinated to the unmarked English versions (Daiches 1964). The BBC's practice of cutting off the London-based "Newsnight" to air the marked "Scottish Newsnight," some of my Scottish acquaintances complained, implies that the BBC sees Scots as provincial enough not to mind the abrupt interruption of international news for their own "regional" news, and as integrated or British enough not to need a separate time slot for "Newsnight Scotland."

Ironically, the "Newsnight" story interrupted on 7 September 2000 was London-based coverage of the plight of an indigenous minority in Australia, but the Glasgow-based news that replaced it provided a platform for discrimination against an indigenous linguistic minority in Scotland. Although concern for the welfare of minority groups is now publicly acknowledged as a positive thing in Scotland, many Scots, feeling the sting of a "cultural inferiority complex" under English rule, have denigrated Gaelic and Gaelic speakers for centuries in a recursive fashion (Irvine and Gal 2000) as discussed in the previous section. After Gaelic speakers ceased to be considered dangerous in the late 18th century (following the defeat of the Jacobite forces at Culloden), Lowland Scots still stigmatized them in class terms, considering them to be peasants, bumpkins, or teuchters.[5] Gaelic remained iconic of that economically and socially debased status, and many Gaelic speakers themselves accepted the idea that Gaelic signified poverty, while English signified upward mobility, thus providing one impetus for Gaelic-English language shift. By the mid-19th century, Scottish race theorists, not coincidentally the earliest theorists of race in Britain, considered Gaelic speakers to be representatives of a separate, degenerate, Celtic race (Fenyö 2000; Knox 1862; Pinkerton 1789). This racialized view is not dominant in late 20th-century Scotland, but the connotations of Gaelic as a marker of a stigmatized ethnicity and class and remain.

Gaelic speakers are acknowledged to be a *linguistic* minority in Scotland, and their minority status in that respect is frequently reiterated. Their ascribed membership in an *ethnic* category in Scottish society is a more problematic issue, however. Gaelic speakers are indistinguishable from the rest of the population in terms of physical features, and have assimilated almost completely to mainstream practices in areas such as dress, social structure, and housing during the past fifty years. Though there is a corpus of distinctively Gaelic personal names and surnames, naming practices in late 20th-century Scotland do not necessarily distinguish Gaelic speakers from non-Gaelic speakers.[6] Many, but by no means all, Gaelic speakers now live on the islands and mainland of the far north-west of Scotland, and a proportion of those Gaelic speakers are crofters, or part-time small-holding tenant farmers. So Gaelic linguistic practices, together with residence in the Highlands and "peasant" status, are almost the only remaining obvious marker of "Gaels" as a distinct ethnic group.

In Scotland as elsewhere in Europe, many still hold a view of language, or rather languages, as intimately tied to nations or nation-states. The "one territory-one state-one nation-one language" concept variously formulated by Herder, Fichte and Humboldt covertly organizes perceptions of language in relation to polity (Blommaert and Verschueren 1992). Gaelic's continued existence from this point of view has posed a problem to Lowland Scots, since English has been identified as the language of the Scottish nation at least since the Union of the Crowns in 1609 (Withers 1984). Thus Gaelic has been elided from the Scottish linguistic landscape in a construction of Scotland's linguistic continuity with England, while at the same time the stereotypical artifacts of the Gaelic culture complex (kilts, tartan, bagpipes, etc.) have been claimed as quintessentially Scottish in a construction of Scotland's cultural distinction from England.

Dorian's concept of linguistic lag as an ethnic marker, developed in her research on the obsolescence of the regional East Sutherland dialect of Gaelic (Dorian 1980; 1981), also illustrates the way in which language indexes ethnicity at the level of Scotland as a whole. In past decades in East Sutherland, according to Dorian, the differing linguistic practices of fisherfolk marked them as a stigmatized group in the eyes of the surrounding crofting and town communities. The stigma persisted over time, because even though the linguistic practices of the fisherfolk changed, the fisherfolk and later their descendants were always considered to be "one step behind" the surrounding communities in their linguistic practices. The first manifestation of fisherfolk being "out of step" was that the Gaelic they spoke was considered more pure than the Gaelic of the surrounding communities. Later, the fisherfolk continued to practice Gaelic monolingualism in contrast to the Gaelic-English bilingualism of their neighbours, then they spoke English less proficiently and with greater Gaelic interference than their neighbours, and ultimately the fisherfolk practiced bilingualism in contrast to the English monolingualism of the surrounding communities. Once the fishing and farming practices were abandoned, and the descendants of fisherfolk "caught up" with the surrounding community in linguistic terms, the means to discriminate between groups faded, and with it the stigma. Thus Dorian concluded that "[t]he ethnic marker is rather the lag than the language" (1980, 38-40).

In other words, Gaelic is not the target of denigration and redemptive efforts for reasons inherent to the language, as the stereotypes proclaim, but for reasons pertaining to the maintenance by a minority group of linguistic practices abandoned by the majority. I argue that this minority group's linguistic difference is perceived as "lag" in the context of a standardizing, nationalist teleology of development, in which Gaelic monolingualism represents the past and English monolingualism represents the inevitable and desirable future, if not the present. Thus Gaelic speakers' differing practices are construed as representing an undesirable state of not having yet achieved an imagined and unreachable goal of national homogeneity (Blommaert and Verschueren 1992).

Undesirable lag among Gaelic speakers is perceived for Gaelic speakers in Scotland as a whole as much as it was for the Gaelic speakers of East Sutherland. As of 2000, all adult Gaelic speakers in Scotland were bilingual in English, as were the vast majority of children. Their bilingualism in the late 20th century, like that of the fisherfolk in the 1970s, was construed by many Scots to represent an undesirable "lag" in the national teleology of Scotland. Scots who subscribe to an ideology of standard English are already defined on its margins by virtue of their own speech habits (Romaine 1982). From their perspective, Gaelic speakers only add an extra dimension of embarrassment when they fail to abandon Gaelic and "catch up" linguistically to the rest of Scotland.[7]

4 Attempts to Reconfigure Gaelic Ethnicity

In the late 20th century, the sentiments expressed in discourses of death and denigration in part constituted responses to the visible results of the Gaelic language planning efforts that accompanied discourses of revitalization and redemption. During the 1990s, a series of high-profile Gaelic language planning efforts came to fruition in the Scottish public sphere. The most prominent of these was an increase in Gaelic-language television programming on BBC Scotland and Scottish Television channels from 1993 onward, some of which was aired in late afternoon and prime time. Other publicly-visible signs of language revitalization programs included the opening of Gaelic-medium units within state-run English-medium schools throughout Scotland, and some bilingual Gaelic-English shop signs in Fort William, Oban, Inverness, and Glasgow. The 1999 opening of the new Scottish Parliament in Edinburgh featured a Gaelic choir, several members taking their oaths in Gaelic, and bilingual English-Gaelic signs, and in 2000 two bilingual Gaelic-English Parliamentary debates were held on government support for Gaelic, and Gaelic medium education.

These language planning programs, particularly Gaelic television programming, were designed to increase the visibility and strengthen the reputation and social position of Gaelic in the whole of Scottish society as well as among Gaelic speakers. Gaelic television especially promoted the national view of Gaelic in Scotland: "The director of the CTG [Gaelic Television Committee] himself acknowledged this 'attempt to make Gaelic central to Scottish identity'" (Cormack 1994, 119). The Scottish tabloid press displayed negative reactions to much of the new Gaelic programming, arguing that they should not have to watch it. A frequent complaint in letters to the editor concerned BBC Scotland's decision to air a Gaelic news program in the BBC's UK-wide "Star Trek: The Next Generation" time slot for several years; therefore, while BBC viewers in England, Wales, and Northern Ireland were watching "Star Trek," BBC Scotland viewers saw the Gaelic news program instead. A newspaper article in 1997 about obscenities in BBC television programming noted that some Scottish viewers found the BBC's Gaelic-language programming more worthy of complaint than English-language obscenities:

[Ms Andrea Calderwood, Head of Drama for BBC Scotland] said the problem BBC Scotland had was not the use of bad language; it was the use of the Gaelic language. They got more complaints from disgruntled viewers about their two-hours-a-week commitment to Gaelic programmes than they did about swear words (Laing 1997).[8]

Such reactions, as well as frequent jibes about the Gaelic news, constituted a rejection of the Gaelic Television Committee's attempt to make Gaelic a more central (or even merely accepted) part of Scottish national identity, "rather than any kind of reasoned reaction to the programmes themselves" (Cormack 1994, 129).

The arguments of Gaelic language planners and advocates have also been rejected when they explicitly utilize the discourse and social framework of race or ethnicity to frame their appeals. In post-devolution Scottish legislation, cultural policy, and public discourse, Gaels have been assigned the status of a "special interest group," equivalent to other groups such as "the disabled" or "gays and lesbians" created by the intersection between identity politics and the state (e.g., Dinwoodie 2000; Boztas 2003). Both representatives of the state and media commentators seem to find it difficult to accept the idea of a separate, linguistically-based Gaelic ethnicity within Scotland, let alone the possibility that that ethnicity could help to define a Scottish ethnicity. Perhaps this is in part because most non-linguistic symbols of Gaelic ethnicity (e.g., kilt and bagpipes) were already appropriated centuries ago in the service of Scottish ethnicity (Cameron 1998).

In a Gaelic column in *The Scotsman* that appeared one week before the episode of "Newsnight Scotland" that I described in the prologue, Alec O'Henley described several Gaelic advocates giving evidence to the Scottish Executive's new commission on racism. He wrote what I heard several other Gaelic proponents say—that if the same denigrating comments in the media described in this chapter were made about Urdu instead of Gaelic, they would be interpreted as ethnic hatred, but when they were made about Gaelic, no non-Gaelic speakers complained that these remarks were prejudicial (O Hianlaidh 1999).

In 2000 only a few other media representatives reacted publicly to the name-calling in a manner similar to Macpherson's and Russell's responses during the "Newsnight Scotland" segment. The week after "Newsnight Scotland," *The West Highland Free Press*, a weekly newspaper based in Skye, printed the following in its gossip column:

> There is a golden rule at BBC Scotland. Whenever Gaelic is being discussed in English, whether on radio or television, it is compulsory to include Alan Brown, a piss-poor columnist for the Scottish edition of the 'Sunday Times', in the line-up.
>
> Brown has made a cottage industry out of sneering at Gaelic and attacking any money spent on it. BBC Scotland regards this as a wonderfully amusing line or argument [sic] and always invites him in to add "balance"—i.e. naked racism—to the debate.
>
> His latest appearance was on the ridiculous "Newsnight Scotland" where he was invited to hold forth on the "rocketing" sums of money (BBC Scotland's word, not ours) spent on Gaelic. Brown obliged by announcing that Gaelic isn't a language at all but a "patois". One can almost hear the bright young things of BBC Scotland squealing with delight at this wonderfully-controversial statement.
>
> Imagine the furore if the BBC in London had run such an offensive item.
>
> Which, of course, they never have ("Clippings from the Phrase Shed" 2000).

This suggests that the BBC in London is far enough away for its employees not to consider Gaelic a threat to their own sense of ethnicity or national identity. However, the BBC in Scotland, which actually contains a Gaelic Department, is considerably closer to the imagined threat of Gaelic. Coincidentally, the *Free Press* columnist noted, that very same week the Press Complaints Commission in London released Gaelic versions of their leaflet on "How to Complain" and their Code of Practice. The anonymous columnist dryly mocked the ambiguity of the leaflet's proffered bilingual complaint service: "It is not quite clear whether one can only complain in Gaelic about Gaelic journalism or whether one can also complain in Gaelic about English journalism." Apart from the *Free Press* column, the "Newsnight Scotland" segment garnered no further comments or complaints that I or my acquaintances could find in the Scottish press. The Scottish branch of the UK's Commission for Racial Equality, which also has a procedure for taking complaints about the media, did not address the issue either.

5 Death and Revitalization: Recycling, Objectification and Distancing

There are several well-documented historical accounts of the sustained denigration of Gaelic speakers and attempts to discourage and suppress the Gaelic language prior to the 1980s, especially in the realm of education (e.g., Campbell 1950; Durkacz 1983; Withers 1984). Therefore, I concentrate my own account on the 1990s to demonstrate how continuous and pervasive the denigration is. In addition to examples of denigrating discourses from the "Newsnight Scotland" segment described in the prologue, I utilize examples from the national media, primarily Scottish newspaper and television examples from the period 1989–2001, as well as older historical examples to trace the origin and development of representations of Gaelic into identifiable discursive traditions.[9] As their provenance demonstrates, the principal groups of people who disseminated these discourses about Gaelic in the late 20th century were those with access to print media: members of the Scottish media, Gaelic language planners and advocates, and North American and European academics in the social sciences. Important to note is the fact that many of the discourses of death and revitalization gain their authority and currency through their academic origins, and repeated quotation and recycling in the media (cf., Hill and Irvine 1993).

The British press, and particularly the Scottish press, was the main media source for criticism of Gaelic in the 1990s.[10] The press is divided into two main types, tabloids and broadsheets. The press sources I analyzed include a number of different types: 1) Scottish tabloid newspapers; 2) national Scottish broadsheet newspapers; 3) some of the UK-wide broadsheet newspapers that circulate north of the border with an added "Scotland" section; and 4) two regional newspapers produced and circulating mainly in the Highlands (*The Press and Journal* and the *West Highland Free Press*). The tone of the British tabloid press, including Scottish tabloids, is distinctive.

British tabloid newspapers utilize a writing style that is aggressive and sensationalizing.[11] Scottish tabloid newspapers, like their English counterparts, position themselves as working class and conservative (Smith 1994, 188–198).[12] The broadsheet newspapers are also called the "quality" papers, in implicit opposition to the tabloids. The broadsheets I analyzed represented a range of political positions, from liberal (*The Guardian*) to conservative (*The Sunday Times*). None of the newspapers' political positions aligned with a completely positive or neutral position on Gaelic except for the two regional Highland papers mentioned.

In addition to newspapers, I include other periodicals like *Science* and *The Economist*, as well as the work of broadcast journalists and producers such as those at BBC Scotland, discussed in more detail below. Gaelic language planners such as John Alick Macpherson work for Gaelic language planning institutions, while other Gaelic advocates like the MSP Mike Russell tend to hold middle class jobs with literacy skills that provide access to the public sphere, such as politician or writer. Academics involved in creating public representations of Gaelic included British and US linguists and British education researchers as well as academics in Scottish universities trained in Scottish Gaelic Studies.

Many of the types of discourse described in this chapter enact distancing (Hill 1993, 147) or "othering" as a way of maintaining the boundaries of linguistic and ethnic groups. All the tropes described here, as used in the Scottish media, fulfill the purpose of distancing Gaelic and its speakers. A journalist might utilize these discourses to establish distance between themself and Gaelic in multiple ways. Gaelic is frequently distanced in space and/or time, with the participant implying or explicitly declaring that Gaelic is a language belonging to a remote, peripheral place far away from "here," or an ancient time, long before "now." By contrast, the "here and now" refers to the participant's own life, Scotland, or the world in general in the present time.

Another type of distancing accomplished in these discourses places boundaries between Gaelic or Gaelic speakers and human cultural and social contexts by objectifying the language. Gaelic becomes a dying person or group of people, a plant or animal or a species of animal, or even an animal or natural sound like the grunting of a pig or the sound of the ocean. The language itself is anthropomorphized in the "language death" metaphor, with a dying language becoming a proxy for dying speakers (cf., Nettle and Romaine 2000), but Gaelic is rarely described as a medium of communication between human beings. In fact, all of these objectifying, anthropomorphizing, and speci(es)fying metaphors for Gaelic erase the historical trajectory of Gaelic in Scotland as a medium of communication, in daily life, in politics, religion, education, and artistic expression, by communities of people in different places at different times. They also erase the long history of government and church intervention against Gaelic language use and transmission in Scotland, particularly in education (Campbell 1950; Withers 1984), and the forced emigrations of massive numbers of Gaelic speakers to the US, Canada and other Commonwealth nations in the previous two centuries (Hunter 1976). Postulating Gaelic and its speakers as comfortably out of reach in the distant past or a faraway place, or as animal or natural object—in the face of living, breathing evidence to the contrary—may indicate the level of threat that some Scots believe Gaelic represents to their sense of self, culture, society, or nation.

Distancing is also frequently created in media discourses about Gaelic by constructing publics of non-Gaelic-speakers, excluding Gaelic speakers from the public discourse as both participants and audiences (Hill 1995a, 198). Such publics are frequently invoked with the use of "we." The audience indexed by the discourses may be a "we" that is constructed as a rational group of English speakers who know that Gaelic revitalization efforts are pointless because Gaelic is a dangerously degenerate habit, or that Gaelic is irrelevant, or that Gaelic is harmless and funny. Or the audience may be a "we" that is constructed as all the people of the Scottish nation, or as a rational group of concerned world citizens, who know that Gaelic must be saved somehow, because it is rich, expressive, or historical, or represents desirable diversity. Utilizing the discourses described in the following section, media commentators seek to objectify and distance Gaelic in all these ways.

6   Discourses of Death and Denigration

The following section describes the various discourses regarding the death and denigration of Gaelic that were expressed in the Scottish media and other publications during the last decade of the 20th century. I have identified at least five such inter-related discourses about Gaelic in these media sources, many of them represented in the "Newsnight Scotland" segment described in the prologue. The discourses about the death of Gaelic posit Gaelic as a living being or group of beings, at or near the end of a life course. The discourses denigrating Gaelic posit other related qualities of the language, based on an ideology of standard English that interprets language variation as deviation or deficit, language change as decay, lack of a written standard as lack of a language, and these perceived negative attributes of speech as negative attributes of speakers (Milroy 2000, 63). Ralph Grillo's discussion of the "ideology of contempt" (Grillo 1989, Ch. 9) and Nancy Dorian's elaboration of his concept (Dorian 1998, 5–12) have both contributed greatly to my identification of these discourses and their relationship to an ideology of standard.

The discourses communicate the following propositions about Gaelic in implicit contrast to English: 1) Gaelic is barbarous or animal-like; 2) Gaelic displays a linguistic deficit; 3) Gaelic is an inherently humourous object of joking and mockery; 4) exposure to Gaelic is onerous or hurtful; and 5) Gaelic is a thing of the past, unsuited for modern times. Although I have separated and numbered these discourses, both for convenience and to convey their extent and variety, the discourses are often combined in actual practice and this list should not be taken as exhaustive (additional discourses and themes are discussed in Chapters 4–6, this volume).

Interesting to note is the way in which metaphor is used in several of these discourses to make cultural sense of the situation of Gaelic-English language contact. English speakers often used metaphors to project meanings onto Gaelic (cf. Fernandez 1986, 31) that they were otherwise unable to construct, as Palmer noted in Irish colonization:

> ...the uncomprehending... could hazard judgements from sounds. In the absence of sense, we register only a jumble of clicks, consonants, aspirants, tones, rhythms, glottal stops. Once sense is added, these sounds acquire the entirely different import that meaning brings. A judgement purely from sound is, by definition, a judgement from ignorance. [...] Description by analogy gives freedom to the listener who wields it; the analogy chosen registers

more the prejudices projected by the hearer than it reflects on any intrinsic qualities of the language itself (Palmer 2001, 29).

The use of metaphor allowed non-Gaelic-speaking commentators to create a set of social meanings for Gaelic as an objectified entity, a "language object." Through metaphor, commentators expressed their prejudices, seeking to depress or elevate the status of Gaelic in the Scottish public sphere according to their predications (Fernandez 1986, 39).

Through repeated disparagement and praise, Gaelic became a "known" quantity with matched opposing sets of characteristics predicated of it. The astonishing continuity of the predications over centuries of Scottish history derives from the continuity of the cultural systems, rather than from the transmission of particular turns of phrase from generation to generation.

6.1   *Gaelic is Barbarous or Animal-like*

Gaelic and Gaelic speakers have often been described explicitly as savage or barbarous, outside the bounds of civilization. Commentators also endowed Gaelic with these characteristics through the use of metaphor and simile. They described Gaelic not as a human language spoken by human beings, but as sounds uttered by animals or birds, or even compared it to a range of flora native to the Highlands.[13] English-speaking observers interpreted the phonology of spoken Gaelic, different as it is from English, as unpleasant sounds, the incoherent utterances of savages or the cries of animals.

Historical precedents for this distancing strategy date back at least five hundred years in Scotland. In the early 16th century, the Scottish poet William Dunbar wrote a carnivalesque scene of Highlanders entertaining the Devil in Hell (Bawcutt 1996, 185):

> *Thae tarmegantis, with tag and tatter,*
> *Full lowd in Ersche begowth to clatter,*
> *And roup lyk revin and ruke.*

> Those devils, in rags and tatters,
> Full loud in Gaelic began to chatter,
> And croak like raven and rook.[14]

Although later writers may not have been aware of the earlier examples, the similarity of metaphors suggests the continuity of a symbolic system. An early 19th-century critic again compared the sound of Gaelic to the sound of birds, in a heated chapter-length diatribe in his book on the Highlands:

> To the non-adept, all languages are equally dark; though the Italian may sound smoother than the Gaelic, (which a genuine Gael denies,) or the bubbling of the Hottentot and the croaking of the Overysselander, appear to be the cries of different animals. A convocation of Turkey cocks, indignant at the intrusion of a scarlet cloak on its debates, resents it in language quite as intelligible as that of the Synod of Highland drovers, and, to common ears, equally varied and copious (Macculloch 1824, 184).

If the Gaelic language sounded no more varied or "copious" than the noise of a flock of turkeys to this author, he was entirely in step with prevailing European colonial attitudes toward the rest of the world's languages. For example, clicks in southern African languages were also compared to the same bird noises as Gaelic: "hens' clucking, ducks' quacking, owls' hooting, magpies' chattering, or 'the noise of irritated turkey-cocks' (Kolben 1731, 32)" (Irvine and Gal 2000, 40).

The repeated pattern of comparing Gaelic and other languages with animal sounds reveals the historical continuity of this colonizing, imperialist attitude of Lowland Scottish and English observers toward Gaelic speakers. Characterizing Gaelic as barbarous or animal-like, of a part with unknown languages from the uncivilized regions of the world, creates an image of a monolithic "other" with uniformly negative qualities (cf., Said 1978). Such a view disregards the perspective of Gaelic speakers themselves (to say nothing of the speakers of other languages who were likewise written off as savages).

The late 20th-century examples seem to have grown out of this earlier colonial tradition, if not through direct influence, then by virtue of their proponents sharing the same strategy of equating "self" with civilization or culture and the "other" with nature (Chapman 1992; Donaldson 1988). Journalists in the 1990s frequently compared Gaelic to the flora, fauna, and natural features of the Highlands, or to the sounds that they make. Scottish tabloid columnist Joan Burnie

(1991) described Gaelic speakers as "heather and vowel bashers" and contrasted them to "the five million Scots who speak normally." Allan Brown described Gaelic speakers as "bracken-munchers" and Gaelic as "a stream of Hebridean twittering," reminiscent of the 19th-century evocations of bird cries (2000a). Another journalist likened a man's Gaelic-accented English speech to an organic substance common in the Highlands: according to the description, he "hissed in an accent as peaty as an Islay distillery" (T. Brown 2000).

Describing Gaelic as animal sounds or as natural substances implies that Gaelic speakers are less than human. They are animals, or at the very least closer to nature; stuck at the wrong end of the evolutionary scale, they are more savage and less civilized than English speakers.

6.2 Gaelic Displays a Deficit

This idea grows out of the concept of Gaelic as barbarous or animal-like, for if Gaelic is believed to be closer to animal than human communication, then while it may be used to communicate emotional states, it lacks the ability to communicate precisely in referential terms the way that civilized, standardized languages such as English can. Differences between Gaelic and English are interpreted to signify that Gaelic lacks features that English possesses; thus the idea is that Gaelic displays a deficit in comparison to English. This concept of comparison manifested in 18th-century Britain and France in relation to the development of a written standard for English and French respectively (Grillo 1989, 173, 179), and Dorian notes that Western dominant-language speakers still generally view minority languages with "ignorance about the complexity and expressivity of indigenous languages" (Dorian 1998, 12). Speakers of a dominant language characterize the minority language—and its speakers—as cognitively deficient by comparison with the standard majority language:

> The standard language is typically considered a rich, precise, rationally organized and rationally organizing instrument; dialects and ethnic minority languages, by contrast, are considered impoverished and crude, most likely inadequate to organize the subordinate world itself and certainly inadequate to organize other worlds (Dorian 1998, 8).

This is the denigrating discourse about Gaelic that has been most obviously dependent on an ideology of standard language, in which words are viewed as units of referential meaning that should ideally bear a one-to-one correspondence with objects and concepts in the world (Silverstein 1979, 197). In any civilized language, these units of referential meaning should ideally be catalogued and codified in a dictionary. Any lack of fit between the units of referential meaning in English and another language indicates, in this view, a shortfall on the part of the other language and its speakers.

The frequently-remarked prevalence of English loan-words in contemporary spoken Gaelic (MacAulay 1986) constitutes one aspect of this lack of fit. English loan-words in Gaelic are interpreted as indicators that Gaelic words in themselves are inadequate, and are believed to call the status of Gaelic as a separate language into question. One scholar of Gaelic noted:

> I have more than once heard it suggested that Gaelic is somehow not really a language, on the grounds that someone talking about cars in Gaelic has been heard to utter the words 'carburettor' [sic], 'sump', 'big end', 'overdrive', or whatever (Gillies 1980, 1).

When an English speaker with no Gaelic language skills hears spoken Gaelic, he or she seems to find the English loan-words to be one of the most distinctive features. In 1999 a taxi driver in Fort William told me that he had picked up Gaelic very quickly while serving with the Royal Air Force on the Isle of Benbecula in the Outer Hebrides. "It's a broken language, you see," he said, explaining that he could understand Gaelic very easily because Gaelic speakers used so many English words in their conversation, "because they didn't have a word for it in Gaelic." A self-appointed critic of Gaelic television posted a similar criticism of English loan-words on his website in 1997:

> Should they have wished, it was quite possible for English speakers to watch ["Telefios," a 5-minute Gaelic news summary program] without the subtitles as Gaelic's development had ended with the Union of the Crowns and enough modern words such as 'helicopter', 'car', and 'cotton mill' could be heard to make out the gist of the news (Rae 1997).[15]

Ironically, the quantity of Gaelic words in historical terms is well-attested in the standardizing mechanism of the dictionary (e.g., Dwelly 1988 [1901–1911]). But such interpretations of a lack or inadequacy in Gaelic also fail to take into account the variety of sociolinguistic reasons why speakers use English lexical substitutions or codeswitching in spoken Gaelic. These may include prestige, comic effect, or the rejection of newly-coined Gaelic words as artificial.

During the "Newsnight Scotland" segment, columnist Allan Brown also implied that Gaelic was compromised in its linguistic status by having an inadequate number of words. Brown described the total number of words in Gaelic as "fourteen thousand fifteen hundred." He appears to have mis-spoken, since this is a fictitious number. In any case, Brown was making the point that Gaelic as a language had a specific total number of words that was less than the number of English words, and that English was adding 20,000 new words every year, while Gaelic, he implied, was not adding new words every year and thus was stagnant or dying. Given the specificity of his estimate, Brown likely arrived at his word-counts for Gaelic and English by counting or estimating dictionary entries, indicating once more the basis of this view in an ideology of standard language that places the highest value on a written standard, codified in part by the word-list of a dictionary, together with the insistence that linguistic difference from the standard represents inadequacy.

Late 20th-century representations of Gaelic also call into question its referential precision. One journalist, writing about the first "Gaelic debate" in the Scottish Parliament in 2000,[16] seized on a grammatical feature of Gaelic that he interpreted as a deficit in order to make a joke about indeterminacy of meaning in the language. The article's title, "They didn't say yes, they didn't say no, so there could not be a conclusion," referred to a 1930s show tune in an example of intertextuality. It began with the following setup:

> Whoever thought up the idea of holding a debate on Gaelic in the Scottish Parliament never took into account that the language has no word for Yes and no word for No. Inevitably the whole thing was bound to be a bit inconclusive—and that was precisely how it turned out (Fry 2000).

This comment, also occasionally made about Irish, does refer to a grammatical feature of the Q-Celtic languages: Irish, Scottish Gaelic, and Manx, do not contain words for "yes" or "no"; instead, the positive or negative declarative form of the original interrogative verb is used to answer the question. This difference from English grammar, however, is interpreted as a lack on the part of Gaelic—Gaelic is seen as missing the words "yes" and "no," and thus missing a definitive way to answer questions, rather than, for example, being seen as possessing a more precise responsive system than English (cf., Dorian 1998, 10).

Such an ideology can extend its focus beyond particular linguistic features to call the entire communicative system of Gaelic into question. As mentioned in the prologue to this chapter, before giving his spurious word-counts for Gaelic and English on "Newsnight Scotland," columnist Allan Brown stated that Gaelic was not in fact a language, but an "idiolect," "a form of code," "a form of patois or argot." In linguistic terms, none of these designations are correct, except perhaps for "code" in the sense employed in "codeswitching" (but see below). Brown may have used the term "idiolect" in an attempt to deny the existence of Gaelic's grammatical system or intra-group communicative function, or to emphasize the idea of Gaelic as an "idiosyncratic" or nonstandardized language, or perhaps just to convey the idea that Gaelic is a dialect of idiots.

The use of "patois" clearly reveals the ideology of standard language, since one definition of "patois" is "a dialect other than the standard or literary dialect" or "illiterate or provincial speech."[17] Another definition of "patois," "the characteristic special language of an occupational or social group," is similar to the definition of argot: "an often more or less secret vocabulary and idiom peculiar to a particular group." The adjectives he used to describe Gaelic are all terms for speech rather than writing, and indicate contempt for what he assumes to be a lack of a written standard. By labeling Gaelic a "patois," "argot" and a "code" (most likely in the popular sense of a "secret code," not the technical linguistic sense as used in "codeswitching"), Brown could be expressing a fear of not being able to understand what is being said in his presence. This same fear is reflected in another column Brown wrote, in which he pretended to infiltrate a fictitious bumbling "Gaelic terrorist group" (see the following section).

6.3   Humour and Mock Gaelic

When Gaelic was the subject of media commentary in the 1990s, it was often treated in a lighthearted or mocking way. Jane Hill identifies this treatment as another important element in a lowering strategy against a minority language, using the example of "mock Spanish" in the US (1993, 1995a, 1995b). As Hill (1993, 149) describes, the humour is one way for English speakers to address the presence of minority language speakers ["the Other"] living in close proximity: "the Other is engaged, but through ironic repetition, accomplished by 'bold' alterations and exaggerations." In this section, I apply this insight to the use of Gaelic in a humourous way, or as the object of humour, in English-language Scottish media.[18] This use is quite different from the affective function that Gaelic may play for Gaelic-English bilinguals, in which Gaelic language use is believed to create or enhance the humour of a verbal performance (Dorian 1981, 78; Weinreich 1953, 174).[19]

From the culturally and economically dominant English-speaking point of view, humour could be found in and easily created from the source materials of the minority language. Publicly-accessible Gaelic source materials had increased in Scotland in the 1990s, as described in the introduction to this chapter. The Scottish public's exposure to spoken and written Gaelic during this time could include Gaelic television programs, as well as a weekly Gaelic newspaper column in the Scottish broadsheet newspaper *The Scotsman*, published in Edinburgh, and in a few regional newspapers in the Highlands.

The humour was expressed through the construction of "mock Gaelic" (parodies of written or spoken Gaelic), and through jokes about Gaelic. A large measure of the humour emerged from the English speaker's perception of incomprehensibility or indeterminate meaning in Gaelic, and the strange noises Gaelic speakers were thought to produce, even when speaking English with a Gaelic accent. A further measure of humour was apparently derived from the presence of English loan-words, as some of the examples in the previous section demonstrate.[20]

Scriptwriters, journalists and columnists presented mock Gaelic on Scottish television and in the Scottish press. For example, in 2000 the BBC Scotland comedy program "Chewin' the Fat" featured a recurring sketch with sock puppets speaking mock Gaelic, with the strategic interjection of English phrases ("Testicular cancer!") providing most of the humour. Columnist Allan Brown also constructed a linguistic parody of Gaelic for a column in the Scottish section of *The Sunday Times* titled "Beware of a gael farce tendency,"[21] which featured the minutes of a fictional meeting of the so-called "extremist Gaelic terror organisation" Sìol nan Gaidheal. The article put English and mock Gaelic words in the mouths of "Gaelic terrorists" such as the following:

> Lt Torcuil MacDonald (lieutenant-at-arms, whisky co-ordinator): Colleagues, comrades. To you all, well done! Or, as the Gaelic has it: Tha an companaidh a Inbhir Nis air deuchainn analach ullachadh a lorgas! [...]
> All: Bhiodh feill mhor! Bhiodh feill mhor! [*sic*] (Brown 2000b)

The mock Gaelic sentences were created by stringing together invented and real Gaelic words; the latter are spelled correctly. In this respect, Brown seems to have engaged closely with the printed Gaelic forms that were the raw material for his mockery, perhaps copying portions from actual Gaelic newspaper articles. The first sentence would be something like "The company from Inverness has [nonsense verb] a test [nonsense adjective or adverb] preparing"; the second one, the nonsensical "a big market would be." Pejorative images of printed Gaelic, Gaelic-accented spoken English, and Gaelic-English codeswitching are also iconically evoked with the addition of extra "h"s, "d"s, "s" and "m" to an English word and a Gaelic word: "Now, to business, not to mention bhuddishnesss" and "Thank you comrade. And thank you commhdraiddh." To an English reader, these letters of the alphabet might seem to be more plentiful in Gaelic orthography than English, and thus they could be considered iconic of printed Gaelic. In addition, for humourous effect Brown mocked the repetitive codeswitching that Gaelic speakers were stereotypically represented as engaging in (Cram 1981), at the same time implying that Gaelic was redundant since Gaelic utterances were always restatements of English ones.

The headline and photos of an article on the 1999 Royal National Mòd[22] in the Scottish tabloid *Sunday Mail* also depicted Gaelic as inherently amusing due to its incomprehensibility and its fun-loving speakers. The tabloid newspaper headline is "It may be Scotland's second language, but it's still all Greek to me" (Keown 1999). The three accompanying color photos show the rosy-cheeked, smiling male author in a number of different situations with captions poking fun at his abilities. The first photo shows him on a platform among several little girls playing a *clàrsach* [small harp], his plump form seated on a tiny stool, his hands on a harp, and his tongue sticking out in a "madcap" expression; the caption reads "CHILD'S PLAY... to the kids at The Mod, that is—Gary sounds as if he's playing the harp with 10 bananas."

The second photo shows the author with his arms around two Gaelic choir members who are drinking in a pub, with the caption "I CAN DO THAT... with choirboys Andrew and pal Peter." The third photo shows him looking bewildered, scratching his tilted head and holding up the program for the Mòd, which features the full event name, "Am Mòd Naiseanta Rìoghail" [The Royal National Mòd] on its cover, with the caption "TONGUE-TIED... Gaelic's still a closed book to Gary."

The photos and headline taken together seem to mock the author for being incompetent in Gaelic arts and literacy. However, they convey a different message when read together with the text of the article, which disparages the Mòd as an extreme minority interest and waste of public money. In this reading, the author is deliberately distancing himself from Gaelic and questioning its status as "Scotland's second language" by proclaiming its utter incomprehensibility. The Mòd competitors posing with Keown in the photos have no idea that the journalist will be writing an article denigrating their language, culture, and activities, and contradicting their optimistic statements about Gaelic. While the Mòd and Gaelic are perhaps good for a party, Keown says, neither are good for much else:

> For many, the Mod is more a week-long bevvy session than a serious cultural celebration. [...] And with that, we embarked on another momentous Mod night of drink and dance with the only Gaelic words worth remembering... Slainte mhath.

6.4   *Ideology of Monolingualism*

The increased visibility of Gaelic in late 20th-century Scotland generated not only joking and mock Gaelic, but also complaints from some journalists about the unpleasant burden of exposure to Gaelic as a foreign language. As part of an ideology of monolingualism, Dorian observes "a belief in the onerousness of bi- or multilingualism" (1998, 12). In this view, speaking more than one language is considered onerous not only at the societal level, but also at the individual level, with no intellectual, social, or financial rewards acknowledged for knowing or learning a second language (Dorian 1998, 11–12). Learning a second language, or even experiencing superficial exposure to it, is believed to cause confusion and impair the cognitive performance of children and adults.

Those journalists who hold the most extreme form of this view feel that having to hear any Gaelic spoken or see any Gaelic written constitutes a burden if not an insult. The offensive exposure includes hearing Gaelic spoken on television (Burnie 1991, Rae 1997), and seeing Gaelic written on signs. Allan Brown described listening to English simultaneous translations of Gaelic during the previously-mentioned Gaelic debate through headphones as an assault on the senses, a form of "pointless torture" (2000a). Ironically, Brown and other Scottish journalists probably command multiple varieties of English already, including both Standard Scottish English and a local dialectalized variety. But this type of multilingualism is erased in the assumed opposition between the monolithic entities of "English" and "Gaelic."

Reading Gaelic on bilingual road signs is also viewed as an imposition.[23] For example, the presenter on "Newsnight" incorrectly implied that if legislation granting a form of official status to Gaelic were passed, then all the road signs on the largest highway in Scotland connecting Glasgow and Edinburgh would be changed to monolingual Gaelic:

> Well, M—M—Mike Russell, c—can you, Mike Russell in Edinburgh, you're drafting a Private Members bill, [Russell: I am.] to try to get this secure status. Now, as critics say, it'll mean that uh, y'know you drive down the M8 in Glasgow, and all the road signs'll have to be in Gaelic, [Russell: That's nonsense–] and if that's not what it means, what precisely does it mean?

Later in the program, Allan Brown said "And on the issue of road signs, even if you go to Glasgow, there's road signs in Gaelic," in a tone of voice implying that this was outrageous. Although a few Gaelic signs had been erected in Glasgow since the mid-1990s, in 2000 there were no road signs; only a handful of Gaelic-English pub signs, the signs on the adjacent offices of the Gaelic Books Council and Comunn na Gàidhlig, and Scotrail's modest English/Gaelic bilingual station platform signs for the West Highland Line, which originates in Glasgow. A single small sign at the main entrance of Queen Street Station in Glasgow read *"Fàilte gu Stèisean Sràid na Bhànrighinn/ Welcome to Queen Street Station."* Complainants elided the fact that most of the relatively rare "Gaelic signs" in Scotland were actually bilingual signs featuring both English and Gaelic, underscoring the all-or-nothing position of monolingual standard language ideology— that there is room for only one language in a national public sphere.

6.5 Social Darwinist Discourse of Death

The major problem with Gaelic or its speakers in the "linguistic social Darwinist" view (Dorian 1998, 10, 12) is an inherent weakness or unsuitability for modern life. This concept as applied to Gaelic speakers originated in the 19th century with the ideas of Spencer, and became more fully developed after the publication of Darwin's theories about the evolution of species (Fenyö 2000, 95, note 12). In this view, Gaelic is a species, the death of which is acknowledged and welcomed as an illustration of the "survival of the fittest" principle. Proponents believe that language shift is proof that the language has failed to adapt to modern life. This view conflates the biological concept of evolution with economic development: the Gaelic language and Gaelic speakers are identified with an embarrassing, economically downtrodden Scottish past, a past that needs to be left behind as quickly as possible to allow the full social, economic, political, and cultural "evolution" of which Scots and Scotland are capable. According to this logic, retaining Gaelic would represent a threat to one's future social mobility, construed as "evolution."

Although the position is not always articulated explicitly, journalists' frequent references to Gaelic as ancient or obsolete remind their Scottish audience that Gaelic is quintessentially of the past. This was the case on "Newsnight Scotland," when presenter Gordon Brewer referred to Gaelic matter-of-factly as "an ancient language" and presenter Isabel Fraser stated in a pre-recorded segment that "The new millennium finds Gaelic at the edge of extinction."

A number of self-appointed anti-Gaelic Scottish and English journalists have expressed this view in the context of praise for the benefits of globalization. For example, Dr. Tim Williams, who writes opinion columns against both Gaelic and Welsh in newspaper articles with titles like "Barbarous brogues no more" (T. Williams 1999) and Michael Glover with columns like "Do Brits really need a second language? English will be the chosen form of world communications and commerce this century" (Glover 2000a, 2000b).

These newspaper columns articulate a schema where monolingual standard English usage represents not only the future, but also the highest possible point of evolution for the entire world in the era of globalization. Therefore, these writers say, Scots ought to be grateful that they can partake in the benefits of globalization as native English speakers, instead of wasting time and money with Gaelic.

In another example, a columnist wrote about her family history in order to argue against revitalizing Gaelic. Like Allan Brown on "Newsnight Scotland," Margaret Morrison provided an opposing viewpoint to a pro-Gaelic columnist in a tabloid feature. She described how one of her Gaelic-speaking great-great-grandfathers from Lewis had "abandoned" Gaelic when he moved to Glasgow for work, and a Gaelic-speaking great-grandfather from Argyll on the other side of her family had "used only English" after likewise moving to Glasgow. She traced this movement as an upward trajectory out of the Highlands and away from Gaelic:

> What happened through several generations of hard-working, aspirational Morrisons, has been mirrored in many other families: when they made their escape from the backbreaking labour of croft life, they left behind the language and culture which went with it (Morrison 1996).

Thus Morrison, like other columnists, identified Gaelic safely with her own personal family past, other families' pasts, and by extension Scotland's past. To strengthen the association of Gaelic with the past, she described Gaelic as "a time-warp language hardly anyone understands," and "this archaic language," and declared that "The harsh reality is that the usefulness of Gaelic to non-native speakers is probably about the same as Aramaic." She described Gaelic revitalization as "Government-aided nostalgia," describing support for Gaelic as a remembrance of things past while making reference to the anti-revitalization component of this ideology.

Positing Gaelic as irrelevant to the present world distances it in space and time; positing Gaelic as an extinct creature or species distances it from human contexts altogether. Journalists portray Gaelic as driven to extinction by forces beyond its control, like the hapless dinosaurs wiped out of existence by global climate change or catastrophe. This view erases the social causes of language shift, which include historically well-attested intervention against Gaelic by the Scottish government since the 12th century CE and the church since the Reformation (Durkacz 1983; Withers 1984).

Sociolinguists studying processes of language shift also find that speakers of minority languages themselves internalize this view, and native Gaelic speakers are no exception. Gaelic speakers themselves come to believe that they must learn English and abandon their original native language, along with their traditional way of life, in order to succeed in the dominant society and economy.

7 Conclusion

Discourses of revitalization and redemption focus on representing Gaelic in a positive light and arguing for its maintenance or support, as dialectical responses to the discourses of death and denigration which argue for the extinction of Gaelic. Both sets of discourses posit stereotypical qualities of Gaelic based in part on an ideology of standard language (Milroy and Milroy 1999), an ideology which includes the following propositions: a civilized or "real" language has a single correct spoken form, which should be based on a single correct written form; linguistic variation is interpreted as inadequacy in comparison with the standard form; language change, including the use of foreign loan-words, is interpreted as decay of the language; negative judgements of speech are "expressed in terms of undesirable moral, intellectual, or social attributes of groups of speakers" (Milroy 2000, 63). Such an ideology, as Milroy again points out, is held widely and tenaciously as common sense in the face of evidence to the contrary, even by the speakers who would be most harshly judged according to its terms.

The stereotypes expressing such judgements of Gaelic represent expressions of anxiety about the relationship of language to ethnicity, and their attempts to renegotiate or reinscribe ethnic boundaries in Scotland. The representations of Gaelic in the media that Scottish journalists and language planners utilize in the late 20th century represent the latest phase in a long historical process, for they continually voice the representations of Gaelic from previous centuries. They also utilize the discursive resources of prior representations to frame their condemnations, observations, and appeals, in a way that highlights the impossibility of finding a purely objective approach to language shift.

Notes

1   This remark referred to Ibrox Stadium, the home of the Rangers Football Club of Glasgow. Ironically, the modern placename is derived from the original Gaelic placename *Àth Bruic*, Ford of the Badger.
2   The corncrake is an endangered species of bird native only to the Outer Hebrides, and still surviving there due to traditional agricultural practices.
3   For example, a sports figure who told ethnic jokes at a sporting dinner in Edinburgh was disciplined by his employer, the Scottish Rugby Union (Chamberlain 2002). However, animosity and discrimination based on ethnic, racial, and religious stereotypes clearly still occurs in the context of "private" discourse and social encounters in Scotland, as Hill (1995a) also describes for the USA.
4   A host of other institutional naming practices follow the same pattern, e.g. "The Arts Council" is the English arts council, while "The Scottish Arts Council" serves Scotland (also see McCrone, Morris, and Kiely 1995, 45). The same situation obtains for Wales, and "Newsnight Wales" is scheduled in identical fashion to "Newsnight Scotland."
5   The definition of the Scots word "teuchter" in the Oxford English Dictionary Online is terse—"A Highlander"—but the entry provides quotations from newspaper articles of 1962 and 1977 that together make the folk connection between the Gaelic language and bumpkin status clear:

> 1962 *Scotsman* 26 Jan. 11 There is ample evidence that she referred to him as a 'teuchter', a word which I understand to mean a country bumpkin. 1977 Times Lit. Suppl. 9 Sept. 1084/2 For the inhabitants of Harris are mainly what most Scots call 'teuchtars'—a word which I had never heard till I had it applied to me by a teacher in a Glasgow school. What is a teuchtar? It is a Lowland Scots imitation of a Gaelic noise, a term of now genial contempt for a crofter or, more generally, for anyone from beyond the Highland line" (Oxford English Dictionary Online 1989).

6   Anglicized Gaelic personal names were in widespread use throughout Scotland in the late 20th century, and English-language personal names

(both traditionally Scottish ones and traditionally English ones) are in common use among Gaelic speakers. Anglicized Gaelic surnames are distributed throughout Scotland, and indeed throughout the area of the original "Gaelic diaspora," including the United Kingdom, North America, and Australia. Moreover, not every Gaelic speaker has a traditionally Gaelic surname, due to intermarriage and other factors.

7   I would argue that this perception of lag, as a component of a larger effort towards homogeneity, accounts in part for the similar experiences of speakers of minority languages across the UK, as well as in France and elsewhere.

8   The word "fuck," considered to be one of the most obscene words in the English language, could be used on BBC television programming after the 9 p.m. watershed. The article noted in regard to obscenities on television that on BBC2, "a programme is allowed an average of five f***s an hour… provided it goes out after the 9pm watershed."

9   I thank the staff of Comunn na Gàidhlig, who formerly kept press clippings about Gaelic in Scotland, for sharing many of these newspaper articles with me while I conducted field research there.

10   Not coincidentally, the newspapers were also a prominent forum for the openly racist criticism of Highlanders, that is Gaels, in mid-19th century Scotland (Fenyö 2000).

11   While US tabloids tend to feature stories about aliens and the paranormal, British tabloids focus on "human interest" stories, albeit often sensationalized, about real human beings.

12   The *Scottish Sun* tabloid and the *Sunday Times Scotland* broadsheet, both notoriously conservative, are owned by the same company, and the *Daily Record* and *Sunday Mail* tabloids are both owned by the same company (Smith 1994, 244). Sunday newspapers are considered separate entities from their weekday counterparts, even when they are owned by the same company and share the same name.

13   Moore (2000, 43) also finds in late 20th-century media coverage of Native American languages "a distinctly 19th century view of the native inhabitants of North America as part of the flora and fauna of the continent, part of its natural landscape."

14   Lines 115–118, translation compiled from Bawcutt's footnotes and glossary. The following several lines relate that although the Devil himself had called for a "Hieland padayne" or Highland festival to entertain him, these Highlanders chattering in Gaelic were too loud for him, so he "smothered them with smoke" in the "deepest pit of hell" according to Bawcutt's translation. The poem is of the "Dance of the Sevin Deidly Sinnis" genre and is identified in anthologies by that name or by its first line, "Of Februar the fyiftene nycht" (Bawcutt 1996, 185).

15   The website was named "Chris Rae's Really, Really New Homepage." The URL was http://www.chrisrae.com/ and according to the page itself, this had been the URL since 16 July 1999.

16   This "Gaelic debate" took place on 2 March 2000 in the new Scottish Parliament. The debate was conducted in both Gaelic and English on the motion, in part, "That the Parliament welcomes the Scottish Executive's programme of action in support of the Gaelic language." The motion was unanimously agreed to. This major public event involving Gaelic was subject to a great deal of commentary in the Scottish press (McEwan-Fujita 2000).

17   Here I employ the US version of Brown's ideology of standard language to consult *Webster's New Collegiate Dictionary*, in a "rhetorical appeal to the published dictionary as the codified authority on what words really mean" (Silverstein 1979, 193).

18   Just as Gaelic is represented and perceived as inherently funny by the Scots, Scottish-accented English is often represented and perceived as inherently funny by the English, and this perception has even been absorbed into US popular culture in the 1990s through the television and film characters of the comedic actor Mike Myers, many of whom feature the same mock Glasgow accent (cf., Irvine and Gal 2000 on fractal recursivity).

19   See Hill (1995, 205, note 14) for the similar and important distinction between "mock Spanish," used by Anglos in the US as a form of humour that indexically reproduces racism, even without explicitly racist intent on the part of the speaker, and "Spanglish," "Caló," or "Border Spanish," used by Spanish speakers as a form or medium of joking and humour among themselves.

20   I believe this phenomenon can be fruitfully compared to early mock Gaelic examples, from a time when face-to-face contact between Highlanders and Lowlanders was becoming more frequent, as Highlanders would come into towns and mingle with and be observed by English-speaking locals.

21   In a tiresome example of intertextuality, the phrase "Gael farce" as a play on the expression "gale force" appears periodically in the headlines of newspaper articles about Gaelic.

22   The Royal National Mòd is an annual national Gaelic music and song competition modelled on the Welsh Eisteddfod.

23   Complaints about bilingual road signs, like complaints about Gaelic television programming and Gaelic medium education, also feature protests against paying for Gaelic language planning efforts with public money, a point that is discussed in detail in Chapter 7.

CHAPTER 4

"Gaelic Doomed as Speakers Die Out"? The Public Discourse of Gaelic Language Death in Scotland

1   Introduction

This paper situates public discourse about Gaelic in Scotland within the context of the wider Anglophone discourse about "minority languages" in general. Such discourse often invokes the views of linguists as scientific or expert knowledge. The construction of scientific knowledge is already itself the subject of scrutiny in the academic field called "history and philosophy of science." More recently, the scope of this field has been extended to cover the science of linguistics (e.g., Crowley 1990). Some linguistic anthropologists have argued that critical analyses of the science of linguistics need to be further extended to include critical analysis of the study of language shift and language obsolescence (see Gal 1989 and others in Dorian 1989; also see Moore 1998 and Hill 2002). That is the purpose of this chapter.

I use the technical terms "language shift" and "language obsolescence" in this paper, rather than the more widely known term "language death," which will itself be an object of scrutiny in the following section. "Language shift" can be defined as the "habitual use of one language … being replaced by the habitual use of another" within a given community (Gal 1979, 1). "Language obsolescence" has been defined in much the same way (Hoenigswald 1989, 347), but linguists often use this term to focus attention on the structural changes in languages undergoing shift, and the theoretical implications of these changes for knowledge about linguistic structure, rather than the social aspects of the process of language shift (e.g., Dorian 1989).[1]

I argue that the study of processes of language shift and revitalization within social science should also include a reflexive study of the academic discourses about these processes, the discourses that social scientists themselves bring to bear on particular languages. It should also include a study of how those discourses are disseminated into the wider public sphere. This paper presents such a study, focusing on the diffusion of academic discourses about language death into the media discourses about Gaelic in Scotland.

The discourse of language death has become a familiar one in the media in recent years, spurred by the growing discussion about globalization and the effects of increased worldwide communication on smaller language communities. Since the 1990s, concerned US linguists have been using print media to issue warnings about the rapid loss of small languages worldwide (e.g., Raymond, 1998).

Similar articles have appeared in the British press, some of which are global in outlook. However, this paper focuses on a group of Scottish and other British newspaper articles from the year 2000 in which British journalists systematically distorted linguists' warnings, transforming them into supposed scientific proof of the imminent death of Gaelic.[2]

In these articles, I identify two different kinds of "discourses of language death," which I define as particular ways of writing about the future of Gaelic and other minority languages. I call these two kinds of discourses "death" discourses and "scientistic" discourses. The death discourses posit Gaelic as a living—or rather dying—organism.

While the death metaphor is compelling, it serves to objectify Gaelic and obscure the actual mechanisms of language shift. The scientistic discourses purport to be based on scientific research and claim to predict the future of Gaelic with absolute certainty, but in fact are based on distorted understandings of linguistics, filtered through preexisting prejudices against Gaelic.

I will begin with a discussion of the way that death discourses are used to describe Gaelic, before turning to the main focus of this paper: the scientistic discourses which misrepresent scientific knowledge in such a way as to assert that it proves the certain and imminent death of Gaelic.

2 The Death Discourse of Language Shift and Obsolescence

Following is a short discussion of the anthropomorphizing metaphor of "language death," commonly used to describe processes of language shift and obsolescence. The idea of "language death" is perhaps the most noticeable element of linguists' discourse about language shift that journalists have borrowed to describe Gaelic. This romanticizing and biologizing metaphor is based on the premise that language is a living organism (see Hoenigswald 1989, 347). This implies that a language has a life cycle, and is an animate object, rather than a learnable human behaviour and symbolic system.

The use of this discourse demonstrates the continued effect of the "pastoral" convention in the understanding of language shift, as pointed out by linguistic anthropologist Susan Gal (1989, 316). This convention is predicated on a romantic notion of the "vanishing primitive," always dying but never quite dead (Clifford, 1986, 112-4). Sarah McKibben (1997; 2000) has analysed the death metaphor's use in describing the situation of Irish (see Ch. 5, p. 127 for further discussion of its origin in 17th century Irish poetry, and speculation on how this may have influenced the metaphor's introduction into Scottish Gaelic poetry).

In the 1930s, warnings of the impending death of Gaelic had already been being issued for such a long time that one commentator expressed frustration with the convention. In his *Introduction to Gaelic Scotland*, published in 1934, Alexander McKechnie described how

> Lord MacKay, one of the judges of the Court of Session, recently stated that he had heard enough of Gaelic being a condemned language for centuries and having to apologise, like Charles I... for being "an unconscionable time of dying" (1934, 11).

Despite these shortcomings, the death metaphor is almost impossible to avoid when discussing language shift. This may be because the very conceptual system of human beings is metaphorical in nature (Lakoff and Johnson 1980, 3). According to Lakoff and Johnson, metaphors structure daily human existence, behaviour, and actions, but they do so in ways which are largely unconscious (1980, 3). Thus, for example, many native English speakers find their everyday attitudes and activities to be pervasively shaped by the metaphorical premise that "time is money" (Lakoff and Johnson, 1980, 7).

We can see the compelling nature of the death metaphor in linguists' focus on the "last speaker" as a trope for illustrating language obsolescence. For example, *Vanishing Voices*, a book about language shift aimed at the general public and co-authored by anthropologist Daniel

Nettle and linguist Suzanne Romaine, features an arresting black and white photograph of Ishi on the cover. Ishi (1861/2–1916), made famous in anthropological circles through the work of anthropologist Alfred Kroeber and his wife Theodora Kroeber, was a California Native American "discovered" in 1911 who was the "last of his tribe" (Kroeber 1981 [1964]) and also the last native speaker of his language, Yahi. *Vanishing Voices* also contains a section with photographs of the "last speakers" of Manx, Eyak, Catawba Sioux, Wappo and Ubykh, and a photograph of the gravestone of the "last speaker" of Cornish.

The focus on speaker death as the mechanism and key point of language death, while certainly dramatic and intuitively logical, is unrealistic. It draws attention away from the main problem in language shift, which is the cessation of intergenerational language transmission (Fishman 1991). Moreover, as linguist Nick Evans has noted (2001), the "last speaker" is considered a prized find by linguists documenting lesser-used languages for posterity, but it can be defined in so many different ways that searching for one can resemble an attempt to reach the vanishing point on the horizon. For example, Evans describes a case where the "last speaker" of an Australian aboriginal language died, only for new "last speakers" to come forward after the funeral; they hadn't wanted to usurp his claim to linguistic and cultural authority during his lifetime. Thus the search for the single last speaker of a language often results in the ongoing discovery of a series of "last speakers" on a sliding scale of criteria for speakershood. As Evans puts it in the title of his article, "The last speaker is dead—long live the last speaker!"

Nonetheless, analyses of minority language situations in the academic literature have built easily on the metaphor of language as a living organism, giving us theories not only of language "death," but also of language "suicide," language "murder" (cited in Crystal, 2000, 87; Edwards, 1985, 51–3), and so on. Nancy Dorian gave us the memorable—and linguistically instructive—image of the East Sutherland Gaelic dialect "dying with its morphological boots on."[3] The cover of linguist David Crystal's 2000 book *Language Death* takes the metaphor in a medicalized direction, depicting a flatlining EKG superimposed over a giant pair of lips tinted blue.

Many linguists, if not their book cover designers, have recognized the problems and the limits of the death metaphor, and have tried to substitute the terms "language shift" and "language obsolescence," at least in their professional accounts. However, the death metaphor has continued to find ready acceptance in the media, in ever more lurid medicalized versions. For example, in one newspaper we find the idea that Gaelic is "on life support" (Johnson and Associated Press 1997), and according to *The Economist*, Gaelic "has just been admitted to the [Endangered Language Fund's] intensive care unit" ("Dying languages: English kills," 1998). The question of whether Gaelic deserves state support even takes the form of a debate over "Do Not Resuscitate" orders: "Now, Gaelic appears to be dying, but is it worth resuscitating the patient?" (see Ch. 3, p. 61).

Unfortunately, the death metaphor and its underlying premise, that languages are living organisms, shift attention away from the actual speakers as human beings. As we all know when we stop to think about it, a language is not a living organism; its *speakers* are living organisms who use the language as a tool; their use is a set of behaviours. However, even this point can be misused in the service of the death metaphor: a 1989 article in *The Independent* described children in a Gaelic-medium unit in Skye as "the last of a dying breed" (Dalrymple 1989, 34), a metaphorical description which is another variation on the romantic pastoral. The figure of speech reintroduces the Victorian-era idea of Gaelic speakers as a separate race—a Celtic race which most Victorians thought of as inferior to the Anglo-Saxon race. But not only are these Gaelic speakers not a separate race, they are not dying. In fact, 31 years later at the time of this book's publication, the oldest of those children may be in their 40s and raising children as Gaelic speakers.

3   The Scientific Discourse of Language Death

Now we move on to the main focus of this chapter, what I call the scientistic discourse of language death. I define this discourse as a particular way of representing linguistic research on endangered languages, with the outcome and even deliberate aim of promoting the idea that there is scientific proof that Gaelic is dying. Obviously, the death metaphors I have just discussed underpin this discourse, but it also relies on people's general understanding of categories of "scientific knowledge" and "expert knowledge" as the most accurate and truthful representations of reality.

I will focus on one major theme of this scientistic discourse of language death: the "100,000 speakers" concept, or the idea that a language needs 100,000 speakers to be viable in today's world. This idea has been represented as a scientific research finding in public discussions about Gaelic. However, if we trace this idea to its origin, we find that it was a speculation rather than the result of a scientific study.

US linguist Michael Krauss originally proposed this concept in a 1992 article that appeared in a special issue of the journal *Language*, the flagship journal of the Linguistic Society of America. The issue was devoted to the theme of endangered languages, edited by the linguist Ken Hale, and featured contributions from many linguists and sociolinguists on the situation of threatened languages around the world (Krauss 1992 is labeled #1 in Figure 4.1).

Krauss's idea was based on a number of informed suppositions and guesstimates. In the following passage, Krauss was attempting to determine how many "safe languages" there are in the world today, that is, languages which are neither endangered nor moribund. His goal was to subtract that "safe" number from the estimated total number of languages in the world, in order to assess how many languages in the world today could soon be lost:

> Let us instead take the approach of calculating the number of languages that are neither "moribund" nor "endangered," but belong to a third category, which I shall term "safe."
>
> For this third category we may identify two obvious positive factors: official state support and very large numbers of speakers. The first does not presently account for much, as there are, as of 1990, only about 170 sovereign states, and the, or an, official language of the majority of these is English (45 cases), French (30), Spanish or Arabic (20 each), or Portuguese (6), leaving only about 50 others… Considering now sheer numbers of speakers, there are 200 to 250 languages spoken by a million or more, but these of course greatly overlap with the official languages category. By including languages with down to half a million we might raise the total by 50, and by going down to 100,000 as a

safety-in-numbers limit, we might perhaps double the total to 600 "safe" languages.

Remember, though, the case of Breton, with perhaps a million speakers in living memory but now with very few children speakers, or Navajo, with well over 100,000 speakers a generation ago but now also with an uncertain future… Bear in mind, moreover, that the median number of speakers for the languages of the world is nowhere near 100,000, but rather 5,000 or 6,000. Therefore, I consider it a plausible calculation that—at the rate things are going—the coming century will see either the death or the doom of 90% of mankind's languages (1992, 7).

One element of Krauss's calculation involved his idea of "safety in numbers." After proposing the potential criteria of having over a half a million or a million speakers to be safe, he settled on 100,000 as an arbitrary "safety-in-numbers limit" for the number of speakers that a "safe" language might be thought to have. Based on this, he estimated a total of about 600 "safe" languages in the world, or 10% of the 6,000 to 7,000 total languages he estimated to exist. That is where we get the figure of "90% of mankind's languages" being endangered, as stated in the last sentence quoted above.

But along with these estimates, Krauss offered a caveat, reminding us that both Breton and Navajo had had over 100,000 speakers in recent history, which still did not protect them from rapid decline. Thus Krauss was aware of the shortcomings inherent in his attempt to estimate the number of endangered languages based solely on such a factor as the number of speakers. Moreover, Krauss also included a second element in his speculation, the idea that official state support was also needed to categorize a language as "safe," which has been omitted from many linguists' and journalists' restatement of the "100,000 speakers" idea.

It is important to bear in mind that the accuracy of Krauss's estimate is fundamentally unknowable, for a number of reasons. First, in order to count something one must first define what is being counted, yet defining what exactly is a language (versus a dialect, for example) is a difficult and ultimately arbitrary task dependent on social as well as linguistic factors (Haugen 1966; Hymes 1984 [1968]). Then there is the problem of determining when a language is actually "dead," as discussed above with reference to the work of Evans. There is also the problem of defining a state of endangerment more generally. Linguist Nikolai Vakhtin notes that assessments of the circumstances of languages are ultimately based on three sources of data: claims by speakers themselves; direct observations, intuitions and guesses by scholars; and "an intermediary option when scholars are themselves speakers, or former speakers" (Vakhtin 2002, 240–1). Vakhtin notes the pitfalls and limitations inherent in each of these sources of data (241–7) and concludes that "prognostications made on the basis of the data the inadequacy of whose sources has been described in this paper are far from trustworthy" (248). As an example he notes that predictions of the imminent death of languages in Northern Russia, based on these types of data, have been ongoing for over one hundred years, and yet the languages are still viable.

Setting this issue aside, we turn to the next step in the transformation of this well-meaning estimate into a statement about the imminent death of Gaelic. A 1998 article by Ken Hale (see #2 in Figure 4.1) utilized Krauss's concept without direct attribution:

> During the coming century, according to some informed estimates, 3,000 of the existing 6,000 languages will perish and another 2,400 will come near to extinction. This leaves just 600 languages in the "safe" category, assuming that category to be languages having 100,000 speakers or more (1998, 192).

Hale's formulation omitted Krauss's extended explanation and qualifiers. He transformed Krauss's plausible calculation of the number of languages not under threat in the world, based on an admittedly arbitrary figure of 100,000 speakers, into a statement of informed estimates based on an unquestioned assumption.

Hale also omitted the idea that state support was necessary to ensure the continued "safety" of a language, which Krauss had proposed, as did many later commentators (although that idea did not escape the notice of every journalist, as will be seen). By the year 2000, Anglophone linguists who worked on smaller languages were well aware of the "100,000 speakers" idea.

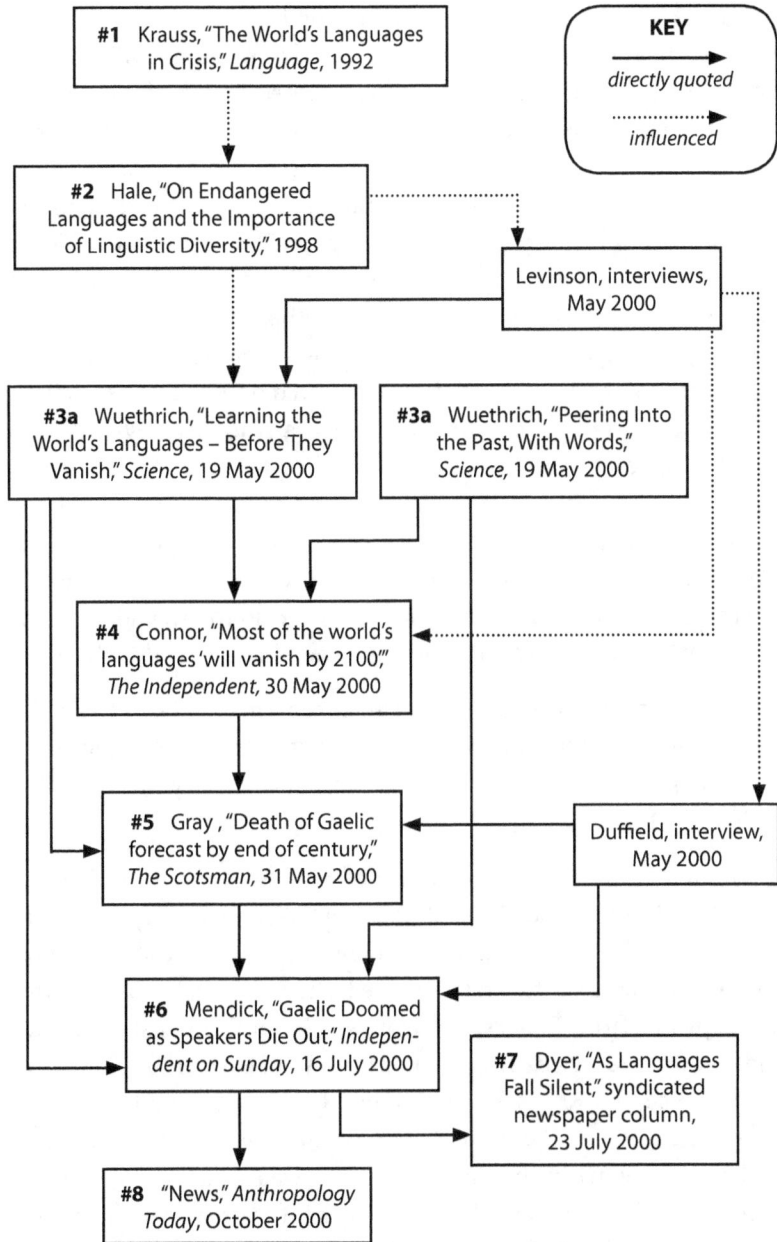

Figure 4.1 The dissemination of the scientistic "100,000 speakers" concept from US & Europe-based linguists, to science media, to Scottish media (who invented false scientific research results about Scottish Gaelic), to British media, to worldwide syndicated media, to UK anthropology.

On 16 May 2000, *Science* magazine published two articles side by side, by the same science journalist, each describing the relationship of "endangered languages" to linguistic research. The longer of the two articles, entitled "Learning the World's Languages—Before They Vanish," described how the study of less-widely spoken languages could contribute to research on whether grammar is innate or learned, and how speech influences thought (Wuethrich, 2000a; see #3a in Figure 4.1). The article quoted the linguists Nick Evans, Ken Hale, Stephen Levinson, Marianne Mithun and several others about the problem of language endangerment, and the importance of preserving endangered languages to provide data for future research on linguistic structure.

As one example, the author described a study by Levinson and another researcher in the Language and Cognition Group at the Max Planck Institute for Psycholinguistics in Nijmegen, the Netherlands, on "how unwritten, often endangered languages express spatial concepts" (Wuethrich, 2000a, 1158). The article started with the estimate that there were 6000 to 7000 languages in the world today, and the assertion that 90% of the world's languages were in danger:

> The world's 6 billion people speak approximately 6000 to 7000 languages, and most experts expect that at least half—and perhaps up to 90%—will disappear in the 21st century (Wuethrich 2000a, 1156).

Thus the author made indirect use of Krauss's estimate which was based on the figure of 100,000 speakers as an arbitrary "safety-in-numbers limit." Given that the journalist attributed the idea to "most experts" rather than to Krauss himself, she most likely obtained this concept not from Krauss, but from the several linguists she interviewed for the piece. This attribution may also demonstrate how widely accepted Krauss's estimate had become among linguists by this time, reaching the status of received wisdom.

The shorter article by the same author was a sidebar to the main one. The sidebar article, titled "Peering into the Past, with Words," described studies that would "offer new insights into the identity of mysterious ancient peoples" by studying, respectively, Nakh-Daghestanian languages of the Caucasus and Celtic languages. The study on Celtic languages was actually a comparison of grammatical features in Celtic and Afro-Asiatic languages, by Orin Gensler of the Max Planck Institute for Evolutionary Anthropology in Leipzig:

> Orin Gensler of the Max Planck Institute for Evolutionary Anthropology in Leipzig, Germany, analyzed Celtic languages, including Irish Gaelic, Scottish Gaelic, Welsh, and Breton. Once prevalent throughout Europe, these languages are now spoken only in the British Isles and Brittany in France... In a forthcoming monograph, Gensler studied 20 grammatical features found in both Celtic and Afro-Asiatic languages... Overall, Gensler found that about half the shared features are rare elsewhere [in 85 other unrelated languages from around the world] (Wuethrich 2000b, 1158; see #3b in Figure 4.1).

This study does not appear to be directly relevant to the idea that a particular number of speakers might be needed to safeguard the future of a language, but it does happen to mention Scottish Gaelic, and presumably because of this, both of these *Science* magazine articles were utilized by other journalists to convey the "100,000 speakers" concept to the Scottish and wider British public, as discussed below.

Moving to the British press, the next article I discuss begins to show how journalists frequently quote or paraphrase linguists' estimates to construct an "expert knowledge" about language death. They present Krauss's original estimates as neutral facts, further increasing the appearance of precision in the generation of "known facts" from the ultimately unknowable and uncountable.

On 30 May 2000, *The Independent* newspaper published an article based loosely on the organizing theme of the first of the *Science* articles, entitled "Most of the world's languages 'will vanish by 2100'" (see #4 in Figure 4.1). The article began:

> Most of the world's 6,000-plus languages will have died out by the end of the century, experts predicted yesterday. Linguists issued fresh warnings about the perilous position of the thousands of languages spoken mainly by adults but increasingly rarely by their children and grandchildren... "Ninety per cent of languages today are spoken by less than 100,000 people. With most languages being spoken by a small number of individuals,

that makes them very vulnerable," said Steve Levinson, of the Max Planck Institute for psycholinguists [sic] at Nijmegen, in the Netherlands (Connor, 2000).

For this article, the *Independent*'s science editor may have obtained a new interview with linguist Stephen Levinson at the Max Planck Institute for Psycholinguistics (not "for psycholinguists"), or he may have simply quoted the interview from *Science* magazine. In any case, the article quoted Levinson referencing Krauss's "100,000 speakers" concept, just as Wuethrich had in her *Science* article about Levinson's research. The article also featured the phrases "experts predict," "scientists estimate" and "linguists estimate," framing subsequent discussion of these figures—and the futures of minority languages that they purported to predict—as knowledge of a very particular type: scientific expert knowledge.

On 31 May 2000, the day after the *Independent* article appeared, *The Scotsman* newspaper published a story titled "Death of Gaelic forecast by end of century" (Gray, 2000; see #5 in Figure 4.1). This article drew on the first of the two *Science* articles (Gray, personal communication), and also possibly on the *Independent* article from the previous day. The major difference between this new article and the previous ones was that this journalist applied the ideas described in the two previous articles directly to Gaelic, in the process actually creating a new story.

The Scotsman article began, "Gaelic could die out by the end of the century if more children are not encouraged to learn the language, a leading linguist warned yesterday." The "100,000 speakers" idea also made its appearance, again as the speech of "experts":

> Experts believe that the only way for a threatened language to survive is to have at least 100,000 speakers and receive full support from the nation state. But just under 70,000 people in Scotland speak Gaelic and, despite unprecedented levels of funding in recent years, Gaelic speakers believe that educational programmes in particular need a huge injection of funding (Gray, 2000).

By juxtaposing these two statements, that a language must have at least 100,000 speakers and that just under 70,000 people in Scotland speak Gaelic, the journalist implied that Gaelic cannot survive.[4]

The article further implied that Levinson, in his capacity as a "leading linguist," had made a public statement specifically about the future of Scottish Gaelic:

> Steve Levinson, a linguist based at the Max Planck Institute for psycholinguists [sic] at Nijmegen in the Netherlands, believes that Irish will survive into the next century, but Gaelic is in serious danger of extinction. Mr Levinson believes that most of the world's 6,000-plus languages will have died out by the end of the century.

However, if one reads the article carefully, one sees that the journalist did not in fact directly quote Levinson about the future of Irish and of Scottish Gaelic; she merely described his beliefs, which she may have extrapolated from his stated position that languages spoken by less than 100,000 people are "very vulnerable."

The idea that this journalist was in fact recycling Levinson's statements from the *Independent* in order to create her own news story is supported by the fact that her article also repeated the identical *Independent* quote from Levinson: "Ninety per cent of languages today are spoken by less than 100,000 people. With most languages being spoken by a small number of individuals, that makes them very vulnerable."[5]

However, the article seems to have utilized the "leading linguist" Levinson's "expert knowledge" to support a statement about the future of Gaelic without his knowledge, and despite the fact that Levinson specialises in studying the Mayan language Tzeltal, not Gaelic.

About six weeks later, on 16 July 2000, *The Independent on Sunday* published an article entitled "Gaelic doomed as speakers die out" (Mendick, 2000; see #6 in Figure 4.1), which was similar to the *Scotsman* article and also drew on both the *Independent* article and the *Science* articles already described. As well as utilizing the discourse of death, this reporter creatively combined the "100,000 speakers" concept as expressed by Levinson at the Max Planck Institute for Psycholinguistics in Nijmegen, the Netherlands, as described in the *Scotsman* article and the first *Science* article, with a different Max Planck Institute study described in the second *Science* article: Orin Gensler's study at the MPI for Evolutionary Anthropology in Leipzig, Germany, on grammatical features in Celtic and Afro-Asiatic languages. The reporter seems to have erroneously reconstituted these two separate elements as a single, but fictitious, study conducted in Nijmegen supposedly "proving" that Gaelic was doomed:

> Researchers at Max Planck Institute in Holland, who have conducted a comprehensive survey of Europe's minor languages, have found that none can survive with fewer than 100,000 speakers. Gaelic has only half that number.

No such study was conducted at any branch of the Max Planck Institute. In addition to creating a fictitious "comprehensive survey of Europe's minor languages" with a fictitious finding "that none can survive with fewer than 100,000 speakers," the journalist also tried to lend credence to this finding by quoting the British linguist Nigel Duffield, who was a guest researcher at the Max Planck Institute at the time. Duffield had already been quoted in the previous *Scotsman* article on the rapid rate of language loss in general and the need for people to be concerned.

However, he was quoted quite differently in this *Independent on Sunday* article. Duffield recalled to me that at the time, several reporters had been trying to reach Stephen Levinson for interviews. One day Levinson was not available, so the secretary of the Language and Cognition Group at MPI gave Duffield's name to reporters instead. At the time of the interview, Duffield was specializing in the theoretical syntax of modern Irish. Presumably because of this focus on Irish, the *Independent on Sunday* reporter called Duffield a "Gaelic expert" and in quoting him, implied that he was qualified to pronounce on the future of modern Scottish Gaelic: "'It is reasonable to think within 100 years Gaelic won't be around,' said Dr Nigel Duffield, a Gaelic expert at the Institute."

Duffield later said that he did not claim to the reporter to be an expert on Scottish Gaelic, since he was not knowledgeable about the particular situation of Scottish Gaelic. Nor had he participated in any study such as the one described in the article. Nonetheless, Duffield observed that the reporter prodded him to apply his general observations on endangered languages specifically to Scottish Gaelic, took his answers out of context, and reframed them as confirmation "that [Gaelic] was doomed" (personal communication, 2002).

One week after this *Independent on Sunday* article, the London-based freelance journalist Gwynne Dyer picked up the story and wrote a syndicated opinion column about it entitled "As Languages Fall Silent." Dyer restated the 100,000 speakers concept, following the *Independent on Sunday* in attributing it to the Max Planck Institute for Psycholinguistics as the finding of a scientific study:

> What enables some minority languages to survive and thrive, while others wither? Numbers, says the Max Planck Institute for Psycholinguistics at Nijmegen in the Netherlands: No language with fewer than 100,000 speakers can hope to survive (Dyer, 2000; see #7 in Figure 4.1).

Dyer did not question the overall validity of the 100,000 speakers concept, but the point of his column was that "numbers" alone would not guarantee the safety of a language. Ironically, he was apparently unaware that Krauss had included the importance of state support in his concept, but Dyer also proposed that political will was also needed to keep a language alive. However, he decided that such political will was missing in Scotland, and thus, he proclaimed, Gaelic was doomed: "Scots Gaelic has not been the majority speech in Scotland for 1,000 years. It could still be revived in theory, but it would take more than just money, and the political will and emotional commitment are probably just not there."

He did not feel that this was a bad thing; taking the opposite position of linguistic conservationists, he claimed that the disappearance of languages worldwide is really just about a reasonable, harmless "consolidation" of human diversity, a view that is a variation of social Darwinism (see Ch. 3, p. 89). Referencing the Monty Python film "The Meaning of Life," Dyer wrote:

> As nature provides us with endless variations on a genetic theme, so the evolution of language as human beings expanded around the globe has given us endless variations on a linguistic theme. But not every sperm is sacred (Dyer, 2000).

Dyer's column was syndicated in approximately 175 newspapers in 45 countries, including the US, Russia, Argentina, Saudi Arabia, and Japan; it was not only published in English, but also translated into less widespread languages like Czech, Finnish, Afrikaans, and Malayalam (personal communication, 2002). Thus the erroneous idea that a scientific study had been conducted proving that no language—including Scottish Gaelic—could survive with less than 100,000 speakers was disseminated worldwide.

Anthropology Today, the newsletter of the Royal Anthropological Institute of Great Britain, was the final whisperer in this high-stakes game of "Telephone"[6] (see #8 in Figure 4.1). The relevant item in the "News" column of the October 2000 issue of *Anthropology Today* is quoted in full here:

> What is the financial value of a living language? Around £12.5 million a year, if you consider how much is spent subsidising the Scottish branch of Gaelic, and apparently to little positive effect. A seemingly terminal decline is in progress, with the number of speakers (mostly in the Western Isles and parts of the western mainland) falling from 79,000 in 1981 to just over 50,000 today. It is estimated that for every child born into a Gaelic-speaking family, four speakers of the language die. And if the findings of the Max Planck Institute in Holland are anything to go by, the future looks bleak. "It is reasonable to think within 100 years Gaelic won't be around," stated Dr Nigel Duffield, an expert on the language at the Institute, in the *Independent on Sunday* (16.08.00) [sic]. A pessimistic outlook that perhaps will not be shared by Scottish nationalists and liberal supporters in London, who want more money spent on saving the language.

Anthropology Today closed the circle by recycling the story about a scientific study proving that a language needs 100,000 speakers to survive back into the academic sphere, where the 100,000 speakers concept originated. Unfortunately this news item may have encouraged British anthropologists to view Gaelic not as part of an indigenous language-culture complex—the orthodox anthropological view—but as an expensive and hopeless cause that is the preserve of special interest groups, reproducing a view that is frequently expressed by popular critics of Gaelic in the Scottish press. The article demonstrates a fundamental misunderstanding of the base of support for

Gaelic; it attributes support mainly to "Scottish nationalists and liberal supporters in London," but Scottish nationalists as a group have never given strong support to Gaelic language maintenance or government funding for it (see Ch. 5, pp. 135–138, this volume), and English "liberals in London" are not generally supportive of Gaelic language maintenance efforts either—when they are even aware of the existence of Gaelic.[7] The article also omits to mention that government support for Gaelic is favoured by the over-lapping groups of (1) many Gaelic speakers who live in Scotland, and (2) parents with children in Gaelic medium education in Scotland. Among other things, this representation of Gaelic illustrates the problems that British social anthropology has had with understanding the value of the anthropological study of British cultures.

The compiler of this item cribbed the first paragraph from the *Independent on Sunday* article already discussed, with a few changes. The compiler further transformed Duffield from a "Gaelic expert" into an expert on Scottish Gaelic, further enhancing his authority to pronounce on the future of the language. The compiler kept the idea that the 100,000 speakers concept was a scientific finding of the Max Planck Institute. An "apparently terminal decline" in *The Independent on Sunday* became a "seemingly terminal decline," and the ostensibly census-based figures of 79,000 speakers in 1981 and just over 50,000 speakers "today" from *The Independent on Sunday* were repeated, together with the reminder that they were "falling."[8]

The constant repetition of the statistics in these and other news stories about Gaelic, together with the descriptors quoted here ("a seemingly terminal decline," "falling," "bleak," and "pessimistic"), constitutes a poetics of statistics that actually intensifies the message in the name of neutral reportage (McEwan-Fujita, 2003, 212–3; see Ch. 6, this volume). The overall effect of the constant recycling of these discourses is to give the impression to anyone who pays attention to the media in Scotland that Gaelic is moribund. This erases, among many other things, the important fact that there are still more than 50,000 living people "out there" speaking Gaelic to one another on a more or less regular basis.

4   Conclusion

Unfortunately, this dynamic of story generation can be typical of the modern media. My goal here has been to show how this dynamic could impact Gaelic in particular. Linguists' original well-meaning warnings about languages in peril were transformed into part of a larger overall pattern of denigration of Gaelic in the Scottish national public sphere. Two sets of preconceptions were involved in this transformation. First is the idea that the purpose of science in general is to generate predictive theories. If this were true, then it would be no surprise for linguistics, as a science, to be expected to generate predictive theories. And if the general public had the idea that this were the case, then it would be no surprise if they assumed linguists' pronouncements to have both scientific validity and predictive value. The second set of preconceptions involves the long-standing prejudice against Gaelic that has been expressed in the Scottish public sphere for the last several centuries and continues today (Durkacz, 1983; MacKinnon, 1974; Withers, 1988; see also Chapters 3, 5, and 6, this volume).

The death discourse about Gaelic can have a number of possible effects on Gaelic speakers and the future of the Gaelic language. First, over-use of this death discourse obscures the fact that "Gaelic" is not in fact a living thing, or an object, but a pattern of learned behaviour and a means of communication between living human beings. Thinking about Gaelic as an object makes it much easier to perpetuate the racist attitudes against Gaelic speakers that have been expressed and enacted for centuries already. The death discourse also obscures the fact that language shift does not take place at the point of speaker death, a key point that must be kept in mind not only when assessing language shift, but also when planning language revitalization activities.

Finally, through repeated exposure to the idea that "Gaelic is dying," there is always the possibility that Gaelic speakers themselves will become more fatalistic about the future of Gaelic, and will enact a self-fulfilling prophecy by failing to transmit the language to the next generation, since "it is dying anyway."

The scientistic discourse about Gaelic may also have its own set of effects on the future of the language. Public officials could use "scientific research results" as justification for their own pre-existing prejudice against Gaelic. Moreover, and most importantly, if public officials believe that linguists have scientifically proven "Gaelic is doomed," then they might feel that public spending on Gaelic revitalization is a waste of money, and attempt to cut off or block funding for Gaelic. Since no linguist possesses the tools or insight to accurately and scientifically predict the future of Gaelic language use in Scotland, we must take precautions not to create self-fulfilling prophecies about its "imminent demise."

In conclusion, the examples discussed here illustrate the important role of constructions of "scientific expert knowledge" by linguists and journalists in public discourses about language shift. We need to keep an eye on the death discourse and the scientistic discourse about Gaelic, and debunk them when necessary, because the replication of these discourses has the potential to become a self-fulfilling prophecy. In other words, discourses of language death have the potential to become a causal factor in the very language shift they purport to describe and predict.

Notes

1   It must be noted that even linguists who use the term "language obsolescence" cannot always escape reference to the concept or metaphor of death (e.g., Hoenigswald 1989, 347; Jones, 1998, 5).
2   I thank the following people for assistance in identifying these sources: Ms. Keira Ballantyne (Department of Linguistics, University of Hawai'i at Manoa), Dr. Nigel Duffield (Department of Linguistics, McGill University), Ms. Edith Sjoerdsma (Secretary, Language and Cognition Group, Max Planck Institute for Psycholinguistics), Dr. Doug Whalen (President, Endangered Languages Fund, Haskins Laboratories, Yale University), and Mr. Ben Zimmer (Department of Anthropology, University of Chicago). I especially thank Dr. James Oliver (Institute of Governance, University of Edinburgh) who alerted me to the existence of the articles mentioning the Max Planck Institute in *The Scotsman*, *The Independent on Sunday*, and *Anthropology Today*, and their factual errors, thus providing the inspiration for this paper.
3   Ironically, although Dorian's studies of Gaelic (e.g., Dorian 1981), have played a major role in scholars' formulation of theoretical models of language shift (Sasse 1992), the Scottish national media seem not to have picked up on this idea. This is perhaps fortunate, given that media sources

could conceivably attempt to utilize her work to further argue for the justification of "letting Gaelic die" in Scotland, although Dorian has never proposed this idea in her own work and instead has argued in favour of Gaelic language maintenance efforts (1987).

4   I analyze the way state financial support for Gaelic is described by the Scottish press in Chapter 6, this volume.

5   The article also repeated the mistaken labelling of the Max Planck Institute for Psycholinguistics as the Max Planck Institute "for psycholinguists," as seen in the passage quoted previously.

6   Or "Chinese whispers" as the children's game is known in the UK, although this name is denigrating to Chinese languages and their speakers.

7   For example, *Guardian* columnist Polly Toynbee, arguably London's most prominent liberal journalist at the time, described efforts to promote the autochthonous languages of Britain and Ireland as "imposing dead languages on wretched children who should be learning live ones" (Toynbee, 2000). Another *Guardian* journalist (Walker, 1999) expressed the view that such initiatives have "a clammy, nativist feel."

8   I must regretfully omit any discussion of the problematic nature of census statistics. However, I briefly note here that reliance solely on census statistics can raise epistemological problems relating to issues of state power (Hacking 1991), the determination of linguistic and ethnic boundaries (Friedman 1997), and the reliability of self-reporting language behaviour (Gal 1979).

CHAPTER 5

Language Revitalization Discourses as Metaculture: Gaelic in Scotland from the 18th to 20th Centuries

1   Introduction

In this paper I analyze discourses of Gaelic language revitalization efforts in Scotland as examples of Urban's (2001) "metaculture" in order to gain a better understanding of how people may attempt and achieve social and linguistic change through minority language revitalization efforts. Metaculture may be defined as "culture about culture," or more specifically cultural forms or practices that comment on other cultural forms or practices, and in so doing impact their circulation. According to Urban, metacultural forms can only make sense, and thus be effective, because they incorporate "a range of prior and seemingly disparate cultural elements" from the past (2001, 5). In incorporating familiar past elements, metaculture actually facilitates the movement of culture in space and in time, pushing it into circulation (Urban 2001, 4). Minority language revitalization efforts are a clear example of metaculture because they are cultural behaviours and forms, yet are also integrally "meta-level", language revitalization efforts, including discourses, are sociolinguistic responses to the linguistic and sociolinguistic changes wrought through processes of language shift. In other words, they are metapragmatic discourses explicitly attempting to change language structure, function, and social usage or undo previous changes (Silverstein 1985). The metacultural forms of minority language revitalization efforts are new, yet they incorporate older elements that allow them to make sense to people and to be effective (Urban 2001, 4).

Scottish Gaelic is a minority language undergoing shift in Scotland. In 1700 it is estimated that about 25–30% of the Scottish population of 900,000 were Gaelic speakers, most of them monoglot (Jones and McLeod 2007, 21). In the first national census to include questions about Gaelic, in 1881, a total of 231,594 Gaelic speakers were enumerated, or 6.2% of Scotland's population. In the 2001 Scottish census, 93,282 people, or 1.8% of Scotland's enumerated 2001 population of 5,062,011, were claimed to have various combinations of skills in understanding, speaking, reading, and/or writing Gaelic.

Discourses utilized by participants in the public discussion of Gaelic in Scotland since the 18th century can be divided into two main categories: discourses of language death and denigration, and discourses of language revitalization and redemption. I define the former as a set of predications about Gaelic and its speakers that participants utilize in order to declare, explain, justify, or advocate for the elimination of Gaelic, and/or to disparage the language or its speakers. I define the latter as responses to the former: a set of predications about Gaelic focused on proclaiming its virtues as justification for its preservation, salvation or revitalization. Although this chapter focuses primarily on discourses of revitalization and redemption, both types of discourses have existed in a dialectical relationship in Scotland for centuries, and both are of importance for understanding semiotically-mediated processes of Gaelic language shift (see Ch. 3).

After a discussion of the historical period in which redemptive and revitalizing discourses about Gaelic first emerged, I shall describe seven different common themes or predications of these discourses, giving historical examples from the 18th through 20th centuries for each and elucidating the fundamental metacultural aspects for each: how the discourses constitute metacultural and metalinguistic commentaries on cultural and linguistic practices, and how previously circulating elements of culture (that is, elements of the presupposed context, Silverstein 2003), including affective stances, ideologies of standard language, and discourses of Gaelic language death and denigration, are dialogically (Bakhtin 1981) contained within each creative revitalizing response (Urban 2001, 222), making it seem familiar and understandable while also limiting the terms of the response.[1]

2 The Context of Emergence

By the 15th and 16th centuries, Lowland Scottish denigration of Highlanders in royal decrees, travel accounts, and popular song had formed a pattern, as discussed in Chapter 3 of this volume. Lowlanders, who spoke Scots and/or Scottish English, portrayed Gaelic-speaking Highlanders as the "other," and assigning them the negative values of barbarousness, dishonour, and animal-like qualities, in implicit contrast to Lowlanders who were civilized, honourable, and of course, fully human (Chapman 1982). The repetition of metaphors in which the sound of Gaelic is compared to the sounds of birds or other animals, for example, is found from the 16th to 20th centuries and suggests the continuity of a symbolic system (see Ch. 3, pp. 79–84).

Explicit meta-level (metalinguistic, metadiscursive, metapragmatic) praise for Gaelic, in contrast to the use of Gaelic as a medium for expression and communication about other matters, seems to have originated in response to this explicit devaluation of Gaelic, in the social and political context of contact between speakers of Gaelic and speakers of varieties of Scots and English. The discourses of revitalization and redemption are clearly responses to discourses of death and denigration. One might therefore suppose that the identification and denigration of Highlanders as Gaelic speakers as such came first in strict chronological terms, and indeed the earliest known examples date from the 14th century CE (Withers 1984, 22). However, as early as the 16th century, the attack and denigration of Highlanders and the defense or valorization of Highlanders were each already being positioned as responses to the opposite position. One of the earliest recorded examples of anti-Highland discourse was framed as a response to pro-Highland, anti-Lowland discourse:

> Montgomerie, in his "Ane Answer to ane Helandmannis Invective" written in the 1550s, went so far as to record "How the first Helandman, of God was maid, of ane horss turd, in Argyle, as is said", and by the same period the difference between Scottish as nationality and Gaelic as a language divorced from Scottishness may even have been explicit in Scottish political circles (Withers 1984, 24).

Therefore, for the period we are discussing in this chapter, from the 18th to 21st centuries, the denigrating discourses cannot usefully be considered as prior to the redemptive discourses, but rather should be considered as always standing in dialectical relationship to them.

The first known explicitly revitalizing and redemptive discourses about Gaelic are contained in 18th-century Gaelic poems that draw on the conventions of the genre of Gaelic panegyric poetry, originally composed in the 13th through 17th centuries by professional poets in praise of noble patrons (MacInnes, 1979). The first poems in praise of the Gaelic language were not only prominent among the very first Gaelic poems to be printed on a press, but were also directly linked with the first attempts at scientific study, preservation, and standardization of Gaelic. The conditions of their composition included the breakdown of the clan system with its noble patronage for the hereditary bardic classes in Gaelic society. Poets were no longer able to make a living as such and were forced to turn to other means of support. Although poets inherited the poetic genres and devices of the Classical period, they broke down the rigid boundaries and in a move "little short of revolutionary," turned from praising "famous men" to praising "women, creatures, things, [and] concepts," including pets, places, ships, bagpipes, whisky, and the penis, as well as the Gaelic language (Black 2007, 114; also see Arbuthnot, 2002).

Thus at the same time that Gaelic poets were culturally utilizing the bardic genres and conventions, they were metaculturally commenting upon them and undermining them, in part as a critique of their precarious new political economic position. That they were redemptively praising Gaelic and heroes of Gaelic at this time marks an emergent "modern" approach to Gaelic not only as a medium of culture, but also as an object of metacultural and metadiscursive commentary; in other words, as a reified language-object. The *moladh* or praise of Gaelic and its "heroes" was the mode of indigenously-inflected modernity most supportive of their own efforts.

The first known poem in praise of Gaelic was the Reverend John Maclean's poem praising Edward Lhuyd for the first scientific research on Scottish Gaelic, one of 13 laudatory poems in Latin, Welsh, and Gaelic printed in the Preface of Edward Lhuyd's 1707 work *Archaeologia Brittanica: an Account of the Languages, Histories and Customs of Great Britain, from Travels through Wales, Cornwall, Bas-Bretagne, Ireland and Scotland* (Ó Baoill 1979, 244–245, 261). Lhuyd's work contained what some call the first Scottish Gaelic dictionary,[2] as well as observations of common features shared by the Celtic languages which demonstrated that they were Indo-European (Campbell and Thomson 1963, xiii, xx–xxii). Lhuyd's study "provided evidence to refute those who condemned the Celtic languages as barbarous dialects—an essential step in their cultural rehabilitation" (Durkacz 1983, 190). Indeed,

> the first 11 of the 13 poems were probably composed in order to counteract in some measure the criticisms of his work which Lhuyd had heard before the publication of *AB* and to which he alludes in his Preface (5th page) (Ó Baoill 1979, 245).

Lhuyd's research took place as the bardic tradition was going out of existence. In 1700, Lhuyd interviewed the Reverend John Beaton, minister of Kilninian in Mull, for his research. Celtic scholar John Lorne Campbell describes the meeting as "altogether exceptional": "the first Celtic scholar, in the modern sense of the word, met one of the last living persons who had had the ancient Gaelic bardic education" (Campbell and Thomson 1963, xxi, 12–15).[3]

Maclean, or Maighstir Seathan as he was known in Gaelic (c. 1680–1756), became a minister in the Isle of Mull in 1702. Scholars speculate that he met Edward Lhuyd in Mull in 1699 or 1700 while a student at University of Glasgow (Ó Baoill 1979, lxiii). Maighstir Seathan may have been one of the two anonymous correspondents who prepared the Scottish Gaelic supplement to the first printed Irish Gaelic dictionary in Lhuyd's volume (Campbell and Thomson 1963, xiv). Maighstir Seathan himself interviewed Rev. John Beaton at the request of Rev. Robert Wodrow, librarian at University of Glasgow, "to obtain… a wide range of information on topics including Highland history, language, tradition, archaeology and manuscripts" which he later conveyed to Wodrow in a letter (Ó Baoill 1979, lxiii). Wodrow had received a "questionnaire on the language and antiquities of the Highlands" in a letter from Lhuyd, and had been extremely eager to contact Beaton after hearing about Lhuyd's discovery of him and his manuscripts (Campbell and Thomson 1963, 3, 22). Maighstir Seathan's encounter, prompted by Wodrow's request, had an impact on the former's praise poem, numbered 17 in an annotated edition of Maclean poets: "Obviously he [Mgr. Seathan] did not forget the information he passed on, for much of the antiquarian content of [poems] nos. 16 and 17 here is to be found in the letter to Wodrow" (Ó Baoill 1979, lxiv, also see 94–95, 100–103).

Maighstir Seathan's poetic praise will be analyzed in detail in the following section. However, its general characteristics can be discussed here. His praise for Gaelic, with its epithets drawn from the bardic tradition, may be viewed as dialogical. He described Gaelic as

A Teanga líonmhur, bhríoghmhur, bhlasda, bhínn,/'san chan'mhain thartrach, líobhtha, ghasta, ghrínn

A widely-spoken, vigorous, sweet and melodious tongue,/A strong, polished, beautiful and accurate language (Ó Baoill 1979, 100–103).

Each of the adjectives may be interpreted in context as a response, presupposing an allegation with a negative valence: Gaelic was not spoken widely but by small and shrinking numbers of people, was not vigorous but weak or unhealthy, was not sweet but unpleasant to hear, not polished but rough and rude, not beautiful and accurate but ugly and vague. Maighstir Seathan piled up the descriptors because these epithets were the very stuff of Gaelic panegyric verse—the conventions of the genre. But we have evidence that these specific negative allegations were made against Gaelic in subsequent centuries (see Ch. 3), so it is not unreasonable to suppose that Maighstir Seathan had already encountered them and was dialogically responding to them.

In the service of the Presbytery of Mull, Maighstir Seathan also had contact with mid-18th-century Gaelic poet Alexander MacDonald (Ó Baoill 1979, lxxiii, lxxvi;), known as Alasdair MacMhaighstir Alasdair in Gaelic (c. 1698–c. 1770) (Thomson 1996, 75–82). Circa 1738, MacMhaighstir Alasdair composed the next known poem praising Gaelic. This one has been called the most influential of the sub-genre of poems praising the language and efforts to revive it (Jones and McLeod 2007, 24). MacMhaighstir Alasdair's poem, titled "*Moladh an úghdair do 'n tsean chánoin Ghailic*" ["The author's praise of the ancient Gaelic language"] (Mac-Dhonuill 1751, 1), was directly influenced in metre and style by Maclean's poem (Ó Baoill 1979, 261, 297). When MacMhaighstir Alasdair published it in 1751, it was the first secular Gaelic verse to appear in print since the poems printed in Lhuyd's preface. MacMhaighstir Alasdair was involved in other pursuits such as Gaelic dictionary making, having started work on *A Galick and*

English Vocabulary in 1728, which was published for use in the schools of the Society in Scotland for Propagating Christian Knowledge, in which he also taught (A. MacDonald and Society in Scotland for Propagating Christian Knowledge, 1741). This dictionary-making activity, his teaching, and his poetical compositions were simultaneously new Gaelic cultural forms, and metacultural and metalinguistic commentaries on Gaelic, aimed at strengthening the social position and reputation of Gaelic.

From the last quarter of the 18th century, more revitalizing and redemptive discourses appeared in connection with the controversies that emerged around James Macpherson's poems of Ossian. First published between 1760 and 1763, they appeared in collected form in 1765 as *The Works of Ossian, The Son of Fingal, Translated from the Galic Language by James Macpherson*. Although Macpherson claimed the poems to be English translations of third-century Gaelic originals, and he later produced an apparent back-translation of some of them, they have in fact been shown to be a pastiche of Gaelic oral literature, English and classical verse, and Biblical styles (Thomson, 1951).

Macpherson put these poems forward in part as an act of cultural rehabilitation or re-valorization. His work was accepted as authentic and valorized throughout Europe, attracting the interest and aesthetic engagement of Herder, Goethe, and Mendelssohn, and the admiration of such figures as Napoleon Bonaparte. At the same time, many public intellectuals such as Samuel Johnson and David Hume questioned their authenticity, and a great deal of ink was spilled in public claims and counter-claims. The Highland Society of Scotland conducted an inquiry into their authenticity following Macpherson's death in 1796, and various treatises attempting to prove or disprove their authenticity continued to be written throughout the 19th century.

Samuel Johnson was a harsh critic of Macpherson and of Gaelic, but Krisztina Fenyö (2000, 20–21) points out that Johnson seems to express contradictory attitudes about Gaelic. In his 1775 account of *A Journey to the Western Islands of Scotland*, Johnson wrote one of the most well-known put-downs of Gaelic as the language of savages:

> Of the Earse language, as I understand nothing, I cannot say more than I have been told. It is the rude speech of a barbarous

people, who had few thoughts to express, and were content, as they conceived grossly, to be grossly understood (Johnson and Boswell 1984, 116).

Those who have been sympathetic to Gaelic have taken Johnson's published comments as a sign that he was completely biased against Gaelic (e.g., Macdhomhnuill 1776, 320, cited in Newton 2000, 192–3; MacKay 1877, xviii; Durkacz 1983). However, Johnson's harsh comments have been interpreted outside of the context of his particular Enlightenment-era approach to language. As the author of *A Dictionary of the English Language* (1755), Johnson did not believe that Gaelic was *hopelessly* deficient; he believed that the shortfall he perceived in the language could be remedied by the development of a written standard:

> After what has lately been talked of Highland bards, and Highland genius [a reference to James Macpherson's poems of Ossian], many will startle when they are told, that the Earse never was a written language; that there is not in the world an Earse manuscript a hundred years old; and that the sounds of the highlanders were never expressed by letters, till some little books of piety were translated, and a metrical version of the Psalms was made by the Synod of Argyle. Whoever therefore now writes in this language, spells according to his own perception of the sound, and his own idea of the power of the letters. The Welsh and the Irish are cultivated tongues. The Welsh, 200 years ago, insulted their English neighbours for the instability of their Orthography; while the Earse merely floated in the breath of the people, and could therefore receive little improvement. When a language begins to teem with books, it is tending to refinement; [...] [with writing] speech becomes embodied and permanent; [...] Exactness is first obtained, and afterwards elegance. But diction, merely vocal, is always in its childhood. [...] There may possibly be books without a polished language, but there can be no polished language without books (Johnson and Boswell 1984, 116).

This passage shows us that in fact, Johnson's comments against Gaelic were motivated primarily by an ideology of standard language in which written language is considered superior to oral language (Milroy and Milroy 1999; see Ch. 9 in this volume). Macpherson had made claims that his poems were translations of 3rd century BCE Gaelic manuscripts in his possession, but these manuscripts did not in fact exist (Johnson and Boswell 1984, 117–118; Fenyö 2000, 20–22).

In expressing his opinion that the Ossian poems were fraudulent, Johnson disputed the antiquity of the entire Gaelic written tradition, hyperbolically denied the existence of any Gaelic manuscripts at all, and completely dismissed the aesthetic, codified, standardized, and literate dimensions of the centuries-old Gaelic tradition of learned poetic composition. Ironically, the highly codified written standard Classical Gaelic of the professional poets had just gone out of use in the previous century, and Johnson's own university, Oxford, had declined to purchase Lhuyd's collection of Gaelic manuscripts after Lhuyd's death (Campbell and Thomson 1963, xiv–xv, 22).[4] Fenyö (2000, 20–22) also notes that the extreme nature of Johnson's comments was likely prompted in part by his love of argument and challenge, his tendency to play devil's advocate, and his propensity for teasing his Scottish friend James Boswell.

Johnson was aware that Gaelic could be written; what he was criticizing in Gaelic was its lack, as he believed, of a standardized orthography, albeit unaware that one had existed (see Ó Baoill 2010, 11–12). Johnson seems to have believed that Gaelic could become a civilized, polished language if only a standardized written form were developed for publishing written works. In the service of this goal, Johnson actually financially supported the publication of the second-earliest Gaelic grammar in 1778, as evidenced by the author's preface (Shaw 1972, xxiii). Moreover, according to Boswell, Johnson shamed the Society in Scotland for Propagating Christian Knowledge into producing the first Gaelic translation of the New Testament, plans for which they had previously cancelled (Boswell 1970, 373–5; Johnson and Boswell 1984, 389–390).[5]

In the late 18th century and on into the 19th, the military subjugation of the Highlands and the popularity and controversy around Ossian contributed to the formation of various societies in London and Scotland to valorize and support the Gaelic language and the Highlands (Daiches 1964; Durkacz 1983, 191–192; Black 1986; Clyde

1995; Robertson 1997). The Gaelic Society of London was founded in 1777, just over 30 years after the defeat of the Jacobite forces at the Battle of Culloden; the Highland Society of London was founded in 1778, and what became the Highland Society of Scotland was founded in 1784 in Edinburgh (Black 1986, 2). McLeod points out that these societies sponsored and inspired new discourses of revitalization and redemption: "In the wake of the Ossianic controversy, the rhetoric of Gaelic cultural self-defence became more insistent, especially in the many celebratory songs composed for Gaelic societies in the Lowlands and beyond" (Jones and McLeod 2007, 25; see e.g. M'Nish 1828).

The later 18th-century examples of revitalizing discourses were connected to the efforts of the Highland Society of London and the Highland Society of Scotland. Donnchadh Bàn Mac an t-Saoir, known as Duncan Ban MacIntyre in English (1724–1812), a poet whose early lifetime overlapped with MacMhaighstir Alasdair's later lifetime, was paid to compose a series of six panegyric poems praising Gaelic and the bagpipes between 1781 and 1789 (MacLeod 1952, 270-299). He recited the premiere of each poem at the Falkirk Tryst piping competition, sponsored by the Highland Society of London from 1781–1783 and by the Highland Society of Scotland from 1784 (Black 1986, 1–2, 7–9). (An analysis of revitalizing discourses from these poems follows in the next section.)

In the early 20th century, Gaelic intellectuals undertook new revitalization efforts motivated by "a new Gaelic-centred form of Scottish nationalism that promoted Gaelic as the national language of Scotland" (Jones and McLeod 2007, 26). One of the most prominent was Ruairidh Erskine of Mar, "whose periodicals (especially *Guth na Bliadhna*, 1904–1925) and other publications endeavoured to modernize the language in various respects, including the development of innovation in literature" (Jones and McLeod 2007, 26). These nationalist discourses of revitalization will be discussed in the following section. In the 1960s, there was a shift to greater activism on behalf of the language, premised on its claimed national significance. In the 1980s, activist efforts were joined (and in some cases supplanted) by the increased professionalization of Gaelic language revitalization efforts in the media, education, and language planning organizations. By the 1990s, journalists and language planners had joined academics and a few politicians in the praising and promotion of Gaelic. This change from century to century indicates that language revitalization efforts are dialectical processes, in which the discourses creating indexicalities for Gaelic are linked to the prevailing cultural values and also to shifts in the political economic position of Gaelic speakers in Scotland.

3   Discourses of Revitalization and Redemption

The seven types of redemptive and romantic praise of Gaelic that I have identified in the Scottish media and other publications make the following predications about Gaelic: (1) Gaelic is a living organism; (2) Gaelic is natural; (3) Gaelic is ancient; (4) Gaelic is "copious," capable of expressing anything, or particularly suitable for certain genres of expression; (5) Gaelic is a national language of Scotland; (6) Gaelic-English bilingualism is good for people; and (7) Gaelic is a valuable commodity. These predications are based on a "metapragmatic theme" that "conceptualizes Gaelic as a thing to be described" (Mertz 1982, 301). The objectification of Gaelic as an animate object marks a meta-level awareness of Gaelic that most likely emerged out of a situation of unequal contact between speakers of Gaelic and speakers of other languages.

This objectification has also arisen, I believe, as part of an ideology of standard language (Milroy and Milroy, 1999), an ideology which includes the propositions that a civilized or "real" language has a single correct spoken form, which should be based on a single correct written form; that non-standard forms are inadequate and inferior in comparison with the standard form; that language change, including the use of foreign loan-words, indicates decay of the language; and that non-standard, negatively evaluated speech indicates "undesirable moral, intellectual, or social attributes of groups of speakers" (Milroy 2000, 63). Such an ideology, as Milroy points out, is held widely and tenaciously as "common sense" in the face of evidence to the contrary, even by the speakers who would be most harshly judged according to its terms.

These predications also include a common element of positive affective stance[6] which can be summarized as the idea "Gaelic is good and deserves support because..." prefacing each one of the seven predications above. Affective stance in language, like other kinds of stance, constitutes a meta-level commentary on language—a metacultural form. The positive affective stance is meant to counter the negative affective stance of attacks on the language and its speakers which the discourses frequently refer to, the most well-known and often-quoted being MacMhaighstir Alasdair's lines about *"mì-rùn mòr nan Gall"*:

> *Mhair i fòs/Is cha tèid a glòir air chall/Dh'aindeoin gò/Is mìoruin mhòir nan Gall*

> Still it [Gaelic] survived/And its voice will not be lost/Despite the deceit/And great ill-will of the Lowlanders (Jones and McLeod 2007, 24).

Speakers' affective stance-taking, which makes affect intersubjectively accessible in discourse (Urban 2009, 42), is thus a key metacultural component in language revitalization discourses; this important point helps us understand the role played by affect in effecting the circluation of culture.[6]

3.1 Gaelic is a Living Organism

The earliest examples of revitalization discourse, 18th-century Gaelic poems, used the metaphor of Gaelic as a living organism. This metaphor implies that a language is not a human behaviour transmitted through socialization, but a living thing that moves through a life cycle.

Maighstir Seathan's poem in praise of Lhuyd, published in 1707 in the preface of *Archaeologia Britannica*, first utilized the metaphor of death and revivification to describe the situation of Gaelic:

> *Air sár o Líath, biodh ádh, is cuimhnu' is buáidh,/do rinn gu húr a dusgadh as a huáimh*

> Good luck, fond memory and success to the great Lhuyd/Who has awakened it [Gaelic] afresh from its grave (Ó Baoill 1979, 100–103).

Robert Campbell, another Gael contemporary with Maighstir Seathan, likewise wrote in his own poem to Lhuyd in the same preface:

> *Do duisgadh riot as anúaigh,/an chanamhuin chruaigh do bhi faoi small*

You have awakened from the grave,/the hardy language that was extinguished (Campbell and Thomson 1963, v).

The metapragmatic and metaphorical awakening of Gaelic from its grave in 1707 presupposes (and further entails) a metaphorical discourse of the death of Gaelic (cf. Silverstein, 2003). These seem to have set the terms for later discourse, for the very title of Alasdair MacMhaighstir Alasdair's self-published 1751 book of poetry containing his praise poem for Gaelic on the first page is *Ais-Eiridh na Sean Chánoin Albannaich*, "The Resurrection of the Ancient Scottish Tongue."

As stated previously, it seems likely that the objectification of Gaelic as a living organism indexes a meta-level awareness of Gaelic that emerged out of a situation of unequal contact between speakers of Gaelic and speakers of other languages. A comparison with the situation of Ireland in this regard is instructive. Sarah McKibben (2000, 89) found that 16th and 17th century Irish poets "developed a literary poetics of cultural crisis" in response to English colonization, culminating in the first known use of the "death metaphor" to describe Irish right at the end of the 17th century in "*Tuireadh na Gaedhilge agus Teastas na hÉireann*" (A dirge for Irish and testimony of Ireland) by Seán Ó Gadhra:

> The poem fuses the elements of the rhetoric of cultural crisis, including the mockery of Irish people who ape English manners, poetry on the "death of Ireland", derisive comments on users of English, and reflections on the lost status of poets and their language. This sober recapitulation condenses prior images into a single metaphor about the language itself. […] Ó Gadhra sees imminent death for Irish not as a vernacular but as a learned language, and he eruditely memorialises himself (by name, in the third person, past tense) and his late colleagues as the last of the scholars. Once more, the metaphoric construct shows its strategic nature, since the poet's stature presumably increases in proportion to the putative decay of the tradition, which Ó Gadhra none the less in fact perpetuates by writing (McKibben 2000, 95).

Thus, ideas about the death of learned Classical Gaelic language and culture were circulating in Ireland at the very time when Lhuyd was conducting research in Scotland and Ireland for his volume. Although there is no evidence extant to suggest any influence on Lhuyd or Maighstir Seathan in this regard (Ó Baoill, personal communication), it is interesting at least to compare the reactions of Irish and Scottish Gaelic poets to deliberate military, political, and sociocultural attacks on their language, culture, and society.[7] For example, in the early 18th century Maighstir Seathan had written the poem "*Ge grianach an latha*" (Though the day is sunny), which like the examples of several other Maclean poets of the previous century dealt with the subject "*dol sìos Chloinn Ghill-Eathain*," the decline of the formerly powerful Macleans who had experienced repeated misfortunes in the 17th century (Ó Baoill 1979, xxxix, 90–99).

The death metaphor has continued to circulate through academia (Dorian 1981; Hoenigswald 1989, 347; McKibben 2000, 96) and in the media to describe Gaelic and other "endangered" languages. Examples are discussed in Chapters 3 and 4, this volume. In the September 2000 "Newsnight Scotland" segment of Chapter 3, guest John Alick Macpherson, head of the Taskforce on Public Funding of Gaelic, countered presenter Gordon Brewer's challenge "Gaelic appears to be dying, but is it worth resuscitating the patient?" with the assertion that there were three possible courses of action: letting Gaelic die, "apply[ing] some palliative care" or using "a radical remedy." Thus Macpherson took up the death metaphor with a positive affective stance, bringing us full circle in a sense with the poem of Maighstir Seathan.

3.2   Gaelic is Natural

While some observers, past and present, have disparagingly likened Gaelic to animal sounds or the flora and fauna of the Highlands (see Ch. 3), others from the romantic era onward made the comparison with nature favorably. One day in 1803, three centuries after the Scots poet Dunbar compared Gaelic speech to the croaking of ravens, the Wordsworths and Samuel Taylor Coleridge went out for a walk around Loch Lomond while on holiday in Scotland. Of that day, Dorothy Wordsworth wrote:

> We stopped suddenly at the sound of a *half-articulate Gaelic hooting* from the field close to us. It came from a little boy, whom

we could see on the hill between us and the lake, wrapped up in a grey plaid… (quoted in Womack 1989, 111, emphasis added).

The boy's Gaelic cries called his human status into question, but also helped to create the mysterious romance of the scene.

Commentators in the 19th and 20th centuries frequently compared the sound patterning of Gaelic preaching and worship to the sound of the ocean (Heath 2002). For example, the folklorist Alexander Carmichael described Gaelic worship in the Outer Hebrides:

> Sometimes the hymn and the prayer are intoned in low tremulous unmeasured cadences like the moving and moaning, the soughing and the sighing, of the ever-murmuring sea on their own wild shores (Carmichael 1972 [1900], 2, quoted in Heath 2002).

Carmichael, the author of the six-volume collection of Gaelic folklore *Carmina Gadelica: Hymns and Incantations Collected in the Highlands and Islands of Scotland in the Last Century*, was favorably disposed towards Gaelic and Gaelic speakers, to say the least. He felt, like many after him, that Celtic Christianity was somehow more spiritual and closer to nature than other forms of Christianity (Meek 2000, 60–66).

In 1999, nearly 500 years after Dunbar, 200 years after Wordsworth, and 100 years after Carmichael, journalists still utilized ostensibly complimentary "natural" metaphors to describe Gaelic and its speakers. A description of Alasdair Morrison, an MSP who was the Minister for Gaelic, the Highlands and Islands, and Tourism at the time, stated that "Gaelic drips from his gob like honey from a spoon…" (McNeil 2000).[8] Another journalist described the Gaelic poet Sorley MacLean giving a reading as "magnificent to hear and to behold—like some old, gnarled tree bent by the wind" (Glover 2000). The positive natural qualities ascribed to Gaelic with these metaphors seem to differentiate them from the disparaging descriptions of Gaelic as barbarous or animal-like seen in Chapter 3. But whether the affect is positive or negative, the metaphors dehumanize Gaelic and remove it from a social context.

3.3   *Gaelic is Ancient*

The invocation of distinguished genealogies in Gaelic panegyric poetry was a convention and a duty of the professional poets (MacInnes 1979). The earliest 18th-century examples of revitalization discourse apply this convention to the praise of Gaelic. Maighstir Seathan's poem in Lhuyd's *Archaeologia Britannica* described the traditional (and mythical) history of the Gaels of Ireland and Scotland as the pedigree of the Gaelic language. A short extract and the editor's notes to these lines demonstrate this:

> 'When the descendants of Gaedheal Glas and of Mílidh,/no faint-hearted race, came from Spain/ [...] When that seed grew great, here and across the sea [i.e., in Scotland and in Ireland],/ Gaelic obtained respect and was valued everywhere [*Air teachd on Spáin, do shliochd an Gháoidhil ghlais,/'sdo shliochd na Míligh 'nfhine nach budh tais;/ [...] Nuair a dhfás a mpór ud mór, a bhos is tháll/'Bhi meas is prís fa 'n Ghaoidheilg ans gach ball*]' (Ó Baoill 1979, 100–101).

> In the pseudo-history of the Gaels drawn up by learned men between the 8th and 11th centuries, using old mythological tales and a large proportion of simple invention, Gaedheal Glas was the ancestor of all the Gaels. He was the son of Scota, daughter of Pharaoh (cf. line 129), and lived in Egypt at the time when the Israelites escaped by crossing the Red Sea (Exodus xiv). He was called *Glas* because of a wound received from a poisonous snake, and was cured by Moses (Macalister, *Lebor Gabála* II, pp. 52, 58–60). Seventeen generations later the descendants of Gaedhal Glas conquered Spain (Ibid, p. 76). Two generations after this they came to Ireland (Ibid, vol. V, pp. 20ff.), their leaders being the sons of Míl, or Míl Easpáine (Ibid, p. 24; *RC*, pp. 308–309). This traditional history, as relayed in the Lowland Scots context (e.g. Bellenden, *Boece*, vol. I, pp. 21–30), had some political importance in Scotland between the 13th century and 1603 (Matthews, 'Egyptians in Scotland'), and perhaps again for a short period after 1707 (*op. cit.*, p. 306)' (Ó Baoill 1979, 262).

Maighstir Seathan also refers to "a thousand years and more" when Gaelic "held first place in the court of kings" (Ó Baoill 1979, 101), which the editor says refers to the time after the sons of Míl had supposedly reached Ireland contemporaneous with the reign of King David in Israel, which was dated by 17th-century manuscript compilers to 1700 BCE (Ó Baoill 1979, 262–263). Mgr. Seathan also claims St. Patrick and St. Columba as Gaelic speakers. As the editor indicates, tracing origins back to Biblical times and lands in premodern historical narratives was not uncommon; the national origin myth of Scotland in medieval times placed the true beginning of the Scottish nation in ancient Egypt, the ultimate validation of Scottish royalty and the nation: "Whatever their political convictions, all Scots concurred in one central tenet of national pride: their country, by virtue of the succession, was the most ancient political fabric in Europe, perhaps in the world" (Donaldson 1988, 6–7).

As mentioned already, Ó Baoill has pointed out that Maighstir Seathan's own interaction with Rev. John Beaton, and subsequent incorporation of this ancient history into his poem, arose out of Lhuyd's own noting of traditional Gaelic history from Beaton (Ó Baoill 1979, lxiii–lxv). Beaton's history itself was derived in part from manuscript sources such as Keating's *Foras Feasa ar Éirinn* (History of Ireland) (Campbell and Thomson 1963, 26), and others which were derived at least in part from Scottish Lowland sources (Ó Baoill 1979, 264).

Alasdair MacMhaighstir Alasdair's praise poem for Gaelic, influenced by Maighstir Seathan's, also included the description of Gaelic's ancient pedigree and its association with the distant past and the Garden of Eden:

'S i labhair Adhamh,/Ann a phárrais féin,/'S ba shiubhlach Gáilic/O bheul álainn Ebh (Mac-Dhonuill 1751, 3–4).

It was [Gaelic] that Adam spoke/In his own Paradise/And Gaelic came fluently/from Eve's beautiful mouth (Jones and McLeod 2007, 25).

In his own series of poems praising Gaelic in the latter half of the 18th century, Duncan Ban MacIntyre likewise described Gaelic as the language of the Garden of Eden, of Noah's Ark, of the prophets, the Israelites in the wilderness, and the parting of the Red Sea, and the language that "won supremacy over every kind of speech" at the Tower of Babel (MacLeod, 1952).[9]

In the wake of the controversy over the authenticity and age of Macpherson's Ossianic poems, some 19th-century Gaelic supporters attempted to prove that Gaelic was indeed ancient. Several wrote voluminously-titled books attempting to prove the ancient pedigree of Gaelic, its affinity with Hebrew, and the claim that the languages of Europe, or all the other languages of the world, were derived from it (e.g., Maclean, 1837; M'Intyre, 1866; MacKay, 1877).

Throughout the 20th century, and into the 21st, the appellation "ancient language" for Gaelic is still a cliché in the media, frequently found in combination with other discourses of revitalization. Returning to our "Newsnight Scotland" example from 2000, when the presenter introduced the story about Gaelic funding, we can see that he moved seamlessly from the life/death metaphor already discussed to the "ancient language" theme:

> Now, Gaelic appears to be dying, but is it worth resuscitating the patient? Tomorrow an official report will call for yet more government money to be spent to keep it going for another few years at least, I'll be talking to the author in a moment. But first, Isabel Fraser examines why an ancient language once spoken by half or more of Scotland's population, is now spoken by only one percent.

3.4 Gaelic is "Copious" or Expressive

This argument counters the assertion that Gaelic is lacking in some way with assertions that Gaelic is "copious," or bursting with words, those units of referential meaning that are needed to describe the world "out there" in standard language ideology (Silverstein, 1996). In response to Samuel Johnson's disparaging remarks about Gaelic published in 1775 (Johnson and Boswell 1984), the Reverend Donald McNicol of Lismore wrote:

> I can aver for truth, before the world, that the Gaelic is as copious as the Greek, and not less suitable to poetry than the modern Italian. Things of foreign or of late invention, may not, probably, have obtained names in the Gaelic language; but every object of nature, and every instrument of the common and general arts, has many vocables to express it, such as suit all the elegant variations

that either the poet or the orator may chuse to make (McNicol 1779, 291–292; quoted in Durkacz 1983, 191).

Durkacz sees this as "a cultural justification for the Gaelic language, perhaps the first attempted" (1983, 191), though he does not take into account the 18th-century examples of Gaelic poetry previously described.

A 20th-century proponent of this view asserted that "The Gaels have a word for it!" or at least that Gaelic can be made to have a word for it, no matter what "it" is (Paterson 1964). The purist dimension of this argument is that borrowing from English should be avoided and new Gaelic words must be coined by language planners to bring Gaelic fully up to date and prove that it is a "modern" language in which one can discuss technology, current events, etc. However, because of the semiotic processes of language shift in which native speakers identify the language with the past (e.g., Mertz 1982), native speakers do not always accept the lexical items that are coined as part of efforts to reverse language shift. The author of *The Gaels Have a Word for It!* noted with frustration the difference between coining new words in English and in Gaelic:

> The point which emerges, however, is that the English speaker, recognising the need for an expanding vocabulary, accepts unquestioningly the terms offered—and uses them. Unfortunately the Gaelic speaker is often too parochially minded to use a properly constituted Gaelic word if Pidgin-English such as *Egsabision, dotair, trenn* ["exhibition," "doctor," "train"] can fill the gap (Paterson, 1964, iv).

However, the Gaelic native speakers Paterson complained about refused the new "properly constituted" coinages proffered instead of English loan-words because the origin of the new words was blatantly in the present, with a specific individual or institution, rather than in common usage. (The use of the English loan-words may have also carried social prestige at the time of coining.)

A theme related to the assertion of "copiousness" is the argument about Gaelic's inherent suitability or even superior ability for particular genres of expression, in implicit comparison with English. This concept in the Scottish Gaelic context arises in part from a dialogical, indigenous aesthetic argument originally made by 18th-century Gaelic poets about the unique beauty of the Gaelic language, within the framework of a panegyric tradition originally directed at the poets' clan chief patrons (MacInnes 1979). For example, Duncan Ban MacIntyre wrote of Gaelic:

> 'S i 's treis' thoirt greis air àbhachd/'S a h-uil' àit 'n téid a luaidh;/ 'S i 's fheàrr gu adhbhar-ghàire,/'S as binne bhlàithe fuaim;/'S i ceòl nam pìob 's nan clàrsach/Luchd-dàn' is dhèanamh dhuan.
>
> 'Tis the most trenchant for a bout of wit,/wherever it is spoken;/'Tis the best for jocularity,/it has the sweetest, warmest sound;/'Tis the music of the pipes and harps,/of minstrels and composers of songs (MacLeod 1952, 273).

As a poet, MacIntyre also described Gaelic's suitability for poetry, and perhaps unsurprisingly this was the area in which poet-commentators, and later proponents of Ossian, felt Gaelic to excel. In the late 18th and 19th centuries, the influence of Macpherson's Ossianic poems and the Romantic movement in general allowed for a favorable reinterpretation of the polarities of the characteristics ascribed to Gaelic speakers, at least for observers sympathetic to the Highlands or to Gaelic (Chapman 1978). The new identification of Gaelic as "the language of Ossian" meant that commentators foregrounded its capabilities related to the functions of poetry, including descriptive and expressive creativity, while erasing its other linguistic capabilities, including descriptive precision, abstraction, and a whole range of social functions.

For example, one Archibald Farquharson published in 1868 an exhortatory volume titled *An address to Highlanders respecting their native Gaelic: showing its and the broad Scotch's superiority over the artificial English for the family and the social circle, and also for lyric poetry*. In another example, Hugh Miller, a journalist sympathetic to the Highlands and Highlanders, wrote in an *Inverness Courier* newspaper review of English poetry by a Gaelic poet:

> The Gaelic, as a language, is singularly rich in the descriptive, but comparatively barren in the abstract. Phrenologists remark nearly the same thing of the Celtic head—the reflective organs

are always less prominently developed than the knowing ones (Miller 1838, cited in Fenyö 2000, 7).

Although Miller highlighted the ability of the Gaelic language, and Gaelic speakers' minds, to deal with the concrete stuff of poetry in the Ossianic mode—"pure description" and "natural imagery"—he doubted the capacity of either the language or its speakers to handle abstract concepts.

The assertion that Gaelic is the best for humour and joking was repeated by Gaelic-English bilinguals during my participant-observation field research in 1999–2000, and similar views have been expressed by speakers of other minority languages (Weinreich 1953, 95; Tsitsipis 1981, 174), probably due to the common experiences of social processes of language shift. This argument of copiousness and superior expressive ability is nearly 200 years old, but late 20th-century journalists supportive of Gaelic still occasionally waxed lyrical about Gaelic's descriptive powers. For example:

> Be warned, if Gaelic is lost, tomorrow's Highlanders will be entire strangers to the subtleties and elegance of a vast body of literature. They will lose a vocabulary of far greater shade and variety than English. (There are at least a dozen Gaelic words for love. There are also, not surprisingly, as many words to describe different kinds of rain.) (MacLeod 1996).

This journalist evokes the modern myth of a hundred Eskimo words for snow as part of a Whorfian perspective on language, but this take on Whorf is a naïve one, not rooted in the reality of indigenous North American languages.[10] The argument is a direct response to the argument that Gaelic displays a deficit in comparison with English, though, still commonly recycled in late 20th-century media (again, see Ch. 3). Here, Gaelic is still compared to English, but Gaelic is not insufficient in referential terms; rather, it is copious, and English instead is the language found lacking.

3.5   Gaelic is a National Language of Scotland

This discourse claims that Gaelic is *a* national language of Scotland, if not *the* national language, justifying the claims by referring to the history of Gaelic as the language of Scotland's monarch, court, and the majority of its population in the early medieval period.[11] Neither Gaelic nor Scots has played any significant role in nationalist politics in Scotland up to the present day: "The advent of nationalist politics in Scotland found the population already politically mobilised as an electorate and enjoying the normal standard of literacy for a developed country—in [Standard English]" (Macafee 1985, 9). That Scottish nationalists never were able to co-opt Gaelic as their own issue is partially due to the fact that "the Gaelic militants of the Scots National League" were expelled from the forerunner of the Scottish National Party in 1933, when the party opted for a Unionist stance and the Gaelic supporters did not (Hanham 1969, 160).

As already mentioned, in the early to mid-20th century, Gaelic-centric Scottish nationalists such as Ruairidh Erskine of Mar promoted a nationalist view of Gaelic. One mid-century Gaelic grammar book, reprinted in 1997, stated at the beginning of Lesson One that:

> Gaelic is the national language of Scotland. It isn't hard to learn… Thousands have mastered Gaelic. Add one more to the number and bring along others. Make Scotland once more a Gaelic Nation (Paterson 1997 [1952], 1).

The Saltire Society published a booklet by the Gaelic professor and poet Derick Thomson which presents not impassioned pleas, but a summary of the history of Gaelic in Scotland to implicitly explain the title, *Why Gaelic Matters* (Thomson 1984). In a brief section called "The language as part of Scotland's identity," Thomson makes a further statement after warning about the dangers of essentialism and over-generalization: "Yet there is probably an irreducible element of Gaelic consciousness in the general make-up of Scots. We can touch lightly on some of the ways in which this comes about and manifests itself" (Thomson 1984, 21). He links the development of this consciousness to experience rather than to any innate qualities, and counts among the experiences the awareness of Gaelic's role in Scottish history, Scots' awareness of family links with the Highlands, acquaintance with Gaelic-speaking people, the use of Gaelic loan-words in English, and general familiarity with Gaelic music. He concludes the section, "This much may be said: Gaelic is one of the touchstones of Scottish cultural and political pride. This is as it should be" (Thomson 1984, 21).

By 1987, anthropologist Sharon Macdonald observed that "[o]n the whole … the idea that Gaelic was part of Scotland's heritage does not seem to have been widely received, and has had its only recognition within the academic realm" (1987, 295). However, in participant observation research she noted that some of the most enthusiastic proponents of Gaelic language revitalization in Scotland claim that Gaelic is of national significance and relevance for Scots (S. Macdonald 1997, 34–43).

The nationalist view of Gaelic gained more support, at least superficially, with the devolution of Scottish government in 1999. The new Scottish Executive and Parliament began to adopt an unofficial position on Gaelic as a symbolic national language with such moves as bilingual Gaelic-English signs in the Scottish Parliament, and the Scottish Executive's appointment of a Minister for Gaelic to replace what was at the time a two-year-old Scottish Office (UK Government) post. The Scottish Parliament appointed a Gaelic Parliamentary officer and convened a committee to work on a dictionary of Gaelic Parliamentary terminology, and hosted a "Gaelic debate" in March 2000, together with two "Gaelic" Parliamentary committee hearings, in October 1999 and May 2000. The debate and hearings were Gaelic-English bilingual events, with simultaneous translation provided from Gaelic into English, though not vice versa. The Scottish National Party MSP Mike Russell participated in the Gaelic debate by reading his own Gaelic speech in support of Gaelic.

Russell appeared as a guest during the September 2000 "Newsnight Scotland" segment on Gaelic funding, briefly expressing a nationalist discourse of revitalization that went beyond Derick Thomson's "pride" to argue for a spiritual component: "…if we can't have a debate about how to save something of vital importance to our nation, our culture, and indeed our souls, then we shouldn't be having a debate at all, we might as well just give up." The "we" indexed by Russell in this case was the Scottish people as a whole discussing "our" nation and culture, but "we" also simultaneously indexed the group gathered virtually in the studio by satellite links, indicating Russell's awareness that what was taking place was not a debate at all.

John Alick Macpherson, the "Newsnight Scotland" guest whose viewpoint was most similar to Russell's, was the Chairperson of the Scottish Executive's Taskforce on Public Funding of Gaelic. This taskforce had produced a report in September 2000 titled "Revitalising Gaelic: A National Asset," the release of which occasioned the "Newsnight Scotland" interview. The report recommended that the Scottish Executive create a small Department of the Gàidhealtachd within the Executive and establish and fund a Gaelic Development Agency responsible to the Scottish Executive and Scottish Parliament. However, it became apparent soon after the segment that these recommendations would not be carried out at that time, calling into question the "national" status of Gaelic.

The "National Cultural Strategy" for Scotland, published in 2000 in a document titled "Creating Our Future: Minding Our Past," indicated the most likely future for Gaelic. The glossy full-color Strategy document included a short section on the languages of Scotland. The document followed the national education guidelines in according no special status either to Gaelic or to Scots as indigenous languages differentiated from immigrant minority languages such as Urdu, Punjabi, and Cantonese in Scotland. The document promised somewhat vaguely that "We shall establish an action group to investigate how the languages and cultural traditions of Scotland"s ethnic minorities can be supported" (25), but it was a "strategy" and not a "policy." When the Strategy was first published, copies were delivered to the Comunn na Gàidhlig office. When an administrative assistant was unpacking the box and handing copies around, I asked if Gaelic was in it. She answered dryly, "Gaelic's on page 25." This was an apt description of the national role of Gaelic envisioned in the new Scottish government's plans—neatly compartmentalized. (Although it is beyond the scope of this chapter to discuss, in 2005 the Scottish Parliament finally passed a Gaelic Language Act, which established Bòrd na Gàidhlig and gradually required devolved Scottish public bodies to develop Gaelic language plans.)

3.6 *Gaelic-English Bilingualism is Good for People*

In the 1990s, the increased visibility of Gaelic generated complaints from some journalists about the unpleasant burden of exposure to Gaelic as a foreign language. This seemingly arises from an ideological-affective complex (see Ch 8, this volume) of anti-Gaelic prejudice and "a belief in the onerousness of bi- or multilingualism" (Dorian 1998, 12). In this view, speaking more than one language is considered onerous at both the societal and the individual level, with no benefits believed to come from knowing or learning a second language (Dorian 1998, 11–12). In fact, in this view, learning another language, or even experiencing superficial exposure to one, is believed to cause confusion and impair the cognitive performance of both children and adults (for a discussion of this belief in relation to Gaelic in Nova Scotia, see Mertz, 1982).

This complex of beliefs, which may be termed an "ideology of monolingualism" or of "subtractive bilingualism," was deliberately countered by Gaelic supporters in 1999 with a new emphasis on an ideology of additive bilingualism (Dorian, 1998) proclaiming that learning or knowing Gaelic in addition to English was beneficial to speakers. The "Johnstone Report," a research study on whether Gaelic medium education disadvantaged primary school pupils academically (Johnstone et al., 1999), was commissioned by the Education and Industry Department of the pre-devolution UK Scottish Office. The report was produced by the Scottish Centre for Information on Language Teaching and Research at Stirling University, and Stirling University education researcher Dr. Richard Johnstone coordinated the research project. The report was released in autumn 1999 and its most frequently repeated conclusion was: "When compared with pupils taught through the medium of English… Gaelic-medium pupils do not appear to be disadvantaged in terms of their attainments in English and mathematics at P5 and P7" (Johnstone et al. 1999, 1).

Comunn na Gàidhlig promoted the results of this report in the national media as part of their effort to encourage Gaelic medium education. They produced a press release welcoming the report and co-sponsored a panel discussion with Johnstone and parents in Inverness in October 1999 at a meeting on the feasibility of a Gaelic-medium primary school in Inverness. Scottish newspapers and a few English ones responded to the press release, covering the report alongside the opening in Glasgow of the first all-Gaelic primary school in Scotland. Each newspaper report repeated the same conclusions stated above, in articles that were neutral in tone. Alluding to the "Johnstone Report" almost a year later on "Newsnight Scotland", John Alick Macpherson stated: "Bilingualism is an advantage. And this has been proven in studies, not only here with Gaelic medium education, but in various countries around the world." This example shows us how revitalization discourse can circulate between the spheres of language planners, academia, and the media.

3.7 *Gaelic is a Commodity*

Another example of the circulation of revitalization discourse between language planners, academics, and the media is provided by the final theme discussed here, the predication of Gaelic as a commodity. This is both an extension and transformation of the objectification of Gaelic in the discourses discussed earlier. It is a response to the discourses and values of capitalism since the late 18th century in which Gaelic was portrayed as a barrier to improvement and economic development of the Highlands, and a barrier to individual economic mobility. It also represents an adaptation of the ideology of neoliberalism, in which "the market" became the moral arbiter of public policy.

Since Margaret Thatcher's time as prime minister in the late 1980s, neoliberal ideologies have saturated the Scottish public sphere and civil society. Given this saturation, it is not surprising that minority language revitalization efforts have become subject to the same set of constraints as other areas of civil society and public policy. The commodification of Gaelic constituted a creative move within those constraints. The process of commodifying the social behaviour of Gaelic language use, transforming it variously into an asset, a market, an economic sector, or an economy, was primarily a discursive process.

The language planning organization Comunn na Gàidhlig (CNAG) played a significant role in the 1990s in fostering an economically-focused type of language planning called "Gaelic development," and in developing and promoting the concept of the "Gaelic economy" as part of this focus. However, when academic consultants eventually elaborated the ideology of a Gaelic economy and specified "Gaelic goods and services" as its concrete realization, the consultants did so without reference to the social act of communicating through the medium of spoken or written Gaelic (McLeod, 2002). The result of this move was that the very issues of Gaelic speaking and transmission were obscured in language planning efforts. Funding for Gaelic revitalization was instead evaluated in terms of its cost effectiveness, defined as its relative ability to produce financial output for each pound of public funds spent on Gaelic, and its relative ability to create numbers of FTEs (full-time equivalent positions), compared to other publicly-funded programs.

One part of this story was the effort by CNAG to promote the discursive construction of the "Gaelic economy" together with Highlands and Islands Enterprise (HIE) by commissioning academic research on the topic. In 1993, HIE and the Gaelic Television committee, with CNAG, jointly commissioned research on "The Economics of Gaelic Language Development" from Alan Sproull, an economist at Glasgow Caledonian University (Sproull and Ashcroft, 1993). One chapter of the report was coauthored by the Director of the Fraser of Allander Institute, a prestigious Scottish economic and policy think-tank at Strathclyde University. The purpose of the study was to inform and influence public policy decisions in regard to Gaelic. These policy decisions would be based on principles of cost effectiveness and value for money; therefore, in that framework it was important for the commissioners of the study to be able to demonstrate with objective research that publicly-funded Gaelic language development programs were a cost effective method of regional economic development in the Highlands, providing good value for money, compared with other regional economic development programs (Sproull and Ashcroft 1993, 7).

In a section titled "Conceptualising the Gaelic Economy," Sproull stated that "From the standpoint of economics, it makes little sense to define [a Gaelic economy] in terms of the acts of production and exchange which are conducted through the medium of Gaelic" (Sproull and Ashcroft 1993, 4). In other words, the Gaelic economy could not be meaningfully defined in terms of either the language of transaction or the language of production, apparently because these two factors could not be reliably measured. The language of transaction could vary from one moment to the next; for example, even in a shop where the employees could speak Gaelic, the language of transaction would be subject to Gaelic-English codeswitching depending on the linguistic competence and social inclinations of customers.

Moreover, focusing on the Gaelic linguistic competence of the producers of goods and services would not allow the measurement of all activities producing "Gaelic goods and services," since not all Gaelic speakers were producing so-called "Gaelic goods and services" while speaking Gaelic (e.g., Gaelic-speaking fishermen producing a catch of prawns) and not all producers of "Gaelic goods and services" were Gaelic speakers (e.g., English-speaking camera operators producing a Gaelic television program). Thus a "Gaelic economy" was defined by recourse to the primacy of vaguely defined Gaelic commodities, rather than with reference to the primacy of Gaelic as a medium of communication between people engaged in acts of production and exchange. The report defined the "supply-side of the Gaelic economy" as "all those activities (and jobs) whose principal purpose is the provision of Gaelic-related goods and services, including the promotion of the Gaelic culture and language." More generally, the report defined the "Gaelic economy" as "the spatial area which stands to gain measurable economic benefits from the further development of the language." This was a geographically-defined concept that was meant to apply to the Outer Hebrides, Skye, and parts of the Inner Hebrides "where Gaelic still is, (or was until very recently), the first language of the community" (Sproull and Ashcroft 1993, 5–6).

The motivation for commissioning the report was indicated in its Executive Summary; it showed that in the neoliberal structure of Scottish development in the 1990s, economic development was increasingly de-centralized. Responsibility for local development was thrown back onto locally-focused agencies such as the local enterprise companies (LECs) of HIE and Scottish Enterprise, along with private and voluntary organizations which HIE and the Government expected to form funding partnerships with the LECs (McEwan-Fujita, 2005; see Ch. 7, this volume). Each of these organizations had a mandate that was defined according to a particular sector of society or the economy. During the 1980s and 1990s "Gaelic" was fully co-opted into this structure and likewise defined as a "sector." The interviews I conducted and the documentation I reviewed made it clear that the extent to which Gaelic language revitalization efforts could proceed (let alone succeed) depended at least in part on participants' abilities to adapt their goals and methods to the prevailing neoliberal orientation.

The further dissemination and utilization of the Sproull report's conclusions was as important as the production of the report itself. After the report was released, CNAG distributed press releases announcing its conclusions that were subsequently written up as newspaper articles. CNAG also utilized the report in its own publications to justify its efforts. For example, in its 10-year progress report, the conclusions of the report were reiterated: a major economic research survey commissioned by Comunn na Gàidhlig in association with HIE and the Gaelic Television Committee (CTG) established that there is a strong relationship between the health and status of Gaelic and confidence and self-esteem within communities. The survey demonstrated that the Gaelic language and culture have considerable potential to confer economic as well as cultural benefits. The minimum estimated size of the overall Gaelic "industry" in 1993 was almost 1000 full-time equivalent jobs and a total contribution to Scotland's Gross Domestic Product (GDP) of £41 million. The report concluded that "policy support for Gaelic activities generates £1 for £1 [pound for pound] relatively more direct jobs than would be the case if the support was given to other sectors of the economy" (Comunn na Gàidhlig 1994, 25).

Not only did CNAG quote and promote the 1993 report, utilizing the economic research as proof of the validity of its efforts, but Sproull himself also re-used it as the main body of an academic article (1996) published in an "economics of language" theme issue of the *International Journal of the Sociology of Language* edited by François Grin. Both the 1993 study and a later study conducted by Sproull and a postgraduate student (Sproull and Chalmers, 1998) illustrate a close relationship between academic research and language revitalization efforts. Although both the 1993 and 1998 reports purported to be economic studies, they also had a strong sociological focus. Both reports involved the conducting of surveys and interviews, and substantial conclusions from both were based on the analysis of results from the surveys. The survey questions were focused on assessing factors such as "social cohesion" and "individual and community confidence." The researchers (and by extension their sponsors) were trying to establish linkages between support for the Gaelic language, positive individual feelings and perceptions of one's community, and economic well-being in order to argue for the positive benefits of public policy support for Gaelic.

The professionalization and corporatization of Gaelic language planning, and the concomitant creation of the "Gaelic economy" concept, did not take place in isolation. Other economically-oriented Celtic language planning efforts in Ireland and Wales provided precedents and exemplars. In Ireland, Bord na Gaeilge (the Irish Language Board) was established in 1978 and had already moved in a neoliberal direction in 1983, a decade before CNAG (Tovey 1988, 63–65). In addition, Údarás na Gaeltachta, the Irish development agency for the Gaeltacht (the Irish government-designated Gaelic-speaking areas in the west of Ireland), which was established in 1979, has a Language and Culture Development Department responsible for integrating Irish social, cultural, and linguistic development with its regional economic development efforts.

Wales also provided a model for economically-oriented "language development." One key participant in the "Gaelic economy" effort mentioned to me in an interview that he was inspired by the organization Menter a Busnes [Enterprise and Business], a Welsh-language economic development company established in Wales in 1989 "which seeks to develop enterprise in its widest sense, and business in particular, as part of Welsh language and culture today" (Menter a Busnes, n.d.).

These precedents, together with the efforts to "develop" Scottish Gaelic, were carried out in the context of the European Union, itself built on the neoliberal principles of the common market. The efforts at each level, the European Bureau for Lesser-Used Languages (EBLUL) at the EU level and CNAG at the national and regional level, were reciprocally used and cited to support one another. For example, EBLUL published a pamphlet titled "The Diversity Dividend" (Price et al., 1997) which made a case for cultural and linguistic diversity being "one of Europe's key resources" for economic growth. This report, authored principally by the executive manager responsible for research and development at Menter a Busnes, proposed an alternative to the modernist paradigm of economic development. It presented case studies of economically oriented language planning projects to prove that economic development did not necessarily require cultural homogenization (Nelde, Strubell, and Williams, 1996). The examples included Slovene and Friulan banking co-operatives, Údarás na Gaeltachta in Ireland, Menter a Busnes in Wales, the Basque co-operative movement Mondragón Cooperative Corporation, business networks in Valencia, Spain, for SMEs (small and medium-sized enterprises), EBLUL's own Economic Development Forum for European Lesser Used Language Communities, Comunn na Gàidhlig's linguistic and cultural tourism project Fàilte—and Sproull's 1993 report "The Economics of Gaelic Language Development."

4 Conclusion

The discourses of revitalization and redemption described in this chapter constitute metacultural and metalinguistic commentaries on the cultural and linguistic practices of Gaelic speaking, commentaries composed of ideological and affective elements. They focused on representing Gaelic in a positive light and arguing for its maintenance or support, in dialogical response to the discourses of death and denigration which argued for the extinction of Gaelic. The representations of Gaelic in the media that Scottish journalists and language planners utilized in the late 20th century represent recent iterations in a long historical process, for they recirculate representations of Gaelic from previous centuries. They also utilize the discursive resources of academic discussions about language shift, bilingualism, and economics to frame their appeals, observations, and condemnations, in a way that highlights the metacultural nature of research and the impossibility of finding a purely objective approach to language shift and revitalization.

Notes

1 Acknowledgements. Above all, I wish to thank Professor Colm Ó Baoill, who originally brought the examples of revitalization discourse in 18th-century Gaelic poetry to my attention, and whose scholarly work, assistance, and mentoring has been invaluable to me. Any errors contained in my work are my sole responsibility. Staff members of the Regenstein Library of University of Chicago, the Patrick Power Library of Saint Mary's University, Halifax, and the Angus L. Macdonald Library of St. Francis

Xavier University, Antigonish, provided valuable resources and assistance.
2   However, Robert Kirk had published a vocabulary with his Bible in 1690 which pre-dates the word-list published by Lhuyd (Black 1986, 16).
3   Beaton's family had served as the hereditary physicians of the Lords of the Isles (Campbell and Thomson 1963, 12). When Beaton died some time before 1715, "In him there passed the last learned representative of a family that had produced scholars for many generations; and only the MacVurichs in South Uist remained to continue the classical Gaelic tradition, and that for only a few more years" (Campbell and Thomson 1963, 22).
4   Proponents of Gaelic immediately set about responding to Johnson's anti-Ossian and anti-Gaelic comments, both in English-language print and in Gaelic oral-literary tradition. The latter is exemplified by Seumas Macintyre's song of dispraise for Johnson, an extended metaphorical satire depicting Johnson as various non-noble creatures and trees, and modeled on a popular panegyric poem abut the death of Alasdair MacDonald of Glengarry, c. 1721, by Sìleas na Ceapaich (Newton 2009, 291–292). Unfortunately the necessity to counter Johnson's statements with statements of fact about Gaelic continues today.
5   Although Johnson was wrong about the lack of old Gaelic manuscripts (Thomson 1951; Gillies 1989), and Gaelic publishing has developed considerably from the 18th century to the present (Thomson 1989), in the late 20th century a writer for *The Economist* magazine took Johnson's 1775 comments literally as a description of the current state of Gaelic: "Their only text is the Bible, and there is no tradition of writing letters" ("Dying languages: English kills," 1998). This utterly incorrect claim suggests the ease and willingness with which external commentators still accept denigrating and false observations about Gaelic rooted in an ideology of standard language.
6   "Ochs (1996, 425) maintains that in stance, the categories of positive and negative affect are universally indexed, together with the affective categories of surprise and intensity/mitigation" (Ch. 8, note 4, this volume).
7   McKibben (2000, 94, note 25) describes how the 17th century saw poets describing the denigration of Irish, and also "a poet of the same generation, Séathrún Céitinn, [to whom] lines of correspondingly elevated praise for Irish are attributed, in "*Is milis an teanga an Ghaeilge*" (The Irish language is a tongue most sweet)." This provides a useful comparison to the 18th-century situation in Scotland.
8   The use of "gob" as a vulgar slang term for the standard "mouth" here is a carnivalesque device of inversion to generate humour, using a vulgar term to describe the mouth of a politician engaged in a formal parliamentary debate; the term may also creatively index the lower class status of the person as a Gaelic speaker (cf., Bourdieu 1991, 86–88 on *guele* vs. *bouche* in French; Chapman 1992, 30).
9   "'N uair a sgaoil na cainntean/Aig tùr aimhreidh mór,/Fhuair a' Ghàidhlig maighstireachd/'San am sim thar gach seòrs'—" (MacLeod 1952, 286).

10   In fact anthropologist Franz Boas identified only four roots (see Martin 1986; Pullum 1991).

11   A related argument on behalf of Gaelic that is no longer in use pertained to the question of British "national" unity: the unity of the United Kingdom. After the formation and success of the Highland Regiments overseas in expanding and consolidating the British Empire, some Gaelic advocates made a plea to retain and support the language in order to maintain Highlanders' superior morale and goodwill, so that they would remain good subjects and brave, hardy soldiers of the Empire (e.g., Shaw 1972 [1778], xvii–xviii; Sinclair 1804, 5–7).

PART THREE

Neoliberalism and Language Revitalization

CHAPTER 6

Neoliberal Discourses of Gaelic Language Revitalization: The "Gaelic Economy" and "Rocketing Spending"

1 Introduction

In the 1990s, professionalized Gaelic revitalization efforts came to be defined largely in relation to the perceived economic aspects of language shift. The Gaelic revitalization project of the late 20th century was to persuade all Scots—Gaelic speakers or not—that Gaelic was useful and valuable in the job market and business. This was a response to the idea that Gaelic was useless for economic and social advancement, a view that has been prominent in popular explanations of Gaelic language shift:

> Contemporary conventional wisdom holds that an inevitable shift from Gaelic must occur in the face of English as the "stronger" language as "progress" destroys the traditional "Highland way of life." Certainly from the earliest times in Gaelic Scotland economic innovation has been associated with the intrusive use of English … In the rhetoric of the [late 19th century] both the Gaelic language and its speakers were seen as impediments to the more productive development of lands and resources in the Scottish Highlands. The supersession of Gaelic and even of the people themselves were generally seen by the advocates of economic development as a necessary prerequisite to progress (MacKinnon 1977, 32–33).

Economic development is one of at least four major social processes through which Gaelic language shift has been taking place in the Highlands of Scotland over the course of several centuries. In MacKinnon's "Gàidhealtachd model" of language shift, the economic development of Gaelic-speaking areas contributed to the shift together with the large-scale removal of Gaelic-speaking population from areas, the influx of new non-Gaelic-speaking incomers to areas, and changes in the power relationship between social groups that caused Gaelic speakers to lose confidence in their system of values and the linguistic matrix in which those values are embedded (1977, 35).

However, it is difficult to determine the extent to which the idea of Gaelic's economic uselessness has been an actual motivating factor of Gaelic language shift in Scotland, or a second-order rationalization of the process of shift. The perception of English language ability as essential for economic success, and Gaelic language ability as a detriment to that success, probably strengthened as subsequent generations of speakers used Gaelic in fewer and fewer domains (Durkacz 1983; Withers 1984). From the late 19th century onward, the *idea* of Gaelic's inherent economic uselessness seems to have been the most relevant factor in language shift:

> In the residual Gaelic areas of northwestern Scotland from the mid-19th century onwards, language-shift from Gaelic to English seems more to be associated with the more abstract qualities of social morale, integrity of the system of values, and confidence in the traditional pattern of socialisation than in the scale and level of advancement of forms of economic development as such (MacKinnon 1977, 35).

In other words, economic factors have shaped Gaelic language shift from the late 19th century to the late 20th century primarily through the indexical link that many Gaelic speakers (and indeed many Scots) have drawn between Gaelic and poverty. However, there also remain the economically-influenced factors of out-migration of Gaelic speakers (for higher education and employment) and in-migration of non-Gaelic speakers (for employment and retirement), as well as the erosion of traditional social structures and a loss of confidence (and interest) in them.

While the possibility of countering a long-held belief about the qualities of Gaelic formed the basis for the new "language development" efforts, the climate of Thatcherism also facilitated the shift to a more enterprise-oriented approach. If the old argument was that Gaelic was economically useless in Scottish society, the new neoliberal argument was that Gaelic was relatively useless in Scottish markets—an argument that opened up a space for proponents to counter-argue that there was in fact a market in which Gaelic could be relatively useful.

The neoliberal ideology of the New Right originated in the late 1970s and blossomed in Margaret Thatcher's Britain (Elliott and McCrone 1987, 496–8). Economic liberalism, or neoliberalism, ideally describes a society in which a framework of laws and social services allows the operation of market forces. While creating a more authoritarian state, Thatcher's government simultaneously exposed the UK economy to the forces of the "free" market in the 1980s (McCrone 1991, 94–95), privatizing state functions, selling off publicly-owned industries and housing stocks, breaking strikes and busting unions. The concept of neoliberalism, well-rehearsed during the Thatcher and Major years, did not lose its grip with the election of New Labour and Tony Blair in 1997. Many of the economic and social changes wrought by Thatcher and Major remained in place.

In addition to neoliberalism, Thatcher's administration gave *heritage* a new prominence in Britain, as both a mode of remembrance and a way of commodifying the past (McCrone, Morris, and Kiely 1995). The British state found heritage a useful concept for reconciling the contradictions of Thatcherism, the neoliberal effort to reduce social relations to market relations, and the neo-conservative effort to further centralize and strengthen the state:

> Such a political strategy was not all that easy to maintain, given its basic philosophical contradictions. In this regard, heritage has two useful functions. On the one hand, it represents considerable cultural capital which can itself be bought and sold, as well as a means whereby commodities can be traded as "authentic." Both involve commodifying the past. [...] On the other hand, heritage is a cultural device for managing as well as for "stage managing" economic change. Conservative regimes in Britain since 1979 have had recourse to claiming the past as a goal for the future. Mrs Thatcher had her "Victorian Values," and John Major his "Back to Basics," while the broad goal of Conservatism since 1979 has been to effect major social and economic change (McCrone, Morris, and Kiely 1995, 30–31).

The political functions of "heritage" in reconciling neoliberalism and neo-conservatism therefore facilitated the commodification of the past, as well as its increased public prominence. Both of these trends paved the way for the more general commodification of culture, through tourism.

Thatcher forced museums and monuments into the marketplace throughout the 1970s and into the 1980s. In the National Heritage Act 1983, the UK Parliament established English Heritage and CADW (Welsh Historic Monuments), and in 1984 they established the Historic Buildings and Monuments Directorate in Scotland. In 1991 the latter became "Historic Scotland" and these three institutions "gained executive agency status … which meant that while they were government-owned, they had the freedom to manage along with the responsibility to return a profit to the government" (Hewison 1987; McCrone, Morris, and Kiely 1995, 16). The 1983 act itself "was fuelled by Mrs Thatcher's desire to make the organizations responsible for protecting traditional heritage more commerically minded." Thus by the 1990s, Historic Scotland had become one among several organizations responsible for marketing the heritage of Scotland, including the National Trust for Scotland, Scottish Natural Heritage, and the Scottish Tourist Board.

Worldwide economic restructuring from the 1970s onward allowed the growth of mass tourism on an international scale (Urry 1990). With the decline in the importance of manufacturing and the increasing emphasis on the service sector in the late 20th century, "culture," like conventionally manufactured items, became another commodity in the new globalized economy (Jameson 1984; McCrone, Morris, and Kiely 1995, 17).

The commodification of culture (in the sense of high culture) and heritage in Britain has been important for the process of economic restructuring and regeneration, particularly in cities. Regional governments, or "local authorities," were at the forefront of this effort in Britain:

> In many British cities, the talk is of the "heritage option" as a means of economic regeneration, and the "culture economy" as a way of achieving post-industrial city status. These culture

industries include traditional ones like museums and cathedrals, but also art galleries, concert halls, orchestras, community arts, TV franchises and the performing arts. ... Cities in turn have invented new titles or adopted existing ones by way of badges of regeneration ... Glasgow as European City of Culture in 1990, Dundee as City of Discovery, Lancaster as Heritage City... (McCrone, Morris, and Kiely 1995, 17–18).

This urban redevelopment, like the rural development of Scotland, has attracted funds not only from the state, but also private developers, heritage organizations, and the European Union. Scotland was in the lead of urban redevelopment, since its towns and cities, unlike England's, received their state funds directly through the economic development organization Scottish Enterprise, previously the Scottish Development Agency (McCrone, Morris, and Kiely 1995, 37).

With the continuing subjugation of social and cultural relations to the market, marketing strategies have increased in importance in Scotland. Political parties and candidates, state-provided social services, and tourism destinations are all promoted through marketing campaigns, whose goal is to sell the Scottish public on one or another idea or practice. Along with marketing came the rise of an important marketing technique in 1990s Scotland—branding. Scottish Enterprise and Locate in Scotland began to use branding in the marketing of inward investment to Scotland by foreign corporations, and the Scottish Tourist Board used it in the marketing of Scottish of tourism within the UK and overseas. The catch-phrase for this trend is "Scotland the Brand" (McCrone, Morris, and Kiely 1995) modified from the traditional song title and appellation "Scotland the Brave." In the late 1990s, in fact, Scotland the Brand was adopted as the name of a Scottish marketing organization whose goal was "to promote the distinctive brand values of Scotland" by promoting specialty products manufactured in Scotland (Scotland the Brand, n.d.).

The ideology of neoliberalism became much greater than Thatcherism, and more ubiquitous, in Scotland as well as the rest of the UK. In the era of New Labour, policymakers continued unquestioningly to treat "the market" as the ultimate measure of public policy. Neoliberal ideologies permeated the Scottish public sphere and civil society:

> One point that has struck home repeatedly during my research has been how deeply Thatcherism has affected all of Scotland's institutions, including its press, even beyond Mrs Thatcher's own fall in 1990. The law, education, arts, and local government establishments have fallen prey to the ideological argument of "market forces," as has the press (Smith 1994, 7).

In Chapter 5 of this volume, pp. 140–145, I noted that with this permeation of neoliberal ideology, Gaelic revitalization efforts became subject to the same set of constraints as other areas of civil society and public policy in Scotland. I examined the discursive process through which the social behaviour of Gaelic language use was commodified and cast variously as an asset, a market, an economic sector, or an economy.

After the political and social changes of the 1980s, Gaelic language planners in the 1990s conceptualized their efforts as "selling Gaelic back to the Gaels" (Crichton 2000): treating "Gaelic" as a raw material, processing it and branding it to add value, and then selling it back to Gaelic speakers. Two distinct senses of "selling" are collapsed into this concept: selling as a metaphor for persuasion, and selling as an economic transaction. However, the commodity that planners hoped people would want to buy was not well defined in these efforts, and it was not the language ability and social interaction that native Gaelic speakers previously obtained or engaged in "for free" through intergenerational transmission of the language.

This chapter describes another phenomenon related to the rise of the economic approach to language planning: the parallel rise of an economic-themed complaint tradition against Gaelic. I revisit the September 2000 "Newsnight Scotland" story that I described at the beginning of Chapter 3. In that chapter, I explored the range of anti-Gaelic "death and denigration" discourses showcased in the segment that were prevalent in the Scottish media in 1999–2000.

In this chapter, I focus on a different set of discourses about Gaelic that emerged in the public sphere under neoliberalism: complaints about public spending on Gaelic revitalization efforts. I demonstrate how these complaints are integrally linked to the neoliberal approach to Gaelic revitalization efforts that started in the 1990s.

2 The Rise of the "Gaelic Economy"

This section traces the role of the organization Comunn na Gàidhlig in fostering an economically-focused type of language planning called "Gaelic development," and in developing and promoting the concept of the "Gaelic economy" as part of this focus. This concept, as utilized in initial planning reports, was only vaguely defined. When academic consultants eventually elaborated the ideology of a Gaelic economy and specified "Gaelic goods and services" as its concrete realization, the consultants did so without reference to the social act of communicating through the medium of spoken or written Gaelic (McLeod 2001). The result of this move was that the very issue of Gaelic linguistic vitality was obscured in language planning efforts. Funding for Gaelic revitalization was instead evaluated in terms of its cost effectiveness, defined as its relative ability to produce financial output for each pound of public funds spent on Gaelic, and its relative ability to create numbers of FTEs (full-time equivalent positions), compared to other publicly-funded programs.

The Highlands and Islands Development Board established Comunn na Gàidhlig (CNAG) in 1984, following its commission of a report on the state of Gaelic in 1982 (MacArthur et al. 1982). CNAG identified four priorities for its efforts: Gaelic medium education, the Gaelic arts, Gaelic broadcasting, and business (Caimbeul 2000, 56). From the beginning, therefore, the organization had at least a partial focus on the role of Gaelic in business. For the first several years CNAG as an organization lobbied for Gaelic medium education provision in Scotland, then helped to create Pròiseact nan Ealan (the National Gaelic Arts Project).

In 1987, Thatcher's UK Government published a White Paper on Broadcasting, the first consultative step to a new legislative Act of Parliament. While Thatcher sought to reorganize British broadcasting in line with her priority on free enterprise, the first director of CNAG saw this as an opportunity to lobby for new funding for Gaelic-language television programming, which had been sparse until that time. CNAG commissioned a report, "The Case for a Gaelic Broadcasting Service," and argued the case with Government representatives on the basis of linguistic and human rights. However, this case met with silence from the Government, and CNAG began to turn more explicitly toward an economic focus. One journalist described the process:

> CNAG saw that raw economics had to be put at [the case's] centre for there to be any chance of success. As one activist reminisced to me during my research for this paper, "After the White Paper we needed a lot of Touche Ross and just a little Saatchi and Saatchi" (Caimbeul 2000, 60).[1]

The first director of CNAG hired a consultant "to report on how Gaelic language programmes might be funded in a more market-tuned system" (Comunn na Gàidhlig 1994a, 13). The consultant was the broadcasting economist Dr. Cento Veljanovski, who was at the time a director of the Institute of Economic Affairs in London, a "pro-Thatcherite think-tank" (Caimbeul 2000, 60). Veljanovski helped to re-cast the case for Gaelic television funding in economic terms:

> Velanowski [sic] was told [by CNAG] to target the issue of why ITV revenue was going out of Scotland at that stage to fund the Welsh S4C [television channel] while Scotland's own linguistic minority had not a television service to speak of. His case was built on two thrusts – the economic benefits to small communities, and a deal where the Scottish ITV broadcasters' existing Gaelic output was maintained in the new broadcasting set-up but topped up by several hundred hours of government-funded Gaelic television programmes (Caimbeul 2000, 60).

Following some private lobbying in London, the Conservative Government consented to the request and in the Broadcasting Act 1990 granted approximately £9 million annually for Gaelic television beginning in 1993.[2] Supporters of Gaelic in Scotland viewed this as a massive and surprising success. In 1991, the first director left CNAG to become the head of the Gaelic Television Committee (Comataidh Telebhisean Gàidhlig, CTG) and a new CNAG Chief Executive was hired.

Meanwhile, also in 1991, the entire organizational structure for economic development in Scotland had been revamped with a more neoliberal focus (MacKinnon 2000b). The Highlands and Islands

Development Board (HIDB) which had been in place since 1965 was dissolved, and a new entity, Highlands and Islands Enterprise (HIE), was formed to take its place. HIE's new responsibility included overseeing a network of ten newly-formed local enterprise companies, or LECs, each one responsible for economic development in a particular local government region of the Highlands: Western Isles Enterprise (WIE), Skye and Lochalsh Enterprise (SALE), Ross and Cromarty Enterprise (RACE), etc.[3] The agenda of HIE and its new LEC network shifted to business development and individual projects. The implications of this transformation for development efforts in the Highlands are discussed in greater detail in Chapter 7 of this volume.

"Development" had always been the point of CNAG since HIDB assisted in founding the organization (Caimbeul 2000). But as social development officers from HIE began to work more closely with CNAG in the early 1990s, they reconceptualized Gaelic language revitalization more completely as a quasi-economic development effort called "Gaelic development." In 1993, the same year the Gaelic television funding started, HIE produced a new "Strategy for Gaelic Development in the Highlands & Islands of Scotland" authored by two HIE social development officers and a lecturer from the School of Scottish Studies at University of Edinburgh (Lingard, Pedersen, and Shaw 1993). The "aim" of the new strategy proposed a connection between the Gaelic language and economic and social development more explicitly than ever before: "Aim: Development of the Gaelic language and culture as a means of raising self-confidence and stimulating economic and social development" (Lingard, Pedersen, and Shaw 1993, 1). The Executive Summary of the report further described the new economistic orientation toward Gaelic:

> The central rationale for the strategy—and for Gaelic development in general—is that commercial activity and economic development do not occur in a vacuum. Active maintenance and development of a community's language, culture and social cohesion, like the environment, is an essential contributing factor to economic and social progress, particularly in fragile areas. The recent dramatic growth of Gaelic based employment supports this: Gaelic with its skills, potential and aspirations

provides a major social and economic asset to be capitalised upon for the future of the Highlands and Islands. In other words, Gaelic is a growth sector (Lingard, Pedersen, and Shaw 1993, 1).

The authors of the report described Gaelic somewhat ambiguously, as both a "growth sector" and an "economic asset" facilitating the success of that sector. HIE published both Gaelic and English versions of the Strategy, for the document aimed at bringing into existence a professional Gaelic world, as described at CNAG in Chapter 10 of this volume.

The Strategy de facto claimed for HIE a responsibility for "developing" Gaelic by virtue of the presence of Gaelic in HIE's targeted geographical area, the Highlands of Scotland. It also claimed the right to delegate this development responsibility to other organizations. HIE expected CNAG to play an important role in "raising the status of Gaelic, particularly with regard to creating employment opportunities for Gaelic speakers" (Lingard, Pedersen, and Shaw 1993, 16). The Strategy described how HIE and its LECs would work together with CNAG to accomplish the newly-defined goal of "language development," which made no mention of reversing language shift:

> The HIE network's future participation in supporting CNAG will be through projects as a minor funding partner, with development on the community level being regarded as of primary importance among CNAG's activities and realised through the close collaboration between the LECs and CNAG on Gaelic development (Lingard, Pedersen, and Shaw 1993, 16).

Fully rationalizing the process of Gaelic development, HIE and CNAG entered into a "Partnership Agreement" from 1993 through 1999, governed by a contract delegating particular responsibilities to each organization. Interaction between the two organizations was facilitated by the fact that the headquarters of HIE and CNAG were within walking distance of one another in the center of Inverness.

In 1993 HIE seconded Roy Pedersen, its Head Social Development Officer and one of the authors of the Gaelic Strategy, to CNAG for just over three years. During his tenure at CNAG, Pedersen put into practice the new development strategy for Gaelic. One of his activities was to write several papers elaborating and publicizing the Gaelic development strategy and present them at Gaelic language planning conferences (Pedersen 1993; 1995b). These papers are notable for their use of the language of economic development, economic forecasting, and quantification, to encompass the work of language planning and revitalization. They began to define and elaborate the concept of a "Gaelic economy" or "Gaelic sector" and the concept of Gaelic as a commodity in that economy.

The first of these papers was "The Dynamics of Gaelic Development" (Pedersen 1993). In this report, Pedersen defined Gaelic development and projected its future progress in terms of quantified "target indicators" in the areas of demography, Gaelic medium education, culture (defined as arts, heritage, and social organizations), and economic development (including media, teaching Gaelic to adults, and cultural tourism). The indicators included two projected sets of figures for each decade from 2001 to 2021, "best expectation" and "limited expectation" development scenarios, for a wide range of factors. These factors included: the total number of Gaelic speakers, the numbers of pupils and students in Gaelic medium education at all levels from pre-school through tertiary, the numbers of Gaelic-medium preschool programs and primary school units, the number of personnel employed at each level of education, the numbers of music festivals held and arts or heritage centres opened, the numbers of professionals employed in these "cultural" endeavours, the numbers of hours of Gaelic television and radio broadcast, and the turnover (in millions of pounds) and the number of full-time equivalent positions in cultural tourism. The quantification represented a new rationalization of language planning as a measurable enterprise.

In this report, future growth was represented by an increase in numbers, and the growth projections were emphasized by listing the projected figures for these categories next to the past figures for 1971, 1981, and 1991. The 1971 and 1981 estimated figures, when compared with the 1991 figures, demonstrated how quickly Gaelic revitalization activities had grown during the 1980s, not least due to the influence of CNAG itself. The 1971 and 1981 figures were zero for the categories of education, music festivals and arts/culture/history centres, and cultural tourism, while the 1991 figures included 84 Gaelic-medium pre-school groups, 30 Gaelic-medium primary school units with approximately 500 pupils and 50 teachers, and 2 fèisean (childrens' Gaelic music tuition festivals). Another type of measure that became visible for the first time in CNAG activities, due to the influence of HIE, was a focus on the number of FTEs, or full-time equivalent jobs, that were projected to be created in each category of effort. In the 1990s, the number of FTEs created became a major standard by which all development programs in Scotland were judged.

In 1995, Pedersen presented another report, "Scots Gaelic: An Economic Force," at the Liverpool conference "Language Planning and Policy in the EU." This paper discussed the four categories into which CNAG divided their language planning efforts (education, economic development, culture, and co-ordination) and "the process by which the interrelated project categories drive forward Gaelic development" (Pedersen 1995b, 2). He re-used the text of this report, together with the 1993 report, in two subsequent papers. The first was "Scots Gaelic as a Tourism Asset," presented at a conference on "Local Identity in Global Culture" at Robert Gordon University in Aberdeen and then published in an edited volume of proceedings (Pedersen 1995a). The second paper was "The Gaelic Economy," which appeared in the edited volume *New Directions in Celtic Studies* as an example of "Celtic praxis" (Hale and Payton 2000; Pedersen 2000). The titles of the papers indicate the deliberate attempt to re-orient thinking about Gaelic: they posit Gaelic to be an "economic force" or a "tourism asset," and implicitly contrast the "Gaelic economy" or a dynamic "Gaelic development" with the prevailing view of Gaelic as an object of language shift and obsolescence as described in Chapters 3 and 4 of this volume. Presenting these ideas to different audiences through conference papers and publications was an integral part of the "index it and they will come" strategy to bring the concept of the "Gaelic economy" into material existence. In other words, if Pedersen could persuade academics and policy-makers to act as though the Gaelic economy existed, then in a sense it would be created.

During the period of his secondment, Pedersen put the concepts outlined in his reports into practice. He led the development of a number of projects including *Sradagan* [Sparks], a youth after-school activity group; *Fàilte* [Welcome], a cultural tourism project; and the Gaelic in the Community Scheme (*Sgeama Gàidhlig sa Choimhearsnachd*), an infrastructure and childcare development project. Pedersen applied for European Regional Development Fund grants for all of these projects through the Highlands and Islands Objective One Partnership Programme. The award of European Regional Development Fund grants significantly shaped and limited these projects, for the ERDF only funded projects of one to three years in duration, and only in conjunction with the EU Member State government. Moreover, although the European Bureau for Lesser Used Languages offered support for educational research and some study visits among small language communities of the EU, in general the European Union did not offer large grants for minority language development,[3] so Pedersen framed these projects as "economic and social development" in the applications. This new approach to development funding was thus born of necessity. Pedersen hired and delegated development officers to set most of these projects in motion before returning to HIE in early 1997.[4] I discuss this in greater detail in Chapter 7, with particular focus on the Gaelic in the Community Scheme.

3   A Neoliberal Complaint Tradition against Gaelic

During the 1990s, as the UK Government and the Scottish Office allocated money for Gaelic medium education and Gaelic television, and the results of this public funding became increasingly visible, the Scottish media developed a new "complaint tradition" (Milroy and Milroy 1999, 24) theme against Gaelic. While commentators still continued to criticize Gaelic in the ways described in Chapters 3 and 4 of this volume, they also began to focus on criticizing public spending for Gaelic revitalization-related efforts. Anti-Gaelic commentators in the media, primarily the Scottish and British national newspapers, proclaimed their opposition to government funding for Gaelic language revitalization efforts on the grounds that Gaelic was already dying or dead, such activities only served a minority interest, and public funding for Gaelic was money ill spent.

Criticism and discussion of public funding for Gaelic continued through the 1990s and achieved new prominence in the autumn of 2000. In autumn 1999, MSP Alasdair Morrison, the Minister for Gaelic, had appointed a national taskforce to examine the issue of public spending on Gaelic. The head of the taskforce was John Alick Macpherson, the deputy director of Comataidh Craolaidh Ghàidhlig [the Gaelic Broadcasting Committee]. The announcement of the formation of the taskforce had caused apprehension among some Gaelic language workers—in his speech announcing the taskforce, the Minister had said that he thought there were too many overlapping Gaelic organizations duplicating each other's efforts. He wished to streamline the process to maximize their efforts and avoid wasting public funding.

The outcome of the taskforce's year-long inquiry into Gaelic revitalization efforts was a report titled "Revitalising Gaelic: A National Asset." The report, called the "Macpherson Report" in Gaelic-speaking circles after the chairman of the taskforce, offered recommendations for improving Gaelic revitalization efforts. The two main ones were the recommendation to create one overarching Gaelic development organization with statutory power, and the recommendation to the Scottish Executive to grant some form of official status to Gaelic.

As already described at length in Chapter 3, BBC Two Scotland aired a segment on this report in an episode of the late-night news discussion program "Newsnight Scotland" on Thursday, 7 September 2000, the night before the report's release to the public. Three guests appeared with presenter Gordon Brewer, who questioned them in a provocative, challenging style typical of British news interviews (Clayman 2002; Greatbatch 1998). John Alick Macpherson had been invited to appear on "Newsnight Scotland" as the chairman of the taskforce that authored the report. Mike Russell, a Scottish National Party MSP, had been invited on the basis that he had become an advocate for Gaelic in the new Scottish Parliament.[5] The third guest was Allan Brown, a Scottish columnist for the "Ecosse" section of the conservative *Sunday Times* newspaper, and a self-appointed Gaelic detractor. Macpherson and Russell were on satellite feeds from the CNAG conference and Edinburgh respectively, while Brown appeared live in the Glasgow studio with Brewer. The theme of the segment was the propriety and effectiveness of public spending on efforts to revitalize Gaelic.

In this chapter I re-analyze the discourse of that BBC interview, and analyze other complaints in the media about public spending on Gaelic revitalization efforts. I identify the ways in which the complainants, like the promoters of the "Gaelic economy" discussed in Chapter 5, made use of neoliberal discourse. I draw my examples from three media articles dating from 1992 to 1999—a 1992 article in *The Economist*, a 1996 article in the Scottish tabloid *Daily Mail*, and a 1999 article in the Scottish tabloid *Sunday Mail*—as well as the 2000 BBC interview.

These sources utilized at least four different interrelated strategies to construct a neoliberally-motivated rhetoric against Gaelic: 1) they portrayed support for Gaelic as a waste of public money, and Gaelic language shift as an issue of individual rational choice; 2) they used juxtaposition and repetition of tropes to convey the idea that public funding for Gaelic was disproportionate to the small number of Gaelic speakers in Scotland; 3) they used deixis to construct an "implied readership" (Reah 2002, 40), a Scottish national audience that excluded Gaelic speakers; and 4) they utilized the reported speech of Gaelic speakers themselves to increase the authority of their negative opinions about the public spending for Gaelic.

In the media examples I analyzed, the first main feature of opinions about Gaelic was their portrayal of Gaelic language revitalization and shift as economic issues of cost-effectiveness and rational choice. As described in Chapter 5, pp. 140–144, CNAG and HIE framed the problem of Gaelic revitalization in part as an economic one. The concept of the "Gaelic economy" was based on a concept of Gaelic as an economic asset. The Macpherson report of 2000 dubbed Gaelic a "national asset."

Commentators opposed to Gaelic likewise increasingly cast their opposition in market terms. They portrayed the market as a mechanism ensuring that the economically fittest cultural formations would survive, and the rest would go extinct, a neoliberal iteration of social Darwinism. Just as the "Gaelic economy" concept erases the social act of Gaelic speaking, the social Darwinist critique of public spending on Gaelic erases centuries of deliberate social interventions against Gaelic, and the involvement of Gaelic speakers and the Highlands in the global economy since the 18th century.

These assertions are in tune with Thatcher's famous claim that "there is no such thing as society" and with neoliberalism's "legitimizing principles of efficiency, accountability and freedom" in the 1980s and early 1990s (Levitas 1998, 113, 115). In this framework, cost effectiveness is transformed into a moral issue:

> In market terms, waste is viewed as immoral and efficiency is seen as the antidote. Since the market is viewed as the most efficient way of managing resources, it is seen as a moral order and the transfer of its hegemony into the world of what was previously the world of the social is part of a moral campaign. The effects of neo-liberalism are held to be that people govern themselves in a liberal and efficient way, involving an emphasis on quality assurance, and a focus upon innovation in practice. Welfarism is relegated to the community and is operated through the principle of the greater good (Williams and Morris 2000, 179).

Post-1997, Blair's "New Labour" placed emphasis on the only slightly altered principles of "efficiency, accountability, opportunity and fairness" (Levitas 1998, 115).

A short sidebar article in *The Economist* in 1992 provides the first example of this discourse. The magazine took note of the Gaelic television grant awarded in the 1990 Broadcasting Act around the time the funds were disbursed to the Gaelic Television Committee. The anonymous article described the £13 million of new spending on Gaelic television using the trope of a per capita breakdown:

> The subsidy, for each of Scotland's Gaelic speakers, is £146 a year—even more, per head, than the £58m that Wales's 500,000 Welsh-speakers get. Britain's 1.5m Hindi-speakers, by the way, get nothing ("Soft-soaping the Gaels," 1992).[6]

The article implied that paying for Gaelic broadcasting was a case of spending the money of the many on a problem of the few. Their approach denied the relevance of Gaelic—and the social problem of Gaelic language shift—for Scottish society as a whole.

Eight years later in 2000, "Newsnight Scotland" repeated this complaint of inequity based on a per capita argument. The news program creatively generated an even larger per capita figure to describe the ratio:

> If we take the £13 million plus the £9 million for Gaelic broadcasting it works out something like £400 per head per year for everyone in this country who actually speaks the language.

Again, this rough calculation was based on the idea that the merit of a publicly-funded project could be assessed by its per-capita cost. The higher the per-capita cost of the project, the more expensive the program was held to be.

Macpherson rejected the presenter's framing of the problem, countering it with the economistic view of Gaelic as a "national asset" that the taskforce report emphasized:

> Well I– I– I don't accept this per capita argument, I think it's specious, and spurious, because that's the argument that the people who are against Gaelic development constantly use. What we have here is a national asset that is in serious decline.

This accounting-style method of discussing the cost effectiveness of publicly-funded programs could be found elsewhere in the British media. Another example, an excerpt from a Scottish media story unrelated to Gaelic, demonstrates the same argument:

> Expensive Mink
>
> Scottish Natural Heritage has been trying to get rid of mink in the Outer Hebrides for a number of years. The animals were released from fur farms in the 1950s and 1960s by environmental campaigners and have bred too successfully in the wild. At taxpayers expense, the organisation has laid 2,500 traps which were baited each day by a dedicated team of trappers. However, in the first year of the £1.65 million project, only 200 mink were caught. *That works out at £1,750 per animal.* But now the organisation is expected to seek more money to extend the scheme (Rampant Scotland 2003, emphasis added).

The "per-animal" expenditure trope used by the commentator to call the efficiency of the program into question is the same as the "per-speaker" expenditure trope used to criticize publicly-funded Gaelic-language programs. In this trope, the assessment of a publicly-funded program's overall effectiveness and indeed worthiness is collapsed into an assessment of its financial efficiency, expressed by dividing the total annual cost of the project by the number of target subjects or units, without taking into account other factors including startup costs and societal benefit. The commentator judges the per capita cost to be too high as a way of passing a negative moral judgement on the program. In this market morality, financial waste is equivalent to moral improvidence. This trope emphasizes an individualized and individualizing assessment of a public policy's ability to address social problems, rather than a consideration of the wider or longer-term social impact of any particular public policy or publicly-funded program.

The presenter of "Newsnight Scotland" further emphasized the individual perspective on language shift over the social perspective, by portraying language shift as the outcome of a set of rational choices by Gaelic speakers:

> But the point, Mike Russell, is, is– is– putting this, or trying to put this in a very neutral way, the point would be that, um, I mean that you say this is a living thing, but the point is the numbers of Gaelic speakers are going down, and presumably the numbers of Gaelic speakers are going down *because Gaelic-speaking families are choosing to have their children educated in English rather than Gaelic*. So in that sense it's a, it's a problem in the Gaelic community more than a problem if you like for, for non-Gaelic speakers ("Newsnight Scotland" 2000, emphasis added).

The presenter makes a metapragmatic assertion of the neutralistic stance he is expected to maintain as an interviewer (Clayman 2002; Greatbatch 1998), but the point in this interview that I emphasize here is the speaker's own emphasis on *choice* as a mode of understanding Gaelic language shift. The presenter continued with this theme of individual choice while speaking to Macpherson:

> John Alick Macpherson, what's your view of that. There is this problem, isn't there. That um, it is *Gaelic families who are having their children taught in English*. To some extent the language may be dying out but *this is self-will from within the community*. Now given that all the millions that have been spent over the past few years haven't really altered that fundamental state of affairs,

it– it– it– it's slightly difficult to see from an outside perspective, how flinging a bit more money at it can really make any difference to it given the overwhelming pressures that Mike Russell's just referred to, on children to be brought up in English so that they can get on in the world.

Thus the "Newsnight Scotland" presenter neglects the larger social relevance of language shift as a social problem, throwing it back onto individual speakers of the minority language, conceptualized as an aggregate of individuals acting in their own economic self-interest. Dorian (1993) discusses the reasons why language shift cannot be adequately understood as the outcome of "free" choices made by a group of individuals, among them the many forms of discrimination and coercion experienced by minority language speakers.

In 1999, the *Sunday Mail* leveled accusations of misspent public money at the Royal National Mòd, the week-long annual Gaelic singing competition modeled on the Welsh Eisteddfod.[7] In the 1990s the Mòd had started to receive a portion of its funding through local enterprise companies (LECs), which since 1991 had formed the apparatus for distributing public economic development funding in Scotland. The Mòd had also achieved greater public visibility in the 1990s when the BBC started televising highlights each night during Mòd week. During the 1990s, several Scottish newspapers started sending journalists to cover the Mòd and write uncomplimentary articles about it. One tabloid article's subtitle was: "Gary Keown finds out why his cash is being spent on the Mod" (Keown 1999).

The theme of the article was that since the Mòd was partially publicly funded, he had personally helped to pay for it. And having paid for part of it entitled him to complain about it; personal interests and public spending became linked through neoliberalism. The author declared, "The Mod is no different, really, to a convention of trainspotters. So why should those who have no interest in Gaelic be forced to pay for part of it?" To make the point that Gaelic was a minority interest, Keown reduced an entire language-culture complex to the level of a hobby—in fact, the hobby with the worst reputation in Britain, popularly considered to be a pointless, time-wasting obsession (see Ch. 3, this volume, for further analysis of Keown's article).[8]

Second, journalists constructed a neoliberal rhetoric against Gaelic with the poetic juxtaposition and repetition of tropes comparing the amount of public money spent on Gaelic revitalization efforts and the number of Gaelic speakers. While most of the complainants expressed prejudice against Gaelic using tropes of death, decline, and distance in time (see Ch. 3), in the 1990s they added complaints against public spending on Gaelic to their anti-Gaelic rhetoric. Journalists had also already been using tropes of declining numbers to describe Gaelic, but in the 1990s they also juxtaposed descriptions of small and decreasing numbers of Gaelic speakers with descriptions of public spending on Gaelic as large and increasing.

The sources I analyzed utilized this pattern of paired tropes repeatedly. For example, the 1996 commentary in the Scottish edition of the *Daily Mail* tabloid stated: "But despite the fact that only a *tiny, dwindling minority* of Scots speak it, a *hugely disproportionate* amount of money is being spent on keeping Gaelic on a life-support system" (Morrison 1996, emphasis added). The 1999 article about the Royal National Mòd in the *Sunday Mail* described the Mòd as "This *overpublicised* celebration of a tongue spoken by a *tiny minority*" (Keown 1999, emphasis added). "Newsnight Scotland" utilized the trope in the introduction to its segment on the Macpherson report:

> The number of Gaelic speakers keeps *falling*. At the end of the last century, more than 210,000 people spoke the language. Ten years ago, that had *fallen* to *fewer* than 70,000. The projected figure for next year could be as *low* as 50,000. Meanwhile, government spending is *rocketing*. £2 million in 1991, £13.2 million next year (emphasis added).

The repetition of these paired tropes contributed to a poetics of neoliberal language death, related to the poetics of statistics described in Chapter 4. It is clear that media commentators use this pattern of tropes to position Gaelic in the worst possible way in the "quality space" of Scottish society (Fernandez 1986).

Third, as well as proclaiming the excessive nature of Scottish public spending on Gaelic, columnists used deixis to linguistically constructed a homogeneous Scottish audience opposed to the spending (Hill 1995; Reah 2002, 36–40). The examples implicitly oppose this imagined group to another imagined group, a minority group of Gaelic speakers that believes public spending on Gaelic is justified and deserved. Commentators used deictics such as "us," "we," and "our" to exclude Gaelic speakers from their construction of a Scottish public. For example, the 1996 *Daily Mail* article began:

> It's one of the last taboo subjects *nobody* in 1990s Scotland dares to discuss. But the issue which has preoccupied *so many of us* in private has finally been aired in public: why are millions of pounds of *taxpayers'* money being spent on a timewarp language *hardly anyone* understands? [emphasis added]

The author used expressions such as *nobody in 1990s Scotland* and *so many of us* to include the reader with herself in her own group. *Taxpayers* further defines this group in neoliberal fashion as a group of individuals with a common financial obligation and interest, rather than as a group of citizens with a common political interest, or even as a social or cultural group with a common cultural or linguistic interest. The author also makes clear that the group in which she includes herself is the majority, both by describing it as *so many of us* and non-Gaelic speakers as *98.6 percent of the population* and *vast swathes of viewers*, and by contrasting this majority group with Gaelic speakers, described as *hardly anyone, only 1.4 percent of Scots*, and *a tiny, dwindling minority of Scots*. All adult Gaelic speakers are fluent in English and read the English-language newspapers as much as non-Gaelic speakers do. Nonetheless, media commentators complaining about the public funding of Gaelic discursively constructed an imagined majority audience of non-Gaelic-speaking Scots disapproving of public funding for the minority concern of Gaelic.

The Economist's portrayal of Gaelic speakers deliberately distanced them from its readers with a slightly different strategy, negative stereotyping. A photo and caption accompanying the article posited Gaelic speakers as objects of mocking address: an incongruous stock photo of a pipe band major in full dress uniform had the caption "Did you set the video, Jock?" ("Soft-soaping the Gaels," 1992). The humour is of the same type described in Chapter 3, which portrays Gaelic (and in this case, Scottishness) as inherently amusing in contrast to anglophone British culture. The pipe band is a stereotypically Scottish institution, originally formed by the Highland Regiments in military service to the British Empire. However, pipe bands are unrelated to Gaelic except insofar as piping was originally a Gaelic cultural tradition, and the earliest members of Highland Regiments were Gaelic speakers. "Jock" is a derogatory ethnonym for a Scottish man that originated in reference to Scottish soldiers, particularly members of Scottish regiments (Oxford English Dictionary Online 1989). The conflation of Scots and Gaels found in this captioned photo, and the title and the first sentence of the article, index an outsider perspective on the issue.

Fourth and finally, media commentators utilized reported speech to enhance the authority of their rhetoric against public spending on Gaelic. Commentators created "double-voiced" discourse (Bakhtin 1981b) with the reported speech of both named and anonymous Gaelic speakers, adding to their own opposition the "moral weight" of selected Gaelic speakers who were themselves skeptical of publicly-funded Gaelic revitalization efforts. Hill and Irvine (1993, 6) note in their analysis of reported speech that "Establishing the authoritativeness of discourse… is particularly important when the discourse serves as the basis for a judgement or a course of action having serious social or personal consequences." This is the type of judgement and action that commentators were encouraging and calling for—a dislike of Gaelic, and/or a cessation of public spending on the support of the Gaelic language.

For example, the anonymously-authored article in *The Economist* used both direct and indirect reported speech of Gaelic speakers to convey a negative judgement of public funding for Gaelic, while making it seem that this judgement had been passed by Gaelic speakers themselves. The article followed a pattern, first describing the negative or pessimistic opinions of a vaguely-defined group of un-named Gaelic speakers, then directly quoting a public figure picked for his presumed authority to speak on behalf of other Gaelic speakers. The figures quoted included a politician, a newspaper columnist, and a television producer, and in each case the article implied that the figure quoted was representative of a larger group of Gaelic speakers. In case of the newspaper columnist, one sentence purported to state the views of "Gaelic-speakers" in general, and the next sentence implied that the columnist MacLeod was a Gaelic speaker whose opinions about funding for Gaelic television exemplify the views of "some Gaelic-speakers" described in the first sentence. Both of these sentences are densely packed with negative descriptors of the funding, the language, and its speakers:

> Even among Gaelic-speakers there are some who doubt that much good will come from this attempt to conserve a threatened language. John Macleod, columnist for the *Glasgow Herald*, scorns the television grant as a politically correct slush-fund wasted on a near-extinct language, creating dreary programmes of no resale value to be made by an upper-middle class Gaelic mafia ("Soft-soaping the Gaels," 1992).

We infer from this passage that "some" Gaelic speakers are doubtful about the effects of the new television programs, but we do not know which ones, except for the specific example of MacLeod. The awarding of a grant to produce Gaelic television programs is described as an *attempt*, which sounds more tentative than *effort*. Moreover, it is an attempt to *conserve*, not revitalize, Gaelic, a *threatened language* (the implied threat, of course, being extinction or death). Whether or not *some Gaelic speakers* actually used these negative words is ambiguous because of the indirect report of the speech. The ambiguity continues in the description of MacLeod's opinions of the funding: "*scorns*" is a strongly negative word; *politically-correct* is a negative expression that implies unreasonable forced catering to a minority interest; *slush-fund* implies crooked management; *wasted* is a strongly negative alternative to *spend*. *Near-extinct* is the language of endangered species and death used to describe Gaelic again, *dreary* a negative judgement word; *no resale value* conveys a neoliberal stance in which the programming, like everything else, should be justified purely by its economic value. Finally, the description of the producers of the programs as *upper middle-class* implies a distance from working-class or rural people, and is paired with *Gaelic mafia* which implies that the people producing the programs are a dangerous, illegal, powerful, underground, clannish business network. The *Gaelic mafia* term was generated from within the ranks of Gaelic speakers to express resentment over the perceived closed power network and financial gain of late 20th-century

Gaelic language planners. The article transforms this more localized concern about upward mobility among Gaelic-English bilinguals themselves into a more generalized criticism of public funding for Gaelic. Through this example and two other instances, the *Economist* was able to express strongly negative rhetoric against public funding for Gaelic, while drawing on the authority of "experts" on Gaelic to augment the moral force or truth value of their own statements.

I have identified four ways in which British and Scottish media sources constructed a systematically anti-Gaelic rhetoric based on the neoliberal presumption that social action and public policy issues can be managed and explained by the principles of free market capitalism. They included the portrayal of Gaelic language shift and revitalization as individualized and economic phenomena rather than social phenomena, the use of paired tropes of large/small and increasing/decreasing to convey that public funding for Gaelic was disproportionate to the small and shrinking numbers of Gaelic speakers; the use of deixis to construct an implied Scottish national audience for their claims that excluded Gaelic speakers; and the use of reported speech to reinforce the authority of negative opinions about public funding for Gaelic. Overall, the framing of the issue in this way could be seen as a response to the effort to discursively define a Gaelic economy. Or more likely, both the rhetoric against public funding for Gaelic and the efforts to promote a "Gaelic economy" developed from the same ethos of neoliberalism that pervaded Scotland, and the rest of the UK, beginning in the Thatcher years and continuing into the tenure of Blair's New Labour.

4 Conclusion

During the 1990s, both Gaelic promoters and public commentators opposed to Gaelic utilized themes of neoliberal discourse in their rhetoric. In the previous decade, the Thatcher Government had introduced a neoliberal privileging of market relations, together with a contradictory neo-conservative emphasis on a strong, centralized state. Thatcher's Government invoked the relatively new concept of "heritage" as one way of reconciling these two aims (McCrone, Morris, and Kiely 1995). The trend toward commodification and valorization of the past as "heritage," together with a restructuring of the world economy in the 1970s, prepared the way for the growth of international tourism and led cities in Scotland and throughout the UK to view the marketing of heritage as a viable option for dealing with economic restructuring and fostering economic development.

This trend continued unabated after the 1997 election of Tony Blair and New Labour, and the trouncing of the Conservative Party in Scotland. New Labour "recogniz[ed] that markets alone produce socially damaging results which are simultaneously inequitable and inefficient" (Levitas 1998, 113) and reintegrated the concept of "society" into an understanding of the market—but the primacy of the market remained, this time as the juggernaut of globalization. Scottish regions and localities continued to be thrown back on their own resources, now under New Labour with discourses of individual responsibility and opportunity. The marketing of heritage gradually expanded to encompass the marketing of culture in general, and grew more sophisticated with the development of branding strategies to "position" localities, ethnicities, and political entities in the market. The Government set up organizations like Scotland the Brand to promote the ethnic distinctiveness of Scotland as a market advantage.

CNAG developed the concept of the "Gaelic economy" and the marketing of Gaelic in this political, social, and economic climate, as had the development- and marketing-oriented Irish and Welsh precedents. The use of economic development strategies to promote language planning, and language planning efforts to promote economic development, is not inherently problematic. But with a lack of firm focus on language planning and standardization, and inadequate state support for Gaelic medium education, the neoliberal turn facilitated an economistic approach that did not help reverse language shift, and in fact ignored the relevance of the social act of communication. Instead, "the Gaelic language" was objectified, and indeed commodified as "Gaelic goods and services" existing independently of the matrix of social interaction through the linguistic medium of Gaelic. Planners and participants tended to lose sight of language use as a human behaviour.

Media criticism of Gaelic in the 1990s only intensified this view, focusing on public funding for Gaelic as an economic issue of cost-effectiveness, and on language shift as the cumulative outcome of free choices of individual Gaelic speakers not to transmit the language. Media critics emphasized the idea that their status as taxpayers (rather than as citizens or subjects) entitled them to criticize public expenditure on Gaelic television, the Mòd Gaelic music festival, and Gaelic medium education. The root of their complaint, however, was that Gaelic was a minority concern, worthy of denigration and irrelevant to the larger Scottish society.

Notes

1 Touche Ross, which later became Deloitte & Touche, was the UK practice of Deloitte Touche Tohmatsu, a major international consulting and financial services firm. Saatchi and Saatchi is a well-known advertising agency responsible for many innovative advertising campaigns building "global brands."

2 The actual amount remained fairly constant for the next ten years at least, which meant a decline in real terms when inflation was taken into account.

3 Support for regional or minority languages in the European Union had been the responsibility of the European Bureau for Lesser-Used Languages (EBLUL), based in Dublin (http://www.eblul.org/). However, a European Court of Justice decision on 12 May 1998 resulted in the European Commission blocking budget lines without legal bases, including budget line B3-1006, "support to regional and minority languages" (Caroline Loup, EC DG XXII, personal communication). This budget line was blocked from 1998 to 2000, cutting off funding not only for research projects but also for EBLUL (Suzanne Romaine, personal communication). A new call for proposals through the Mercator Network of Directorate-General XXII (Education, Training and Youth) of the European Commission (EAC/19/00) was published on 16 September 2000 in Official Journal C 266 (http://europa.eu.int/comm/education/mercator/lang-min.html). The EU discontinued operational funding for EBLUL in 2007, and the organization closed down in 2010 (https://en.wikipedia.org/wiki/European_Bureau_for_Lesser-Used_Languages).

4 Pedersen also persuaded ScotRail (formerly part of British Rail) to adopt Gaelic-English bilingual location signs at selected railway stations. These were the signs marking the West Highland Way rail line. The signs provoked erroneous criticism of "road signs in Gaelic" by newspaper columnist Allan Brown and "Newsnight Scotland" presenter Gordon Brewer, as described in Chapter 3, p. 88, this volume.

5 At the time of the interview Russell was about to introduce a Private Member's Bill to the Scottish Parliament for official status for Gaelic. He

was doing so in the wake of a recent refusal by First Minister Donald Dewar to consider the "Secure Status" bill that the Labour Party had promised it would support in Scotland, and that Comunn na Gàidhlig had been lobbying for since 1997.

6   The expression "soft-soaping" indicates the *Economist*'s editorial view, which was that John Major's Conservative UK Government granted the funding for Gaelic television in order to appease Scottish nationalist sentiments, keep Scots in the Union, and win Scottish support for the Conservative party, which had been extremely low in Scotland since Thatcher was Prime Minister, and continues to be extremely low in 2020. If that was indeed the goal of the funding, it would seem to indicate a misunderstanding of the historical status of Gaelic in Scotland. In any case Tony Blair of the Labour Party won the next general election in 1997, and the Conservatives lost most of their parliamentary seats in Scotland. However, that aspect of the Gaelic television funding is not relevant to this chapter, which focuses on the debate over the funding within Scotland itself.

7   See Thompson (1992) for a history of the Mòd since its inception in 1892.

8   "[R]eaders unfamiliar with the traditional British pastime of 'train-spotting' may find a brief explanation helpful. A reference work detailing all the locomotives operating in Britain appears each year: the object of train-spotting is to 'collect' sightings of as many different trains as possible. This usually involves travelling to a major railway terminus, standing there all day and recording the serial numbers of the trains you observe. (The question 'why?' is more difficult to answer satisfactorily.)" (Cameron 1995, 237).

CHAPTER 7

Neoliberalism and Minority Language Planning in the Highlands of Scotland

1   Introduction

Neoliberalism is a force reshaping cultures and communities worldwide (Comaroff and Comaroff 2000). Small language communities, embedded as they are in majority cultures and states, are not exempt from the effects of neoliberalism (Kockelman 2002; Williams and Morris 2000). This article illustrates the emerging connections in the United Kingdom between neoliberalism as an ideology and style of government, and the practices of publicly-funded minority language planning and policy. The neoliberal orientation to government and civil society has made public funding available to language planners in new ways, but it has also created a new set of conditions to which minority language planners must adhere in order to obtain public funding for their efforts. These conditions marginalize the importance of sociolinguistically informed language planning and goals (Williams and Morris 2000, 200).

Since Margaret Thatcher, Prime Minister of the United Kingdom from 1979–1990, was responsible for introducing neoliberalism to the world in practical form, and thus British minority-language communities were probably among the first to be affected by it, it is appropriate to examine the effects of neoliberalism on the British minority-language community of Scottish Gaelic-speakers in Scotland. The 2001 Scottish census results give a figure of 58,650 Gaelic-speakers in Scotland.[1] This is just over 1% of Scotland's 2001 population of approximately 5.06 million. The vast majority of Gaelic-speakers are English-Gaelic bilinguals, apart from a few preschool-aged children. A further 37,022 census respondents in 2001 indicated that they could understand, read, or write Gaelic, or some combination of these, but not speak it.[2]

Neoliberalism, or economic liberalism, is a political-economic ideology which advocates a shift from a welfare state to an "enabling state" in which individuals' dependency on the state is minimized and instead their responsibility is emphasized (Williams and Morris 2000, 178). The principle of "enabling"

> focuses on the idea of non-directionality, or the claim that states should respond to the needs and expectations of the citizen, rather than directing them towards certain ends. It involves a focus upon the animator state that responds to problems via organization, cooperation and confrontation between public services, elected administration and associations, leading social actors to play a more active role in the solution of social and economic problems (Williams and Morris 2000, 176).

Government ideally exists to facilitate the operation of market forces, with minimal state intervention. The ideology of neoliberalism enacted by governments such as the UK has been far-reaching in its social and cultural effects:

> One might want to say that the generalization of an "enterprise form" to all forms of conduct—to the conduct of organizations hitherto seen as being non-economic, to the conduct of government and to the conduct of individuals themselves—constitutes the essential characteristic of this [neoliberal] style of government: the promotion of an enterprise culture (Burchell 1996, 28–29).

As part of the UK, Scotland has also been subject to the government's "promotion of an enterprise culture." Since the 1980s, neoliberal ideologies have saturated the Scottish public sphere and civil society (M. Smith 1994, 7). As Thatcherism has given way to the era of New Labour, policy-makers in the UK have continued to treat "the market" as the moral arbiter of public spending and policy.

In keeping with this transformation, economic development in Scotland has taken a distinctly neoliberal direction since the early 1990s. In 1991, the entire organizational structure for economic development in Scotland was revamped with a neoliberal focus on "enterprise" (D. MacKinnon 2000b). The Highlands and Islands Development Board (HIDB), which had been in place since 1965, was dissolved, and a new entity, Highlands and Islands Enterprise

(HIE), was formed to take its place. HIE's new responsibility included overseeing a network of ten newly formed local enterprise companies (LECs), each one responsible for economic development in a particular local government region of the Highlands, and named after that region: for example, Western Isles Enterprise (WIE), Skye and Lochalsh Enterprise (SALE), etc.[3] The agenda of HIE and its new LEC network shifted from HIDB's former focus on forestry, tourism, manufacturing, and industrial "growth points" (Alexander 1985, 220), to business development and individual projects.

With the new focus on enterprise, Scottish economic development in the 1990s became a world of acronyms, schemes, initiatives, and programs, of contract employment and public-private partnerships, of "remits" that organizations define for themselves in terms of "leverage," "value for money," and "measurable outcomes." The spending of public funds by HIE and the LECs was carried out through grant applications, award letters, contracts, and invoices. These transactions and the system of which they are a part are believed to operate according to the principle of "governmentality" (Foucault 1991). Anthropologist James Ferguson describes this principle as "the idea that societies, economies, and government bureaucracies respond in a more or less reflexive, straight-forward way to policies and plans" (Ferguson 1994, 194).[4]

For Gaelic language planners in Scotland, neoliberal ideology and practices instilled the new "governmentality" into the process of reversing language shift. Neoliberal influence was particularly apparent in the operation of the joint language-status planning and economic development efforts that have become known as "Gaelic development." Although efforts to promote a minoritized language might seem to run counter to the homogenizing, globalizing effects of the free market, the neoliberal regime also made new sources (or conduits) of public funding available to Gaelic language planners: the EU's European Structural Funds, the UK National Lottery, and public-private partnerships with the LECs and local authorities (i.e., regional councils). In the process, however, language planners became subject to the same set of constraints as other areas of Scottish civil society and public policy. One might say that at the price of their participation in the system, they were co-opted into the neoliberal structure of development in Scotland.

In what follows, I explore the neoliberal development practices of Gaelic language planning in the 1990s–2000s through the example of a particular language development program called the "Gaelic in the Community Scheme/Sgeama Gàidhlig 's a' Choimhearsnachd." The Scheme, as I will call it, is an example of contemporary Gaelic language planning, as well as an excellent example of a typical late-20th-century neoliberal economic development project in Scotland, both in terms of the complexity of the project's funding structure and the external strictures imposed on its goals.

2   The "Gaelic in the Community Scheme"

In 1981, spurred in part by the Scottish census results for Gaelic showing a continuing decline in the total number of Gaelic-speakers in Scotland, the Highlands and Islands Development Board (HIDB) appointed a Gaelic Report Group to assess the current state of Gaelic in Scotland and make recommendations for the future. Following the group's conclusion that a new agency was needed to coordinate Gaelic development (MacArthur et al. 1982), Comunn na Gàidhlig (CNAG) was formed in 1984. CNAG has engaged in a variety of efforts to encourage the use of Gaelic, including the promotion of Gaelic-medium primary-school education, the production of Gaelic radio and television, and lobbying with the British and Scottish governments for official status for Gaelic.

CNAG has also focused on another main area: the promotion of Gaelic through the economic development of rural areas where Gaelic-English bilinguals live. The Western Isles, the area with the largest concentration of Gaelic speakers in Scotland, has been chronically underdeveloped in economic terms and therefore was considered a major target area for such development. According to the 2001 census, approximately 15,811 Gaelic-English bilinguals lived in the Western Isles, out of a total Western Isles population of 26,502. This meant that about 59% of the population of the Western Isles was Gaelic-English bilingual in 2001, with a further 9% or so able to understand but not speak Gaelic.

HIDB's (and later HIE's) rationale for combining language planning and economic development in this way was that improving the economic situation of minority-language speakers living in an economically distressed area such as the Western Isles would give those speakers more opportunities to remain in that area with their families, thus strengthening the social and cultural fabric of the area, including the linguistic practices. A similar approach has also been utilized in Ireland and in Wales (Williams and Morris 2000); the main difference between these examples and that of Scottish Gaelic is that in the case of Gaelic, there has been no legal or official status for the language to date,[5] and little formal corpus planning.

Working within this "language development" framework, HIE and CNAG designed the "Gaelic in the Community Scheme" as a program to award small grants to community groups for their own local-level Gaelic development projects. In 1995, an HIE employee seconded to CNAG completed an EU funding application for the Scheme, which CNAG submitted to the Highlands and Islands Objective One Partnership Programme (HIPP), the body that was responsible for distributing regional development money in the Highlands of Scotland from the EU's European Structural Funds.[6] To match HIPP criteria, the Scheme was designed as a three-year development project to operate in two different regions of the Highlands. CNAG's application was successful, and the European Regional Development Fund, through HIPP, provided 35% of the Gaelic in the Community Scheme's funding (the total amount was £48,000 per year for three years, 1997–1999).

The rest of the funding for the Scheme came from non-EU public sources, as stipulated by EU funding rules. Specifically, it came from five public sources, including CNAG itself, as well as the local government council and the local enterprise company (LEC) representing each of the two regions within the Highlands and Islands in which the Scheme would be run, the Western Isles and Argyll & Bute (see Figure 6.1). After receiving the funding, CNAG hired a coordinator for each of the two areas, and the Scheme began to operate. It awarded smaller grants to local voluntary groups and educational institutions in its two target areas, for projects that were defined by the Scheme as "Gaelic activities."

On its funding application, the Scheme was officially titled the "Gaelic Community Infrastructure and Childcare Facilities Scheme." However, its title was shortened in the promotion literature to the "Gaelic in the

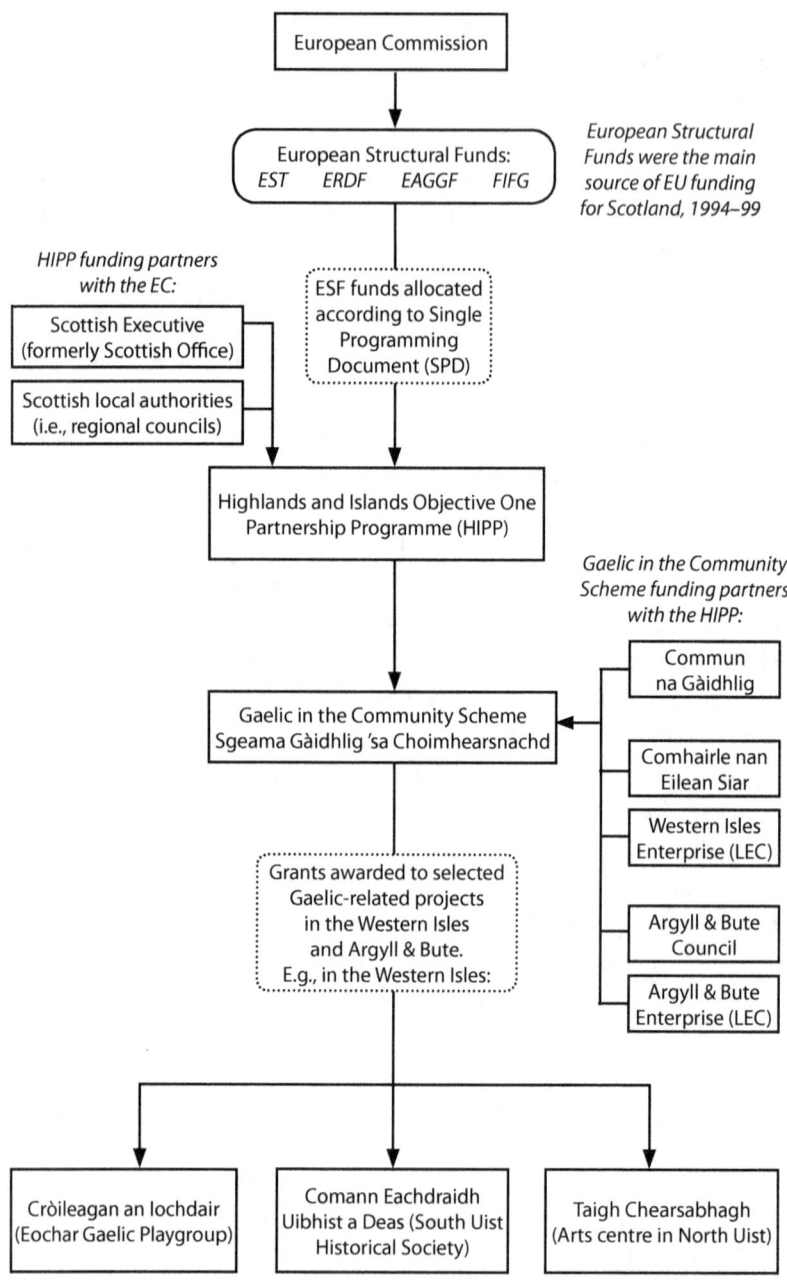

Figure 7.1 The structure of public funding for the Gaelic in the Community Scheme

Community Scheme" or "Sgeama Gàidhlig 's a' Choimhearsnachd." The Scheme assisted with a variety of Gaelic-related projects, including (1) "Gaelic Energy Centres" (providing funds for building renovation and equipment purchase); (2) the employment of "Gaelic staff"; (3) Gaelic-learners' courses; (4) training in childcare; (5) study visits; (6) feasibility studies; and (7) tourist facilities.

During field research in 1999–2000, I observed the administration of this Scheme by the Western Isles area administrator, examined some of the Scheme's Western Isles area files with the permission of CNAG, and interviewed some funding applicants and members of awardee groups. This research has led me to identify three aspects of the Scheme that demonstrate how neoliberal economic development practices can negatively impact Gaelic language planning, even as they seem to facilitate the creation of language-planning programs. The first aspect is the use of both English and Gaelic registers of "development discourse," which may reinforce Gaelic-English diglossia in Gaelic-speaking areas. The second is the problem of unexamined conceptions of "community," which, when operationalized, can reduce the number of opportunities for Gaelic-English bilinguals to speak Gaelic. The third aspect is the quantifiable and economistic nature of the criteria used to assess the success or failure of the Scheme, which do not focus on the actual linguistic behaviour of participants.

3 Neoliberal Aspects of Gaelic Development

The first aspect of the Scheme that poses a challenge to Gaelic language planning is its use of written "development discourse" in both English and Gaelic. Development, as a bureaucratically rationalized activity, requires extensive use of writing and reading. Much of this was carried out in English, but Scheme administrators made deliberate efforts to include Gaelic as much as possible. The Scheme's brochure, application form, and guidance notes were all printed in a bilingual Gaelic-English format. The bilingual presentation of the documents was one way language planners tried to overcome diglossia and create equivalence of meaning and equality of status between Gaelic and English, in the eyes of Gaelic-English bilinguals and the wider Scottish public. Planners believe that Gaelic ought to possess a set of registers parallel to English, to be used in every domain of life in order to carry out the same functions and express the same ideas that English does. Therefore, Gaelic development discourse owes its incipient existence as a register to ideologies of standard language (Silverstein 1987) and translatability.

Scheme administrators used written and spoken forms of both Gaelic and English while administering the Scheme. "Tormod," one of two Scheme administrators, was a native speaker of Gaelic, who wrote some letters in Gaelic for the Scheme business. He said that his own policy was to answer in Gaelic, if someone wrote a letter to him in Gaelic within the context of administering the Scheme. He also spoke in Gaelic to Scheme participants on the telephone.

However, the processes of applying for a Scheme grant and administering Scheme awards involved the creation and usage of many written documents, including not only business correspondence but also minutes and agendas of meetings, application forms, documentation including bank statements, quotations for work to be done or equipment or services to be purchased, planning consent or lease arrangements for buildings, a letter of offer, a letter of acceptance, claim forms, and invoices. Since many of these exchanges involved communication with non-Gaelic speakers, very little of such paperwork was written in Gaelic or bilingual format.

There were also larger societal and ideological reasons why the paperwork was done in English. I asked Tormod why, for example, none of the invoices for costs incurred by participants were written in Gaelic. He explained: "Well, [short laugh] apart from the fact that Gaelic isn't the language of business… [pause] it isn't. There's no point." He went on to point out that the official letters of offer for awards from the Scheme were also written in English. When I asked if the Scheme would ever send out two letters of offer, one in Gaelic and one in English (with the bilingual format mirroring that of the Scheme's application materials), he replied:

No, because it's a legal document. I mean, it's hard enough to understand in English actually. We did do an exercise here quite recently, ah, where um, we translated it. […] But I was thinking about it and I thought, well, you know, [tsk] who's going to uh, read this, and who's going to understand this. There's standard conditions, and there's the legal jargon, and legal jargon kind of, even in English by English standards, it's a little on the, you know ... [pause, tsk] well, plain English it isn't.

This illustrates not only the overwhelming dominance of English in Scottish society, but also the way in which Gaelic and English have come to hold "opposing social connotations" (Eckert 1983, 293) in the context of language shift for many, if not most, adult Gaelic-English bilinguals. Residents in the Western Isles (the Scheme area where I conducted research) tended to conceptualize Gaelic as a locally anchored spoken language of everyday use, not as a written and spoken technical language of specialized use; that place was reserved for English.

These opposing social connotations are reinforced by the contemporary lack of register range in Gaelic relative to English, which has been a result of processes of language shift (MacAulay 1982; Ure 1982). Register creation and elaboration, both ad hoc and planned, is part of the ongoing project of reversing Gaelic language shift. While a "news-speak" register of Gaelic has developed over the past fifty years (Lamb 1999), written and spoken registers of "business," "development," and "legal" Gaelic are still works in progress. This is the case both in the technical sense of corpus planning, and in the social sense of the registers becoming accepted by speakers. Many challenges still remain for both of these aspects. In the technical sense, one commentator described the Gaelic of bilingual brochures as "un-nuanced, colloquial Gaelic," "simultaneously infelicitous, imprecise, and insufficiently attentive to the question of register" (McLeod 1996, quoted in Lamb 1999, 167–168). In the social sense, Lamb notes that the "most daunting issue" of new register formation is Gaelic-speakers "reaching some collective acceptance" about these registers (1999, 143). In the absence of these registers, and with the gradual disappearance of traditional elevated religious and literary registers (MacAulay 1982), native Gaelic-English bilinguals tend to be most comfortable with the spoken register of "everyday Gaelic." This may also impede the acceptance of "development Gaelic," as Tormod noted from his own perspective as a Gaelic-English bilingual development program officer:

> Certainly [...] if you're starting to get into applications anyway you tend to be talking the kind of language that they wouldn't normally talk on a day-to-day level you know. It's all about total project costs and uh, where is your matching funding and, so, you know, it's actually a bit of a strain even for a fluent Gaelic-speaker to be discussing, um, you know, technical aspects of an application in Gaelic.

The lack of skill, practice, and confidence that many adult Gaelic-English bilinguals have with Gaelic literacy also currently mitigates against their developing a level of comfort with emergent writing-based technical registers of development, business, and government Gaelic. On the whole, Gaelic-English bilinguals reach levels of English literacy at least as high as non–Gaelic-speaking Scots do, through participation in the same state education system. However, the shortcomings in Gaelic literacy of many adult Gaelic-English bilinguals are a result of inadequate (or completely absent) formal Gaelic literacy training during their school years.

Finally, the acceptance of Gaelic development discourse as a register is further complicated by the fact that participants generally dislike "development discourse" and related specialist technical registers such as "legal jargon," even in English. The criticism of development discourse by development workers in the Western Isles, who must use the discourse as part of their daily work, suggests an awareness that the increasing use of such discourse disempowers people politically and socially. In interviews with me, participants like Tormod contrasted opaque and obfuscating development discourse to a "plain language" or "everyday language" which was seen as more transparent in meaning. The British press likewise criticized the related neoliberal registers of business and political jargon during the period of my field research. Negative evaluations of specialist registers arise from an ideology of standard language, in which language ideally ought to represent transparently a truthful reality; the unique lexicon of specialty registers seems to lack or exceed the ideal one-to-one relationship between words and things extolled in the ideology of standard language (Silverstein 1987, 8–9).

The second aspect of the neoliberal development process that may negatively impact Gaelic language planning is the way that development programs in general, and the "Gaelic in the Community Scheme" in particular, define their activities with reference to unexamined conceptions of "community." "Community" is a keyword of neoliberalism that indicates the new importance placed on grassroots-level participation in the provisioning of social services (Williams and Morris 2000, 180), but it is ill-defined and contains no explicit conceptualization of linguistic, social, cultural, or economic variation within communities. Unfortunately the way that "community" was defined in the operation of the Scheme without specific reference to language use could help reduce the number of opportunities for bilingual participants to actually speak Gaelic in development-related activities.

The most obvious illustration of the problem of the definition of "community" in the "Gaelic in the Community Scheme" was the name of the Scheme itself. In the previously mentioned ERDF Objective One funding application, the Scheme was officially titled "Gaelic Community Infrastructure and Childcare Facilities Scheme," but as Tormod repeatedly reminded me, the Scheme's title was shortened in the promotion literature to "Gaelic in the Community Scheme" or "Sgeama Gàidhlig sa Choimhearsnachd." His reminders in response to my interview questions seemed to be related to the fact that he frequently had to explain the disjuncture between the Scheme title and its goals to potential Scheme applicants. As Tormod said, some applicants for Scheme funding were confused and occasionally disgruntled to find that the Scheme would not award grants to support every use of Gaelic "in the community," even where the benefit to what they thought of as their community seemed obvious.

The reason for this selective type of funding is that the Scheme was designed to create and support "Gaelic Energy Centres," which were defined as "designated Gaelic spaces," "buildings or rooms within buildings where a diverse range of Gaelic activities can take place." In practice, these consisted mainly of buildings for *cròileagan* (Gaelic playgroups) and local historical society buildings housing visitor centres and museum displays (A. Smith 1999). The focus on "infrastructure" had been designed to fulfill the Highlands and Islands Objective One Partnership Programme's own infrastructure-focused development agenda. Because of this focus, several projects worthwhile from the perspective of language planning were turned down for Scheme funding, including a project to make audio recordings of the Gaelic Bible read aloud for the elderly, and numerous *fèisean*, or children's Gaelic music tuition festivals.

The uneasy fit between the public name of the Scheme and its aims also raises the question of how to define a community with reference to language use, an aspect that—ironically—was entirely omitted from consideration in this Scheme. Instead, "the community" was defined by the Scheme as an entity represented by the "Gaelic voluntary sector." The "Gaelic voluntary sector" was then defined somewhat circularly as being composed of "community groups," which were defined in a very particular way for the "Gaelic in the Community Scheme," as they were for other regional economic development programs. A community group was not considered a legitimate applicant for funds unless it was a "constituted group." A constituted group literally needed to adopt a constitution (most often written in English, though a few were written in Gaelic), and elect officers. Only community groups constituted in this way could apply for development funds; individuals could not.[7]

This setup may have reduced opportunities for Gaelic-English bilinguals to speak Gaelic in the following way: many of the committees of the community groups applying for Scheme funding contained people who could not speak Gaelic. Furthermore, accommodation norms among Gaelic-English bilinguals required that they not speak Gaelic in the presence of a non-Gaelic-speaking individual (see Ch. 8, this volume). These two conditions therefore constrained the amount of business that could be conducted by the groups through the medium of Gaelic, either among themselves or with the "Gaelic in the Community Scheme" program officer.

A third neoliberal aspect of the Scheme potentially problematic for language planning is the use of particular kinds of quantifiable criteria to assess the success or failure of the Scheme. The concept of "measurable outcomes" is regularly applied to plan the activities of development programs and to assess their progress. Cooperation with European Commission guidelines and EU member state-dictated goals for "measurable outcomes" in regional development results in standards of success being set for minority-language planning which measure and quantify enterprise creation, but not actual language use (cf. Urla 1993).

For example, the "project targets" for two years of the "Gaelic in the Community Scheme," as submitted to the European Regional Development Fund, were: to "create 6 [Gaelic Energy] centres; 6 new enterprises, of which 4 will be community enterprises; 12 FTE [full-time equivalent] directly sustainable jobs; 40 childcare places; [and] 30 trainees, of which 6 will be Gaelic cultural heritage management trainees." A 1999 evaluation of the Scheme carried out by a university student summer intern[8] reported that "it was generally agreed that the Scheme has been effectively promoted, managed, and administered" on the basis of a survey of successful and unsuccessful applicants, and concluded that "the Scheme has been successful in meeting its targets as set out in the ERDF (Objective One) application, particularly in terms of creating Gaelic Energy Centres, employment creation and facilitating childcare places" (A. Smith 1999, 2, 37). These targets, while laudable in economic and social terms, do not mention anything about whether participants were actually speaking Gaelic to one another while achieving them.

This conceptualization of development success produces statistics and other quantifications which are generated at several removes from people's daily spoken linguistic practices in the Gaelic-speaking areas in question. Such quantifications miss the nonuniform nature of language ability and use in the context of language shift. For example, since fluency in Gaelic was not a placement requirement, it was quite possible in the Western Isles that Gaelic cultural-heritage-management trainees could be semi-speakers of Gaelic, passive bilinguals, or non-Gaelic speakers altogether, incapable or nearly incapable of using spoken Gaelic on the job. This demonstrates the fetishized nature of the "Gaelic energy centre" concept. In practice, a "Gaelic energy centre" could only generate "Gaelic energy" to the extent that its participants were capable of utilizing the Gaelic language on-site in such a way as to influence those around them to also utilize the Gaelic language on-site.

Thus, the application of "measurable outcomes" could work against the goals of minority-language planning, by eliding the question of whether people were actually speaking the minority language, when defining the goals and assessing the success of the Scheme.[9] In fact, strict adherence to the EU-and member-state-created rules for disbursing grants, together with the bureaucratic division of labor and the accompanying lack of definition of "Gaelic activity" in terms of actual language use, meant that reversing language shift was not in point of fact the goal of the "Gaelic in the Community Scheme." The project officer I interviewed saw reversing language shift as the preserve of education, and as such the responsibility of the local (regional) elected council, Comhairle nan Eilean Siar (Western Isles Council), which administers primary and secondary education (including Gaelic-medium primary-school education). The Scheme, in contrast, was supposed to deal with the EU's and member state's narrowly-defined scope of "community development" through the promotion of various "projects" proposed and run by "community groups" in the "Gaelic voluntary sector."

4   Conclusion

The experiences of local language planning illustrated here demonstrate how the neoliberal orientation of European and state funding has resulted in the exclusion of minority-language planning based on sociolinguistic principles. While the economic goals are significant, thus far language planning under neoliberalism has largely failed to involve sociolinguists, linguistic anthropologists, and others with specialist training in the relationship between language, culture, and society. Just as Williams and Morris point out for Wales, the neoliberal direction has engendered "a shift away from the social sciences as a body of expertise that is capable of guiding any [language] planning activity" (2000, 200).

The sociolinguistic context of ongoing Gaelic language shift, with norms of accommodation to English, limited Gaelic literacy skills among speakers, and the limited register range of Gaelic, has not been taken into account as state-sponsored funding agencies have emphasized neoliberal goals of enterprise and job creation. The use of development discourse, a managerial technology (D. MacKinnon 2000a, 295) required by the neoliberal administrative framework of the EU Structural Funds and Scottish economic development bodies, privileges the use of English. The context of ongoing language shift further mitigates against the acceptance of Gaelic development discourse. It is a testimony to the determination and ad hoc communication skills of Scheme participants that Gaelic is utilized in these programs at all. Further, definitions of "community" in these programs assume a uniform geographically-based conglomeration of individuals, ignoring the fact that the desired target is in fact a language community embedded in a linguistically, socially, culturally, and economically differentiated (and stratified) community. Quantifiable criteria used to measure the success of the Scheme also sidestep the crucial questions of who is speaking Gaelic to whom, where, how often, and why.

The extent to which the devolved Scottish government will utilize a forthcoming Gaelic Language Bill to support Gaelic outside of the neoliberal paradigm remains to be seen. But at this juncture, it seems the government will not necessarily approach the issue from a humanistic rights-based perspective. Neoliberal governance is not based on "some inherent idea of rights as citizen, or even upon universal ethical principles" (Williams and Morris 2000, 176). For example, the 1992 Welsh Language Act

> was an enabling Act rather than one which ensured that rights could be guaranteed. This was commensurate with the political climate where the role of the state was assumed to diminish, and citizens were to assume greater responsibility for their actions, assuming they could be enabled to do so (Williams and Morris 2000, 172).

However, there is a problem with rolling back the state and enabling citizens to be more responsible in "demanding or directing the state to implement [their] will" (Williams and Morris 2000, 198) in regard to a minority language. Gaelic-English bilinguals have been a minority in Scotland for a long time, and as Williams and Morris note for Welsh in Wales, "if minority is conceived as subordinate then the associated deference and low status are not likely to generate a demand for a realignment of language status and services at the local level" (2000, 198). Historically, the Scottish and British states contributed substantially to the shift of Gaelic and other minority languages (Durkacz 1983; Withers 1984). However, at the very moment when the emergent Scottish state could step in to help repair the damage, it seems to be in danger of abdicating its social responsibility and leaving the job up to newly-construed citizen-consumers, "free" to "choose" their stigmatized minority language.

Notes

1 Reliance solely on census statistics can raise epistemological problems relating to issues of state power (Hacking 1991), the determination of linguistic and ethnic boundaries (Friedman 1997), and the reliability of self-reporting language behaviour. I offer the 2001 Scottish census figures here only as a rough estimate.

2 The 2001 census included for the first time a question on whether respondents could "understand" Gaelic, and thus the Gaelic linguistic skills of such respondents (including semi-speakers lacking the confidence to claim that they could speak Gaelic, passive bilinguals, and beginner-level adult learners of Gaelic) may have gone unreported in previous census results. The census results quoted here were provided by Kenneth MacKinnon (2003).

3 At the same time that the Highlands and Island Development Board was transformed into Highlands and Islands Enterprise, the Scottish Development Board was likewise transformed into Scottish Enterprise, overseeing its own network of local enterprise companies in the Lowlands of Scotland (including Dunbartonshire Enterprise, Lothian & Edinburgh Enterprise, and so on).

4 This system changed very little if at all with the devolution of powers to the new Scottish Parliament and Scottish Executive in 1997, which underlines the extent to which governments have accepted the validity of the neoliberal ideology.

5 At the time of writing, both the UK Government and the Scottish Executive had still failed to grant any kind of official or legal status to the Gaelic language in Scotland. However, in 2005 the Gaelic Language Act (Scotland) was passed by the Scottish Parliament.

6 To classify and channel the expenditure of the four European Structural Funds from 1994 to 1999, the EC originally adopted five objectives, ranked and referred to as "Objective One" through "Objective Five." Objective One of the European Structural Funds during this period was "promoting the development and structural adjustment of regions whose development is lagging behind, that is regions whose per capita GDP is less than 75% of the Community average." The other objectives, in descending level of importance and allocations, dealt with areas affected by industrial decline (Objective 2), effects on workers of long-term unemployment and change in production systems (Objectives 3 and 4, respectively), and the agriculture and fisheries of rural areas (Objective 5). Later a sixth objective was added to cover areas with extremely low population density (i.e., the northern portions of Sweden and Finland). The UK Government obtained Objective One status for the Highlands and Islands of Scotland for the period 1994–1999. This set of EU development objectives ended

in 1999, and from 2000–2006 was replaced by a system with a set of only three objectives (known as Objectives One through Three). The objectives then changed again and were Convergence, Regional competitiveness and employment, and European territorial cooperation, from 2007–2013. The categories for allocation of funds changed again in the period 2014–2020.

7   The architects of neoliberal policy and practice intended for such voluntary community groups to form part of the public-private partnership which they expected to do the work that had previously been assigned solely to the government. While Thatcher held that "society" did not exist, Blair's New Labour espoused a communitarian discourse in which "'community' has come to be understood in moral terms which emphasise that 'responsibilities' are the other side of 'rights'" (Fairclough 2000, 37–39). However, such community groups are unelected and together with the LECs (with their appointed, not elected, local boards of directors), they contributed to the eclipse of local democratic representation by unelected, corporatized forms of social organization.

8   In another example of neoliberal public-private partnership, the summer intern's program, the Shell Technology Enterprise Programme, was sponsored by Shell Corporation.

9   These shortcomings have also characterized the "economics of language" approach to minority languages espoused by some economists (e.g. Grin 1996a, 1996b; Sproull 1996). CNAG commissioned both Grin and Sproull at different times to establish and promote the economic value of Gaelic in Scotland to policy-makers and the public (e.g. Sproull and Ashcroft 1993; Sproull and Chalmers 1998). For more discussion see Ch. 5, pp. 140–144, this volume.

PART FOUR

Language Ideologies and Affect

CHAPTER 8

Ideology, affect, and socialization in language shift and revitalization: The experiences of adults learning Gaelic in the Western Isles of Scotland

1   Introduction

At a Presbyterian church service in the Western Isles of Scotland in 2000, I met a Scottish woman in her mid-twenties from the mainland who was studying Gaelic as a second-language learner. We were both living temporarily on the same island in Uist, the southern island group of the Western Isles, where over half the population is Gaelic-English bilingual (see Figure 8.1). I had come there for eight months to do ethnographic research, and she had come to live and work there for the summer hoping to improve her spoken Gaelic ability. She was earnest, friendly, and good-humoured, and I admired her strong determination to speak Gaelic at all times. However, her Gaelic speech was halting, strongly influenced by English phonology, and punctuated by nervous giggles. I wondered at the time if her uncertain manner was exacerbated by the great difficulty she had in finding affordable accommodation and full-time employment in Uist.[1]

When she began to attend the church regularly, she explained to everyone why she had decided to come to Uist, and she always attempted to speak in Gaelic to the Gaelic-English bilingual congregants. When she arrived, I had been attending the church for a few months already as part of my participant-observation fieldwork, and the minister and several congregants immediately directed her to me because "Emily is interested in Gaelic too" or "Emily is good at speaking Gaelic." She and I spoke almost exclusively in Gaelic with each other during the next several months, at church services, social events, and chance meetings. After the first few weeks, however, I began to realize that the Gaelic-English bilinguals at church were repeatedly directing her to me for Gaelic conversation—and speaking to both of us in English most of the time. In so doing, they were effectively denying both of us any extended

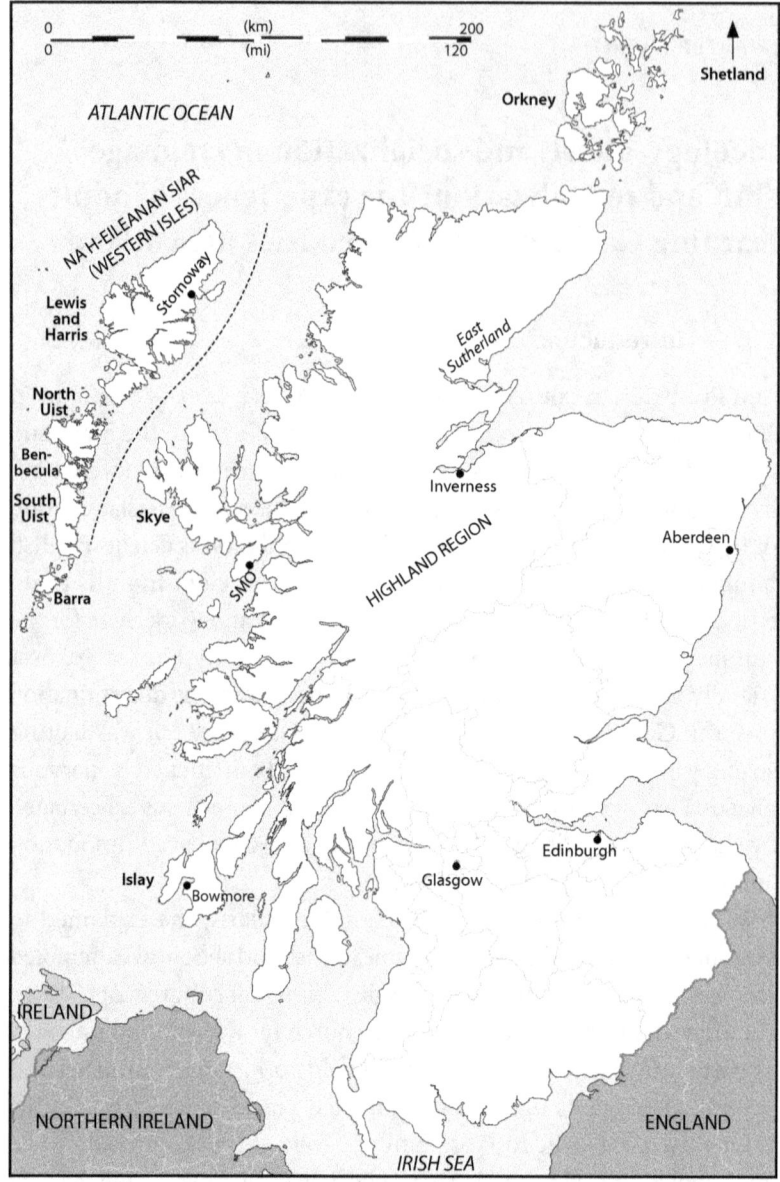

Figure 8.1 Map of Scotland showing Na h-Eileanan Siar (the Western Isles) with the boundary delineated by a dotted line, the Highland region (or Highland Council area), and other islands, towns, and cities mentioned in the book. SMO is Sabhal Mòr Ostaig, the Gaelic college on Skye; East Sutherland is an area in the Highland region. The boundaries of the local authority areas (regions) of Scotland are indicated with grey lines.

interaction with *themselves* in the medium of Gaelic, interaction that we both greatly desired for our own individual reasons.

This woman never complained to me about the situation, but other adult Gaelic learners in Scotland expressed puzzled disappointment or frustration to one another about the reluctance of Gaelic "native speakers" to engage with them through the medium of Gaelic. In Alasdair MacCaluim's 1998–1999 survey of adults learning Scottish Gaelic, 44 out of 643 respondents (6.8%) filled in an open-ended comment section on the survey with comments "critical of native speakers and their treatment of learners" (MacCaluim 2007, 213). Representative comments included "In my experience native Gaelic speakers seem very unwilling (or too impatient) to converse in Gaelic with learners, and help them to improve" and "I cannot understand why native Gaelic speakers I have met are not supportive in maintaining their language and helping learners" (MacCaluim 2007, 266). In 1998 an article titled "Despairing of native speakers," which accused many native Gaelic speakers of a "resentment of learners," appeared in *Cothrom*, the bilingual quarterly magazine of the Gaelic learners' association in Scotland (formerly Comann an Luchd-Ionnsachaidh, now known as Clì Gàidhlig). Similarly, Newcombe noted in her study of adult Welsh learners in Wales, "One of the main problems for learners seeking to practise outside the classroom is persuading native speakers to maintain a conversation in Welsh" (Newcombe 2007, 40).

Ideological mismatches and conflicts between revitalization proponents and ordinary "native speakers" are typical of minority-language revitalization efforts aimed at halting processes of language shift (Dauenhauer and Dauenhauer 1998, Eckert 1983, Kabel 2000, McDonald 1989, Trosset 1986). The first main argument of this article is that, while language ideologies are crucial components of processes of language shift and revitalization (Cavanaugh 2004, Echeverria 2003, Jaffe 1999, McEwan-Fujita 2003, Mertz 1982, Messing 2007), affect is also a crucial component, and ideologies and affect are inseparably intertwined in the linguistic behaviour of participants. The second main argument is that examining language shift and revitalization efforts from a perspective of language socialization (Ochs 1996) allows us to explain how ideology and affect come to be conjoined in participants' linguistic behaviour and interpretation of social conflict.[2]

This is so because a language socialization perspective draws attention to social interaction processes of "novices" being gradually socialized by "experts" through ongoing, recurrent linguistic practices to develop "an understanding of social actions, events, emotions, esthetics, knowledgeability, statuses, relationships, and other sociocultural phenomena" in particular sociocultural contexts (Ochs 1996, 408). Such an approach is productive for the analysis of both language shift, perpetuated by linguistic socialization of children and adults, and language revitalization efforts, in which attempts to linguistically re-socialize both children and adults figure prominently. It is also productive because both language shift and revitalization are locally anchored in face-to-face interaction in which people enact and inculcate broader cultural meanings, ideologies, and structures of affect.

Language shift involves particular kinds of changes over time in the patterns of daily, habitual use of a spoken language[3] in geographically defined communities. Gal (1979, 1) describes language shift as a process in which "the habitual use of one language is being replaced by the habitual use of another" in "bilingual towns, villages, or neighborhoods." Moore (1999, 65) defines it as the process in which "the members of a local speech-community begin pervasively to abandon the use of one linguistic variety in favour of another, regardless of whether or not the language being abandoned continues to be spoken elsewhere." Moore's wording is ambiguous: individuals may abandon the use of a linguistic variety altogether during the course of their own life cycle, but more commonly people seem to maintain the use of a variety with a particular network of interlocutors, while instead linguistically socializing younger individuals primarily or solely in the replacement language (consciously or unconsciously). Thus, changes in daily language use patterns favouring one language over another generally take place from one generation to the next, rather than in the life cycle of single individuals. Fishman (1991, 1) foregrounds this failure of intergenerational transmission in his description of the community context of language shift: "speech communities whose native languages are threatened because their intergenerational continuity is proceeding negatively, with fewer and fewer users (speakers, readers, writers and even understanders) or uses every generation." Although language shift can be very usefully analyzed in regional and national perspective (e.g., Dorian 1981, Withers 1984), language shift essentially involves face-to-face social interaction throughout the individual life cycle and across generations in the family, the home, and the local geographically-bounded community where people encounter their neighbours and experience the local manifestations of the state and the nation through educational, religious, media, and other institutions.

During sociolinguistic processes of language shift, people indexically formulate ideologies of language, or "metapragmatic filters" (Mertz 1982) through which they interpret the macro-level changes they observe around them and according to which they shape their own linguistic and other behaviours (Gal 1978, 1979; Kulick 1992). Ideologies of language may be described as "cultural conceptions of language—its nature, structure, and use—and ... conceptions of communicative behaviour as an enactment of a collective order" (Woolard 1992, citing Silverstein 1987, 1–2; also see Gal 1989, Schieffelin, Woolard and Kroskrity 1998, Silverstein 1979). The formation of language ideologies is "a process involving struggle among multiple conceptualizations" (Woolard and Schieffelin 1994, 58), or rather, struggle among multiple individuals and groups who base their positions on these conceptualizations. People enact ideologies of language shift and revitalization in discourse and other forms of social action (Cavanaugh 2009, Jaffe 1999, McEwan-Fujita 2003, Messing 2007).

Language ideologies are a crucial component of the process of language shift, but I argue that affect is an equally crucial component. I have opted to use the term "affect" instead of "emotion," following the usage of Ochs and Schieffelin (1989, 7), who "take affect to be a broader term than emotion, to include feelings, moods, dispositions, and attitudes associated with persons and/or situations" (cf. Besnier 1990, 420). Scholarship on the anthropology of emotion (Lutz and White 1986) and the linguistic anthropology of language and emotion (Lutz and Abu-Lughod 1990, Wilce 2009) has shown how culturally specific categories of affect are discursively constructed and displayed in linguistically mediated social interaction (Besnier 1990; Cavanaugh 2009, 13; Lutz and Abu-Lughod 1990, 11; Ochs and Schieffelin 1989, 7). While affect is constructed discursively, this process is not a one-way street: established cultural categories of emotion and other kinds of affect also dialectically shape people's metalinguistic discourse and their language behaviour more generally, particularly in situations of language shift. Wilce (2009) advocates including affect, and its embodied dimension, in a broader definition of ideology. However, I believe that it is still useful to keep the terms analytically distinct, because each term can do different work. The concept of ideology as ideational notions or models brings in a consideration of social and power relations more usefully than does the internally focused concept of "attitudes" (Wilce 2009, 115–116), yet I would argue that keeping the concept of affect separate still allows us to consider the intersection between embodiment and social action in language use more effectively than does the ideationally focused ideology.

Affect pervades discourse (Besnier 1990, 421): "Whenever speakers (or writers) say anything, they encode their point of view towards it … The expression of such speakers' attitudes is pervasive in all uses of language" (Stubbs 1986, 1, quoted in Englebretson 2007, 17). Speakers can express affective stance through a multitude of linguistic forms and structures (Besnier 1990, 421; Ochs 1996, 411), and one may observe and analyze speakers' affect by identifying ways in which they index their affective stance in language. Ochs (1996, 410) defines affective stance as "a mood, attitude, feeling, and disposition, as well as degrees of emotional intensity vis-à-vis some focus of concern."

Language ideologies and affect jointly contribute to processes of language shift and revitalization in familial and local community contexts through indexical, dialectical processes of language socialization. As Besnier (1990, 420) notes, principally citing the works of Ochs and Schieffelin, "In many cultures, affect plays a central role in language socialization, and vice versa." Ideologies are never expressed or enacted without the speaker's affective stance toward them being encoded in the discourse. Thus, when experts communicate ideologies to novices, they also communicate their affective stances toward these ideologies through processes of indexicality. As Ochs explains:

> A basic tenet of language socialization research is that *socialization is in part a process of assigning situational, i.e., indexical, meanings* … to particular [linguistic] forms … To index is

to point to the presence of some entity in the immediate situation-at-hand. (Ochs 1996, 410–11, original emphasis)

These indexical, or situational, meanings of linguistic forms are based on contiguity in time, space, or other connection, and may include "temporal, spatial, social identity, social act, social activity, affective or epistemic meanings" (Ochs 1996, 410). Indexes like code choice may be nonreferential (Silverstein 1976), so that a codeswitch (from Gaelic to English, for example) invokes or indexes a particular dimension of a social situation with which it has become "conventionally associated" (Ochs 1996, 411; see also Blom and Gumperz 1972), without contributing to the referential meaning of a communicated proposition (Ochs 1990). The assignment of indexical meanings to minority and majority linguistic varieties and code choices, often in opposing pairs, is a crucial dimension of language shift (Cavanaugh 2009, Kulick 1992, Kuter 1989).

The language socialization processes that contribute to language shift are dialectical and potentially reciprocal, and they occur continuously in the individual life cycle. They occur not only in the socialization of novice children by expert adults, but also in the socialization of novice adults by expert adults. Moreover, as Ochs points out, even if it is asymmetrical, socialization is always potentially bidirectional; novices may in fact socialize experts, and each may "impact each others' discourse knowledge" (Ochs 1990, 302–3). In fact, the power struggle over who gets to play the role of "expert" (and thus of socializer) is one of the anthropologically interesting aspects of language shift and revitalization that can be studied ethnographically (e.g., Hill 1985).

Language shift is a geographically and temporally uneven process that results in the uneven distribution of linguistic skills, ideologies, and affective orientations across populations. Changes in habitual linguistic behaviour do not happen uniformly within any definable social context of shift, whether it is the family, the geographically defined locality or region, state institutions, or the nation-state as a unit (Dorian 1981, MacKinnon 1977). Nor do changes happen uniformly over time in a geographical area; there may be an apparently stable bilingualism for decades or centuries in a region, followed by a

Table 8.1 Gaelic language abilities claimed by respondents in the 2001 Scottish census (source: Table UV12, General Register Office for Scotland, 2005).

Gaelic language abilities claimed by respondents	Number of respondents
Can speak, read, and write Gaelic	31,235
Can speak and read Gaelic but not write	7,949
Can speak but neither read nor write	19,466
Total respondents claiming to be able to speak Gaelic	**58,650**
Can understand Gaelic but not speak, read, or write	27,219
Can read and write Gaelic but not speak	1,435
Can read Gaelic but not speak or write	4,758
Can write Gaelic but not speak or read	901
Other combinations of skills in Gaelic	319
Total respondents claiming non-speaking Gaelic ability	**34,632**
Total respondents claiming some Gaelic language ability	**93,282**

"tip" to the majority language marked by a relatively sudden change in intergenerational transmission practices among the majority of a community (Coleman 1975, Dorian 1981, Mertz 1989).

Therefore, in a situation of language shift, in any given community—or even family—individuals will be found with differing linguistic socialization experiences, which contribute to varying distributions of linguistic skills and varying ideological positions and affective stances on linguistic varieties and language use. (The 2001 Scottish census results illustrate the varying distributions of Gaelic linguistic skills in the case of shift from Gaelic to English; see Table 8.1.) Furthermore, any one of these elements may also shift over time for any given individual, owing in part to further socialization experiences. In a local geographically bounded community undergoing language shift, therefore, people who have been socialized into multiple and conflicting ideologies, and expectations of and affective orientations toward linguistic behaviour, will be in frequent contact with one another.

When people observe language behaviour in others and themselves that does not conform to their ideologized expectations, they take an affective stance as they express their reactions and evaluations. Lutz and White (1986, 406) propose "looking at emotions as one cultural idiom for dealing with the persistent problems of social relationship."

They outline a taxonomy of these persistent and universal problems which includes two problems particularly relevant in processes of language shift:

> 1. the other's violation of cultural codes or of ego's personal expectations (or conflict more generally)... [and] 2. ego's own violation of those codes, including social incompetence or personal inadequacy, and awareness of the possibility for such a failure (Lutz and White 1986, 427).

From this perspective, we can see how language shift and language revitalization efforts generate and express "persistent problems of social relationship" resulting from the mismatch between "cultural codes" or "personal expectations" of behaviour of individuals socialized into different ideologies and affective stances about Gaelic language use.

Expressions of negative affect[4] seem to be common in situations of shift from a minority language to a state-sponsored European language, whether they take the form of grief over the loss (Dauenhauer and Dauenhauer 1995), regret and anger about not having the language passed on to oneself by one's parents (MacCaluim 2007, 267–68; Newton 2005), shame at being a speaker of a minority language, or denigration and contempt from majority language speakers (Bonner 2001; Dauenhauer and Dauenhauer 1998, 64–66; Kuter 1989; Tsitsipis 1981, 1998). However, the language revitalization efforts that are aimed at halting language shift, particularly language-learning efforts, can also generate negative affect among participants. Trosset (1986, 185) applies literature on the anomie and shame of second-language learning in general to the experiences of adult learners of Welsh, discussing the embarrassment of becoming a childlike linguistic novice again as an adult, and the painful process of breaking down the old social identity and forging a new one. Newcombe (2007, 66–70) likewise identifies anxiety as a major barrier to L2 Welsh language learning, using interviews and journals from participants in the Adult Welsh Learners' Project to document the phenomenon.

An important potential source of negative affect in minority language learning seems to be the awareness that adult learners develop of their own and others' inability to measure up to their ideologized expectations. In the case of Jaffe's Corsican university students in the first-year

Corsican language class at the Corsican Studies Institute, their "painful, strangled silence" on the first day of class was the result of their awareness of their own limited Corsican language competence in a context where the essentializing significance of Corsican competence for the Corsican ethnolinguistic nationalist agenda was foregrounded (Jaffe 1999, 200–2). In the case of Gaelic in Scotland, adult learners' ideologized expectations of themselves and others seemed to concern the relative ease with which they expected to learn Gaelic, speak Gaelic to others, and have others speak Gaelic to them, based on their previous language-learning experiences, their residence in a Gaelic-speaking area, and/or their family background with Gaelic. In interviews with me, Gaelic learners described and enacted "Standard Average European" categories of emotion such as blame, shame, fear, uncertainty, bewilderment, envy, and lack of confidence in connection with their efforts to learn and speak Gaelic, whether as an avowed second language or as an avowedly reclaimed inheritance. Before discussing in greater detail the socialization and enactment of ideologies and affect in and by adult Gaelic learners, I shall describe the seven adults I interviewed for this study, and set them in the context of adult Gaelic learning in Scotland more generally.

2   Adult Gaelic "Learners": Context and Description

All adults learning Gaelic in Scotland are now doing so in the context of language shift. Gaelic speakers began to settle in Scotland in perhaps the late 5th century CE, and most of what is now known as Scotland was Gaelic-speaking at one time or another. Since the 13th century CE, Gaelic-speaking areas in Scotland have been shrinking (Thomson 1994, 89–90). By the 19th or early 20th century at least, an influx of English speakers and ideologies of language shift had weakened the Gaelic-speaking social norms of these areas. One native of the Isle of Lewis commented: "What used to happen in our communities, when someone came into our community without Gaelic, they had to learn it to survive. I would say the real decline set in in the late '70s" (F1, #28). By the early 1980s, all Gaelic-speaking communities in Scotland no longer linguistically integrated the new adult members who joined through in-marriage and other forms of in-migration (MacArthur et al. 1982, 14, 16).

Galloway (1995) estimated the total number of adults actively learning Gaelic in Scotland to be approximately 8,000. On the basis of a 1998–99 survey of Gaelic learners, MacCaluim narrowed Galloway's estimate to "fewer than 1,000 fluent Gaelic learners and probably quite a lot fewer" (MacCaluim 2002, 347).

Unlike the Irish state education system, the Scottish education system does not contribute substantially to an increase in the number of people who can claim Gaelic language ability. This is so because Gaelic language education is not compulsory in Scotland at the national level, and in fact it is not available at all in many areas.[5] Nor is Gaelic language ability required for most kinds of state employment, excepting Gaelic-language or Gaelic-medium teaching in the Scottish education system and a handful of other clearly Gaelic-related positions.

The seven adult Gaelic learners interviewed in 2000 for this study lived in Uist (also known as "the Uists," although some dislike this term). It is a group of islands in the southern half of the Western Isles that includes North Uist, Benbecula, South Uist, and several smaller adjoining islands (see Figure 8.1). The Western Isles are the only remaining area of Scotland, and the world, where over 60% of the population is able to speak and/or understand Gaelic.[6] In the 2001 census, 66% of the total population of Uist over the age of three was counted as Gaelic speakers, or 3,206 out of 4,857 people (see Table 8.2).[7] The significance of my interviewees' residence in the Western Isles is that they live in an area where they are more likely to interact on a daily basis with people who were socialized in childhood as Gaelic-English bilinguals. In the ideological framework of learning a state-sponsored majority language like French or Japanese, people normally assume that living in an area where the language is spoken in a community context will increase opportunities for hearing and speaking the language outside the highly controlled classroom context, and thus potentially lead to faster and better language acquisition. However, this is not necessarily the case in minority language situations (Kabel 2000, 135; Newcombe 2007, 41; Trosset 1986).

Because of the small number of subjects, and their non-random recruitment as a convenience sample, I did not perform any formal statistical analyses to correlate responses with sociological factors such as age and occupation; instead, I offer a brief narrative description of the interviewees. However, my interviewees are demographically similar to the respondents in the 1998–1999 survey of 643 adults learning Scottish Gaelic mentioned above, which included 392 respondents living in Scotland (MacCaluim 2007). MacCaluim's description of adult Gaelic learners in Scotland is the most complete in existence, and it helps to demonstrate by comparison that my interviewees were most likely representative of the small group of adults learning Gaelic while living in Uist.

My interviewees were mostly female (five women, two men), which is roughly congruent with the gender distribution of MacCaluim's survey respondents resident in Scotland who were taking evening language courses. A majority of them were women, although for a variety of reasons this does not, as he indicates, prove that more of the adult learners in Scotland are actually women (MacCaluim 2007, 114). The age distribution of my interviewees, who were all in their forties and fifties, was likewise congruent with that of MacCaluim's survey respondents resident in Scotland, 61.6% of whom were aged 40 and over, with the single largest group (23.8%) aged 40–49 (MacCaluim 2007, 115).

In their place of birth and stated nationality, which was congruent in all seven cases, four of my interviewees were Scottish, two were English, and one was US American. This is also reminiscent of the proportions among MacCaluim's survey respondents living in Scotland: 77.3% were raised in Scotland, 14.8% in the rest of the UK, 2.55% in the rest of Europe, 1.3% raised in the United States, 1% in the Commonwealth,

Table 8.2 2001 Scottish census results: Number of Gaelic speakers living in the Uists and Benbecula. Extrapolated from 2001 Census, Table UV12, Knowledge of Gaelic. (Source: Scotland's Census Results Online, General Register Office for Scotland, 2005, http://www.scrol.gov.uk/)

	Total pop w/ Gaelic-spkg ability	Total population	Percentage of Gaelic speakers
North Uist, Berneray & Grimsay	1115	1657	67.3%
Benbecula	701	1249	56.1%
South Uist & Eriskay	1390	1951	71.2%
Total for the Uists	3206	4857	66%

and 0.8% in more than one country (2007, 118). All of my interviewees had moved to Uist as adults sometime between their mid-twenties and late fifties, and had lived there for between 2 and 20 years each. Though they had all made Uist their only home, none of them were considered "locals" in the locally defined sense of having been raised in Uist with at least one parent born in Uist (Burnett 1997). However, while four interviewees had no family connections with Uist, one had a spouse with Hebridean family connections, and two had a Gaelic-speaking parent originally from Uist but had been raised on the mainland of Scotland or elsewhere.

The interviewees had a range of employment statuses: four worked full-time outside the home, one was retired, one was on permanent disability, and one was financially independent and engaged in significant community volunteering. They were all university-educated, and in this regard they were also like the majority of MacCaluim's respondents residing in Scotland, 52.1% of whom had a higher education qualification (MacCaluim 2007, 122–28).

In regard to language ability, two were beginners, one intermediate, and four advanced, by my definition. The beginners had taken only two Gaelic courses over a period of one to two years at the time of the interview. The intermediate-level interviewee had taken several courses over a period of several years and could understand and hold some basic conversations. The advanced interviewees had attained quite high levels of oral, aural, reading, and writing proficiency: they could carry on conversations in Gaelic of varying length, understand conversations and to some extent Gaelic radio broadcasts, read texts written in Gaelic such as newspaper articles, and write letters and homework assignments, some with the use of a dictionary. Prior to interviewing them, I took a course with two of the advanced students, and I sat in on one class session of a course that one of the beginner students took.

When asked, the interviewees described a variety of motives for commencing and continuing the study of Gaelic, including being "keen on languages" in general, wishing to speak the language their parents had spoken, and wishing to learn more about the local culture, which they recognized as distinctively Gaelic.[8] One beginner without family ties to the islands, whom I call "Linda," said "We just thought, well here we are, in the Western Isles, and the way to fit in is to have a go" (X5, #544). "Isabel," who did have family ties, said "[My husband]'s from a Gaelic-speaking family, his parents were still alive, and his mother, she was quite keen that I learned, quite pro-Gaelic, she loved Gaelic with a passion, she was really good about speaking to me in Gaelic, so that was my motivation." In general they seemed to regard their study of Gaelic as based on a combination of personal interest and goodwill; none were studying it for directly instrumental reasons of advancement in employment or in an academic or training course.[9]

One important factor to consider in the overall struggles of both my interviewees and MacCaluim's survey group to attain fluency in Gaelic is the difficulty of finding regular, coordinated language instruction. MacCaluim describes the Gaelic learning infrastructure in Scotland in great detail (2007, 20–75) and concludes that provisions for adults to learn Gaelic are "fragmented, [with] many serious gaps in provision and lack[ing] any overall strategic coordination" (2007, 228). In Uist I found that Gaelic language courses for adults were available from time to time, at various levels, in various formats, and in various venues, and the teachers who offered them were talented and dedicated, but there was no coordination between the offerings and no organized way to progress through a Gaelic language-learning curriculum. This is quite different from the situation described for some other Western European minority language situations, such as Basque in the Basque Autonomous Community (Azkue and Perales 2005). This lack of coordination has been a major factor holding back adults from learning Gaelic to fluency in any great number, as has the sheer difficulty of learning a language as an adult, though the ideological and affective socialization discussed in the following section also significantly shaped their learning experiences.

3   Ideologies and Affect of Language Shift and Minority Language Learning

Now I shall examine the ideological and affective mismatches that arise out of encounters between people with different language socialization experiences in the context of language shift in Uist, connected to my interviewees' efforts to learn Gaelic as a second language. The adult learners interviewed for this study come from a variety of backgrounds; as already mentioned, two of the seven were children of "native speakers" who had not transmitted Gaelic to them in the home, while the other five were Scottish, English, or US American and had no family connections with Gaelic (although one had previously lived and worked in Wales and observed the situation of Welsh). An important additional factor to consider is that the interviewees' expressions of affect were discursively co-constructed with the interviewer, who was known to each interviewee not only as a researcher but also as an adult Gaelic learner with no family connections to Gaelic.

3.1 Socialization of ideology and affect in the family context of language shift

"Alison," one of my advanced-level interviewees who had no family background with Gaelic, reflected on the advantage that she perceived in having a Gaelic-speaking family member: "I have this thing, I see everyone who's become quite fluent in Gaelic, that they're quite a good linguist, or they've got a Gaelic granny in the background that they haven't told you about" (G11, #438). However, the experiences related to me by the two interviewees who had at least one Gaelic-speaking parent did not bear out the imagined advantage of a "Gaelic granny." Both of them had been socialized by Gaelic-speaking parents not to speak Gaelic in the home, and they described and implied mismatched ideologies, expectations, and affective orientations toward Gaelic speaking in the family context that seem to have arisen out of their socialization experiences.

Both interviewees described several kinds of apparent "social relationship problems" (Lutz and White 1986, 406) regarding intergenerational non-transmission of Gaelic in their families. The problems included conflict between themselves and their parents about the non-transmission of Gaelic; conflict between themselves and other kin, particularly siblings and cousins, over the value of Gaelic; and problems both in acquiring Gaelic and in transmitting it to their own children. The problems seem to centre on the previously mentioned themes of "the other's violation of cultural codes or of ego's personal expectations" and "ego's own violation of those codes, including social incompetence or personal inadequacy" (Lutz and White 1986, 427).

We can best understand each of these types of problems if we ask in each case: (i) What is the ideological basis of the cultural code(s) or expectation being violated? And (ii) what kind of affective stance is the interviewee taking in interaction with the interviewer that frames this as a problem? For these learners, the ideological basis might best be described as a bundle of closely related nationalist ideologies of language applied in a language-learning context, including (i) the idea of "native speakers" as naturally produced entities rather than socialized beings, (ii) the accompanying naturalization of intergenerational mother tongue transmission, (iii) the idea of the family as the internally homogeneous unit of language socialization, (iv) the notion that Gaelic-speaking parents could transmit some essential Gaelic ethnic identity to them that would enable them to learn the language more easily (what Dauenhauer and Dauenhauer 1998, 84 term the "genetic fallacy"), and (v) the idea of bilingualism as parallel monolingualisms (Heller 2006). For the parents themselves, on the other side of the ideological mismatch, these covertly essentialist and nationalist ideologies of language learning were most likely countered by ideologies of ensuring the future success of their children by socializing them to speak English (Mertz 1982). Answering the second question posed above, these interviewees took a stance of negative affect as they sketched the dimensions of their own family language socialization experience for the interviewer. The interviewees did not explicitly frame the intergenerational non-transmission of Gaelic by one or both of their parents as a problem, but as Besnier (1990, 428) points out, "affect is most commonly expressed covertly in natural discourse." Affective stance, like other aspects of stance, is also relational and dependent on context (Englebretson 2007, 15). The very fact that these individuals actively undertook to learn Gaelic as adults, after being raised in a family with a Gaelic-speaking parent who linguistically socialized them to speak English instead, implicitly frames their effort as redressing a perceived conflict or failure, and frames the cessation of intergenerational language transmission in their family as a problem.

The first interviewee, "Jean," raised the issue of her family background with me during an interview conducted after we had taken a six-week Gaelic course together (Alison, just mentioned, was also on the course). I did not record the interview; I took largely verbatim typed notes on a computer as I conducted it, and constructed a transcript from these notes immediately afterward. The interview was semi-structured; I was working from a schedule, but tailored it to fit each interviewee's individual situation. A transcript of the relevant portion of our interview follows:[10]

(1)

1	EM:	So are there any people around that you speak to regularly in Gaelic?
2	Jean:	None at all.
3	EM:	Any.
4	Jean:	I could, but I don't.
5	EM:	Not even a bit?
6	Jean:	People speak in Gaelic, and I'll answer in English, or whatever. But I
7		listen. [to people speaking Gaelic] ((pause)) But there's plenty people
8		I could speak to. My parents speak Gaelic.
9	EM:	Where do they live?
10	Jean:	[Mainland city]. My mother's from [island]. My father's from [west
11		coast Highland village].
12	EM:	Oh, on the mainland, so he speaks Gaelic too? That's unusual these
13		days, isn't it, a Gaelic speaker from the mainland?
14	Jean:	{Yes, well, I think he didn't speak Gaelic as much until he met my mother.}
15	EM:	Do you have brothers and sisters?
16	Jean:	I have five brothers and sisters, and none of them are interested in
17		Gaelic. […]
18	EM:	Did your parents speak Gaelic in front of you so that they could talk
19		without you understanding?
20	Jean:	Yes.
21	EM:	What made you decide to start learning it yourself?
22	Jean:	I came here on holiday. It was probably just the same, about seven years
23		ago. I started learning it. ((pause)) But I didn't realize it would take so long.
24	EM:	Do you speak it with your parents?
25	Jean:	Only if I'm asking about my homework and things. Not really. I don't
26		find they're particularly good at ((small laugh)) understanding me.

(N10, #440)

Jean subtly indexed a stance of negative affect through a style of self-disclosure that was constructed through several paralinguistic and discourse-level features. First, she used pauses and a laugh to precede and affectively frame moments of self-disclosure in lines 6–8, 22–23, and 25–26. The first self-disclosure in lines 6–8 revealed to me the existence of her Gaelic-speaking parents, who, she nonetheless implied, she did not speak to in Gaelic. The second self-disclosure in lines 22–23 was an explicit statement of how her Gaelic learning experience had violated her expectations about the amount of effort and time required to learn Gaelic, and the third self-disclosure in lines 25–26 was the reason for her inability to communicate in Gaelic with her Gaelic-speaking parents. The pauses added drama to her disclosure to me, and may have also indexed a reluctance to disclose the information, while the laugh indexed a sense of humourous irony and self-deprecation. The topics of these self-disclosures can be defined as problems of social relationship as defined earlier: (i) violated expectations of others, in this case her parents who did not transmit Gaelic to her as a child and who have difficulty speaking with her in Gaelic now, and (ii) violated expectations of self in the matter of acquiring Gaelic more easily as an adult child of Gaelic-speaking parents.

Jean's interview responses were also distinguished by discourse-level features that constructed a negative affective stance. At certain moments, Jean self-disclosed with terse replies and the gradual, guarded revelation of information. Her responses to my questions were noticeably terse compared with those of the other seven interviewees, sometimes revealing the bare minimum, as seen in lines 1–4 and 18–20. Another example came later in the interview, which is not included in the transcript above:

(2)
EM: Are there any people who greet you regularly in Gaelic, and then switch into English?
Jean: Yeah.... ((she trailed off and didn't volunteer any more))

Jean's tersest replies were on the topic of people *not* speaking Gaelic (despite their apparent ability): Jean not speaking Gaelic to others (although she could), her parents not speaking Gaelic to her (although they could), and other people in the community not speaking Gaelic to her (although they could). Her abbreviated replies, while possibly indicating a more reticent personality, could also be interpreted as affective stance markers constructing negative affect toward the dissonance between ideologized expectations (people who can speak Gaelic will naturally speak it in any given situation) and actual social events (people who can speak Gaelic don't in certain situations). They also mirror and poetically intensify the topic itself: *not* speaking.

During the six-week course we had attended together, Jean had never mentioned her Gaelic-speaking parents to either me or Alison. During our interview, I used our social relationship based on our shared learning experience, and my prior observation of Jean's considerable Gaelic language ability, as a license to gently press her on the point of whether she actually spoke Gaelic to anyone in the Gaelic-speaking community. I explore this point further in the following section, but here I focus on how she spontaneously disclosed information about her parents as Gaelic speakers (lines 5–8), her siblings as uninterested in Gaelic (lines 15–16), and her boyfriend as a Gaelic speaker with whom she did not speak Gaelic. In each case, she disclosed the information in a statement that augmented her direct response to a different question. In a section not included in the transcript above, she even introduced the topic as a non sequitur following a longer sequence of questions and answers about Gaelic speaking in the workplace:

(3)
EM: [Does the organization where you work] have a Gaelic policy?
Jean: No. ((pause)) My boyfriend is from [the island], {he speaks Gaelic}, he would speak if I wanted to. I'm just not good at conversation, my mind goes blank when people speak to me.

When compared to Jean's terse replies to other questions, these self-disclosures are even more noteworthy. Like her pauses, her volunteering of new information in this way created an affective impact on the researcher—it surprised me. And it constructed an affective stance toward the mismatch between her expectations and those of her five siblings: her effort to learn Gaelic as an adult enacted the positive value of Gaelic, while she described in implicit contrast (and conflict) how her five siblings were not interested in Gaelic.

Finally, Jean's self-disclosures are part of an even more complex discursive strategy, a "dance of disclosure" in which she alternated between denying and disclosing her own and others' Gaelic-speaking ability and use to me. Her responses to my line of questioning about whether there was anyone with whom she regularly spoke in Gaelic form a striking sequence of denial and disclosure, which becomes clear when the relevant elements of the transcript are arranged in table form, with the denials shaded (see Table 8.3). Her terse replies to my questions in this dance of disclosure enact the shame and other negative affect of intergenerational language transmission failure for one individual in her own social and familial context of language shift: her sense of social incompetence and personal inadequacy over speaking Gaelic in everyday life, her failure to learn Gaelic quickly, and her failure to interact with her parents in Gaelic, which are framed as failures through negative affect and ideology. Framing her self-disclosures with pauses and a self-deprecating laugh, phrasing them with economy, and doling out information to me in a dance of denial and disclosure, Jean incrementally constructed an account of language shift in her family, her own learning efforts, and her negative affective stance toward these topics.

Table 8.3 Jean's denial and disclosure of Gaelic speaking, Gaelic speaking ability, and availability of Gaelic speakers with whom to speak.

Utterance	Denial or Disclosure
None at all	denial of Gaelic speaking
I could	disclosure of Gaelic speaking ability
but I don't	denial of Gaelic speaking
People speak in Gaelic	disclosure of available Gaelic speakers
and I'll answer in English, or whatever	denial of Gaelic speaking
But I listen {to people speaking Gaelic}	disclosure of Gaelic receptive ability
But there's plenty people I could speak to	disclosure of available Gaelic speakers
My parents speak Gaelic	disclosure of available Gaelic speakers *in family*
I have five brothers and sisters, and none of them are interested in Gaelic	denial of available Gaelic speakers *in family*
I started learning it	disclosure of Gaelic speaking ability
((pause)) But I didn't realize it would take so long	denial of Gaelic ability (qualified)
Only if I'm asking about my homework and things	disclosure of Gaelic speaking *to family* (qualified)
Not really. I don't find they're particularly good at ((small laugh)) understanding me	denial of Gaelic speaking *to family* denial of available Gaelic speakers *in family*

"Graham," the other interviewee with a Gaelic-speaking parent, was the most fluent Gaelic speaker I interviewed. Similarly to Jean, he discussed interaction with his mother in Gaelic, and his mother's Gaelic language ability in the context of family interaction, in poignant terms. I also quote the relevant section of his interview at length here before proceeding with the analysis:

(4)
```
1   EM:       Is there anyone that you speak to exclusively in Gaelic?
2   Graham:   No I don't think so. [...] ...we'll switch between Gaelic and English
3             quite a lot... [...] My mother from time to time, on the phone, not
4             so much face to face.
5   EM:       Why not face to face?
6   Graham:   Face to face you're usually in the company of other people as well.
7             Usually {there's} the company of other family members to consider.
8   EM:       So [your mother] didn't speak Gaelic to you at all as a child?
9   Graham:   No, one or two words. A ghaoil, a lot of kids who've had Gaelic
10            speaking parents {would recognize that one}.
11  EM:       Did you hear much Gaelic growing up then?
12  Graham:   Uhm, not a lot, but that was at a time, and a place in fact, I was
13            born in [large Scottish city], but the family was basically based
14            [overseas in a former British colony] at the time, my father is
15            English, and you're talking [19]50s here, so there were different
16            attitudes around towards little languages like that.
17  EM:       Did you know that your mother spoke Gaelic?
18  Graham:   Oh yeah, we were conscious that mum spoke another language,
19            because we would hear her speak it on the phone to her sisters,
20            we would come here [to the island] for summer holidays, {And
21            my father would occasionally ask my mother} "And how do you
22            say that thing in Gaelic, ((laughing)) how do you get those sounds
23            out" ((guffawing, honking and harumphing in an English accent
24            imitating his father)), she was on a losing streak, she did her best.
25            My cousins spoke Gaelic, cousins of my own age, I remember co
26            versations with them. Because our first family experience was in
27            {another linguistic environment, I was conscious of some people
28            being able to speak more than one language.} I was very envious
29            of my cousins. I remember saying I wished I could speak another
30            language. And they would come back with "Wish I only spoke one."
31  EM:       Do you speak Gaelic to [your children]?
32  Graham:   No, not much. Very little. No, it's partly a confidence thing as well.
33            I mean, I wouldn't, I suppose, the time to have done it would
34            have been from the start, seven years ago now, and that was in
```

35		[Scottish city], it wasn't here, and my Gaelic, I wasn't confident
36		enough in my Gaelic to know if I would be able to handle that, I
37		still don't know the Gaelic for fingers and thumbs, and bibs and
38		things. ((pause)) Once [my younger child] starts at the Gaelic
39		medium unit it may easier or more natural.
40	EM:	((Picking up the thread of an earlier discussion we had about a
41		conference paper I had given, I told him that given my observ
42		tions so far, I didn't think it necessarily would be.))
43	Graham:	It'll be a performance thing for our family. […] It'll always be a
44		conscious thing. (S1, 38 #483)

In his interview, Graham signaled his affective stance toward his family language socialization experience with Gaelic in ways that were quite different from Jean's, but were still subtle, implicit, and at the discourse level. He used general description, voicing, and direct reported speech to index both social and familial disapproval of Gaelic. In lines 6–7 and 12–16, he gave a sense of Gaelic speaking as something that had to be carefully managed in order to avoid disapproval from "other people," "other family members," and "different attitudes around," whether in the home or out in public, on a Hebridean island or in a large Scottish city. Like many children of Gaelic speakers throughout the 20th century, in childhood he heard Gaelic being spoken *around* him, but almost never to him. He seems to have been socialized into the "etiquette of accommodation," analyzed in detail in the following section, in which Gaelic should not be spoken in the presence of, or even within hearing distance of, non-Gaelic speakers. He voiced the disapproval of these un-named others—and of his English father—with the description of "different attitudes around toward little languages like that" in 1950s urban Scotland (lines 15–16). Unlike diminutives in many linguistic-cultural contexts, "little" in this case indexes a diminishment of status, and voices a negative affective stance.

Graham also used reported speech to great effect, constructing his own affective stance by reporting the stance-taking speech of others. First he implicitly contrasted his mother's and his father's own affective stances toward Gaelic. In lines 9–10, he mentioned the "one or two words" of Gaelic that his mother would speak to him as a child, quoting his mother's use of the common Gaelic term of endearment *A ghaoil* ('Love', in the vocative case). Later in the interview, in lines 21–24, he quoted his English father denigrating his mother's Gaelic. The fact that it was denigration was conveyed in Graham's extraordinary mocking imitation of his father, which I described impressionistically in my notes taken during the unrecorded interview (lines 23–24). It was a brief, loud, deep-voiced outburst consisting of rapid alternation between laughter, nasal English-accented mock speech, and clearing of the throat ("harrumphing") interspersed with voiced condescension, mockery, and distancing of Gaelic phonology (*How do you get those sounds out*) (see Ch. 3, this volume on similar mockery of Gaelic in the Scottish press). Graham implied that it was partly through his father's denigration that he became aware of his mother's ability to speak Gaelic. His affective stance is in support of his mother, describing her as repeatedly or inevitably losing a conflict with her husband, and *doing her best* to withstand the denigration of her native language and perhaps to preserve face in front of her children. He had aligned himself with his mother as a Gaelic speaker early in our interview, saying that he had learned Gaelic *because it's my mother's language*, and listing several other reasons before concluding *and {it} seemed to me I should be learning my own*.

Immediately after quoting his father, Graham constructed a poignant contrast between his own and his cousins' desires to speak Gaelic vis-à-vis English, again through indirect and direct reported speech, in lines 25–30. Graham heightened the affective contrast between his monolingual young self who wanted to be bilingual, and his bilingual cousins who wanted to be monolingual, through the juxtaposition of his *I wished I could speak another language* with their *Wish I could only speak one*. In describing interaction with his cousins, Graham was even more explicit in indexing his affective stance of desire to speak Gaelic than he was in describing interaction between his parents.

Both Jean and Graham described and implied mismatched ideologies, expectations, and affective orientations toward Gaelic speaking in their family context. Their accounts to me of their early language socialization experiences demonstrate past and present conflict with siblings, cousins, and parents over the value of Gaelic.

One more issue raised by both Jean's and Graham's interviews regarding the family context of language transmission was that they did not transmit it to their children as a first language. In Jean's case, she did not arrive in Uist until her child was in secondary school. Her child started studying Gaelic as a subject at the local secondary school but soon dropped it because it was "too hard for her to keep up. [...] Her careers advisor told her German would be more useful to her. But she's dropped that now too." Jean herself did not give any indication in the interview that she had ever considered it a possibility to transmit Gaelic to her child. Graham's children were younger when he moved to Uist, but he did not arrive there until after his elder child had already started English-medium primary school on the mainland. Graham again explicitly expressed his affective stance toward transmitting Gaelic to his children as he explained how a "lack of confidence" with the language factored into not attempting to speak Gaelic to his children in the home. Both interviewees mention a number of social factors that did not or could not support them in transmitting Gaelic to their children, including the timing of their own Gaelic study, the timing of their move to Uist, and the state-sponsored institution of the school. Both interviewees also expressed an affective stance through explicit statements of a lack of confidence in their language learning, that probably contributed to the non-transmission of Gaelic to their own children.

Adult learners who were linguistically socialized by a Gaelic-speaking parent or parents, but who acquired Gaelic only incompletely or not at all in the family context, have had very different language socialization experiences than people with no living family connection to Gaelic. However, their particular experiences, skills, and socialized affective orientations toward Gaelic speaking are not usually taken into account in provisions for Gaelic learners in Scotland. For example, I have never seen such experiences acknowledged in the scenarios, dialogues, and other examples in Gaelic language textbooks and teaching materials. Unlike some other minority language situations (e.g., Cavanaugh 2009), in Gaelic revitalization contexts the "adult learner" is usually assumed to be someone who has had no previous exposure to Gaelic in the home.

However, of MacCaluim's 392 survey respondents living in Scotland, 91 (or 23.2%) had at least one Gaelic-speaking parent, which he states is a much higher percentage than would be expected in the Scottish population as a whole (2007, 148–49), and which suggests that adult children of Gaelic speakers who did not transmit the language to them are a significant constituency for Gaelic language-learning efforts. MacCaluim's survey findings about respondents' motivations to learn Gaelic are also suggestive of the same point: respondents in Scotland gave a wide range of reasons for learning, but 16.1% rated as "very important" and 11.5% rated as "quite important" the motivation that "adult members of my family can/could speak Gaelic," with 4.5% of the respondents in Scotland designating this in a separate response as their single "main reason for learning" (2007, 158–9). Eliminating the "not applicable" respondents, MacCaluim further determined that 68.9% of respondents living in Scotland who claimed to have adult family members who can or could speak Gaelic rated this factor as either "very important" or "quite important" in their motivation for learning, and 53.6% of respondents who claimed to live in a Gaelic-speaking area rated this factor as either "very important" or "quite important" in their motivation for learning. In other words, MacCaluim found that "majorities of those living in Gaelic-speaking areas, [and] of those who have or had Gaelic-speaking members of their family … stated that these factors were important in their decision to learn the language" (2007, 159–60). These facts could be usefully taken into account in language planning to support adult learners in the cause of revitalizing Gaelic-speaking residential areas.

3.2 Socialization of affect and ideology in the local context of language shift

The second ideological-affective mismatch concerns the discursive enactment of sociolinguistic boundaries at the local community level. The interviewees' reports of their own and others' linguistic behaviours, and the negative or ambivalent affective stances they took in their reports, show how these adult Gaelic learners were being socialized by some people in their Uist communities not to speak Gaelic in the community.

The ideological mismatch in this case is between "insiders" and "outsiders" in the local community context, who have been socialized into different sets of rules about the appropriate contexts for speaking Gaelic. Uist residents categorize people who settle in Uist as adults as "incomers," a category opposed to "locals." In theory these terms describe, respectively, people who have settled in the area as adults (or whose parents have), and people who were born in the area of at least one parent who was also born in the area (Burnett 1997; Macdonald 1997, 131–40). Throughout the Highlands, people assign sets of opposing values to these two categories: "locals" are believed to belong to the area, to have roots and a history there, while "incomers" are believed not to belong to the area, to lack roots there, and to be "recent and fugitive" (Jedrej and Nuttall 1996, 94–95). In practice, the membership of each group is relative (Jedrej and Nuttall 1996, 173; Burnett 1997); for example, offspring of Uist people raised on the mainland of Scotland and who later settle in Uist do not exactly fit into either category; nor do people from other Hebridean islands who settle in Uist. However, the general equation of Gaelic with "local" and English with "incomer" is still prevalent among Gaelic speakers, and newcomers are socialized into it.

An accommodation norm involving judgements about the particular contexts in which it is appropriate to speak English or Gaelic plays a role in maintaining sociolinguistic boundaries between "incomers" and "locals" in Uist.[11] The central thesis of this norm can be formulated thus: it is rude to speak Gaelic to, or in the presence of, or within earshot of, a person who is not known to be a mother-tongue Gaelic speaker. Such accommodation norms have been documented in slightly differing forms in many European minority language situations, including the "ethic of politeness" observed by Trosset (1986, 68–82) among Welsh speakers, and the "etiquette of accommodation" observed by Woolard 1989 among middle-class Catalan speakers in Barcelona. The development of these practices is a result not only of the increased number of English monolinguals in Gaelic-speaking areas, but also of the historical shift in beliefs and behaviours of Gaelic-English bilinguals, as Susan Gal also noted for Hungarian-German bilinguals in an Austrian village:

> But the presence of monolinguals in local inns and homes did not, it itself, revise linguistic etiquette. What has changed since the 1920s is not so much the pressure exerted by German monolinguals as the responses and conceptions of the bilinguals. They

now acknowledge rather than resist the right of monolinguals to demand use of German in their presence (Gal 1979, 166).

As Gal indicates, "the responses and conceptions of the bilinguals," in other words their ideological-affective stances and behaviours, are the key factors in enacting this etiquette of accommodation.

This accommodation norm appears to have developed as a widespread social practice in Gaelic communities in Scotland by the second half of the 20th century. By the mid-1950s, a noted folklore collector in the Outer Hebrides stated that "Hebrideans nowadays always assume that the stranger is always English speaking" (MacLean 1956–1957, 26).[12] Dorian (1981, 79) noted that this etiquette of accommodation was "almost universally obeyed" in the 1970s among East Sutherland Gaelic speakers on the northeast coast of Scotland. The anthropologist Jack Coleman noted the operation of accommodation norms, which he termed the "Courtesy Rule," in 1973 in Carloway, a Gaelic–English-speaking crofting township on the Isle of Lewis (Coleman 1975, 79–84). One prominent Gaelic scholar from the Isle of Lewis observed flatly, "To behave otherwise is socially unacceptable" (Macaulay 1982, 29). During the period of my fieldwork in 2000, a Uist woman in her sixties explained the norms to me in these terms:

(5)
Och tha, well [...] tha gu math mi– ((cleared throat)) 'se caran *ill-mannered*. Tha (e) gu math *rude* ma tha thu a' dol brudhinn Gàidhlig agus cuideigin ann nach eil a'tuigsinn Gàidhlig, tha mm… ah, chan eil e, chan eil e modhail idir (X4, #497).

'Och yes, well [...] it's very im– ((cleared throat)) it's somewhat *ill-mannered*. (It)'s very *rude* if you're going () to speak Gaelic and someone [is] there who doesn't understand Gaelic, it's mm… ah, it's not, it's not polite at all.'

Her use of the English expressions *ill-mannered* and *rude* in the midst of her Gaelic statement indexed the English position from which judgement is passed on Gaelic in this accommodation norm, while voicing and thus constituting an iconic performance of it.[13]

Her codeswitching, together with the accommodation behaviour more generally, indexed the defensive position of Gaelic–English bilinguals as a group in relationship to English and "monolingual" English speakers. This speaker has been socialized into a system of values in which English speakers hold the superior social and economic position and must always be accommodated. In Lewis in 1973, and in Uist a quarter-century later, locals were very aware that the rest of Britain thought of them as stupid peasants, and that Gaelic language use was considered symbolic of their bumpkin status (see also Cavanaugh 2009, 35–41, 55–62; Tsitsipis 1981). Such views are expressed regularly in the Scottish press (see Ch. 3, this volume). Coleman argues that Gaelic speakers tried to protect themselves from judgements of this kind by avoiding the kinds of behaviours labeled as such, while in the presence of the labelers (Coleman 1975, 78–79).

Coleman (1975, 83) documented how Gaelic-English bilinguals were socialized into this system of behaviour by parental instruction and example in the crofting township of Carloway on the Isle of Lewis. Such early socialization can be continually reinforced by unpleasant social encounters in school, and as adults in public and in the workplace. A Uist woman, "Flora," told a story about her experience working in a local bank branch. Every other year, she said, the Scottish bank's mainland headquarters sent a young and promising male trainee to the island branch to perform a thorough audit. On one of these occasions, the auditor expressed concern that the tellers' use of Gaelic in the workplace might facilitate criminality:

> He just suddenly thought, oh, do you not think they might be trying to rob you if they're talking in Gaelic, you know, they might be trying to rob the place, y'kn– he was saying to the monitor and he tried to stop us speaking in Gaelic (Q1, #513).

Other similar anecdotes from people I talked to in the field indicate that on the mainland of Scotland as well, individuals speaking Gaelic with one another could be subject at any time to insults, directives to stop speaking Gaelic, and even physical violence from bystanders (cf. Gal 1979, 166; Dorian 1981, 80). Judging from the relative infrequency of these accounts in my fieldnotes, such incidents may have been relatively rare in the past few decades. But they did occur, and even one incident could make a lasting impression and influence a person to significantly change his or her linguistic behaviour. Part of the trauma of such incidents is that one never knows when or where they will happen, and they can happen when one least expects them.

Flora's description of a workplace encounter with a customer whom she identified as an adult Gaelic learner demonstrates the impact that this socialization could have on the language "choice" of fluent Gaelic-English bilinguals. Flora described how she found herself on one occasion observing the etiquette of accommodation, despite her stated wishes to do otherwise:

(6)
```
1   Flora:  There's this day this lady came in [to the bank], and, she– I think– if I
2           remember rightly she was a doctor, I can't remember where she was
3           from. But ((pause)) maybe it's just making an assumption when
4           people come in the door, and, you've seen the {people walk
5           (_____), and you think, they'll only have English anyway, so, I don't
6           know whether it was that, that was on the brain but, this particular
7           lady had Gaelic. And she must have either, she must have learned
8           the language, and she was ((laughter started)) fairly proud of having
9           I think, and she was trying to talk to me in Gaelic, I couldn't ((laughter
10          ended)) really talk to her in Gaelic, like, I couldn't. My brain would
11          just not (_____) it, I was speaking to her in English, all the time,
12          didn't matter what she said, I was… ((speech dissolved in a laugh)).
13          And I think, this is odd, you know. Because I knew fine, what I– I was
14          wanting to do, but I– ((pause))
15  EM:     Which was to speak Gaelic?
16  Flora:  Uh huh, but– it just didn't happen. And she was almost out the door
17          before I could– before the brain just switched over and ((pause))
18  EM:     You were able to?
19  Flora:  Yeah.
20  EM:     Was she mad?
21  Flora:  No, she wasn't, but she must have thought it really odd (#513).
```

Here Flora narrated the process of visually identifying and assessing a female bank customer before starting to speak to her.[14] She described making a determination of the customer as an outsider, by definition non-Gaelic-speaking, and speculated that this assessment influenced her brain to override her own will, making her unable to speak in Gaelic to the customer despite the customer's repeated conversational turns in Gaelic. She described a conflict between her brain (lines 6, 10, and 17) and her will to speak Gaelic; slightly different from the Cartesian mind-body split, perhaps this is a modern anatomized version of the Christian "spirit is willing/flesh is weak" trope, with the part of the weak flesh played by the brain. At any rate, Flora's pauses and laughter helped constitute an affective stance of puzzlement, embarrassment, and perhaps even distancing (McIntosh 2009) toward her violated expectations of rational control over her own language choice. Flora had previously stated in our interview that she did not agree with the most extreme enactments of local accommodation norms. She gave me several examples of situations in which she had disagreed openly with other Gaelic-English bilinguals who felt it was rude to speak Gaelic in a particular situation. She was also open to being interviewed in Gaelic by me, and to speaking in Gaelic with me and other adult learners, as both Alison and I had observed.

Flora's anecdote illustrates how this accommodation norm—this nexus of ideology and affect in the speaking body—could shape the behaviour of first-language Gaelic-English bilingual speakers in Uist in their interactions with my interviewees. It could be described as a process in which the local Gaelic speakers (as experts) were socializing the novices into the local pattern of "English to strangers, Gaelic to locals." At the same time, the bilingual experts were socializing the novices into an affective stance of fear and distrust of unknown speakers, and caution around sociolinguistic boundaries.[15]

Most of the adult learner interviewees' descriptions and explanations of speaking Gaelic—or not—to other people in the community were characterized by a negative affective stance. For example, I asked the interviewees a series of questions about whether there was anyone to whom they spoke regularly in Gaelic, and the circumstances under which they did speak to people in Gaelic in their daily lives. In describing their situations, four of the seven interviewees said that they did not speak Gaelic to people very often because of a lack of individual initiative, will, or courage. However, their complex affective stances indicate some dissonance with this explanation, as do their descriptions of negative social reactions from other community members that contributed to their situation of not being able to speak Gaelic, or others not speaking to them in Gaelic. This contradictory position signaled by affective stance, similar to Flora's, shows how the local speakers' etiquette of accommodation may have been gradually inculcated as an embodied ideological-affective complex and rule of sociolinguistic interaction for these interviewees living in the Western Isles.

The best example of blaming lack of interaction in Gaelic on oneself is Jean ("I could, but I don't"), whose responses I analyzed at length in the previous section as a "dance of disclosure" signaling an affective stance of shame about her failure to speak Gaelic. Jean's family experience with Gaelic demonstrated how Gaelic was inaccessible to her despite her having been raised by two Gaelic-speaking parents. Jean's workplace experience also shows how the sociolinguistic boundaries of Gaelic and English speaking invisibly criss-cross social space in bilingual areas. Jean worked in an office with a Gaelic-speaking secretary, where I interviewed her. Soon after the long excerpt quoted in the previous section, the telephone rang while I was asking her about the use of Gaelic in her workplace. We both paused and heard the secretary, "Katag," in the room next door answer the phone in Gaelic and continue talking at length in Gaelic to the person at the other end of the line. Breaking our pause, Jean then volunteered to me, "I hear it a lot, Katag uses Gaelic all the time. I never have to ask her what she's saying." But a few moments later, when I tried to elicit further commentary on patterns of Gaelic use by other community members with her, I was again met with a terse reply:

(7)
    EM: Are there any people who greet you regularly in Gaelic, and then switch into English?
    Jean: Yeah.

She volunteered no further comments on the topic and I did not want to press her, since I had already pressed her earlier. For Jean, it seems that Gaelic was always a little bit out of reach. With her parents on the mainland, she spoke but was not understood; in Uist she understood but did not speak.

When I asked "Who do you speak to regularly in Gaelic?" other interviewees gave similar replies. Alison replied "No one. I do have people that I could speak in Gaelic to, but they have trouble understanding me and it's too much of an effort." Isabel answered the question by referring to one particular person at a local organization and said "I do sometimes speak to him in Gaelic, I could do more if I put my mind to it" (D5, #428).

An energetic and animated woman in her fifties, whom I have already referred to as "Linda," described in her responses not only self-blame, but also particular patterns of interaction with her neighbours that make her socialization experience clear. Early in our interview, Linda made the connection between the etiquette of accommodation and local norms of hospitality, but she still found it troubling that her efforts to speak Gaelic were rebuffed:

(8)
1   EM: What Gaelic lessons or classes have you taken?
2   […Discussion and clarification between EM and Linda followed…]

3   EM: Was it the beginners' class?
4   Linda: Absolute. I had not a clue. We just thought, well here we are, in the
5   Western Isles, and the way to fit in is to have a go.
6   EM: Do you think it did help you to fit in?
7   Linda: No. I think we would have fitted in anyway. Yes. They're nice friendly
8   people that live here. And if you're nice and friendly in return, it
9   doesn't matter what language you speak. Plus the fact that they're so
10   polite, they wouldn't speak Gaelic in front of you anyway.
11   Which niggles a little bit. Because I wish they would. (X5, #544)

Linda's response contains a parallel structure in which *nice friendly people* (locals) and *nice and friendly in return* (ego, the incomer) getting along contrasts with *so polite, they wouldn't speak Gaelic in front of you anyway* (locals) and *I wish they would* (ego, the incomer), who conflict in their orientations to speaking Gaelic. The pauses before and after *Which niggles a little bit* dramatized her explicit complaint even as she minimized it with *a little bit* and *niggles* ('niggle' means 'to gnaw', but its other meanings have connotations of minor and petty). Her affective stance enacted her ambivalence and uneasiness about the discrepancy between Uist natives' standard of friendly and polite behaviour, and her own desire as an incomer to be spoken to in Gaelic.

Linda immediately went on without prompting to give examples of encounters with her neighbours in Uist:

(9)

For instance, one day I plucked up the courage. I was always willing to have a go in a class, but when I'm outside that's different. The neighbour ((pointing out the window)) came down, and I said, *Tha i brèagha*. With the proper enthusiasm. And he said, "That's right." ((laugh)) Even if he hadn't understood it, I wanted a reply in Gaelic! {_____} And I thought, it took me so much effort to do that. It's a nice phrase, {_____} And I said it to someone else, and he said, "Yes! And you've pronounced it correctly, with the emphasis in the right place!" {_____} And I know, and thought, I know (X5, #544).

Linda had learned enough in her beginner Gaelic classes about Gaelic greetings to know how to produce the first pair-part of an appropriate greeting-greeting adjacency pair (Schegloff 2007), with a comment about the weather, such as *Tha i brèagha*, "It's beautiful," using the locally-appropriate feminine pronoun *i* to refer to the weather (which is masculine *e* in other dialect areas). She had also learned how to produce this phrase with a reasonably accurate approximation of Gaelic phonology, as her retelling indicated to me. She expected that an appropriate reply to her comment would have been a comment in Gaelic acknowledging or elaborating on her comment about the weather—something like *Tha gu dearbh* 'Yes indeed'. Such a reply would have completed the adjacency pair of a typical Gaelic greeting.

Instead, in the first brief interaction Linda described, her neighbour violated the turn sequence of the greeting adjacency pair in two ways. First, he initiated a codeswitch from Gaelic to English in the middle of the pair, a switch which Linda implies continued for the remainder of the interaction. Second, he offered a dispreferred response, "That's right," which constituted an evaluation of her Gaelic use and shifted his footing in the conversation from that of an egalitarian neighbour to a hierarchical position of a teacher evaluating a pupil. Although the response also could be interpreted as an agreement with the truth value of her statement, the fact that the comment was an evaluation is made more clear by the codeswitch, and by comparison with her second conversation partner's comment as reported by Linda. This contained an agreement with the truth value of her statement ("Yes") and a separate evaluation of its technical execution ("And you've pronounced it correctly…"). Thus, this English evaluation response violated local Gaelic interactional norms of greeting, codeswitching, and egalitarian social footing (Ducey 1956; Parman 1990).

When Linda spoke in Gaelic to her neighbour, she was attempting to "fit in" to the local community of Uist. Linda had moved into the area, bought a house that had previously been inhabited by a Gaelic speaker, and was learning to speak her neighbour's stigmatized first language. He turned the greeting exchange into an evaluation of the "incomer" by the "local," a switch to judgement by the very person who may have felt that he was usually being judged (see e.g. Hill 1985). Through his meta-level comment on grammar, Linda's neighbour dictated the choice of language, and the position from which to display superior knowledge. He created a conversational disjuncture that indexes a larger social disjuncture between participants who occupy the same geographical space but belong to different sociolinguistic communities with different criteria for membership, and radically different experiences of language socialization.

After relating this anecdote, Linda told me that she wanted a reply, not an evaluation, and looked sad (as I typed in my interview notes at the time). I then asked Linda, "Who do you speak to in Gaelic now? Is there anyone?" She answered:

(10)
>Well not really, because this one ((gesturing out the window to her neighbour)) will only answer me in English. Yeah! I can't think of anyone really. I go into the shop at Drumbeg and try to get my courage up. But I don't.

Linda's explanation of her failure of courage and will, read in the context of her affective stance and her account of her neighbours' behaviour, shows how on some level she seems to be aware of the social nature of the problem. She is actually saying that she doesn't have the courage to override local norms and local definitions of polite behaviour—the courage to be rude by local standards. Blaming herself is a way of remaining humble, and avoiding explicit criticism of her neighbours and fellow community members, while commenting on the social situation.

Strikingly, Jean, Alison, Isabel, and Linda all used the modal *could* in at least one response: There were people they could speak to in Gaelic, or they could do more with Gaelic. This could, I argue, indexes unfulfilled personal expectations of oneself. According to the covert nationalist logic commonly encountered when learning state-sponsored languages like French or Japanese, opportunities for hearing and speaking Gaelic should abound in Uist, a "Gaelic-speaking" area. When the interviewees discussed how their experiences did not match their expectations, their affective stance communicated an awareness that this was a social situation created by their neighbours and coworkers, but they claimed the blame and shame for themselves individually.

This pattern of social interaction, repeated over time in chance encounters in different local community settings—one's garden, the shop, the church—socializes Gaelic learners like Linda into the idea that Gaelic is only for "locals" and English for "incomers," at a time when they still feel uncertain about their linguistic skills. For at least some of the interviewees, this seems to have discouraged subsequent attempts to initiate conversation in Gaelic, except with a trusted interlocutor. Alison commented: "I think you can only speak Gaelic to somebody if there is somebody you know who is sympathetic to you" (G11, #438). This need for trust and general positive affect could even be the result of socialization into the etiquette of accommodation; Coleman (1975, 83) noted the importance of "the element of intragroup trust and acceptance that must be present if local persons are to feel free to speak Gaelic. Such conditions are normally lacking when strangers are present." It seems likely that the "expert" locals were reenacting their own socialization experiences with the "novice" incomers and thus socializing them into the feeling that they could speak Gaelic only with people they trusted. An extended quote from one of the two male interviewees illustrates an affective stance of uncertainty about what "others" think of his attempts to speak Gaelic in conversation:

(11)
> I mean, there are some people who, em, it, I mean, it sounds a bit showy, isn't it, I mean, that's another thing that worries me about my use of Gaelic, is that I feel that, to some extent I have to be in the mood, and not be worried about whether or not they think I'm being a bit showy, and um, almost patronizing. Um, and there is a danger sometimes, the f- when, I mean for example, when I'm up in Stornoway, there is, um, I stay at a place called the [Castle] Guesthouse, which is also very often used by a couple of the local councillors here, and if they turn up for breakfast while I'm there, I'll quite often say, *Madainn mhath, ciamar a tha thu an diugh*, or say, because quite often they'll do the same to me, you know they'll speak, address me in Gaelic, and I'll respond in Gaelic, and just a few salutations and a couple of pleasantries. But I sometimes in the back of my head, I think, you know I wonder if, you know, especially if there are others

> there, who are, say, colleagues, who are also staying there, think I'm trying to be showy and pretentious, almost trying to be teacher's pet with the councillors, and sometimes you feel the environment is not ((pause)) you feel that maybe people think that you're putting on a bit of an act, trying to be clever by giving these bursts of Gaelic, rather than genuinely trying to develop a language. (J11, #484)

Unlike Linda, Jean, and Alison, this interviewee communicated a stance of confidence in his intermediate-level progress and ability in anecdotes he told about his interactions in Gaelic with others in the workplace. However, in this part of the interview, his repeated hedges (*I mean, a bit, isn't it, um, you know*) index the uncertainty that he also explicitly describes: a worry that his work colleagues might perceive his attempts to use Gaelic as "showy" rather than genuine. Graham, the other male interviewee whose interview I analyzed in the previous section, had already apparently been socialized by his own family into observing the etiquette of accommodation: as already mentioned, he referred to "the company of other people to be considered" in explaining why he could not speak Gaelic to his mother face to face, and when I asked Graham if there was anyone who would refuse to speak to him in Gaelic, he said "I don't push it with anyone so I don't know really," meaning that he would not try to force anyone to speak Gaelic with him in the community. This reluctance to "push" or force an interaction to take place through the medium of Gaelic resonates with Hebridean cultural norms of privileging egalitarianism and individual autonomy and avoiding pushiness (Macdonald 1997, 223–5).

Thus, "locals" in Uist, who have been linguistically and affectively socialized to enact the cultural etiquette of accommodation developed over decades if not centuries of language shift, in turn appear to be affectively socializing adult "incomers" in Uist into observing this same ideology of local sociolinguistic boundaries. Ironically, the adult learners are being socialized to enact the boundary from both sides of the fence: on the one side, they are expected to play the part of the English-speaking stranger in "English to strangers," but on the other side, if they persist in speaking Gaelic, they must also learn to be cautious about exactly whom they can speak Gaelic to, identifying their own trustworthy personal in-group members in the learners' version of "Gaelic to locals." Their negative affective stances of ambivalence, unease, fear, self-blame, and shame are richly indexed in their interviews with me, a fellow learner living temporarily in Uist who shared many of their experiences—and affective stances.

3.3 Sociolinguistic mentors and positive affect

When Gaelic learners and Gaelic speakers in Uist enact these ideologies and affective stances, they create hindrances to the acquisition and social use of Gaelic among adult learners. However, in the final section of this article I identify a category of individuals who seem to have done the opposite: they facilitated the acquisition and social use of Gaelic among the adult learners I interviewed in Uist. These fluent Gaelic speakers, whom I term "sociolinguistic mentors," enacted a more inclusive vision of Gaelic speaking. They seem to have ignored the dominant ideologies of language shift and enacted positive affect with adult Gaelic learners, in this case culturally specific feelings of trust and confidence, in speaking Gaelic with them.

Most of my interviewees identified one particular sociolinguistic mentor who had provided a boost to their Gaelic language skills—and positive affect—by regularly interacting with them through the medium of Gaelic. One of the two beginners and five of the six intermediate and advanced learners I interviewed said that they had attained their current level of Gaelic proficiency in part through having daily interaction with at least one particular sympathetic, fluent Gaelic-speaking person in the past, whether it was a coworker, an in-law, a friend, or a boyfriend. This person was willing to speak to them regularly in Gaelic and to make those accommodations that adult second-language learners usually need in order to be able to interact in "real time": to speak more slowly, to help correct mistakes and to supply necessary words and phrases. Linda described her interactions with such a person in a positive affective stance:

(12)
>We used to go to church at "Drumore." This lady "Morag," she always used to come up to me and say ciamar a tha thu an diugh [how are you today], and she'd wait for me to go through the rigmarole. And each day (...) she'd teach me a word about the weather. And of course when I came down here I lost her! (...) But I wish she was down here because she'd help me along. (...) Yeah, she made my night down there! As I saw her coming, I thought, make an effort.

Linda's church acquaintance helped build her vocabulary, fluency, and confidence, as well as supplying her with motivation.

Isabel's main mentor was her husband's mother, who, like some of Nancy Dorian's tenacious and enthusiastic semi-speakers of East Sutherland Gaelic (Dorian 1980, 90–91), had her loyalty for Gaelic sharpened by exile:

(13)
- Isabel: [My husband's mother] was always very kind of positive about it, I'm not quite sure why, she just was. She was a chatty kind of person, never happier than when she was talking in Gaelic. She left [the island] when she was seventeen, and only went back for holidays, she was [living] in London with her family. She was like a fish out of water, she didn't really like London, her only friends were other Gaelic speaking family [people] in London. [Gaelic] represented home, happiness.
- EM: So your husband grew up in London?
- Isabel: Yes. They always went to [the island] for their holidays, back to the family home for six weeks every summer, so he had a fond memory of [the island].

Isabel had another mentor, "Archie," with whom she had worked for a time in an open-plan office:

(14)
Then I didn't do anything [further with Gaelic] till I started work with the [current organization], in 1993, {and met} [my current coworker]'s predecessor, "Archie." He has a similar history to my husband, he was from [island], brought up in [former British colony] and [mainland Scottish city], and he didn't learn Gaelic when he was a child, because his father was not a Gaelic speaker. Same as my husband [who didn't learn it because only his mother was a Gaelic speaker]. But again he had an interest in Gaelic because of his mother, and when he went to university he started to learn Gaelic, his mother was very helpful. She was really really really particular about his pronunciation, so people say he has good [island] Gaelic, she wouldn't rest till he had the pronunciation right, she also taught him lots of idioms, {the sort that} you couldn't learn unless someone was telling them to you. He ended up with excellent Gaelic, but understood what it was like to be a learner. So when I was sharing a room with him, a pro-Gaelic person, a bit like you have, he asked me about (…). And he then sort of started to speak to me quite a lot in Gaelic, he understood my difficulties. While I was sharing a room with him, my Gaelic improved tremendously. So that was good.

Archie had one Gaelic-speaking parent, but his family socialization experience seems to have been different again from both Jean's and Graham's, a good example of the wide variety of language socialization experiences and affective orientations found in situations of language shift, and of the way that people can become linguistically resocialized after childhood.

Alison described her mentor, a former boyfriend who had also had a higher level of contact with non-native Gaelic speakers:

(15)
> I used to go out with someone from [crofting township], a native speaker [named "Tormod"]. He said my Gaelic wasn't good enough for him to be able to converse with me, but once my Gaelic got better with "Donnie's" {class}, I could say enough for him to understand it and he could say more back. Anything I wanted to know I could ask him. He gave me an awful lot of idiomatic Gaelic and Uist expressions. I think I went to Donnie's classes, and then it was years before I went to his next classes, and {he said, you've improved so much, how did you improve, and I said I studied it on my own.} And now, to an extent, I miss that, because I'm with "Nick" and Nick doesn't speak Gaelic... ((Later in the interview)) Tormod and I just went out five years ago. {Then we were just friends, then Nick came along and he didn't like another man being around and Tormod stopped talking to me.} [Tormod] was the only person I knew who would sit down, and make me speak Gaelic, and that was just because he was used to learners.

Tormod, a crofter, had gotten into a regular pattern of hosting students from Sabhal Mòr Ostaig, the Gaelic college on the Isle of Skye:

(16)
> ...if the Department of Agriculture have a student who wants to spend time, they'll ring him up, or if Sabhal Mòr have a student who wants to learn Gaelic, they'll ring him up. {They always seem to ring him up.} He's very good at teaching people Gaelic, because he has dealt with languages {and learners}.

However, at the time I interviewed them, all of the adult learners who had identified a particular mentor for Gaelic conversation had lost their mentors. Alison's romantic relationship with her mentor had ended, and her new partner did not approve of their remaining friends. Linda described above what happened when she moved from a temporary home on one island to their permanent home that had just been renovated on a neighbouring island. The others had lost their mentors through such circumstances as the death of the mentor or a change of employment, and new mentors had not come into their lives at the time I interviewed them. One factor preventing these learners from having more interaction through the medium of Gaelic, then, was that their trusted, sympathetic mentors were not easy to replace in the circumscribed routines of home, work, and worship. In these quotidian situations, many if not most of the Gaelic-English bilinguals they encountered displayed discomfort when faced with non-fluent and/or non-local attempts at Gaelic speech.

More research is needed to determine why some people become sociolinguistic mentors and others do not. However, at this point it is clear that some fluent Gaelic-English bilinguals in Uist and elsewhere have at least partially escaped or overcome the affective and ideological socialization into local sociolinguistic boundaries that is characterized by the situation of shift from Gaelic to English. In interviews, some first-language Gaelic speakers told me about occasions when they defended their right to speak Gaelic in the face of public criticism from strangers, and contested other first-language Gaelic speakers' insistence on speaking English when nearby non-Gaelic speakers were not directly involved in the conversation. Many of them took some pleasure in assisting adult Gaelic learners. In other cases, fluent Gaelic speakers apparently felt secure enough in their own spoken Gaelic ability, their dialect form, and/or their literacy abilities, to be able to spontaneously volunteer assistance or to offer it when asked. Formal education in Gaelic would seem to be one possible factor influencing people's approach, but not the only one.

4   Conclusion

Adult second-language learners face considerable challenges, particularly when the target language is as structurally dissimilar to their own first language as Gaelic is to English. This article clearly demonstrates, however, that factors related to language structure, individual learning proclivities, and infrastructure for language teaching and learning are not the only challenges facing adults who learn minority languages such as Scottish Gaelic. Adult minority-language learners also must deal with the familial and local-level impact of the sociolinguistic and cultural conditions of language shift, which includes the ideological and affective stances that have become culturally entrenched among native Gaelic speakers through micro-level language socialization practices.

The sociolinguistic boundaries between English-speaking "incomers" and Gaelic-speaking "locals" described in this article extend throughout geographically defined Gaelic-speaking communities and are enacted in familial and institutional contexts, sometimes even contrary to the stated will of the enactors. These enacted ideologies and affective stances create conditions that impede interaction through the medium of Gaelic between adults learning the language and adults who already speak Gaelic as a first language. This furthers the process of language shift in two ways: First, it removes opportunities for adults to practice or improve their Gaelic speaking ability; and second, it removes opportunities for adults to assist in socializing other community members (whether younger or older) into the public, daily use of Gaelic in one of the few remaining areas in the world where Gaelic is available as a community language to more than half of the inhabitants.

The ideologies and affect of language shift also shape and limit the opportunities being made available to adults to learn Gaelic in the context of language revitalization. For example, the situations, emotions, experiences and abilities of people with Gaelic-speaking parents, who were ideologically and affectively socialized into language shift in childhood, are overlooked in the types of courses offered to learn Gaelic and in Gaelic language revitalization efforts more generally. The affective impact of this socialization may be strong. One of MacCaluim's Gaelic Learners' Survey respondents in Scotland gave a personal view on the topic:

> I have asked myself why I am bothering with this language many times. Not having been brought up in the Highlands, I don't understand all the taboos associated with this language. All I know is that my father didn't speak his native language to me and, being brought up in Glasgow I didn't have the option to study Gaelic, even to O Grade. These things made me angry and upset as a young adult, especially the fact that the only time I heard Gaelic was when adult family members wanted to exclude

me from their conversation. Gaelic has probably been spoken in my family for hundreds of years and I feel upset and guilty that it has stopped in my generation, even though I had no choice about learning it as a child. When I hear Gaelic, it often makes me want to cry. It sounds very right, but it's still something I'm excluded from. I'm still on the wrong side of the language barrier, and it feels like many native speakers are dismissive of my very broken Gaelic. ... The only young people who will speak Gaelic with me are other learners. I find that very sad and discouraging, except that the other learners are very enthusiastic. I wish I understood the psychology of this language and why people are so reluctant to speak it—including my own father. ... To be honest, I don't have the courage, or insensitivity (?) to speak Gaelic to people no matter what. If my attempts to murder the Gaelic language in conversation are met with annoyance or impatience, I desist. Maybe I am a coward because even if a sympathetic Gaelic speaker is around, I find it hard to speak Gaelic to them if other people are overhearing who: (a) don't speak or understand Gaelic and resent it being spoken in case Gaelic speakers are using the language to exclude them; (b) are fluent speakers who are liable to laugh at my attempts to speak their language; (c) are young people who understand and / or speak Gaelic and seem to resent my attempts to learn Gaelic. I'm not sure why but they seem to see it as uncool and something which doesn't fit into everyday life. As a person who is still young, I find it hard not to be influenced by the attitudes of other young Gaels (MacCaluim 1997, 267–68).

Despite the infrastructural, cognitive, and social barriers, though, the interviewees living in Uist managed to make significant progress in learning Gaelic. In addition to their own ability and effort, they benefited from interaction with sociolinguistic mentors who did not allow sociolinguistic boundaries laden with negative affect to prevent them from speaking to Gaelic learners in Gaelic. The socialization experiences and other factors that influence some Gaelic speakers to become socio-linguistic mentors remain to be investigated, but the interactions they foster with Gaelic learners prove that the micro-level socialization of both affect and ideology is crucially important in language revitalization efforts as well as processes of language shift.

These adult learners are motivated to contribute to reversing Gaelic language shift in Scotland: among MacCaluim's 1998–99 survey respondents living in Scotland,

> The reason for learning most commonly quoted as being very important was *I would be helping to keep Gaelic alive*, which was said to be very important by 67.9% of Scottish respondents and as quite important by another 25%. [...] This was also the most frequently chosen main reason for learning, picked by 25.8% of respondents in Scotland. This shows a high level of concern with the well-being of Gaelic and suggests that most respondents do not see their learning of Gaelic as a purely personal pastime, but rather see it as part of the effort to reverse language shift in Scotland (MacCaluim 2007, 158).

But unless more and better ways can be found to increase local community-level opportunities for these individuals to speak Gaelic, and to build Gaelic-speaking social networks, there is a serious risk that their efforts will remain at the level of personal achievement and fail to contribute substantially to revitalizing Uist as a distinctively Gaelic-speaking area. In regard to the situation of adult learners of Welsh, Newcombe (2007, 114–15) states that "There is an urgent need to investigate further the relationship between native speakers and learners and find ways to enable the two groups to work together more productively." Newcombe makes suggestions for facilitating support for learners outside the classroom, such as schemes to pair native speakers with learners, a national friend/mentor system, drop-in centers for learners and native speakers (particularly in urban areas where the minority language is not a community language), marketing initiatives to make natives speakers more aware of learners' needs, and training for native speakers committed to language revitalization in how to converse with learners (Newcombe 2007, 115). Such initiatives, if incorporated into Scottish Gaelic revitalization efforts, might help to revitalize Gaelic in areas where it has traditionally been spoken as a community language.

Notes

1 *Tapadh leibh* to the anonymous interviewees who generously shared their time and experiences with me. My deep gratitude goes to Christina Bratt Paulston, Nancy Dorian, Barbara Johnstone and two anonymous reviewers who read and commented in detail on an earlier version of the manuscript, leading me to reconceptualize it substantially. I am also grateful to Jillian Cavanaugh, Alexandra Jaffe, Scott Kiesling, Kendall King, Lindsay Milligan, and Rachel Reynolds, who offered many suggestions for improvement and/or recommendations of relevant literature. Previous versions were presented to the Harvard Celtic Colloquium; the Department of Linguistics, University of Pittsburgh; Rannsachadh na Gàidhlig 2008 at St. Francis Xavier University, Antigonish; and the Department of Anthropology of Saint Mary's University, Halifax. I thank the audiences, especially the members of Sgoil Ghàidhlig an Àrd-Bhaile, Halifax, for their valuable feedback and encouragement.

2 Cavanaugh 2009 has outlined the "social aesthetics of language" as another key approach to the intertwining of ideology and affect in a situation of minority language shift. Cavanaugh 2004 also describes nostalgia as an ideological-affective discourse of language shift among Bergamasco speakers in northern Italy.

3 Or a signed language (Nonaka 2004), but not a written language.

4 Ochs (1996, 425) maintains that in stance, the categories of positive and negative affect are universally indexed, together with the affective categories of surprise and intensity/mitigation.

5 However, in the first year and sometimes second year of secondary school (S1 and S2), Gaelic language education is effectively compulsory as a learner's subject for some students in some schools in the Highland and Eileanan Siar (Western Isles) regions. This is decided at the school level rather than at the regional level (Moray Watson, personal communication).

6 General Register Office for Scotland, 2005. The map shows that in the civil parishes of the Western Isles, 60–<75% of the population aged 3 and over were enumerated as Gaelic speakers, with the exception of the civil parish of Stornoway on the Isle of Lewis, where 40–<60% were enumerated as Gaelic speakers.

7 These 2001 census figures were obtained by creating a custom composite table using the Scottish Census Results Online (SCROL) website, http://www.scrol.gov.uk. From the main page, the "SCROL analyser" function was selected, then the topic "Cultural," and the table "Knowledge of Gaelic." The table was then created by selecting the geographical area option of "inhabitable islands" and checking boxes to include Benbecula, Berneray (North Uist), Eriskay, Grimsay, North Uist, and South Uist. These islands together comprise the civil parishes of North Uist (Berneray, Grimsay, North Uist) and South Uist (Benbecula, South Uist and Eriskay).

8   This must be stated explicitly, since not all residents of the islands seemed to fully recognize or care that they were living in an area that was ethnolinguistically distinctive and different from other regional and local cultures of Scotland (or England, for that matter).

9   Adults studying Gaelic as part of an academic course would most likely be in residence at Sabhal Mòr Ostaig (the Gaelic college on the Isle of Skye), the Celtic and Gaelic Departments of the Universities of Aberdeen, Glasgow, and Edinburgh, or in the teacher training programs of the School of Education in University of Aberdeen or Strathclyde University.

10   Transcription conventions used in this chapter include the following (partially adapted from Schegloff 2007):

(a) (single parentheses) enclose the author's best guess about what was uttered indistinctly in recorded interviews;

(b) single parentheses enclosing a space () indicate that something was said in a recorded interview, but that what was said cannot be identified;

(c) [brackets] enclose words which are supplied by the researcher either to add clarifying information, or substitute generic information for identifying placenames and personal names, e.g. [the island] to substitute for the real name of an island;

(d) an ellipsis in brackets [...] indicates utterances omitted from the transcription;

(e) {braces} indicate words that were paraphrased by the researcher in written notes of unrecorded conversations and interviews;

(f) ((double parentheses)) enclose the researcher's descriptions of events, e.g. ((laughter)) and ((pointing out the window)); and

(g) "Quotation marks" enclose the first instance of a pseudonym. Subsequent uses of the pseudonym appear without quotation marks. The author gave culturally and linguistically appropriate pseudonyms.

(h) Letter-number combinations and numbers with preceding hashes, such as (G1, #34) are reference codes from the author's field notes.

11   Here I refer to politeness as a folk or "emic" concept used by Gaelic-English bilingual speakers, not the technical linguistic concept of politeness.

12   Newcombe (2007, 40) quotes a commentator on a similar situation in Wales in the mid-1970s: "In Wales, the language for speaking to strangers is English" (Jacobs 1976, 14).

13   At first she began to say the word *mi-mhodhail* "impolite," but then used the two English alternatives. It is possible that she may have been accommodating to my perceived Gaelic linguistic ability by using the English words. However, moments later when still talking about the same topic, she used the Gaelic word *modhail* "polite."

14   Coleman (1975, 90–93) described how Carloway villagers, socialized into the etiquette of accommodation, would make a quick evaluation of an unfamiliar person's hair, clothing, posture, and other features that would indicate whether the person was island-born or a stranger, in order to judge whether to speak Gaelic or English to the person (see also Woolard 1989 on Catalan).

15   In this article I have chosen to focus on the ideological and affective aspects of socialization into the etiquette of accommodation. However, there are possible additional factors that help explain the reluctance of some native Gaelic speakers to engage in Gaelic conversation with adult learners. One point mentioned by three of my interviewees (Jean, Isabel, and Alison) was that some native speakers had a difficult time understanding their spoken Gaelic, and/or accommodating their own spoken Gaelic so that the learners could understand them. However, since ideological and affective factors (language attitudes, stereotypes) seem to play a part in accommodation and in mutual intelligibility between speakers of different varieties (Street and Giles 1982, Wolff 1959), it is not possible to determine to what extent local socialization into the observance of sociolinguistic boundaries accounts for these phenomena, compared to the role that lexical, structural, and phonological differences between the learners' Gaelic and the locally spoken varieties play. Newcombe also discusses a different reason why some native Welsh speakers are reluctant to keep conversations going in Welsh: the insecurity of native Welsh speakers about their own Welsh language proficiency (2007, 43–44). This may also be a factor in the situation of Gaelic, particularly with native Gaelic speakers who incompletely acquired Gaelic in the family context, and/or who received no or insufficient formal education in Gaelic. However, in the data gathered for this paper, the only clear evidence of native speakers' insecurity about their own Gaelic arose in connection with Gaelic literacy activities (specifically, Gaelic language course homework). I treat this issue separately in Chapter 9, dealing with what I call the "ideology of literate speakerhood," a standard language ideology in which Gaelic-English bilinguals compare their literacy in English to their lack of literacy in Gaelic, and express shame related to their lack of literacy skills in their native language.

CHAPTER 9

Ideologies and Experiences of Literacy in Interactions between Adult Gaelic Learners and First-Language Gaelic Speakers in Scotland

1 Introduction

This paper explores the way that shared ideologies and differing experiences of literacy may shape social interactions between adult Gaelic learners and adult first-language Gaelic speakers.[1] A number of adults learning Gaelic in Scotland have reported negative reactions from some first-language Gaelic speakers concerning their attempts to speak and write to them in or about Gaelic (e.g. MacCaluim 2007, 213, 266–72; MacPhàdruig 1998; Walker 1998). In Alasdair MacCaluim's 1998–1999 survey of 643 Gaelic learners, among the 46 open-ended comments respondents made about the relationship between learners and native speakers of Gaelic (MacCaluim 2007, 213), several raised Gaelic literacy in particular as a problem or point of difference between learners and native speakers:

> The few local native Gaelic speakers here can't read and write easily and feel inferior and do not want to encourage learners—so we make no progress (MacCaluim 2007, 266).

> One of the biggest problems for learners is the attitude of certain speakers of Gaelic (who claim to be "native," although their ability to write the language and their understanding and familiarity with the written form is often minimal) who will belittle any attempt to learn the language; the frightening thing is that some of these people are (fairly senior) schoolteachers in the Highlands. It is not a common attitude, but a small number of repeated posts to various internet newsgroups have managed to destroy the morale of a large number of learners (MacCaluim 2007, 267).

> Though I have strong links to Lewis and spend one week in four there, I still learn more Gaelic from classes etc. than from the

people around me. Other people always speak to me in English as a matter of politeness and apologise if they inadvertently slip back into Gaelic. They regard my attempts to speak Gaelic as embarrassing and unnecessary and always answer in English. At the same time they are astonished and mystified by the fact that I read Gaelic books and write to them in Gaelic while I am away (MacCaluim 2007, 271–2).

These commenters express a number of opinions and observations about Gaelic literacy and first-language Gaelic speakers, including the idea that many do not read and write Gaelic well, the idea that a lack of Gaelic literacy skills somehow undermines one's "native speaker" status, and the "astonishment" and "mystification" on the part of "native speakers" when confronted with the learner's desire to read and write in Gaelic.[2] How do these kinds of negative reactions and judgements among adult Gaelic learners and first-language Gaelic speakers relate to participants" ideologies about Gaelic and English literacy?

I propose that Gaelic-English bilinguals and English-speaking Gaelic learners in Scotland share what might be called an "ideology of literate speakerhood" inculcated through the state education system. I define this ideology as the unexamined assumption that a "speaker" of a language is someone who has ideally mastered both speaking and writing the language, and moreover has acquired these skills in relation to a standardized form of the language. Both first-language Gaelic speakers and Gaelic learners have been socialized into this ideology, but they approach it from different perspectives that have been shaped by their different language socialization and education experiences. On the one hand, most adult Gaelic learners take literacy in their first language for granted and model their language-learning efforts on their education in both English and "foreign languages" in school and at university. They approach the acquisition of Gaelic literacy as a normal and fundamental part of second language learning. On the other hand, a substantial proportion of Gaelic-English bilinguals received little or no formal education in their first language, Gaelic, and were educated in a system that subordinated Gaelic to English—when it recognized Gaelic at all.

When Gaelic-English bilinguals who do not feel confident in their Gaelic literacy skills encounter Gaelic learners who display Gaelic literacy skills or an interest in acquiring such skills, the encounter may prompt these bilinguals to reflect on their Gaelic literacy skills and interpret them through the ideological filter of literate speakerhood. This may result in feelings of lack or inadequacy in their first-language literacy ability, expressed as negative affect to Gaelic learners. These reactions may in turn be misinterpreted as signs of personal animosity, exclusivity, a deliberate withholding of information, or even inauthenticity by adult learners, who mistakenly assume that any speaker of Gaelic must also be a proficient reader and writer of Gaelic.

2 National Institutional Ideologies of Literacy and Standard Language

In literate societies where English is the dominant language, such as the UK, people tend to conflate spoken and written language in everyday discourse: they often talk and write about writing in terms of speech (e.g. "In her book, the author says…"), and talk and write about speech in terms of writing (e.g. "Doubt has a silent b") (Stubbs 1980, 22; Halliday 1989, xv). Most people in these literate societies view speaking and writing as two different ways of expressing "the same thing" and privilege writing over speaking in many areas of life; this may be termed a "litero-centric" discourse.

The litero-centric discourse in which written and spoken language are intertwined is a core feature of standard language ideology. Calling a standard language an "ideology" may seem odd, because popular views of language in the US and the UK tend to define standard language as an actually existing entity. However, Milroy and Milroy (1999, 19) instead advocate conceptualizing language standardization as an ongoing historical process, and standard language as an ideology, "a set of abstract norms to which actual usage may conform to a greater or lesser extent." Ideologies of language more generally have been defined as "cultural conceptions of language—its nature, structure, and use—and […] conceptions of communicative behaviour as an enactment of a collective order" (Woolard 1992; also see Silverstein 1979; Schieffelin, Woolard and Kroskrity 1998). Thus a "language ideology" approach foregrounds the ways in which people link language use, including literacy practices and standardization, with the enactment of social relationships and the construction of social and cultural group membership and hierarchy. Silverstein (1996, 286) describes the fundamentally ideological nature of language standardization in linguistic communities where it has taken hold:

> Standardization ... is a phenomenon in a linguistic community in which institutional maintenance of certain valued linguistic practices—in theory, fixed—acquires an explicitly-recognized hegemony over the definition of the community's norm. People defer—on grounds varied as a function of their positions in the community, to be sure—to the authority of such institutions to articulate the community's norm. Hence, "best" users of the language, that is, at least, those who would be "best," strive to achieve this Standard linguistic practice, the control of which as part of the functionally differentiated norm becomes an index of "best speakerhood."

Thus "best speakerhood," based on a person performing spoken and written language practices asymptotic to the abstract norms of the written standard, is promoted by institutions which maintain valued linguistic practices—for example, English literacy—and inculcate their hegemony over the definition of a linguistic community's norm. This ideology of standard wholly or partially supersedes other definitions of a linguistic community's norm based on oral usage.

Technologies and practices of reading and writing, controlled and cultivated by institutions such as the school, play a vital role in initiating and maintaining a standard language as ideology and hegemony (Silverstein 1996, 286). Milroy and Milroy further describe the process of objectification and naturalization of the standard through the dictionaries, grammars, and textbooks that are the tools of hegemonic institutions such as schools and universities:

> Thus, the writing system serves as one of the sources of prescriptive norms, and prescription becomes more intense after the language undergoes codification (as in eighteenth-century England), because speakers there have access to dictionaries and grammar-books, which they regard as authorities. They tend to believe

that the "language" is enshrined in these books (however many mistakes and omissions there may be in them) rather than in the linguistic and communicative competence of the millions who use the language every day (Milroy and Milroy 1999, 22–3).

These assumptions have been inculcated in people through schooling, most obviously in recent times through the school subjects of "English" and "modern languages." The type of literacy referred to here is "schooled literacy": the ability to write in "grammatically correct" fashion using "correctly spelled" words, consulting grammar books and dictionaries as points of reference for "correct usage." At this point it must be noted that sociolinguists who study literacy as a socially and culturally constructed phenomenon use the term "literacies" to convey "the pronounced heterogeneity of literacy experiences both within and across social groups" (Street and Besnier 1994, 534–5). From this perspective, "schooled literacy" is just one among many different kinds of literacies, albeit one imbued with enormous social power and significance in contemporary middle-class Western life. In schooled literacy the social process and institutional context of schooling "determines what counts as acceptable literate knowledge" (Cook-Gumperz 2006, 10–11). One major aspect of this standard language ideology, with its conflation of spoken and written language, is what I call the "ideology of literate speakerhood": the assumption that a "speaker" of a language is also ideally a reader and writer of a standardized version of that language.[3]

3 The Ideology of Literate Speakerhood in the Context of Gaelic in Scotland

The standards of speakerhood can be different in speech communities where the variety in question is not subject to the ideology of standard language or assumptions of literate speakerhood. For example, Dorian (2010, 262) identified the local criteria for best speakerhood of the isolated unwritten dialect of East Sutherland Gaelic (henceforth ESG) based on extensive linguistic fieldwork in the village of Embo in the 1960s and 1970s. ESG speakers in the latter half of the 20th century were all bilingual in English, and they were aware that their Gaelic dialect was very divergent from western Gaelic forms. Dorian notes that in Embo ESG, the foremost element in producing speech admired by community members was sheer verbal (rather than strictly linguistic) skill. Verbal skill encompasses such things as the ability to draw on a rich lexicon effectively, to tell stories with a point, to recount or allude to a local repertory of well-known anecdote, to compliment or to insult with subtlety or verve, to converse with liveliness, to prevent or fill awkward conversational gaps, and generally to maintain and make use of the verbal tradition of the community (including material such as proverbs, local rhymes, songs, by-names, prognostications, and the like). The more of these abilities a speaker had, the more admired her or his speech was likely to be (Dorian 2010, 262).

As Dorian observes, "Conformity to conservative grammatical norms was not a requirement for success in these facets of speaking well." Although Dorian's interlocutors apparently registered "speech performance that conforms to traditional models of [ESG] grammar" at some level, they almost never positively commented on it (Dorian 2010, 263). More important than grammatical conservatism in determining best speakerhood in Embo ESG was overall verbal skill, and also speaker loyalty to ESG: the willingness to use the variety as a "preferred medium of communication" even despite less than full grammatical proficiency in ESG, and despite full proficiency in English. These factors, together with social standing in the community in more stratified communities (Bloomfield 1964; Evans 2001; Dorian 2010) could serve as indices of "best speakerhood" for speakers of a variety without a codified written form. Such measures of speaking well may be difficult to acquire or even to conceptualize for adult Gaelic learners who have not experienced language as an exclusively oral medium of communication since early childhood, and who have been measured all their lives by the standard of standard language, and concomitantly socialized into the ideology of literate speakerhood.[4]

Dorian's description of "verbal skill" in the orally-mediated Gaelic community of Embo evokes the disappearing world of Gaelic oral tradition in Gaelic-speaking communities of the Highlands and islands documented by folklore collectors in the 19th and 20th centuries. Following the collapse of the clan system with its learned orders in the 17th and 18th centuries, and the Highland Clearances in the 19th century, most Gaelic speakers were gradually cut off from both the "high" and the "low" oral and literary Gaelic traditions that had existed. Calum Maclean (1956–1957) noted that story-telling in the *taigh cèilidh* [cèilidh house] had faded from the Hebrides by the mid-20th century. As English became the exclusive language of the state, the schools, and literacy in Gaelic-speaking areas, it seems likely that many Gaelic speakers in local community contexts gradually stopped seeing Gaelic as the language of knowledge, learning, and a wider *Gàidhealtachd* or Gaelic-speaking region, and instead began to see Gaelic as only a local, spoken language most suitable for interaction with kin and neighbours (Eckert 1983, 293–4 describes such a process occurring in Occitan; for Gaelic see Ch. 8, this volume).

Orally-transmitted informal education in spoken Gaelic and local cultural practices has continued in abbreviated form in family and community contexts through the latter half of the 20th century (Murray 1989). However, many adult first-language Gaelic speakers have received little formal schooling in Gaelic language skills and even fewer have received formal education in other subjects through the medium of Gaelic. The history of Gaelic in Scottish education was for over three centuries one of antipathy, neglect, and absolute refusal in most quarters to acknowledge that Gaelic-speaking children might most easily learn to read and write in their first language, even if the eventual goal was the introduction of English (Campbell 1950; MacLeod 1966). Due to a lack of systematic, consistent national directives for many years, Gaelic speakers' experiences of Gaelic education in the national system have varied according to factors such as year of birth, local authority area, geographical location, and even particular school and teacher. Until at least the mid-20th century, "Individual teachers in some schools in the Highlands and Islands did, over the years, make appropriate use of Gaelic as a teaching medium, but such provision was sporadic and independent of the official education system" (Dunn and Robertson 1989, 44).

Even after efforts began to introduce bilingual education systematically into the official system, these efforts were confined to particular local authority areas. For example, the Inverness Education Scheme begun in 1960 in the Hebridean areas of Inverness-shire described by MacLeod (1966) was applied somewhat unevenly across particular districts and implemented according to the personal judgement of teachers (MacLeod 1966, 326–7). Even the later Bilingual Education Project, whose aim was "to produce Gaelic/English bilinguals with a mastery of the skills of understanding, speaking, reading and writing in both languages" (Murray and Morrison 1984, 16), could not run in all 59 Western Isles primary schools that existed at the time in the new Comhairle nan Eilean Siar area: it ran from 1975–1978 in 20 primary schools, and 1978–1981 in 34 schools. Nigel Grant noted that in 1985 when Gaelic medium education began, "there were fewer Gaels with access to Gaelic medium education than without it" (Grant 1996, 157).

Additionally, adult first-language Gaelic speakers who received instruction in primary school are unlikely to maintain or further develop their Gaelic literacy skills in any way comparable to their English literacy skills, unless they have gone on to study Gaelic at secondary school or in further or higher education, and/or have taken one of the rare Gaelic-essential positions of employment in Scotland. Thus as a result of the social, political, and economic conditions of language shift, including a lack of full state support for systematic Gaelic literacy education for Gaelic-speaking children in Scotland, many first-language Gaelic speaking adults are either out of practice and uncomfortable reading and writing Gaelic in a variety of contexts, or unable to read and/or write it at all. The 2001 Scottish census results seem to support this conclusion. As illustrated in Table 9.1, the total number of 2001 census respondents returned as Gaelic speakers in Scotland is 58,650 (GROS 2005, Table UV12). Of these, 31,235 claimed to be able to speak, read, and write Gaelic, 19,466 claimed to be able to speak Gaelic but neither read nor write it, and 7,949 claimed to be able to speak and read Gaelic but not write it.

Although census statistics are problematic in many ways, as a rough guide it seems significant that 27,415 census respondents, or 46.7% of those who claimed Gaelic speaking ability, also claimed either partial or absent Gaelic literacy skills.[5] In contrast, most adults studying Gaelic as a second language have been socialized to approach the learning of Gaelic through the lens of schooled literacy. Reading and writing are often the primary modalities of studying Gaelic; taking notes, writing on the board, consulting dictionaries, reading

Table 9.1 Gaelic language abilities claimed by respondents in the 2001 Scottish census (Source: Table UV12, General Register Office for Scotland, 2005)

Gaelic language abilities claimed by respondents	Number of respondents
Can speak, read, and write Gaelic ("literate speakers")	31,235
Can speak and read Gaelic but not write	7,949
Can speak but neither read nor write Gaelic	19,466
Subtotal: Respondents claiming Gaelic speaking ability with partial or no Gaelic literacy skills	**27,415**
Can read and write Gaelic but not speak	1,435
Can read Gaelic but not speak or write	4,758
Can write Gaelic but not speak or read	901
Subtotal: Respondents claiming no Gaelic speaking ability but some Gaelic literacy skills	**7094**
Can understand Gaelic but not speak, read, or write	27,219
Other combinations of skills in Gaelic	319
Total: Respondents claiming any Gaelic language ability	**93,282**

literature aloud, and completing written English-Gaelic translation exercises and other homework (which may be checked or graded for correct spelling, vocabulary, and grammar) are some of the main language learning activities in the classroom.[6] The teacher may speak to the students about and/or in Gaelic, and have the students speak to one another in Gaelic, and audio recordings of Gaelic speakers and language exercises may be listened to outside the classroom, but even these activities are generally engaged in with a writing utensil and paper at the ready, for the purposes of transcription and translation exercises. Well-meaning Gaelic learners transfer the concern for correctness of spelling, grammar, and pronunciation of the written word, acquired in formal schooling in relation to English and "modern languages," to Gaelic. Indeed, most adult learners, whose childhood acquisition of English has been augmented and superseded by years of formal education, may not consciously be aware of any other way to engage in second language acquisition than this litero-centric model developed for the acquisition of a state-sponsored, writing-based codified standard language.[7]

What most adult first-language Gaelic speakers in Scotland do share with most adult Gaelic learners is a formal schooling through the medium of English, usually in either the Scottish or the English education system (though indeed the US and Commonwealth education systems are all similar in this regard, as are the continental European systems with their own state-sponsored languages). This formal education has inculcated "schooled literacy" as I have just described, as part of an ideology of standard English in which the standardized written form of a language is the most highly valued, forms of speaking which most closely approximate to this standard written form are also highly valued, and a "speaker" of a language is understood as someone who has mastered not only speaking but also reading and writing a standardized form of the language. Schooled literacy in an official standardized state language is considered a political and cultural ideal by state governments across the developed and underdeveloped world. Thus as one might expect, after the new devolved Scottish government was formed in 1999 the Scottish Executive quickly moved to address concerns about English literacy in Scotland:

> In June 2000, the Scottish Executive announced new political commitment and financial support of £24 million for adult literacy and numeracy, the first significant investment for over 20 years. Learning Connections, a team based within Communities Scotland, was charged with developing and delivering a strategy for improving basic skills. The then Minister for Enterprise and Lifelong Learning, Henry McLeish, launched the adult Literacy 2000 team, which over six months focused on how to raise standards in Scotland. The resulting document, *Adult Literacy and Numeracy in Scotland*, was published in 2001 (National Literacy Trust, n.d.).

The 2001 report mentioned above never explicitly identified the language in question as "English," but it described 800,000 adults with weak or nonexistent English literacy skills in Scotland, although no clear source is given for this figure.[8] Clearly a great deal of money and energy is still being spent on improving English literacy in Scotland (and on publishing reports about it); since the 2001 report, two reports from HM Inspectorate of Education have followed: "Changing Lives: Adult Literacy and Numeracy in Scotland" (2005) and "Improving Adult Literacy in Scotland: An evaluation of adult literacy provision delivered by colleges, local authority community learning and development services and prisons in Scotland" (2010).

Why is literacy in English considered so important to achieve across the entire population in Scotland? The 2001 Scottish Executive report gives a number of reasons, which the authors acknowledge are specific to this social, cultural, political and economic context:

> Ministers have articulated a vision of a modern vibrant Scotland, all of whose citizens are equipped to fulfil their potential. Improving literacy and numeracy will be crucial to that process, so that everyone has the skills to lead fulfilling lives and play a full part in family and community life. Raising literacy and numeracy levels will help promote a wide range of Government policies and priorities such as social justice, health, lifelong learning and economic development. In an increasingly globalised economy, Scotland's future prosperity and competitiveness depends on building up the skills of her existing workforce and improving the employability of those seeking work. But improving literacy skills can also provide the first steps to learning other languages, promoting understanding in a multicultural society, and accessing a whole range of life opportunities. An inclusive society is also a literate society (Scottish Executive Enterprise and Lifelong Learning Department 2001, 7).

Here we can see articulated the cultural ideal of schooled English literacy in Scotland. In this ideal, literacy makes people's lives more self-realized and fulfilling, allows them to better fulfil their obligations to kin and the local community, helps them understand other cultures and get along with one another more easily, and makes them better workers and citizens of the state, not least by maximizing their contribution to the state's competition against other states in a globalized economy. Literacy skills are considered a positive component of selfhood, as the 2005 HM Inspectorate of Education report noted:

> The report confirms that the [national adult literacy and numeracy] initiative [undertaken following the 2001 report previously quoted] is having a positive impact on individuals' lives, and includes impressive personal testimony from many

learners. Literacies programmes are making important contributions to individuals' sense of self-worth and self-confidence (HM Inspectorate of Education 2005).

For Gaelic speakers formally educated in this cultural context, schooled Gaelic literacy may very well take on similar cultural meanings to schooled English literacy. And in turn, Gaelic speakers may also transfer the stigma of non-literacy in English, conveyed by the term "illiteracy," to non-literacy in Gaelic. The potential shame of non-literacy in one's first language Dauenhauer and Dauenhauer describe the role of Tlingit speakers' negative emotions such as pain, fear, shame, and embarrassment in Tlingit language shift in Alaska. The pressure to perceive traditional linguistic practices as bad was applied and perpetuated through the ideologies of the schools and churches throughout the 19th and 20th centuries (Dauenhauer and Dauenhauer 1998, 64–6).

Expressions of negative emotions seem to be common in situations of shift from a minority language to a state-sponsored European language, including grief over the loss (Dauenhauer and Dauenhauer 1995), regret and anger about not having the language passed on to oneself by one's parents (MacCaluim 2007, 267–8), shame at being a speaker of a minority language (Bonner 2001), and denigration and contempt from majority language speakers (Dauenhauer and Dauenhauer 1998; Kuter 1989; Tsitsipis 1981).

An anthropological approach to emotion as universally experienced, yet constructed in particular cultural contexts, can help us understand the source of some first-language speakers' shame about non-literacy in Gaelic. Lutz and White (1986, 406) see emotions as culturally specific ways of dealing with persistent and universal problems in human social relationships. They offer a taxonomy of such problems, of which two are particularly relevant to the issue of how people feel about literacy and non-literacy. They are "1. the other's violation of cultural codes or of ego's personal expectations (or conflict more generally) … [and] 2. ego's own violation of those codes, including social incompetence or personal inadequacy, and awareness of the possibility for such a failure…" (Lutz and White 1986, 427).

If we apply these concepts to the situation under discussion, we can see that by the late 20th century, schooled literacy constitutes just such a "cultural code" in Scotland, and through schooling and family socialization it may also come to constitute a "personal expectation" for many Scots. Concomitantly, such a cultural code would cast the absence of schooled literacy as "illiteracy"—a lack or a failure of some kind. There is a difference between adult Gaelic learners and first-language Gaelic speakers as far as the range of meanings they are able to construct for their own Gaelic and English language abilities in light of such a cultural code or personal expectation. Of the 392 adult Gaelic learners resident in Scotland surveyed by Alasdair MacCaluim, 71.4% aimed to become "fluent in speaking, reading and writing Gaelic" (MacCaluim 2007, 152). A further 5.6% aimed to become "fluent in reading and writing Gaelic," bringing the total respondents including Gaelic literacy in their language learning goals to 77%. In contrast, 14.5% selected oral fluency only—"I would like to become fluent in speaking Gaelic"—as their level of target fluency. We may assume that virtually all of these respondents were already proficient in both spoken and written English. From this perspective, we can see how encounters between adult Gaelic learners and first-language Gaelic-English bilinguals concerning Gaelic literacy may generate "problems of social relationship." Members of both groups share the cultural code or personal expectation of a set of behaviours—writing and reading in their spoken languages—but they do not share the same language socialization and education experiences in regard to Gaelic. This difference may lead to differing positive and negative emotional orientations toward the issue of Gaelic literacy, expressed linguistically through affective stances.

One example illustrates the way that different levels of Gaelic literacy ability may intersect with the ideology of literate speakerhood to prompt expressions of shame and inadequacy. The example is a written exchange between an adult learner (the author) and a first-language Gaelic-English bilingual. In 2003 I sent an email message to a white-collar public employee in the Western Isles requesting information about a Gaelic-related event that had been covered in the local newspapers. This employee had been identified to me as the person who had facilitated the event and could give me more information about it. I wrote the first half of my e-mail message to the employee in Gaelic—painstakingly, dictionary in hand—and the second half in

English, hoping in this way to demonstrate how serious I was about studying Gaelic while not taking an "all-Gaelic-or-nothing" position (and indeed making the assumption that written Gaelic could convey this message just as well as spoken Gaelic could). The e-mail sent to me in reply warmly offered the information I requested, and also stated:

> Your written Gaelic is excellent, putting me to shame! I do apologise for not writing back so, but—although fluent, and a native-speaker born-and-bred—my literacy (in the Gaelic written word) borders on abysmal. I have simply got out of the way of it over the years, but I aim to address this increasing deficiency through practice.

Why does the respondent state that I put them to shame, by writing an e-mail message to them partly in Gaelic?[9] And why would the respondent feel it necessary to state their intention to rectify the situation? The stance of shame articulated explicitly by the respondent, which might also be defensiveness to defuse anticipated disapproval from me as a pro-Gaelic researcher, does not simply come from their awareness of their inability or lack of confidence to write back to me in Gaelic. As already discussed, I believe it is a result of two combined factors: 1) being formally educated and well-practiced in English literacy, and minimally educated in Gaelic literacy and unaccustomed to using it on a daily basis; and 2) being aware of the disparity between one's English and Gaelic writing abilities from the perspective of an ideology of literate speakerhood, in which one is expected to be literate in a language that one can speak. The contrast with this person's demonstrated literacy in English makes the non-literacy in Gaelic seem like even more of a "deficiency," as the person termed it.

In this and other situations it is easy to see how, in the very act of seeking language learning help from first-language Gaelic speakers, Gaelic learners may display Gaelic reading and writing skills that some first-language Gaelic speakers lack, and thereby inadvertently demonstrate what first-language speakers label as a superior Gaelic language proficiency (superior because it is derived from formal education)—even if the learners themselves would disagree with such an assessment.

4 Conclusion: Implications for Future Research and Revitalization Efforts

The participants on both sides of the interactions I call "literacy encounters" seem to share a set of assumptions about written and spoken language in which written skills are prioritized and a speaker of a language is also ideally assumed to be a reader and writer of a language. That is, speaking skills and literacy skills are assumed to be ideally co-present and equally well developed in any given individual, for every language the individual is able to speak. This paper has discussed the disparities in Gaelic literacy abilities and attitudes across the Gaelic-speaking and Gaelic-learning population, and the positive and negative emotions that may be involved in recognizing and giving meaning to one's own Gaelic literacy abilities, or lack thereof, in light of the hegemonic ideology of literate speakerhood.

As the 2001 census results in Table 9.1 show, a substantial proportion of Gaelic speakers in Scotland were reported as having only partial or no Gaelic literacy skills—27,415, or 46.7% of the 58,650 respondents who were reported to be able to speak Gaelic. As already discussed, this is most likely due to the uneven provision and uptake of Gaelic-medium and Gaelic-language education. As Table 9.2 shows, when these figures are broken down by age (albeit in the very unevenly divided age groups provided by the GROS), we find a substantial proportion of partially-Gaelic-literate and non-Gaelic-literate Gaelic speakers in every age group for respondents aged 5 and over. The percentage of self-reported Gaelic speakers who reported partial or no Gaelic literacy skills does vary: it ranges between 24% and 56%, with age groups from 5–11 and 24–90+ ranging from 39–56% and the age group 12–15 with the lowest percentage of partial- or non-Gaelic-literate speakers at about 24%.

This lower figure for respondents aged 12–15 may be accounted for by the numbers of pupils studying Gaelic as a subject in secondary school, where reading and writing form a major part of the curriculum and examinations. Whether this 2001 percentage indicates a permanent increase in the proportion of Gaelic-literate speakers that will register on the 2011 census, or a temporary increase in every cohort of 12–15 year olds that diminishes as pupils leave school and some discontinue the study or use of Gaelic, remains to be seen. More sophisticated analysis of the 2001 census data and comparison with data from other census years will be necessary in order to understand what if any statistical trends may be in progress. In any case, however, it seems likely that among every group of first-language Gaelic speakers in Scotland aged 5 and over, a literacy skills continuum has existed and will likely continue to exist for some time. At one end of the continuum are those Gaelic speakers who are highly formally educated in Gaelic grammar and literacy and use these skills in daily life, and at the other end are those Gaelic speakers who lack any formal education in how to read and write Gaelic.

How might the ideology of literate speakerhood, negative affect, and the differences in literacy skills among different groups of Gaelic speakers impact Gaelic language revitalization efforts? Disparate experiences and attitudes between some Gaelic language learners and some first-language Gaelic speakers make it more difficult for adult Gaelic learners to contribute to the revitalization of Gaelic as a language of daily use in multiple spoken and written domains. They may labour in their classroom-based literacy endeavours, yet be excluded and/or exclude themselves from using Gaelic in daily spoken contexts. Meanwhile, many Gaelic-English bilinguals who use the language in daily life never received training in Gaelic "schooled literacy," and may avoid or even disdain any context in which schooled literacy becomes relevant.

When one becomes aware of literate speakerhood as an ideology, one may more easily refrain from assuming that every Gaelic speaker is also a Gaelic reader and writer. Since almost half of Gaelic speakers reported themselves to be partially-literate or nonliterate in Gaelic, the experiences, attitudes, and linguistic practices of this population should be taken into account in language planning efforts as much as the experiences, attitudes, and practices of speakers who acquire and regularly practice Gaelic literacy skills. An explicit understanding of the disparities and range of skills and attitudes across Gaelic-speaking communities can help in defining desirable language planning goals and target audiences or populations. For example, from the understanding that some Gaelic speakers feel negative emotions about their Gaelic literacy, efforts might follow to communicate the value and

Table 9.2 Gaelic language abilities claimed by respondents in the 2001 Scottish census, broken down by age (Source: Table UV12, General Register Office for Scotland, 2005, with additional data provided by request from the General Register Office for Scotland, 21 August 2009). Percentages are rounded to the nearest tenth of one percent.

	A. ALL PEOPLE (total enumerated population of Scotland)	B. Gaelic speakers total (columns C + D + E total)	C. Speaks, reads and writes Gaelic	D. Speaks but neither reads nor writes Gaelic	E. Speaks and reads but cannot write Gaelic	F. %age of Gaelic speakers reporting full Gaelic literacy skills (column C as a %age of B)	G. %age of Gaelic speakers reporting partial or no Gaelic literacy skills (columns D + E as a %age of B)
All People	5062011	58650	31235	19466	7949	53.3	46.7
0-2 years	161519	317	17	285	15	5.4	94.6
3-4 years	115355	611	45	540	26	7.4	92.6
5-11 years	435574	3928	2362	1274	292	60.1	39.9
12-15 years	259617	2896	2191	556	149	75.7	24.3
16-24 years	566477	5385	3280	1601	504	60.9	39.1
25-34 years	699397	6612	3589	2233	790	54.3	45.7
35-59 years	1757439	20550	10911	6732	2907	53.1	46.9
60-69 years	500849	7810	3781	2656	1373	48.4	51.6
70-79 years	372440	6448	3096	2169	1183	48.0	52.0
80-89 years	164230	3315	1622	1130	563	48.9	51.1
90+ years	29114	778	341	290	147	43.8	56.2

uniqueness of Gaelic orality to new adult learners, to defuse tension between learners and first-language speakers through opportunities and training for structured oral interaction, or to offer consistent and non-judgemental Gaelic literacy training to adult first-language speakers in urban or rural areas.

To increase knowledge and to focus language revitalization efforts, more research is needed on ideologies and practices of Gaelic literacy. In addition to more generation and analysis of survey data, much can be gained from taking an ethnographic approach to ideologies and practices of Gaelic literacy in Scotland (e.g., Pollock 2006), following the lead of literacy scholars like Collins (1995), Collins and Blot (2003), Street (1995), and Street and Besnier (1994). Such research can help us understand the many different ways in which Gaelic speakers define, view, and pursue Gaelic literacy practices. For example, first-language Gaelic speakers may practice not only schooled Gaelic literacy but also multiple kinds of home-taught and community-based Gaelic literacies, including Gaelic Bible literacy and Mòd song text literacy. Different speakers might categorize these literacy abilities differently in their census responses—for example, one person who claims to be only able to read the Gaelic Bible but no other Gaelic texts may claim to be able to read Gaelic, but another respondent with the same literacy skills may claim not to be able to read Gaelic.

Speakers also develop a wide range of affective orientations to Gaelic literacy activities pursued in contexts as varied as primary school, secondary school, college, university, home, religious worship, choir practice, training workshops, and the workplace. Census questions, broad in scope and based on self-assessment, are not able to give a nuanced view of people's language behaviour and ideologies in the way that ethnographic field research using the methodologies of participant observation, interviews, surveys, and proficiency tests can.

When considering the role of Gaelic literacy in Gaelic language revitalization efforts, language planners must also take into account the overlapping but potentially conflicting literacy orientations of states and minority language groups. Modern states have come to view the literacy rates of their populations as indicators of development tied to economic productivity. Many states worldwide claim literacy rates of 95–100% of the population (UNESCO Institute for Statistics, n.d.), but these statistics can be manipulated by defining the criteria for literacy and criteria for membership in enumerated categories of persons in various ways. For example, some states may only include citizens in their count, and some states use the completion of a certain level of compulsory education as a proxy for literacy, without regard for factors such as school attendance or performance. Often statistics do not even specify the language in which literacy is being measured, but the official state language is usually unmarked and assumed.[10]

The UNESCO Institute for Statistics did not have data on literacy rates in the United Kingdom as a whole, and thus the authors of the United Nations *Human Development Report 2009* chose to use a figure of 99% literacy in the United Kingdom to calculate the UK's place in the 2007 Human Development Index (the report does not indicate how the figure was selected) (UN 2009, 171,175). However, it is clear from Scotland's previously discussed concern with adult literacy that the English-speaking population of Scotland (which also encompasses Gaelic-speaking Scotland) is not "fully" literate in English, and this is not explainable solely by the presence of people for whom English is a second or additional language. Thus total literacy in a given population is not necessarily an achievable goal even in a standardized form of an economically powerful "world language" with the considerable resources of a state supporting the effort.

Minority language speakers may take on the state's orientation to literacy, striving to attain full minority-language literacy among their own populations of speakers through systematic education with development-related goals. However, they may also take different perspectives on the relative values and uses of literacy and orality in the minority language, both as a legacy of their own oral cultures and histories and as a response to their minoritized position vis-à-vis the state. One example of the ongoing valorization of non-literate cultural standards for "speaking well" comes from Irish. Coleman (2004) describes the technique of "personation," or acts of imitating other people using direct quotation, as a foundational element in Irish-language conversation and verbal art, including witticisms, narratives of poetic speech, and lyric song. Personation enacts a sociolinguistic ideology that "locates linguistic value in a universe of known or knowable persons and social types, as opposed to other discourses which locate linguistic value in referential transparency or in an idealized national past" (Coleman 2004, 409). Coleman notes that "…Gaeltacht verbal art [using personation] plays an important role in resisting ideological assaults from without" including the assaults of purist ideologies of Irish produced in the name of the post-colonial Irish nation and technocratic discourses of Irish–English equivalency and translatability produced by the Irish state (2004, 408). This counter-hegemonic understanding of what it means to be a good speaker of Irish illustrates one way in which some Irish speakers resist or subvert the norms of nation-state inspired standardization and schooled literacy, and favour contemporary practices derived from norms rooted "in the linguistic and communicative competence of the people who use the language every day," to paraphrase Milroy and Milroy (1999, 23).

For as long as human language has existed, purely oral, non-written languages have existed, and children have acquired their first language largely through hearing and speaking. Moreover, prior to the development of nationalism and nation-states, literacy was not generally cultivated society-wide but was rather the preserve of particular groups or classes in most societies, including Gaelic society. Thus a split or continuum of skills between literate and non-literate first-language Gaelic speakers, or between literate Gaelic learners and non-literate Gaelic first-language speakers, is not inherently problematic. But such a split *is* problematic in a state context where indigenous Gaelic literacies and oralities have been denied and devalued for over 400 years, and narrowly-defined schooled literacy is valued so highly that it helps define the very worth of a language and a culture. It is problematic in a globalized political economic context where minority group existence is justified with reference to the economic productivity of its speakers as bilinguals, when that productivity depends on developing and using "parallel monolingual" standard literacy skills in two languages (Heller 2007; see note 3). And it is problematic to the extent that the revitalization of Gaelic in Scotland is staked on creating a self-sustaining community of fully-literate balanced Gaelic-English bilinguals when nearly half of Gaelic-English bilinguals are partially-literate or non-literate in Gaelic. In these contexts, the spectrum of definitions and practices of Gaelic literacies must not be taken for granted, but must be studied ethnographically and taken into account in the planning of Gaelic language revitalization efforts.

Notes

1 The author wishes to thank the anonymous reviewer as well as Nancy Dorian, Kelda Jamison, and Vanessa Will for their very helpful comments on the manuscript. The General Register Office for Scotland staff generously provided an age and sex breakdown of the data in Table UV12 of the 2001 Scottish Census results. The author is also grateful to the following members of the Language Policy e-mail list for replying to a query about statistics on state literacy rates: Rusiko Amirejibi, Anthea Fraser Gupta, Kathryn Howard, Francis Hult, Joseph Lo Bianco, and Dave Sayers.

2 Other important aspects of the relationship between adult Gaelic learners and first-language Gaelic speakers, including the "etiquette of accommodation" to English among first-language speakers, are discussed and analysed in McEwan-Fujita 2010a (see Ch. 8, this volume).

3 A corollary to standard language ideology is the ideology of bilingualism or multilingualism "as a set of parallel monolingualisms, not a hybrid system" (Heller 2007, 5). In other words, the idea that a multilingual person would possess a parallel and equivalent set of linguistic skills (including literacy) in each of his/her languages (generally defined as standard languages), rather than a "hybrid system" in which multilingual speakers practice constant codeswitching and mixing, and use different varieties (or languages) in different settings for different purposes. Heller states that this ideal of multilingualism as parallel monolingualisms has gained favour in francophone Canada since the 1960s as linguistic minorities have emphasized "access to multiple cultural and linguistic resources" rather than essentialized ethnic identity in order to assert their legitimacy and worth in both the national context and the globalized economy (2007, 4–5).

4 Dorian's 20th-century ESG speakers also practiced a variety of literacies, including English-language "schooled literacy," and for at least one individual an ad hoc self-taught Gaelic literacy prompted by the requests of the researcher (Dorian 1981, 80–92; Dorian 1990).

5 The analysis of census statistics here is complicated by the fact that "literacy" and "partial literacy" are themselves ideologically constructed concepts subject to a wide range of definitions and interpretations, not least by respondents who self-report their Gaelic language abilities. For example, the parents who reported that their children under the age of 2 could read and write Gaelic (Table 9.2, Column C) were probably reporting this in anticipation of the child's future development of such abilities, based on factors such as the speaking of Gaelic in the child's home and/or plans to place the child in Gaelic medium education. A more helpful, but no less socially constructed, benchmark of total "literacy" would be proficiency at schooled literacy in a standard language confirmed by standardized testing. Therefore I take the census statistics at face value here only for the purpose

of generally demonstrating that there are disparities in literacy abilities among Gaelic speakers in Scotland.

6 The Ùlpan and Total Immersion Plus (TIP) models that have been adapted and developed more recently for Gaelic language teaching in Scotland and Nova Scotia, Canada respectively feature a much stronger focus on speaking skills. At the time of writing the author had not yet had the opportunity to study or experience these methods in depth, and thus they are not included in the general description of adult Gaelic language education given here.

7 The California Master-Apprentice Program is a deliberately designed counter-example that helps demonstrate how pervasive the literacy-dominant approach to language learning is, and the challenges it poses for teaching and learning minoritized languages that are non-written and/or lack a strong writing tradition and a standardized form (Hinton 1997; Hinton et al. 2002).

8 The report does mention English six times in the context of describing "people with English as a second or additional language" as target populations, and once in a case study of apparent first-language English speakers: "Margaret and Douglas are both visually impaired. Douglas decided to improve his English skills, because he was becoming increasingly involved with voluntary groups, taking on PR and secretarial functions" (Scottish Executive Enterprise and Lifelong Learning Department 2001, 32). To its credit, the report also calls for greater understanding of the situation of Gaelic speakers described in this paper: "Further work is required to identify the literacy, numeracy and oracy needs of adults whose first language is not English and the needs of fluent Gaelic speakers who have not developed their literacy skills in that language" (*ibid.*, 12).

9 I purposely use the gender-neutral singular pronoun "they" to conceal the correspondent's gender.

10 Many states, including the USA, do not enumerate the speakers of particular languages in their census.

CHAPTER 10

Working at "9 to 5" Gaelic: Speakers, Context, and Ideologies of an Emerging Minority Language Register

1   Introduction

Scottish Gaelic is a minority language that has been undergoing language shift since approximately the 12th century CE in Scotland (Withers 1984).¹ Gaelic is currently the focus of language planning and revitalization efforts in Scotland. One interesting aspect of these efforts is the emergence of an ethnolinguistically identified Gaelic-speaking middle class, a number of whom have become "professional Gaels," or "language workers" as I term them (after the "culture workers" of Whisnant 1983). This chapter explores the way these language workers negotiate the emergence of "professional Gaelic" as a register in the white-collar office workplace.

A register may be defined as "a variety of language associated with situation and purpose" (following Biber 1993; Lamb 1999, 141). Language shift entails an ongoing loss of registers as well as domains and speakers. In Scottish Gaelic, for example, Meek (1990, 11) has noted the progressive loss of command of an upper register of Gaelic based on the language of the Gaelic Bible among Protestant Gaelic speakers born after 1950. Language revitalization often leads to the deliberate or ad hoc creation of new registers which extend an endangered language into new areas of use. For example, Lamb (1999) has described and documented the emergence of "Gaelic news-speak" as a media register.

Register formation is a sociolinguistic process (Biber and Finegan 1993), as are the planning and development of minority and endangered languages. Thus an ethnographic perspective on register formation in a minority language situation can complement a purely linguistic description. In fact, an ethnographic perspective on language revitalization more generally is essential to a full understanding of the phenomenon. Only an ethnographic perspective can show us the processes of language revitalization: the motivations and the daily negotiations of speakers in their social and cultural contexts. My ethnographic analysis is based on four months of participant observation research and interviews conducted in 1999 and 2000 with workers at Comunn na Gàidhlig (CNAG), a Gaelic language planning organization in Scotland.

2 Description of Speakers

Prior to the 18th century, traditional Gaelic society was highly stratified (MacInnes 2006). During the social, economic, and military upheaval of the 18th century, Gaelic-speaking society lost its upper class (the clan chiefs, who became culturally and linguistically anglicized), its learned classes (including hereditary physicians, lawyers, poets, and pipers, whom the clan chiefs could no longer support) and its middle class (the tacksmen, or estate managers, who elected to emigrate). The remaining population of Gaelic speakers was disproportionately impoverished and oppressed, and Gaelic speakers became stereotyped as poor, illiterate peasants, the lowest of the low; Gaelic likewise was assigned the same social significance.

The relatively recent social re-stratification of Gaelic speakers as a group, with the emergence of an ethnolinguistically self-identified "Gaelic middle class" (MacKinnon 1996) may be organizing linguistic variation in Gaelic into a new register of "professional Gaelic."[2] However, the stereotype of Gaelic as a peasant language remains strong in the Scottish public consciousness (see Ch. 3, this volume).[3] Thus ambiguity and conflict among Gaelic speakers (to say nothing of non-Gaelic-speaking Scots) over the very meaning of the social re-stratification in relationship to ethnicity and language is part of the process of register formation. Therefore, my analysis of professional Gaelic focuses on the diverse speakers, sociocultural contexts, and conflicting ideologies of the emerging register.

"Professional Gael" is an ambiguous term; in theory it could refer to professionals of any kind who are Gaelic-English bilinguals. In practice it usually refers only to the relatively small group of Gaelic-English bilinguals professionally employed in the promotion of the Gaelic language. However, educated Gaelic-English bilinguals who work in white-collar professions of all kinds form the demographic basis for this smaller group, and they appear to be increasing in numbers in Scotland (MacKinnon 1996).

"Professional Gael" was not originally coined as a positive term. An anthropologist who studied the Gaelic college Sabhal Mòr Ostaig on the Isle of Skye described the term as:

> a derogatory concept in the Gaelic community used to refer to people who have capitalized on their identity, especially their linguistic and cultural capital, to get involved in Gaelic development, Gaelic broadcasting, or comparable areas (Gossen 2001, 314).

Local Gaelic speakers on the Isle of Skye used the term "half mockingly, half enviously," to describe the ambitious administrators of the Gaelic college (Gossen 2001, 314), and indeed many Gaelic speakers in the Hebrides have viewed economic and social success ambivalently (see for example Jedrej and Nuttall 1996; Macdonald 1997). An ideology of egalitarianism has been enforced in Gaelic-speaking communities such that any individual who appeared to be more successful than others would be open to criticism in the community. Outsiders ("incomers") have often been encouraged to take positions of local leadership (Parman 1990), and locally-born Gaelic speakers have achieved academic or professional success on the mainland, away from the Gaelic-speaking areas. In such circumstances it is not surprising that Gaelic speakers who have sought success openly, particularly through the promotion of Gaelic language and culture, have been criticized by other Gaelic speakers.

A major challenge for professional Gaels who are language workers is to create and negotiate in practice a "9 to 5" or professional Gaelic office environment. The phrase "9 to 5" is familiar to Gaelic speakers from the Dolly Parton song of that title, and I use it to evoke the type of compensated full-time white-collar work that is done in bureaucratically rationalized offices from 9:00 a.m. to 5:00 p.m., Monday through Friday, as opposed to shift work, agricultural or fishing work, offshore work, domestic work, etc. A "Gaelic office" is a hybrid space: on the one hand, it is an office of the bureaucratically rationalized Western (and more specifically British) type, a form of social, economic, and spatial organization where full-time, middle-class work is performed. As such it is embedded in a social and cultural infrastructure dominated by English: all of the workers are bilingual in English, and most of the goods and services received by such an office are provided by non-Gaelic speakers, including postal delivery, repair of office machines, etc.

On the other hand, a Gaelic office is also a site where the business of the office is deliberately conducted as much as possible through the medium of spoken and written Gaelic, and Gaelic linguistic activities are prioritized over English ones. But because the process of language shift has progressively restricted Gaelic language use, lexicon, and registers to non-commercial and informal contexts, most Gaelic speakers (and indeed most other Scots) have come to believe that Gaelic is not suitable for business. They associate Gaelic most strongly with domesticity and rural labor. The dual nature of a Gaelic office as both "Gaelic-oriented" and "white-collar professional" thus necessitates ongoing lexical and pragmatic innovations to extend Gaelic into the business domain. This means that on a daily basis the CNAG workers must negotiate between the practice of professional Gaelic and their own understandings of Gaelic developed mostly in the island-based domains of family and village-level community.

3   The Gaelic Office: Context and Description

"Gaelic offices," defined as Gaelic-oriented bureaucratic professional work environments, are still rare in Scotland. The vast majority of offices, shops, and other businesses in Scotland use Scottish varieties of English; from the 18th century until recently, this even included organizations that concerned themselves explicitly with the support of Gaelic language and culture and the well-being of poverty-stricken Gaelic speakers in the Highlands. One of these organizations, An Comunn Gàidhealach (ACG), began to use Gaelic internally in its operations in the late 1980s, though not without objections from some staff and members who feared that this change would alienate the many ACG members who were "supporters" of Gaelic but unable to speak it themselves.

The English milieu in Gaelic-focused organizations changed relatively recently with the founding of the Gaelic language planning organization Comunn na Gàidhlig (CNAG) in 1984. The first head of CNAG was the instigator of an informal "Gaelic office" policy within CNAG itself. By 1999–2000, most if not all of the organizations with deliberately Gaelic-oriented offices were the ones such as CNAG that were directly involved in Gaelic language revitalization efforts. They included An Comunn Gàidhealach, Comataidh Craoladh Gàidhlig (the Gaelic Broadcasting Committee, formerly Comataidh Telebhisean Gàidhlig, the Gaelic Television Committee), Pròiseact nan Ealan (the National Gaelic Arts Project, originally part of CNAG), Comhairle nan Sgoiltean Àraich, and the BBC offices of Radio nan Gàidheal in Stornoway and Inverness, as well as BBC Alba within BBC Scotland in Glasgow.[4]

As part of a twelve-month period of anthropological research in Scotland for a larger project, I spent three months in 1999 and one month in 2000 based in the CNAG head office in Inverness. During this time I also made two one-week side trips to the Stornoway branch office on the Isle of Lewis.

When I arrived at CNAG in 1999, my communicative skills were typical of the classroom-educated language student; I spoke Gaelic hesitantly, although I could understand, read and write it reasonably well. By the time I returned to CNAG in 2000 for the final portion of my field research there, I could speak Gaelic more fluently after having had more practice and experience over the year. I conducted my field research in both Gaelic and English, with the goal of being sensitive to the linguistic preferences of my interlocutors and the ways in which these preferences were shaped by context. However, the issue of language choice in field research on a minority language is a difficult one, and I explore its implications elsewhere (McEwan-Fujita 2003).

While conducting research at CNAG, I went to the office nearly every weekday for participant observation and interviewing. While taking notes, doing research in CNAG's collection of press clippings, and making arrangements to interview people, I occasionally assisted with minor administrative tasks such as clipping newspaper articles, photocopying, and collating. During and in between these activities I had short conversations with participants on various topics relevant to my research.

In addition to participant observation, I formally interviewed every staff member based in the Inverness and Stornoway offices at least once, using a schedule containing questions about linguistic upbringing, education, current linguistic usage, work history, and current activities at CNAG. I conducted four interviews entirely in English, six interviews almost entirely in Gaelic, and two in a combination of Gaelic and English.

The daily business of the CNAG office revolved around several areas. These included the promotion of Gaelic medium education among Scottish parents and future primary-school teachers, lobbying with the Scottish Executive (formerly the Scottish Office) and the new Scottish Parliament for official status for Gaelic, and general activities to publicize Gaelic in Scotland. Personnel also administered a number of shorter-term projects part-funded by the European Union.

The twelve people working at the headquarters of CNAG during my research were a diverse group of Gaelic speakers in terms of their geographical origins: they represented one mainland Gaelic-speaking area on the northwest coast and five Hebridean islands (Skye, South Uist, North Uist, Scalpay, and Lewis).[5] Ten of the twelve were fluent native speakers of Gaelic who had grown up in homes where both parents spoke Gaelic. Of the other two workers, one had grown up in a home with one Gaelic-speaking parent. By her own account she had not fully acquired Gaelic in the home, but had learned Gaelic to fluency at Sabhal Mòr Ostaig, the Gaelic college on the Isle of Skye. The other worker had grown up as a non-speaker of Gaelic in a home without Gaelic and learned Gaelic to fluency as an adult. All of these people were also fully fluent and literate in English. Thus the CNAG office was a place where Gaelic-English bilinguals speaking different Gaelic dialects mingled and spoke to one another face to face in Gaelic; this inter-dialectal interaction is another important aspect of Gaelic offices which I discuss elsewhere (McEwan-Fujita 2003).

The CNAG workers were also a diverse group in terms of their individual Gaelic linguistic abilities and habits. All of the CNAG workers were fully bilingual in Gaelic and Hebridean or Highland English (Clement 1997; Sabban 1984), as are the vast majority of present-day Gaelic speakers.[6] All of the island-born speakers spoke the particular Gaelic dialectal varieties associated with their district and island of origin. The mainland-born worker who was a non-native fluent speaker made a choice to utilize the dialect form of her district of residence. The other mainland-born worker, the former semi-speaker, spoke a form of Gaelic lacking distinctive dialect features; she had learned to speak Gaelic fluently at Sabhal Mòr Ostaig in Skye.

Because of changes over the years in the geographical organization of the education system and in the role of Gaelic in the schools, workers of different ages had quite different experiences with Gaelic in their schooling. Additionally, some workers born before about 1965 had been Gaelic monolingual when they entered primary school, although some with older siblings had learned English from them prior to entering school. They also had different experiences with Gaelic in their working lives; some had never worked in a Gaelic-related position prior to working for CNAG, while two had come to CNAG after working at a Gaelic publishing company. Two others had used spoken Gaelic occasionally in previous positions working with the public in the Highlands, specifically in interactions with elderly people who preferred speaking Gaelic.

Despite a wide range of schooling and employment experiences, all the CNAG workers appeared to be highly competent in Gaelic literacy skills.[7] For virtually all CNAG workers, as for most native Gaelic-English bilinguals, the use of written Gaelic was almost entirely confined to the work domain. They did not write extensive personal correspondence in Gaelic, although they might include a short phrase in a greeting card. Some individuals with prior Gaelic publishing experience or greater confidence were more involved in proofreading and correcting Gaelic grammar and spelling in written documents. Most of the workers had well-thumbed Gaelic-English dictionaries on their desks which I saw them consulting regularly.

In the office environment of CNAG, staff members would engage freely in English codeswitching and borrowing in informal situations, as did Gaelic speakers in Uist, according to individual inclination and ability. The informal situations in which people spoke this "everyday" Gaelic peppered with English words and phrases included conversations and informal meetings between staff members, and their telephone conversations. As Dorian also noted for East Sutherland Gaelic (1981, 101), the number of English loan-words seemed to be a marker of the degree of formality of Gaelic in the CNAG office. During formal events and in written communications, CNAG workers minimized their use of English loans and avoided codeswitching. The formal events included semi-annual board meetings, the Annual General Meeting (AGM), public speaking engagements, and interviews on BBC Radio nan Gàidheal. The formal written communications, which included press releases, letters, minutes of meetings, and reports, were usually produced in a bilingual English-Gaelic format.

The daily activities of the office included the use of both spoken and written Gaelic. Spoken Gaelic was used in telephone conversations, in casual interactions and meetings between co-workers, and in interactions with other Gaelic speakers, whether they were employees of other Gaelic revitalization organizations, or Gaelic speakers doing business with CNAG (by, for example, installing computer systems). Written Gaelic was used in the creation and distribution of letters, e-mail, faxes, and memos; telephone messages; and company publications including brochures, reports, and meeting minutes and agendas.

However, the CNAG office was completely encompassed by an English-speaking world, and English intruded frequently on the Gaelic office. All the computer software was English-based and included the widely-used Microsoft word processing, spreadsheet, internet browser, and e-mail programs.[8] The majority of the reference books in the office, apart from Gaelic dictionaries, were printed in English. The workers also had to accommodate to the world of English to communicate with the milkman, the postman, parcel deliverymen, and other service providers who could not speak Gaelic.

Telephone callers who could not speak Gaelic were sometimes surprised by CNAG staff answering the phone in Gaelic. On one occasion, the receptionist "Catriona"[9] answered the phone as usual by saying "*Feasgar math, Comunn na Gàidhlig*" [Good afternoon, Comunn na Gàidhlig], and the person on the other end of the line said "I'm sorry, I don't speak Gaelic. Do you speak English?" Catriona, who had apparently grown frustrated with such reactions, told me what the caller said and complained "I just speak Gaelic, I haven't got two heads, and I'm not thick!" My field research and regular review of the Scottish press in 1999–2000 indicated that average non-Gaelic speakers in Scotland, even the ones who telephoned CNAG, still perceived bilingualism or multilingualism as something rare and not always entirely welcome, particularly when it did not involve a prestige European language such as French or German.

Other callers, as well as the postal service, also regularly mistook Comunn na Gàidhlig for An Comunn Gàidhealach, whose headquarters were also located in Inverness. For example, in early October 1999 the CNAG receptionist was constantly interrupted by telephone callers requesting information about the Royal National Mòd—the annual Gaelic singing competition organized not by Comunn na Gàidhlig but by An Comunn Gàidhealach. The Royal Mail also regularly misdelivered correspondence to CNAG that was addressed to An Comunn Gàidhealach. This particularly seemed to happen when the envelope was addressed entirely in Gaelic, despite the fact that since the late 1980s the Royal Mail had officially allowed mail to be addressed in Gaelic as well as English, with the promise of accurate delivery contingent on the use of the postcode.

In the remainder of this chapter, I discuss two pragmatic aspects of the language workers' professional Gaelic in the workplace: 1) workers' evaluations of their own and others' lexical choices; and 2) the problem of developing business etiquette in Gaelic, with a focus on greetings.

4   Evaluations of Lexicon in the Gaelic Office

On a daily basis the CNAG workers were negotiating between the practice of professional Gaelic on the one hand, and their own understandings of Gaelic developed for the most part in the island-based domains of family and village-level community on the other hand. The constitution of this new register involved an acceptance of the very possibility of Gaelic being used in an office domain, as well as the development of strategies to make it possible.

One aspect of this ongoing negotiation was the ambivalence that the fluent bilingual workers expressed about "new Gaelic" words and expressions. Some of my interviewees saw them variously as inauthentic, ridiculous, unaesthetic, viscerally unpleasant, or rigidly purist. In some cases they simply said they didn't like the words. For example, in a Gaelic conversation with "Dòmhnall," a part-time contract employee, about my research activities, I said *"Rinn mi mòran agallamhan"* [I did a lot of interviews]. He repeated the word *"agallamhan"* [interviews] a few times, then commented in English, "I never heard the word until about two years ago. I don't like it very much." (#144).[10]

"Sìne," a full-time employee, expressed a desire for adult Gaelic learners to simply use an English word rather than a newly-coined Gaelic word (#517). This was a sentiment I heard often in various contexts, for the workers themselves frequently used English words in their spoken Gaelic and considered this to be appropriate in everyday informal conversation—even in the Gaelic office. For example, in a casual Gaelic conversation that took place between Sìne, me, and a visiting local businessman, the visitor noted with amusement that a non-native Gaelic speaker who was prominent in Gaelic language planning insisted on always calling the Apple Macintosh computer *Ubhal Mac an Tòisich*, a combination of the Gaelic word for "apple" and the original Gaelic form of the surname Macintosh (#72).[11] As the visitor related how he had insisted that an "Apple Macintosh" is an "Apple Macintosh," Sìne and I laughed heartily, finding the earnest desire to translate absolutely everything into Gaelic amusing since it was out of keeping with the sociolinguistic norms of codeswitching in the Gaelic-speaking areas from which most of the CNAG workers originated.

Sometimes the conflict between cultural authenticity and linguistic propriety was acute. One evening, just before leaving the office for the day, "Anna" asked her supervisor "Ailig" who was staying late if she should put on the answering machine. She asked the question in Gaelic, but used the English word "answering machine." Ailig answered her in Gaelic, saying not to turn it on, because he was expecting some phone calls. I then left the office with Anna, and as we were walking away and talking about something else, she suddenly said to me, "*Inneal-freagairt*, I should have said! But it sounds so silly to say it." She had just remembered that there was a new Gaelic word for answering machine. She seemed to be caught between two genuine, strong, and conflicting impulses: a feeling of responsibility to use Gaelic, and a feeling of ridiculousness for using "new" Gaelic. After some more thought, she said, "I know I should be saying them but it just sounds so strange to say these words. [...] My parents have a completely different way of speaking than I do." I asked her how so, and she just said that anything she said, they would have a different way of saying it in Gaelic (#129).

However, most of these same workers, working as they did with written Gaelic, did use the "new" Gaelic words themselves. When constructing documents with English-Gaelic parallel translations, they might use *An Stòr-Data Briathrachais Gàidhlig*, the book form of the computerized database word-list produced by Sabhal Mòr Ostaig. The database includes many new Gaelic translations for "modern-day expressions," including the names of UK acts of parliament and various Scottish national and voluntary bodies in English (Vathjunker 1992/93). Anna, who felt conflicted about the Gaelic word for answering machine, would also devise new Gaelic words herself if she did not like the new Gaelic words she found in the *Stòr-Data*—I watched her doing this while composing written documents. "Mairead," who fielded many telephone calls and processed a great deal of paperwork, noted all the new Gaelic words that she encountered in her work, like "*iomairt*" [initiative], and complained that sometimes she needed a dictionary to decode them. But she followed this comment with "The thing is, the more you do it, the more you get used to it" (#189). Indeed, I noticed that at other times Mairead used such words without comment. And a senior employee, "Donalda," who had a positive attitude about Gaelic language change, observed at length in Gaelic:

> *Feumaidh sinn faclan ùra… 's tha faclan ùra a' tighinn a-steach dhan a' chànan, dhomhsa, mar chomharradh gu bheil an cànan beò, 's gun an cànan ga chleachdadh. 'S gum feum an cànan atharrachadh, mar a tha an dòigh beatha againn ag atharrachadh.*

> We need new words… and new words are coming into the language, to me, as a sign that the language is alive, and that the language is being used. And that the language must change, as our way of life is changing. (#546)

New words were more than acceptable to Donalda; they were a sign of the adaptation of both Gaelic and Gaelic speakers to a changing world, a positive sign of the continued existence of Gaelic. This shows the diversity of attitudes towards new lexical items, as workers negotiate a way forward through the conflicting demands of cultural authenticity and register development.

5   Professional Gaelic: Professional Manners, Gaelic Greetings

Verbal expressions of etiquette in the context of the Gaelic office are another important aspect of language workers' professional Gaelic where we can see the emergence of new usages as well as negotiation over the forms it should take and the meanings it should carry. When the practice and ideology of professional business are transplanted to a Gaelic-speaking domain, the professional manners must accompany them; or rather, when Gaelic language use is imported into a professional business domain, professionalism must be translated into Gaelic. One area in which we can examine this practice is the area of greetings. The particular greetings used at CNAG, and the commentary surrounding them, provided a way for workers to deal with the contradictions that characterize the extension of Gaelic into the professional realm. CNAG workers were essentially negotiating a way between the ideal of an all-Gaelic office which encompasses linguistic practices of professionalism and business manners, and the ideal Gaelic core of authenticity which indexes a rural, agricultural, domestic island-based environment and their own origins in that environment.

Telephone greetings provide one example of this negotiation between professional Gaelic and rurally-based Gaelic. Catriona, the receptionist at the main CNAG office in Inverness, always answered the telephone before noon with, "*Madainn mhath, Comunn na Gàidhlig*" [Good morning, Comunn na Gàidhlig]. After noon, she would say "*Feasgar math, Comunn na Gàidhlig*" [Good afternoon, Comunn na Gàidhlig]. Mairead, mentioned earlier, did the same. This telephone greeting served the purpose of communicating to callers that the organization was a Gaelic one. It also signaled to Gaelic-speaking callers that they could conduct the telephone conversation in Gaelic. This was important, since Gaelic speakers generally tended to assume that people unknown to them could not speak Gaelic. A bilingual English-Gaelic greeting was not used; the rationale for this was never discussed, but if English was used at all, it could very likely have prompted even many Gaelic-speaking callers to accommodate to the English usage, and therefore in some sense could have compromised the mission of the office. No doubt it could also be cumbersome.

It must be noted that without the receptionist specifically answering the phone in Gaelic, the fact of CNAG being a "Gaelic organization" would not in itself have guaranteed to potential callers, or created the expectation in them, that the person who answered the phone could actually speak Gaelic. For example, as previously mentioned, the nearby headquarters of An Comunn Gàidhealach in Inverness had been an English-speaking office for many years.

"*Madainn mhath*" and "*Feasgar math*" were presented as standard Gaelic greetings in many Gaelic courses for adult language learners. They are the first phrases listed under the "Meeting Friends/Getting Acquainted" section in the phrase book *Everyday Gaelic* (MacNeill 1991). During my research in the CNAG office, several workers and the chief executive would often greet me with "*Madainn mhath* Emily" in the morning when I first came into the office.

However, Anna contested the practice of saying "*Madainn mhath*" on the telephone. She said that she wouldn't say "*Madainn mhath*" when she answered the phone because it sounded wrong, unnatural, and artificial. She interpreted it as a direct calque on English and a sign of English manners:

> *Madainn mhath* doesn't make sense. *Madainn mhath* is something that makes you stick out as a learner. If you're only wanting to be polite, to me "good morning" is an English thing to say [...] For me, I find *madainn mhath* and *feasgar math*, I find that so daft saying it. And people kind of look at you... If I want to say it, I'll just say "Good morning, Comunn na Gàidhlig" [on the telephone], but {pause, change to a musing tone} that gives the wrong impression. But then, Gaelic has changed so much that in the business world it's almost acceptable to say, *madainn mhath* and *feasgar math* (#36).

Implicit in Anna's back-tracking on the preference for "Good morning" in English was the idea that it would give the wrong impression to callers to greet them in English, because CNAG was supposed to be a Gaelic organization. I noticed that Anna had in fact developed her own strategy for answering the phone to avoid "*madainn mhath*" while still greeting callers appropriately as the representative of a Gaelic organization. She said "*Hallo, Comunn na Gàidhlig*" using the Gaelicized form of "hello," which was a borrowing from English and a common greeting in Gaelic-speaking areas (MacAulay 1982, 29). "*Hallo*" could be perceived as more linguistically neutral: a more authentically Gaelic greeting than "*madainn mhath*," less obviously English than "good morning," and indeed Gaelic enough not to trigger Gaelic speakers to accommodate to a perceived use of English.

Anna seemed to be thinking through the issue as she talked, and in her extended commentary, there was an acknowledgement of the professionally-motivated language change wrought by the Gaelic revitalization movement, together with a resistance to that change. Anna recognized the necessity of corpus planning and language change in order to utilize Gaelic in new domains; she noted for example that a college economics course would require the use of a standardized academic language, and a Gaelic-medium economics course at Sabhal Mòr Ostaig, where she herself had studied, would therefore require the use of a standardized Gaelic academic language. However, she resisted the idea of change in the dialectal, spoken form of Gaelic: "But I don't accept that you have to have spoken Gaelic standardized. […] I just see this kind of nightmare scenario where they only […] understand what they hear on the radio." By "they," she meant young people learning Gaelic in the present.

The question of standardization, together with the different social values assigned to Gaelic and English codes (Blom and Gumperz 1972), were the issues at the heart of our discussion of greetings. When I asked Anna what the preferable alternative to "*madainn mhath*" would be in daily face-to-face Gaelic conversation, she said that people would simply comment on the weather as a greeting, rather than saying "good morning." She then related the use of comments on the weather as greetings to the social context of older Gaelic speakers living around the house where she grew up, in a rural district of a Hebridean island. She observed that in 1999, her parents' three closest sets of neighbours were in their 50s, 70s, and 80s respectively, "so this whole concept [of saying *madainn mhath*] doesn't work" for Anna to greet her parents' neighbours in this Gaelic-speaking area, when she visits. This rural island context, both familial and familiar, as well as the particular age range of the interlocutors, is the context that "authentic" Gaelic indexes for many fluent native speakers. Anna's dichotomy between the "crazy" standardized spoken Gaelic greeting "*madainn mhath*" and the authentic, non-standardized comments on the weather is one example of how the native Gaelic speakers working at CNAG remain partial to the idea of "Gaelic" as a spoken variety of idiomatic Gaelic with dialect features indexing their rural, island district of origin and an older age set.

However, while Anna valued this particular context for Gaelic language use, she also recognized reluctantly that it was changing: "Over the last ten years things have changed drastically. It's more anglified. There's not the same amount of mixing as there used to be, [with] people going around to each other's houses. So there's not as much mixing of generations" (#36). In fact, she said that when she was young, the same neighbours of her parents would only speak English to her. She explained that "Older people don't expect children to speak Gaelic, so they just speak to them in English."[12] But, she noted, once the neighbours knew she worked "in Gaelic," they spoke Gaelic to her with no problem.

If "*madainn mhath*" was considered inauthentic Gaelic by some Gaelic-English bilinguals, how did it come to be part of the canon of Gaelic greetings taught to adult Gaelic learners, and an acceptable way to answer the telephone in a Gaelic office?

According to the ideology of standard language (Silverstein 1996, 292), there ought to be a Gaelic equivalent for every English word and expression (see for example Paterson 1964). Every foreign-language dictionary and phrasebook constructs its equivalencies according to this ideology. Moreover, since traditional interlocutor-specific greetings are not so easily taught or learned, teachers of Gaelic may have wished to provide a simpler standardized Gaelic morning greeting equivalent to the standard English one.

The linguistic standardization of Gaelic greetings is also an aspect of professionalization, the issue most relevant to the institutional context of Gaelic language use at CNAG. One fluent Gaelic speaker who had learned Gaelic as an adult attributed the promotion of the use of "*madainn mhath*" as a substitute for the English "Good morning" to Sabhal Mòr Ostaig (SMO), the Gaelic college in Skye. This explanation relates to SMO's original mission from its founding in 1974, which was to provide business education through the medium of Gaelic and thus transform the Gaelic language into a viable tool for business in Scotland. This required transposing Gaelic from the family domain to a white-collar office domain, creating a new lexicon—and pragmatics—as part of a new register of Gaelic.[13] The chief executives of CNAG continued this mission by professionalizing their language revitalization efforts in the 1980s and 1990s.

6 Conclusion

This ongoing effort to professionalize Gaelic highlights the linguistic and social change that Gaelic-speaking areas in particular, and Gaelic speakers in general, have been undergoing in the latter half of the 20th century. More and more Gaelic speakers are becoming professionals of various kinds, and most of them are still moving up and moving out of the traditionally Gaelic-speaking areas of the Hebrides, and settling across the mainland of Scotland. Those among them who become "professional Gaels," earning a livelihood by contributing to the project of Gaelic language revitalization, must negotiate in practice how best to extend the language into a new register. As they see it, they must find a way to "professionalize" Gaelic while remaining true to their own authentic—and non-professional—Gaelic ethnic origins.

Notes

1   Gaelic dialects have become obsolescent in most of the formerly Gaelic-speaking areas of Scotland (e.g., Dorian 1981). Offered here only as a rough guide, the 2001 Scottish census results list 58,650 Gaelic speakers in Scotland; this is just over 1% of Scotland's population of about 5.06 million. A further 37,000 census respondents indicated that they could understand, read, or write Gaelic, or some combination of these, but not speak it.
2   This contrasts with the situation of dialect death described by Nancy Dorian in the localized and isolated Gaelic-speaking area of East Sutherland, where Gaelic speakers all belonged to the same lower socioeconomic class throughout most of the 20th century (Dorian 1981, 152).
3   This sentiment was articulated, for example, in a 1995 editorial in *The Scotsman* newspaper, which stated that the Gaelic language is "a low level peasantish sort of debris." A columnist named Margaret Morrison, writing in the *Daily Mail* tabloid newspaper in 1996, declared that when her ancestors "made their escape from the backbreaking labour of croft life, they left behind the language and culture which went with it."
4   One former BBC Radio nan Gàidheal employee told me that he believed that the Gaelic radio division had struggled with maintaining a

Gaelic-medium office, however, because they shared work space with English-language BBC radio divisions. My limited observation seemed to support this idea: in 1999 I attended a BBC staff party in Inverness, where colleagues from Radio Highland and Radio nan Gàidheal mingled. Nearly all conversation during the party was conducted in English.

5   All of these people did not have the same employment status with CNAG. Nonetheless, they all maintained office space at CNAG or regularly used CNAG facilities, and in so doing, interacted on a regular basis with one another. To highlight this common experience they shared in the workplace, while recognizing the differences in their employment status, as a group I term them "workers" rather than "employees."

6   The only exceptions are some pre-school age children.

7   However, other Gaelic-speaking professionals who did not work in directly Gaelic-related jobs had widely varying levels of literacy.

8   The national Scottish curriculum development organization Learning and Teaching Scotland launched a Scottish Gaelic version of Open Office software in 2005. However, the field research on which this article was based was conducted in 1999–2000, before this software existed.

9   A gender-matched and culturally-appropriate Gaelic pseudonym was used for each participant to preserve anonymity.

10   Numbers in parentheses are the author's fieldnote record numbers. Long quotations are given exactly as transcribed from tape-recorded interviews, whereas short quotations are from written fieldnotes.

11   This literal (albeit ungrammatical) translation thus brought full circle the international linguistic transformation of the Gaelic surname *Mac an Tòisich*, meaning "son of the chief": from its beginning as a Gaelic clan or family name, to anglicized Scottish surname (variously spelled MacIntosh, Macintosh, or McIntosh), to a US American surname (again MacIntosh, Macintosh, or McIntosh), to the name of a variety of apple popular in the US (Macintosh apple), to the appellation of a globally-popular US brand of personal computer (Apple Macintosh), which was then translated back to Gaelic (*Ubhal Mac an Tòisich*), albeit ungrammatically, since the construction should have used the genitive case: *Ubhal Mhic an Tòisich*. It should be noted that the person reporting this usage may have been the one responsible for omitting the genitive case, rather than the original user.

12   A CNAG employee from a different Hebridean island also noted the same phenomenon with her own children and her neighbours.

13   However, Sabhal Mòr Ostaig was not the sole origin of this practice. Nancy Dorian (personal communication) noted that a native Gaelic-speaking teacher at a school in Sutherland enthusiastically used and promoted the expression "*Madainn mhath*" as a greeting in his community, decades before the founding of Sabhal Mòr Ostaig.

PART FIVE

New Speakers and Reversing Language Shift

CHAPTER 11

Gaelic Revitalization Efforts in Nova Scotia: Reversing Language Shift (RLS) in the 21st Century

1   Introduction

Scottish immigrants and their descendants have been speaking Gaelic in Nova Scotia since the last quarter of the 18th century. Gaelic users and supporters are working to revitalize the language in the province in the early 21st century. This chapter demonstrates how academic studies of endangered languages apply to the situation of Nova Scotia Gaelic. The level of endangerment of Nova Scotia Gaelic is determined by using original and expanded versions of Joshua Fishman's Graded Intergenerational Disruption Scale (GIDS). After reviewing some critiques of the scale in light of linguistic anthropology, a new expanded GIDS tailored specifically to Nova Scotia Gaelic is presented which lists the situation, priorities, recommended actions and challenges of each stage of revitalization. The scale can help clarify and guide efforts to reconstruct Gaelic as a spoken language of daily community-based use. Finally, previous 20th-century revitalization efforts are assessed and recommendations are made for goal-setting and coordination between all institutions and voluntary groups involved with Gaelic.

2   Current Situation and Demographics

Scottish Gaelic speakers began emigrating from Scotland to Nova Scotia in the last quarter of the 18th century; the main period of emigration lasted 1770–1840. They came over largely in chain migrations of entire families and communities, adapting to the New World while maintaining and developing their Gaelic language, culture and oral traditions through to the 20th century (Kennedy 2002, 18–19).

The intergenerational transmission of Gaelic from parents to children in homes ceased on a community-wide basis in the 1930s and

1940s in Cape Breton. The timing of this shift was identified through linguistic anthropology field research in Cape Breton, including interviews and Gaelic-language proficiency tests conducted with Gaelic speakers in the communities of Mabou and the North Shore in 1978–1979 (Mertz 1982). The actual intergenerational language shift from Gaelic to English as the language of child-rearing most likely occurred in the previous generation, when the Gaelic-English bilingual parents of children born in the 1930s and 1940s were raised themselves in both Gaelic and English by parents who had been extensively exposed to English in their schooling and employment-related emigration. This conclusion was reached through historical research and the results of a door-to-door survey conducted in Christmas Island and the North Shore in 1990 (Dembling 1991).

A 5% sample produced from the 1901 census results reports Gaelic as the fourth most commonly spoken language in Canada after English, French, and German (Dembling 2006, 206). The sample indicates that the total Gaelic-speaking population of Canada was approximately 90,000 out of 5.37 million, with about 50,000 living in Nova Scotia. In the 1931 census, the number of Gaelic speakers living in Nova Scotia was about 24,000 (Dembling 2006, 207). Twentieth-century Canadian census figures reported by Cosper (1998) show the decline of Gaelic in Nova Scotia since this time, although since 1941 the reported number of "Gaelic" speakers has included both Scottish and Irish Gaelic (Dembling, personal communication, 27 May 2012). The 1941 Canadian census reported 12,065 people with Gaelic as a mother tongue in the province; the 1961 census reported 3,702 people with Gaelic as a mother tongue and the 1981 census reported 1,270 people in Nova Scotia with a "Celtic language" as a mother tongue.

Just as in the 20th-century census, speakers of Scottish Gaelic were not enumerated separately in the 2006 Canadian census statistics (Statistics Canada 2007). Instead, the statistics reported numbers of Gaelic speakers in the two unclear and potentially overlapping categories already mentioned. The first is "Gaelic languages," which could include speakers of both Scottish Gaelic and Irish.[1] The second is "Celtic languages," which could include speakers of Scottish Gaelic, Irish and Welsh. The total reported population of Nova Scotia in 2006 was 913,462. Based on a 20% sample of respondents (those who completed the long census form), the census results reported 890 speakers of "Gaelic languages" in the Province of Nova Scotia, of whom 245 were reported in Cape Breton Island and 200 in the provincial capital of Halifax, with the rest elsewhere in the province. Of these 890 speakers of "Gaelic languages" in the Province as a whole, 460 reported "Gaelic languages" as a mother tongue, whether Irish or Scottish Gaelic.[2]

3   Reversing Language Shift (RLS) and the Graded Intergenerational Disruption Scale (GIDS)

Gaelic in Nova Scotia may be classified as a language that is undergoing a shift and which is the subject of revitalization efforts. In this section I shall define these terms, and then describe and critique a model that assesses just how "endangered" or "vital" a given language may be. The model also includes recommended actions to take in order to reverse language shift at each stage of the process, and, in the following section, I shall apply the model to analyze the particular situation of Nova Scotia Gaelic.

"Language shift" can be defined as a process in which "the habitual use of one language is being replaced by the habitual use of another" in "bilingual towns, villages, or neighbourhoods" (Gal 1979, 1). In such contexts, it is possible for an individual to abandon speaking a language in his or her own lifetime, but more often the way language shift works is that people maintain the use of that language with members of a particular social network throughout their lifetime, and speak a different language to children and others outside that network (Kulick 1992; Gal 1978; also see Ch. 8, p. 236 in this volume).

Users of the language undergoing a shift, or their descendants, may engage in "language revitalization" to try to change this situation. Joshua Fishman, a sociologist of language, has defined language revitalization in a specialized way as "reversing language shift" (RLS): "the theory and practice of assistance to speech communities whose native languages are threatened because their intergenerational continuity is proceeding negatively, with fewer and fewer users ... or uses every generation" (Fishman 1991, 1). More generally, language revitalization can be defined as "the attempt to add new forms or new functions to a language which is threatened with language loss or death, with the aim of increasing its uses and users" (King 2001, 4).

Fishman proposed the Graded Intergenerational Disruption Scale (GIDS) as a tool to determine a language's relative vitality or endangerment on a scale "from full use by many users to no use by any users" (Lewis and Simons 2010, 105). The greater a language's level of endangerment, the further along it is in the process of shift, with the ultimate outcome of shift being language "death" or obsolescence. The scale also suggests the actions that are most important to take in order to ensure the continuation of a language at any given level or stage of endangerment (Fishman 1991, 81). Fishman originally described the GIDS in narrative form, but he later restated it in the form of a table which is adapted here as Table 11.1.

The name of the scale, "Graded Intergenerational Disruption," indicates that its main concern is the degree to which transmission of the language from one generation to the next has been disrupted or maintained. This disruption occurs because when speakers stop transmitting a language from one generation to the next, they lose the main way of creating new fluent speakers in a culturally acceptable context, and hence of reproducing their language community. Therefore, Fishman insists that GIDS stage 6, "intergenerational [language] usage within the confines of the home, family, neighbourhood and face-to-face community" (1991, xii), should be encouraged and stabilized first and foremost in RLS efforts. Although efforts to achieve stages 5 through 1 on the scale are often attempted, and may even seem more urgent and feasible, they will not contribute to reversing language shift unless they also support transmission of the spoken language in homes, families, neighbourhoods and communities.

The GIDS is a powerful tool; it "remains the foundational conceptual model for assessing the status of language vitality" (Lewis and Simons 2010, 104). It has also been criticized for shortcomings, both conceptual and technical. The conceptual points will be dealt with in the following section. To address some of the technical shortcomings, linguists from SIL International have proposed a new version called the Expanded Graded Intergenerational Disruption Scale or EGIDS (Table 11.2), which incorporates the endangerment evaluation scale developed by linguists for UNESCO in 2003, and the language vitality categories developed for SIL International's *Ethnologue*, which aspires to list, describe and categorize all of the world's known languages.[3]

Table 11.1 A summary of Fishman's Graded Intergenerational Disruption Scale (GIDS) adapted from Fishman (2001, 466) and Lewis and Simons (2010, 3). The chart should be read from the bottom up, starting at Stage 8.

STAGE	SITUATION	GOAL
1	The language is used for local and regional mass media and government services	Using the language in education, work sphere, mass media and governmental operations at higher and nationwide levels
2	The language is used in the local or regional work sphere	Using the language in local and regional mass media and government services
3	Children attend schools providing some or all education through the medium of the language	Using the language in the local/regional (i.e. non-neighbourhood) work sphere, both among in-group members and out-group members
4	The language is used orally by all generations and is effectively used in written form throughout the community	Setting up schools that offer some or all instruction in the minority language, either public or private, and either substantially under majority curricular and staffing control or substantially under in-group curricular and staffing control
5	A new generation of children are learning to speak the language as a first language	Setting up schools for literacy acquisition in the language, for the old and young, outside of and supplementary to their compulsory education
6	A cohort including teenagers, younger adults and parents of young children use the language in daily life	Restarting intergenerational mother tongue transmission of the language in an intergenerational and demographically concentrated home-family-neighbourhood-community context
7	Cultural interaction in the language primarily involving the community-based older generation(s)	Creating a cohort including teenagers, younger adults and parents of young children who speak the language comfortably with one another and with older people
8	The only remaining speakers of the language are members of the grandparent generation	Reconstructing the language as it was actually used, and adult second language acquisition of the language

The original GIDS in Table 11.1 has eight stages, while the EGIDS in Table 11.2 has 13 levels, although the new levels are still numbered to correspond clearly to Fishman's GIDS stages. The column marked "UNESCO" correlates the UNESCO Atlas designations of degree of endangerment with the numbered levels. The column marked "Label" incorporates the SIL *Ethnologue* vitality categories and characterizes the overall level of use (Lewis and Simons 2010, 110).

Most of the new levels have been added at the threatened end of the scale, where the authors felt that the most clarification was needed in order to use the scale as a tool to classify the state of endangerment and assist revitalization efforts. For example, the EGIDS subdivides the goal of GIDS Stage 6, "The language is used orally by all generations and is being learned by children as their first language" into Level 6a "Vigorous/Safe" and Level 6b "Threatened/Vulnerable," with the difference between them being that at Level 6a, "The language is used orally by all generations and is being learned by children as their first language" for all children of the child-bearing generation, while at Level 6b this is only the case for some children of the child-bearing generation. These designations are problematic, but they represent an attempt to capture the complexities of language shift in a diagnostic tool.[4]

Levels 0, 9 and 10 are totally new, with level 0 corresponding to international use of the language for many functions—a new ultimate "Safe" category—and levels 9 and 10 further adding to the endangerment end of the scale. Level 9, "Dormant," was incorporated from the 16th edition of the *Ethnologue*, to which it had been added in response to "editorial correspondence from members of ethnic groups who objected to the label of 'extinct' even though no remaining first-language speakers could be identified" (Lewis and Simons 2010, 109).

The authors acknowledged that the general direction of language shift (metaphorically "upward" toward revitalization or "downward" toward obsolescence or death) is as important to consider as the individual stages, and here we see a disjuncture between Fishman's original narrative formulation of the GIDS and its EGIDS adaptation. The original, described as "a typology of disadvantaged languages and ameliorative priorities," is written in an "upward" direction, with recommendations and encouragement for revitalization proponents (Fishman 1991, 81–121). However, the reformulated EGIDS (Table 11.2) keeps the typology and omits the "ameliorative priorities," resulting in a scale that is based on language shift in a "downward" direction. This does not accord well with the perspective of those engaged in language revitalization efforts.

Table 11.2 EGIDS – Expanded Graded Intergenerational Disruption Scale adapted from Fishman 1991 (reproduced from Lewis and Simons 2010: 8)

LEVEL	LABEL	DESCRIPTION	UNESCO
0	International	The language is used internationally for a broad range of functions.	Safe
1	National	The language is used in education, work, mass media, government at the nationwide level.	Safe
2	Regional	The language is used for local and regional mass media and governmental services.	Safe
3	Trade	The language is used for local and regional work by both insiders and outsiders.	Safe
4	Educational	Literacy in the language is being transmitted through a system of public education.	Safe
5	Written	The language is used orally by all generations and is effectively used in written form in parts of the community.	Safe
6a	Vigorous	The language is used orally by all generations and is being learned by children as their first language.	Safe
6b	Threatened	The language is used orally by all generations but only some of the child-bearing generation are transmitting it to their children.	Vulnerable
7	Shifting	The child-bearing generation knows the language well enough to use it among themselves but none are transmitting it to their children.	Definitely Endangered
8a	Moribund	The only remaining active speakers of the language are members of the grandparent generation.	Severely Endangered
8b	Nearly Extinct	The only remaining speakers of the language are members of the grandparent generation or older who have little opportunity to use the language.	Critically Endangered
9	Dormant	The language serves as a reminder of heritage identity for an ethnic community. No one has more than symbolic proficiency.	Extinct
10	Extinct	No one retains a sense of ethnic identity associated with the language, even for symbolic purposes.	Extinct

Therefore, Lewis and Simons also produced an alternate version of the EGIDS (Table 11.3), with levels 6b through 9 reframed as moving toward revitalization rather than extinction. For example, the EGIDS Stage 6b "Threatened"—"The language is used orally by all generations but only some of the child-bearing generation are transmitting to their children"—is re-conceptualized as the Revitalization EGIDS Stage 6b, "Re-established": "Some members of a third generation of children are acquiring the language in the home with the result that an unbroken chain of intergenerational transmission has been re-established among all living generations" (Lewis and Simons 2010, 117).

4 Sociolinguistic and Cultural Factors Impacting Assessment of Endangerment

The GIDS and EGIDS are tools for comparative and macro-level analysis. Yet anthropological studies of language shift at the micro-level, the local or community level, show us that much of what is salient and important to understand about each situation of language shift actually happens at the level of cultural ideologies, affective experiences, and face-to-face interaction, in the context of particular historical experiences (Gal 1978; King 2001,17–21; Kulick 1992; Mertz 1982; Ch. 8, this volume). Linguistic anthropological analyses also contribute several points about the nature of communities and language use that must be incorporated into any assessment of language endangerment and priorities for revitalization. Three of these points are described here.

1. Language shift and revitalization efforts are uneven, both demographically and ideologically. The stages of language shift represented in the GIDS and EGIDS are not always sequential or mutually exclusive, and revitalization efforts never proceed smoothly or without contestation. As will be discussed in the following section, multiple stages of both shift and revitalization can be occurring simultaneously in different areas of any given geographical region. Multiple stages can even be occurring in the same time frame within a given family, a point that follows on from the observation that families are not homogeneous sites of language transmission (see point 2 below). Moreover, as can be seen in Table 11.4, column V, "Main Challenges," cultural and ideological factors play key roles in processes of language shift and revitalization efforts (Dauenhauer and Dauenhauer 1998).

Table 11.3 Revitalization EGIDS Levels (reproduced from Lewis and Simons 2010, 117)

LEVEL	LABEL	DESCRIPTION
6a	Vigorous	The language is used orally by all generations and is being learned by all children as their first language.
6b	Re-established	Some members of a third generation of children are acquiring the language in the home with the result that an unbroken chain of intergenerational transmission has been re-established among all living generations.
7	Revitalized	A second generation of children are acquiring the language from their parents who also acquired the language in the home. Language transmission takes place in home and community.
8a	Reawakened	Children are acquiring the language in community and some home settings and are increasingly able to use the language orally for some day-to-day communicative needs.
8b	Reintroduced	Adults of the parent generation are reconstructing and reintroducing their language for everyday social interaction.
9	Dormant	Adults are rediscovering their language for symbolic and identificational purposes.

Revitalization efforts are subject to the multiple and conflicting ideologies of participants, and can engender encounters laden with both positive and negative affect (see Ch. 8–9, this volume).

2. Children are socialized not only in families, but also in communities. Assumptions about how children are socialized to speak a native language must be expanded. A "mother tongue" is not only or necessarily learned from a child's mother. Families and homes are not necessarily institutions where parents reproduce biologically or linguistically. Siblings in the same family can develop very different levels of competence in the first language of the parent(s) (Spolsky 2009), and can also develop different ideologies and affective orientations toward the minority language depending on birth order, education experiences, emigration and other factors (e.g., Dorian 1980).

Many supporters and detractors of Fishman's GIDS overlook his point that the entire home-family-neighbourhood-community nexus is included in the support of intergenerational transmission, including neighbourhood institutions (1991, 92–93). This nexus encompasses not only parent-child and grandparent-grandchild relationships, but also many other kinds of language socialization relationships (see Ochs 1990, 302–303). Adults can socialize other adults and can socialize children of all ages in many capacities (extended family member, family friend, teacher, coach, lunchroom supervisor, religious leader, store clerk, etc.). Children can socialize each other and can socialize adults, as well. In fact, any "expert" can socialize any "novice," as long as the people involved take the roles of expert and novice in interaction. Canadian education researcher Mark Fettes (1997) expands on the idea that multiple kinds of social relationships besides home-based and parentally provided immersion can help to reverse language shift: "any meaningful long-term relationship conducted in the language helps to establish an intergenerational network of relationships."

3. "Community" can be defined in many different ways. There are multiple ways of conceptualizing minority-language speakers as a community or communities, and these impact the assessment of a language's level of endangerment. In Nova Scotia, a "Gaelic community" can be defined in two different ways: (1) as a traditional geographically defined locale where people speak Gaelic to one another in face-to-face settings in daily life (a town, village, district, island, etc.), or (2) as "communities of practice" which are defined as "groups of people who share a concern or a passion for something they do and learn how to do it better as they interact regularly" (Wenger 2006). A Nova Scotia-wide[5] Gaelic community of practice is composed not of Gaelic-speaking localities where individuals encounter one another in daily life, but rather of Gaelic-speaking individuals who gather and work together in smaller communities of practice at multiple levels (Wenger 1998). Gaelic communities of practice include social networks of friends and acquaintances (including digitally mediated networks), voluntary organizations, Gaelic language classes, cultural and recreational events, and part-time & full-time employment. Although a sense of geographical place is culturally significant and important to community members, and travel times and fuel costs constrain their mobility, 21st-century Gaelic communities of practice are built more fundamentally around members' shared concern and passion for Gaelic, their shared learning experiences and regular interaction at planned events than around chance daily encounters and shared residence in a locale.

5   Nova Scotia Gaelic: Level of Endangerment and RLS Priorities

How endangered is Nova Scotia Gaelic, and where is it currently positioned on the EGIDS? I have created the Nova Scotia Gaelic EGIDS (Table 11.4) to help answer this question. The table adapts the numbering and wording of Fishman's original GIDS stages (Table 11.1), the terminology and some expanded numbering of the Lewis and Simons EGIDS shift and revitalization scales (Tables 11.2 and 11.3) and the points made above. For each stage, separate columns describe the starting point (II), the recommended goal (III), specific actions to achieve the goal (IV), and the major challenges, both ideological-emotional and technical-practical (V). The GIDS framework is not often presented in a table form tailored to one particular language situation, but this format (inspired by Dauenhauer and Dauenhauer 1998) allows for greater inclusion of relevant local and cultural factors in the scale. Separating the starting point from the goal helps to clarify the difference between these two for each stage, and to highlight the key role of the goals in the scale; these points are not as clear in previous summary versions of the GIDS (Fishman 2001, 466; Lewis & Simons 2010, 3).

Assessing the situation from the perspective of a Nova Scotia-wide community of practice, Gaelic is at GIDS Stage 8. I shall discuss this in greater detail but first must make the point that although revitalization efforts are ongoing in a community of practice, language shift is also still advancing or already completed in most traditional geographically-bounded communities that were formerly Gaelic speaking. In most areas of its former heartland, Cape Breton Island, Gaelic is at EGIDS Stage 8b "Nearly Extinct": "The only remaining speakers of the language are members of the grandparent generation or older who have little opportunity to use the language" (Table 11.3; also see Table 11.4, stage 8, column II). For most other geographical areas in eastern Nova Scotia where Gaelic was spoken in the 18th through 20th centuries, for example in Pictou and Antigonish Counties, it is currently at EGIDS Stage 9 "Dormant": "The language serves as a reminder of heritage identity for an ethnic community. No one has more than symbolic proficiency." Gaelic is also "Dormant" in the Halifax area: families and individuals migrated from Cape Breton

Table 11.4 The Nova Scotia Gaelic EGIDS. Selected stages of Fishman's Graded Intergenerational Disruption Scale or GIDS (1991, 81-111) and Lewis and Simons' Expanded GIDS or EGIDS (2010), adapted to the situation of Gaelic in Nova Scotia. NOTE: Scale is to be read from the top down.

I. STAGE	II. STARTING POINT	III. GOAL	IV. HOW TO ACHIEVE	V. MAIN CHALLENGES
10	*Extinct:* In many formerly Gaelic-speaking areas, no one retains a sense of ethnic identity associated with Gaelic, even for symbolic purposes	*Rediscovered:* Make people, particularly those of Scottish ancestry, aware that one-third of people in Nova Scotia have Gaelic-speaking ancestors and that Gaelic is still spoken in Nova Scotia	Public, voluntary and personal awareness efforts, consciousness-raising, advertising, marketing, encouraging the use of written, spoken and sung Gaelic in public	People's lack of knowledge about provincial and family history; Gaelic is written out of history books, and knowledge of its existence suppressed Logistical and financial limitations of advertising and marketing
9	*Dormant:* Gaelic serves as a reminder of heritage identity for some members of the Gaelic and Scottish ethnic communities in Nova Scotia, but no one has more than symbolic proficiency (e.g., using the phrases "Ciad mìle fàilte" and "Ciamar a tha sibh?")	*Rediscovered:* Adults rediscover their language for symbolic and identificational purposes (including symbolic displays of written Gaelic, memorization and performance of song texts, and casual participation in social events and language courses)	Public, voluntary and personal awareness efforts, consciousness-raising, advertising, marketing, encouraging the use of written, spoken and sung Gaelic in public Make people aware that the Gaelic language is a unique aspect of Nova Scotian culture and a preferred vehicle of Gaelic culture, and that there are opportunities to learn and speak Gaelic in present-day Nova Scotia	Joking, animosity, willful ignorance and lack of interest from non-speakers, including people claiming Scottish ethnicity Logistical and financial limitations of advertising and marketing Many adults' satisfaction with remaining at this level or lack of resources (time and money) to take their Gaelic-learning efforts further

| 8 | *Rediscovered yet Moribund:* Some adults use Gaelic for symbolic purposes, but the language is only spoken natively by elderly people, some of whom are socially active (EGIDS 8a, Moribund), but most of whom have few opportunities for social interaction (EGIDS 8b, Nearly Extinct) | *Reintroduced:* Reconstruct spoken Nova Scotia Gaelic for multiple social uses

Build a core group of middle-aged adult Gaelic learners and users (who may be geographically scattered) | Locate as many Gaelic-speaking elders as possible and socially re-integrate them into Gaelic-medium interaction

Documentation: record everyday spoken-language, expressions, oral traditions from native speakers

Create courses and programs in which adults acquire Gaelic as a second language

Bring native Gaelic-speaking elders into contact with interested adults through the medium of Gaelic | Possible social isolation or poor health of elderly people; possible refusal to identify themselves as speakers of a formerly stigmatized language

Setting documentation goals: dialects, words, expressions, discourse genres (conversation, childcare, storytelling, etc.)

Coordinating community-level and academic documentation efforts

Archiving documented language and utilizing it in teaching materials so that it is accessible to learners

Designing Gaelic language curricula and teaching methods that are both effective and culturally acceptable

Adults obtaining language instruction of sufficient duration and intensity to attain fluency in Gaelic—more than a few hours per week

Selecting a target Gaelic variety to acquire—which dialect, which teachers

Difficulty of acquiring accurate pronunciation of Gaelic as a second language

Possibility that Internet-based interaction and Gaelic cultural events (singing, instrumental music, dance, storytelling) may not lead to acquisition of daily spoken language |

I. STAGE	II. STARTING POINT	III. GOAL	IV. HOW TO ACHIEVE	V. MAIN CHALLENGES
7	*Reintroduced*: Gaelic is used for cultural interaction primarily by adults who are middle-aged and older ("beyond child-bearing age"), with one another and with elders	*Reawakened*: Build a cohort including teenagers, younger adults and parents of young children who comfortably and regularly speak Gaelic as a second language with one another and with older people.	Create "communities of practice" where young people witness adults speaking Gaelic (based on geographical proximity, social networks and regular, enjoyable gatherings and events). Generate interest in Gaelic among teenagers and young adults and parents of younger children Provide effective instruction in spoken Gaelic for teenagers, young people and parents Create youth groups, parenting groups and family-friendly multi-generational events	Competing with majority culture and English-medium jobs to attract interest and time commitment of young people Parents' inability to attend Gaelic classes and events without childcare Insufficient level of Gaelic instruction in public education and universities for bringing students to spoken fluency Universities' not being allowed to release contact information of Gaelic students/alumni to facilitate network building Traditional geographical communities no longer the basis for daily Gaelic use; must plan for "communities of practice" based on shared orientations to Gaelic Different needs and characteristics of different Gaelic communities of practice (e.g. rural vs. urban) Competition with, rather than medium of, family and leisure activities Gaelic cultural activities (e.g. singing, music and dance) not necessarily supporting acquisition of daily spoken Gaelic by parents, young adults, adolescents and children

| 6 | Reawakened: A cohort that includes teenagers, younger adults and parents of young children is using Gaelic as a second language with each other and older people | Re-established and Revitalized: Children are raised in Gaelic in the home and/or daycare, by parents, grandparents and/or other caregivers

In this way, a new cohort of first-language Gaelic speakers is created

Gaelic speakers are demographically concentrated in multigenerational communities, or at least gather regularly face-to-face

Gaelic-speaking communities are reinforced by the support of local institutions | Encourage and support Gaelic speakers who become parents to use Gaelic in the home when raising children

Train young adults and older adults to be Gaelic-medium childcare providers

Create Gaelic-medium daycare and preschools to support families

Develop other "family-friendly" Gaelic institutions and events | Most new Gaelic users' lack of language skills, registers and confidence to speak Gaelic to children

Some new Gaelic users' possible transmission of a hybridized, anglicized Gaelic to children

Children raised speaking Gaelic become socially isolated from other Gaelic speakers

Support of Gaelic by one parent only

Other challenges continue as at Stage 7 |

I. STAGE	II. STARTING POINT	III. GOAL	IV. HOW TO ACHIEVE	V. MAIN CHALLENGES
5	*Revitalized and Vigorous:* Children are learning Gaelic as a native language, starting at age 0-3. Gaelic is spoken by people of all generations with one another informally in daily life (child-parent-grandparent, older-younger, expert-novice)	*Written:* Children acquire "guided" Gaelic literacy to support their speaking abilities All Gaelic-speaking community members acquire literacy which can indirectly and directly support Stage 6 RLS goals (indirectly in terms of symbolic identity and status; directly in terms of intergenerational social interaction)	Provide Gaelic literacy instruction to children and adults at the local or community level, under Gaelic community control (for example, incorporate basic Gaelic literacy instruction into children's Gaelic-medium programs such as summer camps and extracurricular activities) Develop goals, a curriculum and lessons for providing basic Gaelic literacy instruction	Lack of fluent adult Gaelic speakers who are also literate in Gaelic Some speakers' cultural preference for orality and oral cultural forms Gaelic orthography challenging for literate English speakers Possibility that Gaelic literacy activities may substitute for, not support, intergenerational transmission of spoken Gaelic Possibility that community-based literacy instruction be seen as competing with the schools

| 4 | Written: There is a Gaelic community of children and adults who understand and speak conversational Gaelic and can read and write basic Gaelic | Educational: Children attend schools providing some or all education in Gaelic

The schools represent Gaelic cultural space, and are not just agencies for the transmission of "neutral" (majority) knowledge, skills and attitudes. Ideally, they are publicly funded (like Fishman's type 4b schools) but substantially controlled by Gaelic speakers (like Fishman's type 4a schools, e.g., Conseil Scolaire Acadien Provinciel in NS). | Obtain the legal right and funding to set up Gaelic-medium public schools. (Depend on parental demand, lobbying by Gaelic voluntary groups, political goodwill, political patronage and federal or provincial official status legislation.)

Build schools, create an administrative framework

Develop a Gaelic-medium curriculum following NS provincial guidelines

Develop new Gaelic teaching materials for the curriculum (books, activities, lesson plans)

Train fluent Gaelic-speaking teachers

Ensure that schools are "indigenized" in their operations, personnel, program revision and control, budgets, etc. | Possibility of conflict between culturally appropriate Gaelic-medium subject matter and teaching methods and majority anglophone federal and provincial guidelines for a literacy-based school curriculum

Possibility that adult Gaelic users will view Gaelic-medium schools for children as the saviour of Gaelic, and feel that they have no personal responsibility to socialize children in Gaelic outside of formal education

Necessity of a written standard or norm for the development of written educational materials

Possibility that education activities, most of which are literacy-related, will be based on a standardized form of Gaelic that is not accessible or acceptable to traditional native speakers

Parents' view that their children's future employment prospects are linked to English-medium schooling

Public opposition to use of public funding for Gaelic-medium schools |

I. STAGE	II. STARTING POINT	III. GOAL	IV. HOW TO ACHIEVE	V. MAIN CHALLENGES
3	*Educational:* People educated in Gaelic seek work, but also wish to maintain ethnolinguistic identity and revitalize their communities in economic terms	*Trade:* Gaelic is used by adults in the work sphere outside of the Gaelic community, beyond the sphere of education already implied in Levels 5 and 4	Discussion omitted here	Discussion omitted here
2	*Trade:* Gaelic is transmitted in home and community, taught in schools and used in some work situations	*Regional:* The beginning of the "Big League": Gaelic is used in "lower" governmental services and mass media	Gaelic Affairs provincial government office is in place Further discussion omitted here	Discussed omitted here
1	*Regional:* Gaelic is used in "lower" governmental services and mass media.	*National:* Gaelic is used in some higher level educational, occupational, governmental and media efforts	Discussion omitted here	Discussion omitted here

to the Halifax area, and many know that they had Gaelic-speaking parents, grandparents, great-grandparents or ancestors. Therefore, when these areas are considered as traditional geographically based communities, Gaelic is in the end stages of language shift, although in these areas there is also a great deal of goodwill toward Gaelic which could still be mobilized to help both people themselves and the language. It is only within intentional communities of practice, composed mainly of active groups of adult Gaelic learners, that we can assess Gaelic as in the process of being at Stage 8 of revitalization.

The twin goals of GIDS Stage 8, the reconstruction of spoken Nova Scotia Gaelic for multiple social uses and the creation of a core group of fluent middle-aged Gaelic users, are currently being pursued by individuals, a range of voluntary groups and institutions, and the Gaelic Affairs division of the Nova Scotia Department of Communities, Culture and Heritage. Adults are learning Nova Scotia Gaelic by teaching and taking language courses and participating in various cultural events and organizational activities. The introduction of "Total Immersion Plus" style Gàidhlig aig Baile (GAB) classes in Nova Scotia in the past decade appears to have strengthened this stage, as has the development in recent years of the Bun is Barr program based on the California Master-Apprentice program developed by Hinton et al. for aboriginal languages (Hinton 1997; Hinton, Vera and Steele 2002).

The essential measure of success at this stage is whether a "core group" of adult speakers has yet been created. However, "core group" is a fundamentally ideological concept, and its existence cannot be assessed in purely quantitative terms. Future research may be able to quantify how many adults are currently involved in Gaelic-language learning, how much time they spend learning and their levels of fluency and use. A documented increase in the number of fluent speakers would indeed be a very helpful point of reference, but in itself does not guarantee the formation of a core community of practice that can work together to reverse language shift.

However, an evaluation of whether this core group exists can still be made with reference to progress through the GIDS stages. On the basis of recent participant observation and experience, it is clear to the author that members of the adult Gaelic-speaking community of practice in Nova Scotia do strongly wish to sustain the language, but as of the time of writing in 2011, the community cannot yet support the attainment of GIDS Stages 7 and 6.

How close is the Nova Scotia Gaelic community of practice to the starting point of Stage 7, where Gaelic is being used for regular social interaction primarily by adults who are middle-aged and older? As already mentioned, this is a question not only of how many middle-aged and older users there are (enough to sustain regular interaction and a variety of voluntary activities), but also a question of the proficiency level of those users (how many are fluent) and the frequency of their Gaelic-medium interactions (which is partly though by no means wholly a function of their physical proximity). My assessment is that currently there are not enough fluent middle-aged Gaelic users who interact with each other frequently enough in Gaelic to form a solid social network base for sustaining progress toward the goal of Stage 7: to create a "younger cohort of [Gaelic]-as-a-second-language-users" (Fishman 1991, 90), a cohort including teenagers, younger adults and parents of young children who regularly speak Gaelic as a second language with one another and older people.[6] As was the case throughout the 20th century, the people who are currently working for and in Gaelic are spread too thinly on tasks both central and peripheral to RLS, and risk burning out. Other Gaelic speakers have been "brain drained" away from the province.

Even if the community were considered to have already advanced to the starting point of Stage 7, the challenges of achieving the Stage 7 goal of creating a cohort of fluent Gaelic-speaking young adults and parents of young children are still very great. Devoting time to Gaelic learning is difficult for parents of young children. Participation in adult Gaelic evening classes and many Gaelic events in the province requires leaving one's young child(ren) with a non-Gaelic speaking caregiver. This creates a situation in which Gaelic learning tends to be an activity for retirement-age adults. Attracting parents and young adults is also difficult because Gaelic also has to compete with other highly valued family and leisure activities, such as hockey, rather than serving as a medium for such activities. Gaelic RLS supporters are competing with the majority English-medium culture and its employment opportunities to attract the interest and time commitment of young people. When Gaelic does capture their interest in public education and universities, the courses do not bring students to fluency, and most students of Gaelic melt back into the general populace after graduation rather than integrate into a Gaelic community of practice.

There is some progress toward the Stage 7 goal: approximately ten to fifteen young adults in their twenties have become fluent in Gaelic during the past five years or so through a combination of university courses, courses at the Gaelic college Sabhal Mòr Ostaig in Scotland, Gàidhlig aig Baile classes, and the Bun is Barr master-apprentice program. They are actively involved in a Nova Scotia Gaelic community of practice; for example, periodically over the past two years, one person has held a Gaelic immersion week for young adults on the North Shore. However, we do not know how the number of young adults involved now compares to the number of young adults involved in Gaelic in the 1970s, or the 1990s.

Where is Nova Scotia Gaelic with respect to achieving the all-important RLS goal of Stage 6, intergenerational transmission of Gaelic in the home-family-neighbourhood-community context? This goal is highlighted in bold type in Tables 1 and 4 to indicate its importance as the foundation or keystone of RLS. Some individuals in eastern Nova Scotia are making efforts to transmit Gaelic to children in the home. I have identified fewer than twenty families in eastern Nova Scotia with one or more children aged 0–18 in which one parent can speak Gaelic, and two families in which both parents can speak Gaelic, in which one or both parents are making, have recently made or plan to make attempts to speak Gaelic to the children. There is enormous diversity among these families both in terms of their geographical areas of residence (scattered across eastern Nova Scotia) and the type of family (two-parent or single-parent, "original" or blended, biological or adopted children). Gaelic usage patterns are similarly diverse among the parents in these families, with a Gaelic-speaking parent attempting to use all Gaelic, some Gaelic, or a few words and phrases. Some parents working on Stage 6 goals experienced the interruption of intergenerational transmission in their own lifetime, or married into a family that did, and others are introducing Gaelic into their families for the first time ever or for the first time within living memory.

These parents are dedicated, but what is still missing to achieve the goal of Stage 6 is not only greater numbers but also the "neighbourhood-community" element of the "home-family-neighbourhood-community" nexus which can be built up when the goal of Stage 7 is achieved. As described already in the third section of this chapter, children are socialized not only in families, but also in communities, and the entire home-family-neighbourhood-community nexus is included in the support of intergenerational transmission, including neighbourhood institutions (Fishman 1991, 92–93) such as voluntary organizations. This nexus encompasses many kinds of language socialization relationships, as already mentioned (Ochs 1990, 302–303).

When new efforts to revitalize Nova Scotia Gaelic are placed on the EGIDS, one can see more clearly how they relate to the priority of achieving the goal of intergenerational transmission at Stage 6. Some efforts support the goals of Stages 8, 7 and 6 directly, some indirectly and some perhaps not at all. For this reason, Fishman's original GIDS description advocates treating "higher-order" RLS efforts with caution until intergenerational transmission has been achieved, lest resources and efforts be diverted inappropriately. This does not mean that no higher-order efforts should be attempted; sometimes they seem essential to overcoming centuries of oppression and denigration of the language (Fishman 2001). For example, the 2006 establishment of the Office of Gaelic Affairs, now a division of the Department of Communities, Culture and Heritage in the Nova Scotia provincial government, is a highly significant recent achievement at GIDS Stage 2 and 3, bringing Gaelic into governmental services and the (non-education-related) work sphere. Gaelic Affairs supports the goals of Stages 8, 7, and 6 directly: it produces publicity materials which may bring more adults from Stage 9 into Stage 8, runs its own Stage 8 project (Bun is Barr), materially supports another Stage 8 effort (the teaching of Gàidhlig aig Baile courses to adults) and provides grants to community groups whose projects may work toward the goals of Stages 8, 7 and 6.

On the other hand, Gaelic is also taught in some public primary schools, which might initially be considered an example of GIDS Stage 4. However, Gaelic can only be taught as a subject to some children in selected public primary schools in Antigonish County and Cape Breton Island, which is very different from the Stage 4 goal of a Gaelic-medium school with a culturally Gaelic curriculum under the control of Gaelic-speaking administrators (see Table 11.1 and Table 11.4). A place for Gaelic in Nova Scotian public schools has only been achieved through strenuous effort, and is maintained and developed through many hours of hard work, both paid and voluntary, by dedicated and talented individuals. But the level of "foreign" language instruction that is allowed to be provided in Nova Scotia public schools has never supported pupils to attain fluency in Gaelic, or even in French (which is not only one of Canada's federal official languages, but also a living and heritage language of many Nova Scotians). Thus, the limited way in which Gaelic is currently allowed to be taught in the schools draws some of the most concentrated efforts to assist Gaelic, but it does not appear to directly support the attainment of Stage 6, intergenerational transmission. It supports Stages 10 and 9: it may make more parents and students aware of Gaelic as a "real" language with a history in the province, and may awaken an interest in some parents and students to learn their heritage language after the "critical period" for children's language acquisition is past.

6 A Historical Perspective on RLS: 20th-Century Revitalization Efforts

The Nova Scotia Gaelic EGIDS presents the recommended way forward if a community of practice wishes to revitalize Gaelic as a spoken language of daily use. However, the scale cannot account for all relevant factors, and a brief review of previous revitalization efforts produces a more sobering assessment of the obstacles to attaining GIDS Stage 6 and reversing Gaelic language shift in Nova Scotia.

In looking at accounts of "Gaelic revival" in 20th-century Nova Scotia, we find that while language shift progressed gradually from EGIDS Level 6a, through 6b and 7, to 8a, 8b and 9 (Table 11.2), concurrent Gaelic revitalization efforts did not successfully move beyond the goal of GIDS Stage 8, creating a significant group of fluent adult speakers who are middle-aged and older (Table 11.4). Mertz summarized efforts to revitalize Gaelic in eastern Nova Scotia from the 1920s through 1980 (1982, 187–227) and noted that:

> There have been revival attempts emanating from [Sydney, Antigonish and St. Ann's] at sporadic intervals throughout much

of the twentieth century. Yet these separate attempts have generally failed to unite the disparate groups supporting Gaelic in Cape Breton—or in Nova Scotia as a whole. Aside from [these three centres], there have also been many individual attempts by members of rural communities in Cape Breton, and by residents of communities elsewhere in Nova Scotia, to teach Gaelic (Mertz 208–209).

These efforts helped to cast Gaelic in a new light for Cape Bretoners, as something of value, in contrast to the many years of denigration and neglect it had received. In this sense, they were extremely positive, as Dorian (1987) notes for revitalization efforts of East Sutherland Gaelic and other minority languages undergoing language shift. However, in many of these efforts, "a precise examination of the message conveyed reveals that it involved a revival of interest in Gaelic more than a revival of language use" (Mertz 1982, 219).

Mertz found four factors common to the efforts from the 1920s–1980: 1) the revival attempts were made by educational elites or professionals; 2) people who initiated revival attempts were either from "away" or were Cape Bretoners who had spent considerable time away from the island; 3) the division between predominantly Catholic and Protestant areas played out as a mutual avoidance and lack of interaction between people in these areas with respect to Gaelic revitalization efforts; and 4) a divide between the urban centre of Sydney and the rural areas of Cape Breton also manifested itself in the lack of coordination of revitalization efforts (209–11).

Dembling assessed journalistic accounts of the 1990s "Gaelic revival" in Cape Breton and found that while one article referenced an increase in the number of Gaelic students at St. Francis Xavier University, almost everything else referred to as "Gaelic revival" in the media related to the prominence of professional recording artists, most of whom were not actually learning Gaelic. Census statistics notwithstanding, it was not possible to say how many Gaelic speakers or learners there were in the province, and that is still the case today. Dembling did find that the counter-culture, "bottom-up" trend of the 1970s brought by the hippies and folklorists was still positively influencing revitalization efforts to focus more on ordinary people's experiences (1997, 67–68). Tartanism was downplayed, while community-organized efforts such as Féis an Eilein were initiated and the *Am Bràighe* newspaper was launched.

Dembling also found that the influences of the 1970s carried through to the 1990s in the classroom. Gaelic classes featured increased local cultural content, immersion, role-playing and visits from native speakers (1997, 77). These gains may not have necessarily translated into greater numbers of learners becoming fluent, but there is no way to know without having counted. Dembling did carry out a survey of sixty-six adult Gaelic learners in 1996–7 and found that respondents were enthusiastic, but "the trend from the sample would indicate that only a few learners persist to the higher levels of fluency" (106).[7] Most of the survey respondents also indicated that they did not feel they had enough opportunities to speak Gaelic (113). At the same time, a handful of Gaelic learners who had achieved fluency and some recent native-Gaelic-speaking immigrants from Scotland were raising their children in Gaelic (64–65).

Across the 19th and 20th centuries, dedication, energy and talent were poured into Gaelic revitalization activities: teaching, writing, publishing, musical events, folklore collection, raising children in Gaelic. Many people have strongly wished to revitalize the language. For example, Malcolm MacDonald, a Gaelic instructor at the Gaelic College, wrote in the College's short-lived newspaper *The Canadian-American Gael* (which was published 1943–1948):

> *Feumaidh sinn an dìleab phrìseal so ionnsachadh do'n oigridh le bhi 'ga bruidhinn anns na dachaidhean... agus ma nì sinn an ni so, cha'n eil teagamh nach dean iadsan an ni ceudna ri'n gineal.*

(We need to impart this precious legacy to the younger generation by speaking it in the homes... and if we do this, no doubt they will do the same with their children.) (CAG 1 [14], qtd. and trans. in Dembling 1997, 56).

But thus far, despite a very strong desire for revitalization among Gaelic users, and strenuous efforts among some, the shift from Gaelic to English has not yet been reversed. In 2012 all remaining geographically based communities where Gaelic was a language of daily use have shifted to EGIDS Stage 8a, "Severely Endangered," or 8b, "Critically Endangered" (Table 11.2). Revitalization efforts have not moved beyond GIDS Stage 8. Stage 7 has not yet been achieved, let alone Stage 6 (Table 11.4).

7 Conclusion

The GIDS and EGIDS are useful tools, but they are limited and static. They do not take account of unique local conditions, and they do not predict or describe the events of the past or the future. They can be used to help formulate a set of goals and define the intermediate steps that are needed to reach those goals. In this way, the scales are useful tools for language revitalization goal-setting and planning. This assessment is presented in order to identify some of the ideological-emotional and technical-practical barriers to Gaelic revitalization.

As is often noted in situations of language shift, nothing can substitute for the positive will of Gaelic users themselves to change the current situation. But as the 20th century shows, positive will alone has not been enough to move from GIDS Stage 8 to Stage 7 and eventually to Stage 6. What is still missing? Coordination and cooperation.

The Gaelic community of practice must work together in several related areas:

(1) Agreement by voluntary groups and public institutions on clearly-defined RLS goals for Nova Scotia Gaelic—are most participants content at Stage 8, or do enough people want to work toward Stage 6 to make it worthwhile? (See Table 11.1).

(2) Improving the design, implementation and funding of Gaelic-language acquisition beyond current levels in order to significantly increase the numbers of adults being brought to fluency.

(3) Coordinating efforts of voluntary groups and public institutions so that all resources support agreed RLS goals as effectively and efficiently as possible, and pooling ideas to identify new funding sources and create innovative forms of cross-institutional support.

(4) Positive acknowledgement of a diverse Nova Scotia Gaelic community of practice encompassing the passions and practices of rural and urban, young and old, conservative and innovative, oral tradition-oriented and literacy-oriented, Cape Breton-oriented and Nova Scotia/Scottish-oriented, Canadian-born and immigrant, novice

and old-timer, and heritage learner and new Gaelic user. These aspects of diversity cross-cut the Nova Scotia Gaelic community of practice, and it is my belief that each and all could potentially be acknowledged, validated, included, and deliberately planned for without threatening any of the others.

Notes

1   In theory it could also include Welsh, since anglophone folk understandings of the Celtic language family sometimes mistakenly identify Welsh as a "Gaelic language" rather than a Celtic language, even erroneously referring to it as "Welsh Gaelic."
2   The 2011 census results on language were not available at the time of writing, but they were released in 2012.
3   SIL International (www.sil.org), formerly known as Summer Institute of Linguistics, is an evangelical Christian linguistics organization. Some linguists and indigenous peoples find their missionary activities and orientation offensive, although SIL has also made major contributions to language documentation and community language revitalization worldwide. SIL's *Ethnologue* publication is available online at www.ethnologue.com.
4   The designations "all" and "some" are based on the concept of ethnic groups as bounded and internally homogeneous, a point for which Fishman's RLS theory has been criticized. "All" users of a language will never be doing the same thing in a situation of language shift (or indeed in any other situation). Thus "all" and "some" should be interpreted not as quantifiable percentages of a population, but as the cultural-ideological positions "normatively" ("all" meaning either taken-for-grantedness or the explicit position that "all members of our group do this, or all members should") and "selectively, no-longer-normatively" ("some"). At the heart of language shift is this shift from the "old norm" of socializing children in one language, to the "new norm" of socializing children in another language. The question of what percentage of residents in a geographically bounded community or region makes this shift before it becomes the "new norm"—in other words, the demographic point of "tip"—is still open to investigation (Ó Giollagáin 2011). The point of tip is more likely located in the realm of ideological changes and accompanying shifts in behaviour by key individuals in various social networks (Mertz 1989).
5   Or more accurately, eastern Nova Scotia-wide.
6   I base this assessment on the efforts of a voluntary organization in 2011–2012 to run a weekly family-oriented Gaelic event in the Halifax area, and observation of other Gaelic events taking place 2010–2012 in different areas of Nova Scotia.

7   This was a non-random sample carried out in 1996 of individual Gaelic learners in Halifax and elsewhere, students in Gaelic courses at St. Francis Xavier University in Antigonish and University College of Cape Breton in Sydney (now Cape Breton University), a Gaelic Day at St. Francis Xavier, a weekend immersion event in Margaree and the Gaelic festival Féis an Eilein in Christmas Island. Dembling was not allowed to survey adult summer students at the Gaelic College because the leadership at the time refused; they objected to the inclusion of questions about the Gaelic College on the survey (1997, 79).

CHAPTER 12

"Ìle ga Bruidhinn": A community-based Gaelic dialect revitalization proposal

1 Introduction

Language revitalization may seem simple, but it is as difficult and complex as any other deliberate effort to change human behaviour. Yet social scientists and practitioners have already discovered a great deal about how language death and revitalization processes work. Their research-based theories and recommendations, together with more general insights about the nature of language and learning, should inform the design of minority language revitalization programs.

In this paper I introduce the concept and rationale for a proposed community-based Gaelic revitalization project, provisionally titled Ìle ga Bruidhinn ("Islay speaking her/it", with "her"/"it" referring to the Gaelic language). The paper describes how language revitalization research supports the principles and planning of Ìle ga Bruidhinn. The project's fundamental principle is that "a theory of language renewal must begin with the speakers, with people 'doing language' together in meaningful ways, and work out from there" (Fettes 1997). Getting native Gaelic-speaking people to spend a lot of time talking with people who want to learn from them, supported by a structured Gaelic immersion course in an existing local Gaelic institution, can renew the transmission of distinctive local varieties of Gaelic to future generations. According to research by Will Lamb on the use of Gaelic dialects by teachers in Gaelic medium education (GME) in Scotland, all local and regional Gaelic dialects except those of Lewis and South Uist will disappear within a few generations in Scotland if new means are not found to restart their transmission and promote their use (Lamb 2011).

2 Project Overview

The project design features intensive residential adult Gaelic language instruction using the Ùlpan system, in a particular dialect form of

Gaelic, supported by intensive interaction with trained native dialect speakers in a community setting. The proposed community setting for the project is Bowmore on the island of Islay, and the institutional setting is Ionad Chaluim Chille Ìle, located just outside Bowmore.

At the end of the 19th century, and through much of the 20th century, Gaelic was strong in Islay. Duwe's (2006) assessment of census statistics from 1881 through 2001 concluded that the future of Gaelic in Islay was severely weakened but could be improved with the efforts of local institutions:

> Gàidhlig in the southernmost Hebrides still suffers from decades of neglect and ignorance. The basis for a possible consolidation of language use is rather limited and the language community has a strong bias towards the older generation. Educational provision is not on a comparable level with other islands in the Inner Hebrides. This in itself provides the main potential for future growth. Improvements could easily be accomplished through intensified pre-school provision and dedicated second language teaching in local primary schools. Future positive impacts can be expected by the extension of activities around Ionad Chaluim Chille (2006, 22-23).

The 2011 census counted 835 people with Gaelic language ability aged 3 and older in Islay as a whole, or just over one-quarter of the total island population of 3228. According to my observations and conversations in 2011, Islay Gaelic is still spoken by some of these people, but not all. Although Gaelic use was not widespread in Bowmore, the area of concentrated population closest to ICC, Gaelic had been a language of daily use amongst many people in Bowmore within living memory. In the 2011 census, 140 speakers and 51 understanders of Gaelic were counted in Bowmore.

The main elements of the proposed project are as follows. The participants would include:

- 14 adult students to be brought to functional fluency in spoken Gaelic, with 10 or more of these from Islay and up to 4 from elsewhere;
- up to 56 local speakers of Islay Gaelic (up to 4 per student)

who would be trained and paid to serve as sociolinguistic mentors to the students, interacting with them in Gaelic and supporting and enhancing their classroom learning;
- 8–12 new and experienced Ùlpan tutors, required to be Islay Gaelic speakers, who would receive new or supplementary tutor training for the project;
- 2 project administrators (one full-time, and one part-time).

The activities of the project would consist of the following: developing a new pilot Islay dialect edition of the Ùlpan course, providing to students 9 weeks of daily Ùlpan adult Gaelic language instruction and practice (totaling 324 classroom hours); developing and piloting a training course for Islay Gaelic-speaking community members to become sociolinguistic mentors to the adult learners, paying these mentors to provide a further 54 hours of structured, classroom-based, Gaelic-medium interaction with the students, and paying these mentors to provide approximately 500 further hours of facilitated daily interaction with the students, in the form of various social activities and events outside the classroom. Communal morning and evening meals would also provide a daily focus for informal Gaelic-medium interaction between tutors, students and Gaelic-speaking catering staff. Dormitory-style accommodations are envisioned, but local home-based accommodations would also be considered if enough local Gaelic-speaking hosts could be found (accommodations are an extremely important aspect of the project, but are also contingent on available local resources and the budget). Overall, the project would aim to provide around 882 total hours of Gaelic instruction and exposure per student. Further details not included here would be developed in cooperation with the sponsoring institution according to the availability of local resources and funding.

The immediate objectives of the project as proposed are 1) to bring a core group of people to functional fluency in Islay Gaelic—to the point when they can start speaking Gaelic on their own in the community setting, and then continue learning and increasing their fluency through normal daily interaction and practice, 2) to train new Gaelic tutors who can go on to teach local varieties of Gaelic in Argyll & Bute region, 3) to create meaningful paid work for local Gaelic speakers in

Islay, and 4) to bring new Gaelic-related income directly into a fragile island economy.

The short-term goals of this project are 1) to make more Ìlich (Islay people) aware of how unique and valuable the Islay dialect is as a resource for local knowledge, culture, leisure, and the local industries of whisky and tourism; 2) to re-instill and strengthen confidence and pride in Islay Gaelic among all Ìlich; 3) to persuade more people who know Islay Gaelic to use Islay Gaelic on a daily basis, especially with prospective speakers; and 4) to increase awareness of, and positive feelings towards, Gaelic among Argyllshire residents in general.

The long-term goals of the project are 1) to strengthen and increase the Gaelic identity of Islay by increasing public and private Gaelic use; 2) to reverse the impending disappearance of the Islay dialect by restarting its transmission to new speakers in Islay; 3) to reverse the disappearance of Gaelic as a spoken language of daily use in Argyllshire more generally, especially in its traditionally Gaelic-speaking communities; and 4) to create a project with a training program component that Ionad Chaluim Chille Ìle could export to the heartland communities of other Gaelic dialect areas throughout Scotland and the diaspora.

3 Rationale: Language Revitalization Theory and Practice

The remainder of this paper describes some of the language revitalization and education research and theories that support the principles and planning of Ìle ga Bruidhinn.

3.1 *Language Shift, Revitalization, and Reversal: Defining the Terms*

Language shift is defined as a process in which "the habitual use of one language is being replaced by the habitual use of another" in "bilingual towns, villages, or neighbourhoods" (Gal 1979, 1). Although language shift can be analyzed from regional and national perspectives, it is essential to keep in mind that language shift—and efforts to reverse it—involve face-to-face social interaction in local settings (McEwan-Fujita 2010a, 30; see Ch. 8, this volume). As MacKinnon wrote over 30 years ago, "the line of bilingualism runs through every home and meeting place in Gaelic Scotland" (MacKinnon 1984, 505).

Language revitalization can be defined generally as "the attempt to add new linguistic forms or social functions to a language which is threatened with language loss or death, with the aim of increasing its uses and users" (King 2000, 4, 23). The most well-known approach to language revitalization, "Reversing Language Shift" (henceforth RLS), is defined by sociologist of language, Joshua Fishman, as "the theory and practice of assistance to speech communities whose native languages are threatened because their intergenerational continuity is proceeding negatively, with fewer and fewer users […] or uses every generation" (Fishman 1991, 1).

The most serious obstacle to RLS occurs when the transmission of a language from one generation to the next stops altogether. Recognizing this, Fishman insists that "intergenerational [language] usage within the confines of the home, family, neighbourhood and face-to-face community" (Fishman 1991, xii) should be encouraged and stabilized first and foremost in RLS efforts.

In fact, Fishman recommends that if intergenerational transmission in this nexus has not yet been achieved or stabilized, then all language planning efforts should be evaluated according to how well they support it, and prioritized accordingly. Furthermore, he asserts that making higher-order efforts "to control the language of education, the workplace, the mass media and governmental services, without having sufficiently safeguarded [intergenerational transmission], is equivalent to constantly blowing air into a tire that still has a puncture" (1991, xii). This is all the more true in the case of endangered local dialects, which are already under pressure from both dominant dialects and standardization in these domains.

The recent report on the community language survey in Shawbost, Isle of Lewis, indicates that intergenerational transmission of the language "has all but ended" in one of the strongest "Gaelic-dominant" areas in the Western Isles and indeed in the whole of Scotland (Munro et al. 2011, 4). Since Shawbost was one of the strongest areas, one may surmise that other Gaelic-speaking areas of Scotland are in a similar state at best. This is a crucial time for efforts to reverse Gaelic language shift.

Schools are not effective on their own in reversing Gaelic language shift or transmitting vernacular Gaelic. Oliver (2002, 164), Pollock

(2006, 239), and O'Hanlon (2012, 288) have conducted research showing that Gaelic medium education (GME) pupils tend not to speak very much Gaelic outside of educational contexts. O'Hanlon found that among the GME pupils surveyed and interviewed by her, there were a small number, who, after the transition to the first year of secondary school, "cited home and community-based language use" as a potential or intended future use of Gaelic (O'Hanlon 2012, 233, 236–237, 309) and so GME certainly may contribute to the future use of Gaelic by adults with children in home and community. However, GME combined with an absence of intergenerational transmission may also be contributing to the anglicization of the language and its divergence from traditional regionally-based spoken varieties, as demonstrated by data from GME pupils on Skye (Landgraf 2011), Lewis and Glasgow (Nance 2013, 2014).

Thus from the perspective of RLS, Gaelic medium education could be seen as "pumping air into a leaking tire" as long as intergenerational transmission of Gaelic is not secure, even though GME does seem to contribute to an "individual level personal identification" with Gaelic for some pupils (O'Hanlon 2012, 311). Likewise, other educational efforts like Gaelic (Learners) Education in secondary schools do not directly achieve RLS, although they can indirectly support it (Milligan 2010). In short, schools seem to be effective in RLS insofar as they can support and supplement the transmission of Gaelic in the home-family-neighbourhood-community nexus, not as a substitute for it. Thus while GME is important and necessary for overall national revitalization, there needs to be a primary focus on the "home-family-neighbourhood-community" nexus right now in order to maximize the opportunities for reversing Gaelic language shift in Scotland.

3.2   *Reversing Language Shift: Theoretical Challenges*
Some academics have criticized the way that Fishman prioritizes language transmission in families above all else in his Graded Intergenerational Disruption Scale or GIDS (Darquennes 2007 and Milligan 2010, 77 describe these criticisms). Some who criticize this priority feel that it detracts from the important role of other factors such as minority-language schooling (Romaine 2006, 465), educational

and work institutions (Edwards 2006, 6), or socio-economic mobility (Strubell 2001, 261) in revitalizing a language.

In particular, the question of socio-economic mobility should be addressed. Since the 1990s, sociologists and economists of language have been claiming that the development of minority-language-related employment can play a key role in reversing the negative socio-economic value of a language, which will in turn persuade more people to raise their children in the minority language (Darquennes 2007, 64–65).

A major question is: which should come first, national development of education and employment opportunities in Gaelic, or support of intergenerational transmission in families and local communities?

A great deal of Gaelic language policy in Scotland over the past few decades has been focused on improving socio-economic mobility through the nexus of Gaelic medium education and Gaelic-essential employment. These creative, impressive, and wide-ranging efforts, operating within the limits of the neoliberal framework imposed by Thatcher and successive Westminster governments, have involved building up Gaelic media, promoting a "Gaelic economy", and promoting Gaelic medium education throughout Scotland.

However, considering the state of intergenerational transmission in Shawbost as a barometer, at least as much attention should be devoted to the intergenerational transmission of the endangered language (and indeed endangered dialects) within the family, neighbourhood, and community, as to the active quest for "family-external mechanisms" that could generate greater use of the endangered language.

Nancy Hornburger and Kendall King, two prominent academics who research and advocate for minority language revitalization in Latin America, also recognize the overall importance of adults transmitting the language to children prior to and outside of school in a critique of Fishman's GIDS model. They criticize only its fixed place at a certain stage in Fishman's GIDS model: "it seems important to locate this all-important dimension of RLS outside the stages, as either an overarching or underpinning essential to all of them, to be pursued at all times" (2001, 186).

Having said that, we should not place overwhelming emphasis, pressure, or blame on parents in regard to intergenerational transmission.

Many two-parent families have only one Gaelic-speaking parent, most families are nuclear without live-in grandparents, and two-parent and especially single-parent families are under stress with many demands on their time. Many families, and most women with young children working outside the home, rely on paid or unpaid childcare.

Many of Fishman's supporters and detractors overlook his point that the entire home-family-neighbourhood-community nexus is included in the support of intergenerational transmission, not just nuclear families (1991, 92–93). This nexus encompasses not only parent-child and grandparent-grandchild relationships, but also many other kinds of language socialization relationships (Ochs 1990, 302–03). Adults can socialize other adults, and adults can socialize children of all ages in many capacities, not just as parents. Children can socialize adults as well. Multiple kinds of social relationships besides home-based immersion can help to reverse language shift—as Fettes says, "any meaningful long-term relationship conducted in the language helps to establish an intergenerational network of relationships" (Fettes 1997). For example, anecdotal evidence suggests that in some 20th-century minority-language communities, young men underwent some kind of apprenticeship or initiation into local traditional subsistence-based activities, and in so doing, also acquired their community language as teenagers or young adults, even though they had not learned it as children in the home. Language—and dialect—revitalization programs can be designed to foster and support such relationships.

3.3 Reversing Language Shift: Practical Challenges

In additional to conceptual challenges, there are also more practical challenges to RLS. Although the sociolinguistics and language planning literature divides life neatly into separate domains, which can be useful for guiding and challenging our thinking, RLS is not so simple or straightforward. As Dauenhauer and Dauenhauer (1998) have pointed out, based on their experience with native language revitalization in Alaska, technical, ideological and emotional issues pose major challenges to language revitalization.

These challenges manifest clearly in the effort to involve adult second-language learners in RLS. Based on a review of RLS theory supporting his survey of adult Gaelic learners in Scotland, Alasdair

MacCaluim has described how adult learners could potentially contribute to RLS by "parenting Gaelic-speaking children, filling Gaelic-related jobs and consuming Gaelic products and services" (MacCaluim 2007, 75). Furthermore, adults are useful to RLS not only as parents, workers, and consumers, but also as speakers in social relationships with other speakers, forming multigenerational social networks and communities. They can strengthen the fabric of the "neighbourhood-community" portion of the family-home-neighbourhood-community nexus as already proposed. Moreover, adult learners can make very significant contributions to the revitalization of particular regional dialects (e.g., Wentworth 2005).

But adult learners cannot contribute directly to RLS in this way unless they can also make the leap from "learner" to "speaker" in their self-identification and practice. Based on his own research and others' from the preceding decade, MacCaluim noted that "few Gaelic learners are able to reach fluency in the language" due to "the gaps and inadequacies in the Gaelic learning infrastructure" in Scotland (2007, 74).

Although these gaps are in the process of being addressed for Gaelic through Ùlpan and other projects funded by Bòrd na Gàidhlig, adult minority-language learners must deal with other challenges besides poor provision. These include the challenges of learning as adults, and especially the ideologically and emotionally-charged behaviours entrenched among many native Gaelic speakers. These behaviours include:

(a) enacting an etiquette of accommodation, trying to be polite by switching to English in social situations where a non-Gaelic speaker is present, or a less-than-fluent speaker attempts to speak Gaelic (common in minority language situations; see Trosset 1986, 68–82; Gal 1979, 166; Dorian 1981, 79; Woolard 1989); and

(b) maintaining sociolinguistic boundaries by defining Gaelic exclusively as a "local language", speaking Gaelic in a way that delimits "in-group" boundaries to include family, friends, and neighbours, and exclude others, and expressing resentment or intolerance for adult learners and non-native spoken Gaelic.

I have discussed how these attitudes are not only enacted by native Gaelic speakers, but also inculcate negative affect into Gaelic learners living in Gaelic-speaking areas (McEwan-Fujita 2010a; see Ch. 8, this volume). I have witnessed many poignant situations over the years where Gaelic is "everywhere and nowhere": people who desperately wish to learn and practice Gaelic are surrounded by Gaelic speakers, and hear Gaelic being spoken to others every day, but their own access is blocked.

These problems contribute to language shift in two ways. First, they close off opportunities for adults to practise or improve spoken Gaelic and become fluent speakers. Second, they remove opportunities for fluent adults to assist in socializing other community members (younger or older) into the daily use of Gaelic in the last remaining Gaelic-speaking areas in the world.

Adult learners on the whole are motivated to contribute to reversing Gaelic language shift in Scotland: among MacCaluim's 1998–99 survey respondents living in Scotland, almost 93% indicated that "I would be helping to keep Gaelic alive" was either very important or quite important to them as a reason for learning Gaelic (MacCaluim 2007, 158).

But adult learners' efforts are failing to help revitalize Gaelic-speaking areas as such. They will continue to fail in supporting RLS unless more and better ways can be found to increase community-based opportunities for adults to move from "learning" to "speaking" Gaelic, and to building Gaelic-speaking social networks (see Ch. 8, p. 235, this volume).

It is a mistake to discard the goodwill of learners, or to channel it solely into institutions serving learners. It is also a mistake to discard one of Scotland's most precious resources in the effort to revitalize Gaelic: the very significant number of "understanders" (passive or receptive bilinguals) and "lapsed" or "former" speakers. In the 2001 census, 27,219 people were returned as understanding but not speaking, reading, or writing Gaelic. Could they be drawn into a revitalization effort in greater numbers, if their partial acquisition of Gaelic was re-framed in a positive light? In the situation of Innuttut and Innu-aimun in Labrador, linguists who designed teacher-training programs described such people as the "last chance generation" to reverse language loss in particular families, and noted that their unique needs are rarely met in conventional language courses (Johns and Mazurekewich 2001, 362).

Finally, it is a mistake to turn our backs on native Gaelic-speaking communities, even—or rather especially—in the face of the Shawbost report. Suggestions of how to support adult learners outside the classroom have been made by Lynda Pritchard Newcombe for Welsh, including schemes to pair native speakers with learners, a national friend/mentor system, drop-in centers for learners and native speakers, marketing initiatives to make native speakers more aware of learners' needs, and training for native speakers committed to language revitalization in how to converse with learners (Newcombe 2007, 115). Such initiatives, if incorporated into Gaelic revitalization efforts, could help to revitalize Gaelic in areas where it has traditionally been spoken as a community language (McEwan-Fujita 2010a; see Ch. 8, this volume). Many of these suggestions are incorporated into the proposed project.

3.4   The Role of "Heartlands" in Reversing Language Shift

During the conference "Maintaining and Revitalising Minority Languages in their 'Heartlands'" held at Sabhal Mòr Ostaig in September 2011, there was little theoretical discussion of why Gaelic-speaking heartlands are desirable to maintain and revitalize. Therefore I offer definitions and concepts here from the perspective of linguistic anthropology, which specializes, among other things, in studying relationships between language, territory, and ethnicity.

A minority language "heartland" can be defined as a community, area, region, or territory of a nation-state where: (a) a language was historically spoken by a significant population but is now minoritized or obsolescent, and (b) the local or regional culture is at least partially recognizable as bearing the same ethnonym designation as that language. It is also often the case that "native" or first-language practitioners of the language-culture complex still live there in greater demographic concentration than elsewhere in the nation-state.

Here I offer a list of reasons why minority language "heartlands" should be given the fullest consideration in RLS efforts:

(a) Immersion: A heartland can potentially provide a demographic concentration of native speakers in a single geographically-defined area. This concentration can contribute to creating an immersion situation if native speaker mentors can be trained and encouraged to overcome negative affect and ideological conceptions, and strategically placed to speak to learners.

(b) Motivation: Simply put, people are more likely to learn to speak a language when there is someone they want to talk to in that language. Heartland areas provide motivation as well as immersion—in this case a place to visit or live, where one can build more fulfilling local relationships and participate more deeply in local culture through the medium of Gaelic.

(c) Most effective transmission of existing language-culture complex: when the chain is broken and traditional first-language speakers are gone, it will be much more time-consuming, effortful, and possibly expensive to (1) create new speakers recognized as having anything culturally in common with fluent "traditional" or "native" speakers; and (2) maintain some continuity with the Gaelic "language-culture complex" of the past. Change is inevitable, and new cultural forms are being developed that use Gaelic as a medium of expression, but such cultural forms are more likely to be accepted as "authentically" Gaelic rather than inauthentically derivative from the majority culture when developed by people who have been socialized as Gaelic speakers in a particular Gaelic-speaking community (also see below).

(d) Strengthening cultural confidence and ability to assimilate global influences: By the early 1980s, all Gaelic-speaking communities in Scotland had ceased to linguistically integrate new adult members who joined through in-marriage and other forms of in-migration (MacArthur et al. 1982, 14–16). The author has frequently heard people contrast Gaelic speakers with Welsh speakers who seem to possess a greater confidence in their language and greater belief in the necessity and ability of outsiders to learn it if they wish to live in those communities. Even in a globalized world, with change all around us driven by new technologies and transnational corporations, people can continue to adapt globalized cultural practices and goods to their own local forms and purposes through processes of "glocalization" (Inda and Rosaldo 2004). They seem to be more able to do so when they possess an intangible "cultural confidence" allowing them to absorb and transform non-local influences while maintaining a strong sense of group identity, group worth, and continuity with the past. Cultural confidence is a positive affective (or emotional) stance toward one's culture, potentially including one's language; hence, the need to account for emotions in the transmission of Gaelic and the socialization of new speakers.

(e) Anchoring authenticity of political claims: ideologies of nationalism which link language and territory still guide the public policy of state governments and permeate people's daily lives (Billig 1995). Social scientists know that "homelands" and "heartlands" are socially constructed, but they are still powerful nationalist tropes. The continued existence of a Gaelic-speaking heartland provides the strongest possible political justification for public funding that a minority language policy can have, as opposed to language policy for a world language like English or French.

As the recent survey results from Shawbost show, we cannot take any Gaelic-speaking community for granted as a heartland; "the community" must be continually maintained and built up, and even re-created to an extent (as is proposed in this project). Deliberate design and support of community-based language revitalization is desperately needed in the "heartlands" which were hit the hardest by language shift and loss in the first place. Unfortunately, a community that has been undergoing language shift for decades may not be in the best position to spontaneously re-organize its resources to reverse language shift.

To support Gaelic communities like Shawbost and Bowmore, I propose combining three elements in a Gaelic dialect revitalization project: 1) academic expertise in language shift and revitalization, 2) a successful structured language teaching program with a tutor training component, and 3) an existing Gaelic institution with strong ties to its local community. These combined resources are then offered to train and empower community members to do their own revitalization, and even to export it to other communities.

4 Language Revitalization: Theoretical and Applied Suggestions

Following are further theoretical and applied insights based on anthropological research, which are incorporated into the proposed project.

4.1 Theories of Learning in RLS Project Design

The community-based educational aspects of this project are based on the learning theories developed by anthropologist Jean Lave and computer scientist Etienne Wenger, who collaborated on an ethnographic study of learning through apprenticeship through which they developed the concepts of "legitimate peripheral participation" (Lave and Wenger 1991) and "communities of practice" (Wenger 1998) as new perspectives on learning.

Lave and Wenger propose that learning is fundamentally social in character. It does not take place in individuals' heads. It takes place through an interactional process called legitimate peripheral participation (henceforth LPP), in which newcomers are allowed to participate in a community of practice, initially by observing old-timers, and then by gradually increasing the intensity and complexity of their participation until they become full participants (Lave and Wenger 1991, 29).

LPP takes place in the context of a community of practice, of which newcomers eventually become full members. Communities of practice are defined by Wenger as 'groups of people who share a concern or a passion for something they do and learn how to do it better as they interact regularly' (Wenger 2006).

If we apply the community of practice concept to minority language speakers, then we cannot take geographically-bounded local communities for granted as minority-language speech communities. Instead we must try to create conditions for the formation and maintenance of Gaelic-speaking communities of practice where learning can take place. This effort must be made just as much in traditional geographically-based communities as within institutions such as GME, tertiary education, and workplaces (McEwan-Fujita 2013; see Ch. 11, this volume).

Lave and Wenger make an important distinction between learning and "intentional instruction" or teaching. Intentional instruction often takes place in classrooms, but they believe that instruction is not "in itself the source or cause of learning" (1991, 41). In other words, what is explicitly taught in a classroom does not always have any direct or causal relationship to what is learned. In fact, students in a classroom may learn things through peripheral observation and imitation that are very different from the goals of the intentional instruction. What do adult Gaelic learners actually learn in traditional adult Gaelic education? They may learn how to be good students in a classroom, how to read and write Gaelic, how to watch the clock—and how to speak English at the tea-break!

All too often, they also learn "learners' Gaelic": fixed phrases such as *"Ciamar a tha thu?" "Tha gu math"* [How are you? I'm well] and simple structures such as *"Tha mi…"* and *"Tha e…"* [I am… It is…]. These structures signal that they are learning Gaelic. But it is very hard to make the leap from these to natural spoken Gaelic with conventional classroom-based instruction alone.

Apprenticeships can feature some intentional instruction along with legitimate peripheral participation. The "Ìle ga Bruidhinn" project will implement intentional instruction through the Ùlpan program, because many adults can learn grammatical structures effectively through classroom-based instruction. At the same time, this will be supplemented by placing the students in situations where they interact with native speakers on a daily basis, practicing speaking in real-time with the structures introduced in the Ùlpan course. The students' initial legitimate peripheral participation (listening and observing) will gradually grow into a practice of speaking Islay Gaelic. And in fact what appears to be the supplementary aspect of this programme, the time spent with native speakers where there is no overt teaching, will be the time when they learn how to be speakers themselves.

Another crucial component of LPP and communities of practice is access:

> To become a full member of a community of practice requires access to a wide range of ongoing activity, old-timers, and other members of the community; and to information, resources, and opportunities for participation (Lave and Wenger 1991, 48).

To whom do adult Gaelic learners have access? In other words, with whom do they interact principally, through the medium of Gaelic? Mostly other adult learners, and a few teachers. They are often sequestered from first-language Gaelic speakers, either through residence outside of Gaelic-speaking areas, or through the enactment of sociolinguistic boundaries as previously mentioned. In fact, adult learners and non-native fluent speakers may form their own communities of practice instead, with new cultural meanings—and new forms of Gaelic.

From an anthropological point of view, this is an interesting cultural phenomenon. But from a pro-Gaelic revitalization point of view, when walls are built up between native Gaelic-English bilinguals and people who desire to learn Gaelic as a second language, Gaelic linguistic and cultural forms tend to be lost and replaced by English ones, rather than transformed into new Gaelic forms. The walls must consciously be taken down, which is what the proposed program is designed to do.

Through their legitimate peripheral participation in ongoing practice (Lave and Wenger 1991, 64), learners also gradually acquire a new identity as a member of a community of practice. This identity may also be construed as membership in a culture: "An extended period of legitimate peripherality provides learners with opportunities to make the culture of practice theirs" (Lave and Wenger 1991, 95).

Too often, however, adult Gaelic learners in Scotland are socialized into a new identity as perpetual Gaelic learners rather than as Gaelic speakers. The challenge for language revitalization is finding ways for people to develop identities not as Gaelic learners but as daily Gaelic users. It cannot be done simply by redefining everyone who can say a few words as a Gaelic speaker (as suggested by Moffat 1995). It cannot be done by funding and designating buildings as "Gaelic infrastructure" without any attention to the abilities and practices of the occupants (McEwan-Fujita 2005; see Ch. 7, this volume). It *can* be done by involving people in a community of practice of daily Gaelic speakers, through providing access to old-timers and opportunities for LPP.

Learning through LPP provides not only a new identity, but also motivation: "Acceptance by and interaction with acknowledged adept practitioners make learning legitimate and of value from the point of view of the apprentice" (Lave and Wenger 1991, 110). As they learn through practice, apprentices see that there is a viable way of using Gaelic in the world, and a setting where it is appropriate to do so. Adapting Lave and Wenger's wording above to describe the program proposed here, the community of fluent and residual Islay Gaelic speakers and their productive relations with the island and the wider world will provide the apprentice learners with continuity-based "futures" as Gaelic speakers.

4.2 Emotions, Cultural Ideologies, and Language Socialization in RLS Project Design

Language shift and revitalization are often understood to be fundamentally socio-economic processes, as the discussion around the economics of language revitalization demonstrates. However, linguistic anthropology research has shown that emotions and cultural ideologies (or cultural value systems) are fundamental rather than secondary components of language shift and revitalization (Kulick 1992; Gal 1978; McEwan-Fujita 2010a; 2010b; see Ch. 8, this volume). Emotions and cultural value systems are filters through which people interpret material reality, and they are also forces shaping people's actions which create new material realities. Therefore, successful language revitalization efforts should take into account emotions and cultural ideologies in their planning (Dauenhauer and Dauenhauer 1998; McEwan-Fujita 2010a; 2010b; see Ch. 8–9, this volume).

Emotions and cultural ideologies are transmitted through processes of language socialization. Language socialization is a combination of language acquisition and cultural socialization (Ochs and Schieffelin 1984). It is defined as a social interaction process in which "novices" are gradually socialized by "experts" through ongoing, recurrent linguistic practices to develop "an understanding of social actions, events, emotions, aesthetics, knowledgeability, statuses, relationships, and other socio-cultural phenomena" in particular sociocultural contexts (Ochs 1996, 408). Cross-cultural ethnographic research on childrearing has established that affect is a central part of language socialization (Ochs and Schieffelin 1984; Besnier 1990). This means that one acquires language and culture in ways that are inextricably intertwined with emotions.

Language teaching specialists also now recognize that emotions are an integral part of language learning. Second language acquisition specialists recommend fostering positive emotions, or positive affect, in foreign language learning as a way of increasing its effectiveness (Arnold 1999). For example, Oxford (2011) devotes an entire chapter of the book *Teaching and Researching: Language Learning Strategies* to affective language learning strategies, strategies that can be used to manage students' emotions for the purpose of maximizing their language learning. Oxford shows that in language learning, the emotional aspects are just as important as the cognitive aspects, if not more so. She metaphorically labels affective strategies as "electricity workers", because they are as important in making language learning work as electricity is in making devices work. Electricity is also an invisible force; this aspect of the metaphor highlights the fact that explicit recognition of the key role of affect has been almost wholly absent from strategies aimed at minority language revitalization.

Therefore, I recommend planning for positive affect in the learning process, to counteract decades of negative emotions about Gaelic in the lives of participants living in a context of Gaelic language shift. This is achieved principally through several efforts: 1) creating and providing training workshops for mentors before the teaching component starts, which address potential areas of negative affect such as speaking Gaelic to non-fluent speakers (McEwan-Fujita 2010a; see Ch. 8, this volume) and talking about Gaelic literacy (McEwan-Fujita 2010b; see Ch. 9, this volume); and 2) planning enjoyable social activities for the mentors and students to do together through the medium of Gaelic. The island of Islay, for example, an area rich in Gaelic culture and history, natural beauty, and whisky distilleries, has no shortage of possibilities for enjoyable group activities.

5 Conclusion

In conclusion, this chapter has presented selected aspects of a new proposed project to revitalize a particular endangered dialect of Gaelic in a community-based setting, through a combination of classroom-based dialect instruction and facilitated interaction between learners and trained native dialect speakers.

This proposal is offered as a model that could be introduced in any area where a project funding application can be made, a local institution can host and collaborate on the project's development, and enough fluent speakers of a desired dialect or variety can be found to train as mentors.

References

Alexander, Sir Kenneth. 1985. "The Highlands and Islands Development Board." In *The Economic Development of Modern Scotland 1950–1980*, ed. R. Saville, 214–232. Edinburgh: John Donald.

Arbuthnot, Sharon. 2002. "A context for Mac Mhaighstir Alasdair's *Moladh air Deagh Bhod*." In *Rannsachadh na Gàidhlig 2002*, ed. C. Ó Baoill, N.R. McGuire, 163–170. Abderdeen: An Clò Gaidhealach, Aberdeen.

Ardener, Edwin. 1989. "The Voice of Prophecy: Further Problems in the Analysis of Events." In *Edwin Ardener, The Voice of Prophecy and Other Essays*, ed. Malcolm Chapman, 134–154. Oxford: Blackwell.

Ardener, Edwin. 2007. *The Voice of Prophecy and Other Essays*, 2nd edition, ed. Malcolm Chapman. Oxford: Berghahn Books.

Arnold, Jane, and H. Douglas Brown. 1999. "A map of the terrain." In *Affect in Language Learning*, ed. Jane Arnold, 1–24, Cambridge: Cambridge University Press.

Arnold, Jane, ed. 1999. *Affect in Language Learning*. Cambridge: Cambridge University Press.

Azkue, Jokin, and Josu Perales. 2005. "The Teaching of Basque to Adults." *International Journal of the Sociology of Language* 174, 73–83.

Bakhtin, Mikhail. 1981. *The Dialogic Imagination: Four Essays by M.M. Bakhtin*. ed. Michael Holquist, transl. Caryl Emerson and Michael Holquist. Austin: University of Texas Press.

Barrowclough, Anne. 1999. "Rob and Ewan both want a wife." *The Times*, 12 February, 21.

Bauman, Richard. 1984 [1977]. *Verbal Art as Performance*. Prospect Heights, IL: Waveland Press.

Bauman, Richard. 1986. *Story, Performance, and Event: Contextual Studies of Oral Narrative*. Cambridge: Cambridge University Press.

Bauman, Richard and Charles L. Briggs. 2003. *Voices of Modernity: Language Ideologies and the Politics of Inequality*. New York: Cambridge University Press.

Bawcutt, Priscilla. 1996. *William Dunbar: Selected Poems*. London: Longman.

Bendix, Regina. 1997. *In Search of Authenticity: The Formation of Folklore Studies*. Madison: University of Wisconsin Press.

Besnier, Niko. 1990. "Language and Affect." *Annual Review of Anthropology* 19, 419–51.

Biber, Douglas. 1993. "An Analytical Framework for Register Studies." In *Sociolinguistic Perspectives on Register*, ed. Douglas Biber and Edward Finegan, 31-56. New York: Oxford University Press.

Biber, Douglas, and Edward Finegan. 1993. *Sociolinguistic Perspectives on Register*. Oxford: Oxford University Press.

Billig, Michael. 1995. *Banal Nationalism*, Thousand Oaks, CA

Black, Ronald I. 1986. "The Gaelic Academy: The Cultural Commitment of the Highland Society of Scotland." *Scottish Gaelic Studies* 14, 1-38.

Black, Ronald I. 2007. "Alasdair mac Mhaighstir Alasdair and the new Gaelic poetry." In *The Edinburgh History of Scottish Literature, Volume Two: Enlightenment, Britain and Empire (1707-1918)*, ed. S. Manning, I. Brown, T. O. Clancy, M. Pittock, 110-124. Edinburgh University Press.

Black, Ronnie. 1998. "Tàmailt air" [Review of *Reimagining Culture* by Sharon Macdonald], *The Scotsman*, 15 April, 14.

Blom, Jan-Petter, and John J. Gumperz. 1972. "Social Meaning in Linguistic Structure: Code-switching in Norway." In *Directions in Sociolinguistics: The Ethnography of Communication*, ed. John Gumperz and Dell Hymes, 407-34. New York: Holt, Rinehart & Winston.

Bloomfield, Leonard. 1964. "Literate and Illiterate Speech." In *Language in Culture and Society: A Reader in Linguistic and Anthropology*, ed. Dell Hymes, 391-6. New York: Harper & Brothers.

Bonner, Donna M. 2001. "Garifuna Children's Language Shame: Ethnic Stereotypes, National Affiliation, and Transnational Immigration as Factors in Language Choice in Southern Belize." *Language in Society* 30, 81-96.

Boswell, James. 1970. *Life of Johnson*. Oxford University Press.

Bourdieu, Pierre. 1991. *Language and Symbolic Power*. Transl. G. Raymond, M. Adamson. Cambridge, MA: Harvard University Press.

Boztas, Senay. 2003. "Gaelic in 'gay' status protest." *The Sunday Times*, 20 April. Accessed 23 April 2003. http://www.timesonline.co.uk/article/0,,2091-652425,00.html.

Briggs, Charles. 1988. *Competence in Performance: The Creativity of Tradition in Mexicano Verbal Art*. Philadelphia: University of Pennsylvania Press.

Brown, Allan. 2000a. "A Tongue Lashing from the Gaels." *The Sunday Times*, 20 February 2000. Accessed 2 February 2001. http://www.sunday-times.co.uk/news/pages/sti/2000/02/20/stiecoeco01003.html.

Brown, Tom. 2000. "It Might Be Gaelic But They're Still Talking Nonsense." *The Daily Record*, 3 March 2000, 8.

Brown, Wendy. 2003. "Neoliberalism and the End of Liberal Democracy," *Theory and Event* 7(1). Accessed 17 July 2009. http://muse.jhu.edu/login?uri/=journals/theory_and_event/v007/7.1brown.html.

Bruford, Alan. 1978. "Recitation or Re-Creation? Examples from South Uist Storytelling." *Scottish Studies* 22:27–44.

Bucholtz, Mary and Kira Hall. 2006. "Identity and Interaction: A Sociocultural Linguistic Approach." *Discourse Studies* 7 (4–5), 585–614.

Burchell, Graham. 1996. "Liberal government and techniques of the self." In *Foucault and Political Reason: Liberalism, Neo-liberalism and Rationalities of Government*, ed. A. Barry, T. Osborne, and N. Rose, 19–36. Chicago: University of Chicago Press.

Burnett, Kathryn A. 1997. "Negotiating Home: Categorisation and Representation of Identity among Indigenous and Incoming People of Uist, in the Outer Hebrides." PhD diss., Glasgow Caledonian University.

Burnie, Joan. 1991. "The Voice of Today: Bitch Hunt is War on Women." *The Daily Record*, 21 May 1991, 19.

Bwrdd yr Iaith (the Welsh Language Board). n.d. Accessed 2 November 2002. http://www.bwrdd-yr-iaith.org.uk/en/aboutus.php?cID=93&xID=159.

Caimbeul, Tormod. 2000. "The Politics of Gaelic Development in Scotland." In *Gaelic Identities/Aithne na nGael*, ed. Gordon McCoy and Maolcholaim Scott, 53–66. Belfast: Institute of Irish Studies, Queen's University Belfast and Ultach Trust/Iontaobhas Ultach.

Caird, J. B., and H. A. Moisley. 1961. "Leadership and Innovation in the Crofting Communities of the Outer Hebrides." *Sociological Review* 9(1):85–102.

Callan, Hilary. 2004. "Ardener, Edwin William." In *Oxford Dictionary of National Biography*, ed. H. C. G. Matthew and Brian Harrison, 365–366. New York: Oxford University Press.

Cameron, Deborah. 1995. *Verbal Hygiene*. New York: Routledge.

Campbell, D. and MacLean, R. A. 1974. *Beyond the Atlantic Roar: A Study of the Nova Scotia Scots*. Toronto: McClelland & Stewart.

Campbell, John Francis. 1969 [1890]. *Popular Tales of the West Highlands, Orally Collected. With a translation by J. F. Campbell*. Detroit: Singing Tree Press.

Campbell, John L. and Derick Thomson. 1963. *Edward Lhuyd in the Scottish Highlands 1699–1700*. Oxford: Clarendon Press.

Campbell, John Lorne. 1950. *Gaelic in Scottish Education and Life: Past, Present and Future*. Edinburgh: W. & A.K. Johnston.

Campbell, John Lorne, and Donald MacCormick. 1969. *Hebridean Folksongs: A Collection of Waulking Songs by Donald MacCormick in Kilphedir in South Uist in the Year 1893*. Oxford: Clarendon Press.

Carmichael, Alexander. 1972 [1900]. *Carmina Gadelica: Hymns and Incantations with Illustrative Notes on Words, Rites, and Customs, Dying and Obsolete*. 6 vols. Edinburgh, London: Oliver and Boyd.

Carter, Ian. 1974. "The Highlands of Scotland as an Underdeveloped Region." In *Sociology and Development*. ed. E. de Kadt and G. Williams, 279–311. London: Tavistock Publications.

Cavanaugh, Jillian R. 2004. "Remembering and forgetting: Ideologies of language loss in a northern Italian town." *Journal of Linguistic Anthropology* 14, 24–28.

Cavanaugh, Jillian R. 2009. *Living Memory: The Social Aesthetics of Language in a Northern Italian Town*. Malden, MA: Wiley-Blackwell

Chamberlain, Gethin. 2002. "Former Rugby Star Carpeted over Racist Jokes." *The Scotsman*, 2 February. http://www.thescotsman.co.uk/index.dfm?id=124922002.

Chapman, Malcolm. 1978. *The Gaelic Vision in Scottish Culture*. Montreal: McGill-Queen's University Press.

Chapman, Malcolm. 1982. "'Semantics' and the 'Celt.'" In *Semantic Anthropology*, ed. David Parkin, 123–143. London: Academic Press.

Chapman, Malcolm. 1989. "Introduction." In Edwin Ardener, *The Voice of Prophecy and Other Essays*, ed. Malcolm Chapman, vii–xxviii. Oxford: Blackwell.

Chapman, Malcolm, 1992. *The Celts: The Construction of a Myth*. New York: St. Martin's Press.

Clark, Peter. 1995. "Who Needs the Gaelic?" *The Scotsman*, "Weekend" magazine, 11 March, 24.

Clement, David. 1997. "Highland English." In *The Celtic Englishes*, ed. Hildegard L. C. Tristram, 301–307. Heidelberg: Carl Winter Universitatsverlag.

Clifford, James. 1986. "On Ethnographic Allegory." In *Writing Culture: The Poetics and Politics of Ethnography*, ed. James Clifford and George Marcus, 98–121. Berkeley: University of California Press.

Clifford, James and Marcus, George E., eds. 1986. *Writing Culture: The Poetics and Politics of Ethnography*. Berkeley: University of California Press.

"Clippings from the Phrase Shed." 2000. *West Highland Free Press*, 15 September 2000, 11.

Clyde, Robert. 1995. *From Rebel to Hero: The Image of the Highlander, 1745–1830*. East Linton: Tuckwell Press.

Cole, John W. 1977. "Anthropology Comes Part-Way Home: Community Studies in Europe," *Annual Review of Anthropology* 6, 349–378.

Coleman, Jack David Bo. 1975. "Language Shift in a Bilingual Hebridean Crofting Community." PhD diss., University of Massachusetts.

Collins, James. 1995. "Literacy and Literacies." *Annual Review of Anthropology* 24, 75–93.

Collins, James and Richard K. Blot. 2003. *Literacy and Literacies: Text, Power, and Identity*. Cambridge: Cambridge University Press.

Comaroff, Jean; and Comaroff, John L. 2000. "Millennial Capitalism: First Thoughts on a Second Coming." *Public Culture* 12 (2), 291–343.

"Company." 2002. *A Dictionary of Business*. Oxford University Press/Oxford Reference Online. Accessed 12 March 2003. http://www.oxfordreference.com/views/ENTRY.html?subview=Main&entry=t18.001214.

Comunn na Gàidhlig. 1994. *Ag Obair Dhuibhse [Working for you; a ten-year report]*. Inverness: Comunn na Gàidhlig.

Connor, Steve. 2000. "Most of the world's languages 'will vanish by 2100.'" *The Independent*, 30 May. Available from URL: www.independent.co.uk/story.jsp?story=3024. accessed 15 July 2005.

Constantinidou, Evi. 1992. "Local history and identity in a coastal village in East Sutherland, Scotland: A social anthropological study." DPhil thesis, Dept. of Anthropology, University of Oxford.

Cook-Gumperz, Jenny. 2006. "The Social Construction of Literacy." In *The Social Construction of Literacy*, ed. Jenny Cook-Gumperz, 1–18. Cambridge: Cambridge University Press.

Cosper, Ronald. 1998. "Language in Nova Scotia." In *Language in Canada*, ed. John Edwards, 355–71. Cambridge: Cambridge University Press.

Coxon, Philip. 1988. *A Curlew in the Foreground*. Newton Abbot: David & Charles.

Crichton, Torcuil. 2000. Interview. Segment on the Macpherson Report with Gordon Brewer interviewing Allan Brown, John Alec Macpherson, and Mike Russell. "Newsnight Scotland." BBC Scotland, 7 September.

Crowley, Tony. 1990. "That Obscure Object of Desire: A Science of Language." In *Ideologies of Language*, ed. John E. Joseph and Talbot J. Taylor, 27–50. New York: Routledge.

Crystal, David. 2000. *Language Death*. Cambridge: Cambridge University Press.

Daiches, David. 1964. *The Paradox of Scottish Culture: The Eighteenth-Century Experience*. Oxford: Oxford University Press.

Dalrymple, W. 1989. "The Last of the Gaels." *The Independent Magazine*, 14 October, 34–37.

Darquennes, Jeroen. 2007. "Paths to language revitalization." In *Contact Linguistics and Language Minorities / Kontaktlinguistik und*

Sprachminderheiten / Linguistique de Contact et Minorités Linguistiques, Plurilingua 30, 61–76.

Dauenhauer, Nora Marks, and Richard Dauenhauer. 1995. "Oral literature embodied and disembodied." In *Aspects of oral communication*, ed. Uta M. Quasthoff, 91–111. Berlin: de Gruyter.

Dauenhauer, Nora Marks and Richard Dauenhauer. 1998. "Technical, Emotional, and Ideological Issues in Reversing Language Shift: Examples from Southeast Alaska." In *Endangered languages: Current Issues and Future Prospects*, ed. Lenore A. Grenoble and Lindsey J. Whaley, 57–116. Cambridge: Cambridge University Press.

Dembling, Jonathan. 1991. "Ged a Tha Mo Ghàidhlig Gann: Cape Breton's Vanishing Gàidhealtachd." BA thesis, Hampshire College.

Dembling, Jonathan. 1997. "Joe Jimmy Alec Visits the Gaelic Mod and Escapes Unscathed: The Nova Scotia Gaelic Revivals." MA thesis, Atlantic Canada Studies, Saint Mary's University.

Dembling, Jonathan. 2005. "You Play It As You Would Sing It: Cape Breton, Scottishness and the Means of Cultural Production." In *Transatlantic Scots*, ed. Celeste Ray, 180–197. Tuscaloosa: University of Alabama Press.

Dembling, Jonathan. 2006. "Gaelic in Canada: New Evidence from an Old Census." In *Cànan & Cultar/Language & Culture: Rannsachadh na Gàidhlig 3*, ed. Wilson McLeod, James Fraser and Anja Gunderloch, 203–14. Edinburgh: Dunedin Academic Press.

Dinwoodie, Robert. 2000. "Gaels and Disabled Lose Out in Bill Vote." *The Herald (Glasgow)*, 8 June 2000.

Donaldson, W., 1988. *The Jacobite Song: Political Myth and National Identity*. Aberdeen: Aberdeen University Press.

Dorian, Nancy C. 1970. "A Substitute Name System in the Scottish Highlands." *American Anthropologist* 72, 303–319.

Dorian, Nancy C. 1972. "A Hierarchy of Morphophonemic Decay in Scottish Gaelic Language Death: The Differential Failure of Lenition." *Word: Journal of the International Linguistic Association*, 96–109.

Dorian, Nancy C. 1973. "Grammatical Change in a Dying Dialect." *Language: Journal of the Linguistic Society of America*, 413–438.

Dorian, Nancy C. 1977. "The Problem of the Semi-speaker in Language Death." *International Journal of the Sociology of Language* 12, 23–32.

Dorian, Nancy C. 1978a. "The Dying Dialect and the Role of the Schools: East Sutherland Gaelic and Pennsylvania Dutch." In *Georgetown University Round Table on Languages and Linguistics*, 646–656.

Dorian, Nancy C. 1978b. *East Sutherland Gaelic*. Dublin: Dublin Institute for Advanced Studies.

Dorian, Nancy C. 1978c. "The Fate of Morphological Complexity in Language Death." *Language*, 54 (3), 590–609.

Dorian, Nancy C. 1978d. "The Preservation of the Vocative in a Dying Gaelic Dialect." *Scottish Gaelic Studies* 13 (Part 1), 98–102.

Dorian, Nancy C. 1978e. Review of Kenneth MacKinnon, "Language, Education and Social Processes in a Gaelic Community." *Language in Society* 7, 137–140.

Dorian, Nancy C. 1980a. "Language Shift in Community and Individual: The Phenomenon of the Laggard Semi-Speaker." *International Journal of the Sociology of Language* 25, 85–94.

Dorian, Nancy C. 1980b. "Linguistic Lag as an Ethnic Marker." *Language in Society* 9, 33–41.

Dorian, Nancy C. 1981a. *Language Death: The Life Cycle of a Scottish Gaelic Dialect*. Philadelphia: University of Pennsylvania Press.

Dorian, Nancy C. 1981b. "The Valuation of Gaelic by Different Mother-Tongue Groups Resident in the Highlands." *Scottish Gaelic Studies* 8, 169–182.

Dorian, Nancy C. 1982a. "Defining the Speech Community to Include Its Working Margins." In *Sociolinguistic Variation in Speech Communities*, ed. Suzanne Romaine, 25–33. London: E. Arnold.

Dorian, Nancy C. 1982b. "Language Loss and Maintenance in Language Contact Situations." In *The Loss of Language Skills*, ed. Richard D. Lambert and Barbara F. Freed, 44–59. Rowley, MA: Newbury House Publishers.

Dorian, Nancy C. 1985. *The Tyranny of Tide*. Ann Arbor: Karoma Publishers, Inc.

Dorian, Nancy C. 1986. "Making Do with Less: Some Surprises along the Language Death Proficiency Continuum." *Applied Psycholinguistics* 7, 257–276.

Dorian, Nancy C. 1987. "The Value of Language-Maintenance Efforts Which Are Unlikely to Succeed." *International Journal of the Sociology of Language* 68, 57–67.

Dorian, Nancy C. 1990. "Writing without Reading: An Illiterate Imperfect Speaker's Adventures in Writing Gaelic." In *Celtic Language, Celtic Culture: A Festschrift for Eric P. Hamp*, ed. A. T. E. Matonis and Daniel F. Melia, 218–44. Van Nuys, CA: Ford & Baillie.

Dorian, Nancy C. 1993a. "A Response to Ladefoged's Other View of Endangered Languages." *Language* 69, 575–579.

Dorian, Nancy C. 1993b. "Stylistic Variation in a Language Restricted to Private-Sphere Use." In *Sociolinguistic Perspectives on Register*, ed. Douglas Biber and Edward Finegan, 217–232. Oxford: Oxford University Press.

Dorian, Nancy C. 1994a. "Comment: Choices and Values in Language Shift and Its Study." *International Journal of the Sociology of Language* 110, 113–124.

Dorian, Nancy C. 1994b. "Varieties of Variation in a Very Small Place: Social Homogeneity, Prestige Norms, and Linguistic Variation." *Language* 70, 631–696.

Dorian, Nancy C. 1997. "Telling the Monolinguals from the Bilinguals: Unrealistic Code Choices in Direct Quotations within Scottish Gaelic Narratives." *International Journal of Bilingualism* 1, 41–54.

Dorian, Nancy C. 1998. "Western Language Ideologies and Small-Language Prospects." In *Endangered Languages: Current Issues and Future Prospects*, ed. Lenore A. Grenoble and Lindsey J. Whaley, 3–21. Cambridge: Cambridge University Press.

Dorian, Nancy C. 2001. "Surprises in Sutherland: Linguistic Variability amidst Social Uniformity." In *Linguistic Fieldwork*, ed. Paul Newman and Martha Ratliff, 133–151. Cambridge: Cambridge University Press.

Dorian, Nancy C. 2009. "Age and Speaker Skills in Receding Languages: How Far Do Community Evaluations and Linguists' Evaluations Agree?" *International Journal of the Sociology of Language* 200, 11–25.

Dorian, Nancy C. 2010. *Investigating Variation: The Effects of Social Organization and Social Setting*. Oxford: Oxford University Press.

Dorian, Nancy C., ed. 1989. *Investigating Obsolescence: Studies in Language Contraction and Death*. New York: Cambridge University Press.

Ducey, Paul. 1956. "Cultural Continuity and Population Change on the Isle of Skye." Faculty of Political Science New York: Columbia University

Duncan, William J. n.d. "Taransay Side School, September, 1921 – July, 1929." *Brochan* [annual magazine of Sir E. Scott School, Tarbert, Harris], 24–25.

Dunn, Catherine M. and A. G. Boyd Robertson. 1989. "Gaelic in Education." In *Gaelic and Scotland – Alba agus a' Ghàidhlig*, ed. William Gillies, 44–55. Edinburgh: Edinburgh University Press.

Dunn, Charles W. 1953. *Highland Settler: A Portrait of the Scottish Gael in Nova Scotia*. Toronto: University of Toronto Press.

Durkacz, Victor. 1983. *The Decline of the Celtic Languages: A Study of Linguistic and Cultural Conflict in Scotland, Wales and Ireland from the Reformation to the Twentieth Century*. Edinburgh: John Donald.

Dyer, Gwynne. 2000. "As Languages Fall Silent." *Star Tribune* (Minneapolis, Minnesota, USA), July 23, 23A.

"Dying languages: English kills." 1998. *The Economist* [US Edition], 6 June, 83.

Echeverria, Begoña. 2003. "Language Ideologies and Practices in (En)gendering the Basque Nation." *Language in Society* 323, 383–413.

Eckert, Penelope. 1983. "The Paradox of National Language Movements." *Journal of Multilingual and Multicultural Development* 4 (4), 289–300.

Eckert, Penelope and McConnell-Ginet, Sally. 1992. "Think Practically and Look Locally: Language and Gender as Community-Based Practice." *Annual Review of Anthropology* 21, 461–490.

Edwards, John. 1985. *Language, Society and Identity*. Oxford: Blackwell.

Edwards, John. 2006. "Players and Power in Minority-group Settings." *Journal of Multilingual and Multicultural Development* 27 (1), 4–21.

Elliott, Brian, and David McCrone. 1987. "Class, Culture and Morality: A Sociological Analysis of Neo-Conservatism." *Sociological Review* 35, 485–515.

Englebretson, Robert. 2007. "Stancetaking in Discourse: An Introduction." In *Stancetaking in Discourse: Subjectivity, Evaluation, Interaction*, ed. Robert Englebretson, 1–25. Amsterdam and Philadelphia: John Benjamins.

Ennew, Judith. 1978. "The Impact of Oil-Related Industry on the Outer Hebrides, with particular reference to Stornoway, Isle of Lewis." PhD thesis, Dept. of Anthropology, Cambridge University.

Ennew, Judith. 1980. *The Western Isles Today*. Cambridge: Cambridge University Press.

Evans, Nicholas. 2001. "The Last Speaker is Dead – Long Live the Last Speaker!" In *Linguistic Fieldwork*, ed. Paul Newman and Martha Ratliff, 250–81. Cambridge: Cambridge University Press.

Fairclough, Norman. 2000. *New Labour, New Language?* New York and London: Routledge.

Farquharson, Archibald. 1868. *An Address to Highlanders Respecting Their Native Gaelic: Showing Its and the Broad Scotch's Superiority over the Artificial English for the Family and the Social Circle, and also for Lyric Poetry*. Edinburgh, Glasgow, Oban, Inverness, Stornoway: Maclachlan and Stewart; W. Love; J. Miller; J. Noble; W. Gilchrist Macpherson.

Fenyö, Krisztina. 2000. *Contempt, Sympathy and Romance. Lowland Perceptions of the Highlands and the Clearances during the Famine Years, 1845–1855*. East Linton: Tuckwell Press.

Ferguson, James. 1994. *The Anti-Politics Machine: "Development," Depoliticization, and Bureaucratic Power in Lesotho*. New York: Cambridge University Press.

Fettes, Mark. 1997. "Stabilizing what? An Ecological Approach to Language Renewal." In *Teaching Indigenous Languages*, ed. Jon Reyhner, 301–18. Flagstaff, AZ: Northern Arizona University.

Fishman, Joshua A. 1965. "Bilingualism, Intelligence and Language Learning," *The Modern Language Journal* 49 (4), 227–237.

Fishman, Joshua A. 1991. *Reversing Language Shift: Theoretical and Empirical Foundations of Assistance to Threatened Languages*. Clevedon: Multilingual Matters.

Fishman, Joshua A. 2001. "Can Threatened Languages Be Saved?" In *Reversing Language Shift Revisited: A 21st Century Perspective*. Clevedon: Multilingual Matters.

Foucault, Michel. 1991. "Governmentality." In *The Foucault Effect: Studies in Governmentality. With Two Lectures by, and an Interview with, Michel Foucault*, ed. Graham Burchell, Colin Gordon, and Peter Miller, 87–104. Chicago: University of Chicago Press.

Friedman, Victor. 1997. "Observing the Observers: Language, Ethnicity and Power in the 1994 Macedonian Census and Beyond." In *Toward Comprehensive Peace in Southeastern Europe*, ed. Barnett Rubin, 81–105 and 119–26. New York: Council on Foreign Relations.

Fry, Michael. 2000. "They Didn't Say Yes, They Didn't Say No, So There Could Not be a Conclusion." *Scottish Express*, 3 March.

Fullerton, Tom. 1999. "Cash and Marry for Islanders." *The Express*, 6 February, 27.

"Gaelic revival myth scotched by student." 1996. *Times Higher Education Supplement*, 12 January.

Galloway, John M.K. 1995. "The Role of Employment in Gaelic Language Maintenance and Development." PhD diss., University of Edinburgh.

Gal, Susan. 1978. "Peasant Men Can't Get Wives: Language Change and Sex Roles in a Bilingual Community," *Language in Society* 7 (1), 1–16.

Gal, Susan. 1979. *Language Shift: Social Determinants of Linguistic Change in Bilingual Austria*. New York: Academic Press.

Gal, Susan. 1989. "Language and Political Economy." *Annual Review of Anthropology* 18, 345–67.

Gal, Susan. 1989. "Lexical Innovation and Loss: The Use and Value of Restricted Hungarian." In *Investigating Obsolescence. Studies in Language Contraction and Death*, ed. Nancy C. Dorian, 313–331. Cambridge: Cambridge University Press.

General Register Office for Scotland. 2005. "Map 2: Parishes in Scotland by the percentage of people aged 3 and over who speak Gaelic, 2001." Accessed 8 December 2007. http://www.gro-scotland.gov.uk/files/gaelic-rep-english-appendix.pdf.

General Register Office for Scotland. 2005. Table UV12: Knowledge of Gaelic. Accessed 29 February 2008. http://www.scrol.gov.uk/.

Gillies, William. 1989. "A Century of Gaelic Scholarship." In *Gaelic and Scotland – Alba agus a' Ghàidhlig*, ed. William Gillies, 3–21. Edinburgh University Press, Edinburgh.

Glazer, Konstanze. 2007. *Minority Languages and Cultural Diversity in Europe: Gaelic and Sorbian Perspectives.* Clevedon: Multilingual Matters.

Glover, Michael. 2000a. "Do Brits Really Need a Second Language? English Will Be the Chosen Form of World Communications and Commerce This Century." *The Scotsman*, 11 May 2000, 16.

Glover, Michael. 2000b. "Just another slip of the tongue." *The Independent*, 31 July 2000. Accessed 19 June 2001. http://www.independent.co.uk/ story.jsp?dir=1&story=8306&host=1&printable=1.

Gossen, Andrew. 2001. "Agents of a Modern Gaelic Scotland: Curriculum, Change, and Challenge at Sabhal Mòr Ostaig, the Gaelic College of Scotland." PhD diss., Dept. of Anthropology, Harvard University.

Grant, Nigel. 1996. "Gaelic and Education in Scotland – Developments and Perspectives." *Scottish Gaelic Studies* 17, 150–58.

Gray, Alison. 2000. "Death of Gaelic forecast by end of century." *The Scotsman*, 31 May.

Grin, François. 1996a. "Economic Approaches to Language and Language Planning: An Introduction." *International Journal of the Sociology of Language* 121, 1–16.

Grin, François. 1996b. "The Economics of Language: Survey, Assessment, and Prospects." *International Journal of the Sociology of Language* 121, 17–44.

Hacking, Ian, 1991. "How Should We Do the History of Statistics?" In *The Foucault Effect: Studies in Governmentality: with Two Lectures by, and an Interview with, Michel Foucault.* ed. G. Burchell, C. Gordon, and P. Miller, 181–195. Chicago: University of Chicago Press.

Hale, Ken. 1992a. "Language Endangerment and the Human Value of Linguistic Diversity." *Language* 68 (1), 35–42.

Hale, Ken. 1992b. "On Endangered Languages and the Safeguarding of Diversity." *Language* 68 (1), 1–3.

Hale, Ken. 1998. "On Endangered Languages and the Importance of Linguistic Diversity." In *Endangered Languages: Language Loss and Community Response*, ed. Lenore A. Grenoble and Lindsay J. Whaley, 192–216. Cambridge: Cambridge University Press.

Halliday, Michael A. K. 1989. *Spoken and Written Language.* Oxford: Oxford University Press.

Hamp, Eric P. 1989. "On signs of health and death." In *Language Obsolescence*, ed. Nancy C. Dorian, 197–210. Cambridge: Cambridge University Press.

Hanham, H. J. 1969. *Scottish Nationalism.* London: Faber and Faber.

Harris, Gillian. 1999. "Islanders hope £700,000 grant will woo wives." *The Times*, 5 February.

Haugen, E. 1966. "Dialect, Language, Nation." *American Anthropologist* 68 (4), 922–35.

Heath, Julie. 2002. "Liberty and Tradition: Sound Patterning in Hebridean Prayer and Preaching as Poetic Device and Linguistic Sign." In *Rannsachadh na Gàidhlig 2000*, ed. Colm Ó Baoill and Nancy R. McGuire, 25–33. Aberdeen: An Clò Gaidhealach.

Heller, Monica. 2006. *Linguistic Minorities and Modernity: A Sociolinguistic Ethnography*, 2nd edition, London: Continuum Books.

Her Majesty's Inspectorate of Education. 2005. "Changing Lives: Adult Literacy and Numeracy in Scotland." Accessed 14 June 2010. http://www.hmie.gov.uk/documents/publication/clalns.html.

Her Majesty's Inspectorate of Education. 2010. "Improving Adult Literacy in Scotland." Accessed 14 June 2010. http://www.hmie.gov.uk/ documents/publication/ialis.pdf.

Herzfeld, Michael. 1987. *Anthropology through the Looking-Glass: Critical Ethnography in the Margins of Europe*. Cambridge: Cambridge University Press.

Hill, Jane H. 1985. "The Grammar of Consciousness and the Consciousness of Grammar." *American Ethnologist* 12, 725–37.

Hill, Jane H. 1995. "Mock Spanish: A Site for the Indexical Reproduction of Racism in American English." Language & Culture: Symposium 2. Accessed March 12, 2002. http://www.language-culture.org/colloquia/symposia/hill-jane/.

Hill, Jane H. 2002. "'Expert Rhetorics' in Advocacy for Endangered Languages: Who Is Listening, and What Do They Hear?" *Journal of Linguistic Anthropology* 12 (2), 119–33.

Hill, Jane H., and Judith T. Irvine. 1993. "Introduction." In *Responsibility and Evidence in Oral Discourse*. ed. Jane H. Hill and Judith T. Irvine, 1–23. Cambridge: Cambridge University Press.

Hinton, Leanne. 1997. "Survival of Endangered Languages: The California Master-Apprentice Program." *International Journal of the Sociology of Language* 123, 177–91.

Hinton, Leanne, Matt Vera, Nancy Steele, and Advocates for Indigenous California Language Survival. 2002. *How to Keep Your Language Alive: A Commonsense Approach to One-on-One Language Learning*. Berkeley, CA: Heyday Books.

Hoenigswald, Henry M. 1989. "Language Obsolescence and Language History: Matters of Linearity, Leveling, Loss, and the Like." In *Language Obsolescence: Studies in Language Contraction and Death*, ed. Nancy C. Dorian, 347–354. Cambridge: Cambridge University Press.

Hornburger, Nancy and Kendall A. King. 2001. "Reversing Quechua Language Shift in South America." In *Can Threatened Languages be Saved? Reversing Language Shift, Revisited: A 21st Century Perspective*, ed. J. A. Fishman, 166–94. Clevedon, UK: Multilingual Matters.

Hymes, Dell. 1984 [1968]. "Linguistic Problems in Defining the Concept of 'Tribe.'" In *Language in Use*, ed. John Baugh and Joel Sherzer, 7–27 Englewood Cliffs, NJ: Prentice-Hall.

Inda, Jonathan Xavier, and Renato Rosaldo, eds. 2004. *The Anthropology of Globalization: A Reader*. 2nd ed. Malden, MA: Blackwell.

Irvine, Judith T., and Susan Gal. 2000. "Language Ideologies and Linguistic Differentiation." In *Regimes of Language*, ed. Paul Kroskrity, 35–84. Santa Fe: School of American Research.

Jacobs, N. 1976. "Learning Welsh 3." *Planet* 34, 14–15.

Jaffe, Alexandra. 1996. "The Second Annual Corsican Spelling Contest: Orthography and Ideology." *American Ethnologist* 23, 816–835.

Jaffe, Alexandra M. 1999. *Ideologies in Action: Language Politics on Corsica*. Berlin: Mouton de Gruyter.

Jamison, Kelda. 2010. "The Conundrum of Kurdish Literacy: Inscription and Population in Contemporary Turkey." Presentation to the Anthropology of Europe Workshop, University of Chicago, 13 May.

Jedrej, Charles, and Mark Nuttall. 1996. *White Settlers: The Impact of Rural Repopulation in Scotland*. Luxembourg: Harwood Academic.

Johns, Alana and Irene Mazurekewich. 2001. "The Role of the University in the Training of Native Language Teachers." In *The Green Book of Language Revitalization in Practice*, ed. Leanne Hinton and Ken Hale, 355–66. New York: Academic Press.

Johnson, M. and Associated Press. 1997. "Scottish Gaelic on life support," *Calgary Herald*, 13 September.

Johnson, Samuel and James Boswell. 1984 [1775]. *A Journey to the Western Isles of Scotland and Journal of a Tour to the Hebrides*. London: Penguin Books.

Johnstone, Richard, Wynne Harlen, Morag MacNeil, Bob Stradling, and Graham Thorpe. 1999. *The Attainments of Pupils Receiving Gaelic-medium Primary Education in Scotland*. Stirling: Scottish Center for Information on Language Teaching and Research [SCILT] on behalf of the Scottish Executive Education Department.

Jones, Charles, and Wilson McLeod. 2007. "Standards and Differences: Languages in Scotland, 1707–1918." In *The Edinburgh History of Scottish Literature, Volume Two: Enlightenment, Britain and Empire (1707–1918)*.

ed. Susan Manning, Ian Brown, Thomas Owen Clancy, and Murray Pittock, 21–32. Edinburgh: Edinburgh University Press.

Jones, Mari C. 1998. *Language Obsolescence and Revitalization: Linguistic Change in Two Sociolinguistically Contrasting Welsh Communities.* Oxford: Clarendon Press.

Kabel, Lars. 2000. "Irish Language Enthusiasts and Native Speakers: An Uneasy Relationship." In *Aithne na nGael/Gaelic identities*, ed. Gordon McCoy and Maolcholaim Scott, 133–38. Belfast: Institute of Irish Studies, Queen's University Belfast and Ultach Trust/Iontaobhas Ultach.

Kennedy, Michael. 2002. "Gaelic Nova Scotia: An Economic, Cultural, and Social Impact Study. Halifax: Nova Scotia Museum." Accessed 29 September 2012. http://museum.gov.ns.ca/site-museum/media/museum/Gaelic-Report(1).pdf.

Keown, Gary. 1999. "It May Be Scotland's Second Language, But It's Still All Greek to Me." *Sunday Mail*, 17 October, 25.

Kiesling, Scott. 2006. "Language and Identity in Sociocultural Anthropology" In *Encyclopedia of Language and Linguistics, Vol. 5*, 2nd edition, ed. Keith Brown, 495–502. Oxford: Elsevier.

King, Kendall A. 2001. *Language Revitalization Processes and Prospects: Quichua in the Ecuadorian Andes.* Clevedon: Multilingual Matters.

Kockelman, Paul. 2002. "Subjectivity as Stance under Neoliberal Governance: Language and Labor, Mind and Measure, among the Q'eqchi'-Maya." PhD diss., Department of Anthropology, University of Chicago.

Krauss, Michael. 1992. "The World's Languages in Crisis." *Language* 68 (1), 4–10.

Kroeber, Theodora. 1981 [1964]. *Ishi: Last of His Tribe*. New York: Bantam Books.

Kulick, Don. 1992. *Language Shift and Cultural Reproduction: Socialization, Self, and Syncretism in a Papua New Guinean Village*, Cambridge: Cambridge University Press.

Kurt C. Duwe. 2006. *Gàidhlig (Scottish Gaelic) Local Studies, Vol. 16: Ile, Diùra & Colbhasa (Islay, Jura & Colonsay)*, 2nd ed. Hamburg.

Kuter, Lois. 1989. "Breton vs. French: Language and the Opposition of Political, Economic, Social and Cultural Values." In *Investigating Obsolescence: Studies in Language Contraction and Death*, ed. Nancy C. Dorian, 75–89. New York: Cambridge University Press.

Labov, William. 1972. *Sociolinguistic Patterns*. Philadelphia: University of Pennsylvania Press.

Laing, Allan. 1997. "BBC Swears by Four-Letter Word." *The Herald (Glasgow)*, 8 August, 3.

Lakoff, George, and Mark Johnson. 1980. *Metaphors We Live By*. Chicago: University of Chicago Press.

Lamb, William. 1999. "A diachronic account of Gaelic News-speak: The development and expansion of a register," *Scottish Gaelic Studies* 19, 141–171.

Lamb, William. 2008. *Scottish Gaelic Speech and Writing: Register Variation in an Endangered Language*. Belfast: Cló Ollscoil na Banríona.

Lamb, William. 2011. "Is there a future for regional dialects in Scottish Gaelic?" Paper presented at "Linguistic Attrition; Linguistic Creation" Symposium, University of Aberdeen, 3 December.

Landgraf, Sìleas. 2011. "The self-awareness and attitudes of school children towards Gaelic." Presentation at "Maintaining and Revitalising Minority Languages in their 'Heartlands'" conference, Sabhal Mòr Ostaig, September

Lave, Jean and Etienne Wenger. 1991. *Situated Learning: Legitimate Peripheral Participation*. Cambridge: Cambridge University Press.

Lawson, Bill. 1997. *The Isle of Taransay: A Harris Island in its Historical Setting*. Taobh Tuath (Northton), Isle of Harris: Bill Lawson Publications.

Lethbridge, T. C. 1952. "Excavations at Kilpheder, South Uist, and the problem of the brochs and wheelhouses." *Proceedings of the Prehistoric Society* 18:176–193.

Levitas, Ruth. 1998. *The Inclusive Society? Social Exclusion and New Labour*. London: Macmillan Press Ltd.

Lewis, M. Paul and Gary F. Simons. 2010. "Assessing Endangerment: Expanding Fishman's GIDS." *Revue Roumaine de Linguistique* 55 (2), 103–20. http://www.lingv.ro/resources/scm_images/RRL-02-2010-Lewis.pdf.

Lutz, Catherine and Geoffrey M. White. 1986. "The Anthropology of Emotions." *Annual Review of Anthropology* 15, 405–36.

Lutz, Catherine, and Lila Abu-Lughod, eds. 1990. *Language and the Politics of Emotion*. New York: Cambridge University Press.

Macafee, C., 1985. "Nationalism and the Scots renaissance now." In: Görlach, M. (Ed.), *Focus on: Scotland*. John Benjamins, Amsterdam, 7–17.

MacArthur, John M.M., et al. 1982. *Cor na Gàidhlig. Language, community and development: The Gaelic situation*. Inverness: Comunn na Gàidhlig.

MacArthur, John M.M., Fred Macaulay, Catriona MacDonald, Martin Macdonald, Donald J. MacKay, Finlay MacLeod, Duncan MacQuarrie, and Cailean Spencer. 1982. *Cor na Gàidhlig. Language, Community and Development: The Gaelic Situation*. Inverness: Highlands and Islands Development Board.

MacAulay, Cathlin. 1998. "Gaelic: A study of language maintenance and shift in the Scottish Gaidhealtachd." PhD thesis, University of Hertfordshire.

MacAulay, Donald. 1976-78. "The Writing of Scottish Gaelic: Uses of Convention and Innovation." *Transactions of the Gaelic Society of Inverness*, 50, 81-96.

MacAulay, Donald. 1978. "Intra-Dialectal Variation as an Area of Gaelic Linguistic Research." *Scottish Gaelic Studies* 13 (Part 1), 81- 97.

MacAulay, Donald. 1979. "The State of Gaelic Language Studies." In *Languages of Scotland*, ed. A. J. Aitken and Tom McArthur, 120-136. Edinburgh: W & R Chambers.

MacAulay, Donald. 1982a. "Borrow, Calque and Switch: The Law of the English Frontier." In *Language Form and Linguistic Variation. Papers dedicated to Angus Macintosh*, ed. John Anderson, 203-237. Amsterdam: John Benjamins B. V.

MacAulay, Donald. 1982b. "Register Range and Choice in Scottish Gaelic." *International Journal of the Sociology of Language* 35, 25- 48.

MacAulay, Donald. 1986. "New Gaelic?" *Scottish Language*, 120-125.

MacCaluim, Alasdair. 1998. "A' Cur Clach Chlaon air a' Chàrnan / Adding an Oblique Stone to the Cairn" [Review of Reimagining Culture by Sharon Macdonald], *Cothrom* 16, 52-54.

MacCaluim, Alasdair. 2002. "Periphery of the Periphery? Adult Learners of Scottish Gaelic and Reversal of Language Shift." PhD thesis, University of Edinburgh.

MacCaluim, Alasdair. 2007. *Reversing Language Shift: The Social Identity and Role of Scottish Gaelic Learners*. Belfast: Clo Oiscoill na Banrighna.

Macculloch, John. 1824. *The Highlands and Western Isles of Scotland, Containing Descriptions of Their Scenery and Antiquities, with an Account of the Political History and Ancient Manners, and of the Origin, Language, Agriculture, Economy, Music, Present Condition of the People, &c. &c. &c. Founded on a Series of Annual Journeys between the Years 1811 and 1821, and Forming an Universal guide to that country, in letters to Sir Walter Scott, Bard*. London: Longman Hurst Rees Orme Brown and Green.

Macdhomhnuill, R. 1776. *Comh-chruinneachaidh Òrannaigh Gàidhealach [the Eigg Collection]*. Duneidiunn [Edinburgh].

Mac-Dhonuill, Alastair [Alexander MacDonald]. 1751. *Ais-Eiridh na Sean Chánoin Albannaich; no, An nuadh Oranaiche Gaidhealach*. Author, Edinburgh.

MacDonald, Alexander, and Society in Scotland for Propagating Christian Knowledge. 1741. *A Galick and English Vocabulary, with an Appendix of the Terms of Divinity in the Said Language. Written for the Use of the Charity-Schools Founded and Endued in the Highlands of Scotland*. Edinburgh: Printed by R. Fleming and Sold by Mrs. Brown, Society in Scotland for Propagating Christian Knowledge.

MacDonald, Fraser. 2003. "Geographies of Vision and Modernity: Things Seen in the Scottish Highlands." DPhil thesis, Oxford University.

MacDonald, Fraser. 2011. "Doomsday fieldwork, or, how to rescue Gaelic culture? The salvage paradigm in geography, archaeology and folklore, 1955-1962." *Environment Planning D: Society and Space* 29(2):309–335.

MacDonald, Fraser, ed. 2004. "Colloquium: Susan Parman's Scottish Crofters: A Historical Ethnography of a Celtic Village," *Journal of Scottish Historical Studies* 24 (2), 159–181.

Macdonald, Sharon. 1987. "Social and Linguistic Identity in the Scottish Gàidhealtachd." PhD thesis, Department of Anthropology, Oxford University.

Macdonald, Sharon. 1997a. "A People's Story: Heritage, Identity and Authenticity." In *Touring Cultures: Transformations of Travel and Theory*, ed. Chris Rojek and John Urry, 155–175. New York: Routledge.

Macdonald, Sharon. 1997b. *Reimagining Culture: Histories, Identities and the Gaelic Renaissance*. Oxford: Berg.

Macdonald, Sharon. 1997. *Reimagining Culture: Histories, Identities and the Gaelic Renaissance*. Oxford: Berg.

Macdonald, Sharon. 1999. "'A bheil am feur gorm fhathast?': Some Problems Concerning Language and Cultural Shift." *Scottish Studies*, 186–197.

MacGaffey, Wyatt. 1991. Review of *Edwin Ardener: The Voice of Prophecy and Other Essays* by Malcolm Chapman. *American Anthropologist* 93(4), 972–973.

MacGregor, Alasdair Alpin. 1952. *The Western Isles*. London: Hale.

MacIlle Dhuibh, Raghnall. 2011. "'Cuir' mi ás an fhearann thu': Leabhraichean ùra." The Scotsman, 18 June, 36

MacInnes, John. 1979. "The Panegyric Code in Gaelic Poetry and its Historical Background." *Transactions of the Gaelic Society of Inverness* 50, 435–498.

MacInnes, John. 2006. *Dùthchas nan Gàidheal: Selected Essays of John MacInnes*, ed. Michael Newton. Edinburgh: Birlinn.

MacKay, Charles. 1877. *The Gaelic Etymology of the Languages of Western Europe and More Especially of the English and Lowland Scotch, and of Their Slang, Cant, and Colloquial Dialects*. London: Published for the author by N. Trübner and Co.

MacKay, Margaret A. 2004. "Voices, Names, Words: Scottish Crofters and Scottish Ethnology." In "Colloquium: Susan Parman's Scottish Crofters: A Historical Ethnography of a Celtic Village," *Journal of Scottish Historical Studies* 24 (2), 169–172.

MacKinnon, Danny. 2000a. "Managerialism, Governmentality and the State: A Neo-Foucauldian Approach to Local Economic Governance." *Political Geography* 19, 293–314.

MacKinnon, Danny. 2000b. "Rural Governance and Local Involvement: Assessing State–community Relations in the Scottish Highlands." Unpublished mss. University of Aberdeen.

MacKinnon, Kenneth. 1974. *The Lion's Tongue: The Story of the Original and Continuing Language of the Scottish People.* Inverness: Club Leabhar.

MacKinnon, Kenneth. 1977. *Language, Education and Social Processes in a Gaelic Community.* London: Routledge and Kegan Paul.

MacKinnon, Kenneth. 1981. "Scottish Opinion on Gaelic: A Report on a National Attitude Survey for An Comunn Gàidhealach Undertaken in 1981." Hatfield: School of Business and Social Sciences, Hatfield Polytechnic.

MacKinnon, Kenneth. 1984. "Scottish Gaelic and English in the Highlands" in *Language in the British Isles*, ed. Peter Trudgill, 499–516. Cambridge, UK: Cambridge University Press.

MacKinnon, Kenneth. 1984. "Scottish Gaelic and English in the Highlands" in *Language in the British Isles*, ed. Peter Trudgill, 499–516. Cambridge, UK: Cambridge University Press.

MacKinnon, Kenneth. 1996. "Social Class and Gaelic Language Abilities in the 1981 Census." *Scottish Gaelic Studies* 17, 239–249.

MacKinnon, Kenneth. 2003. "Census 2001 Scotland: Gaelic Language Abilities by Age Group and Country of Birth." In *Bòrd Gàidhlig na h-Alba: New Thinking for a Fresh Start?* http://www.arts.ed.ac.uk/celtic/poileasaidh/newthinking/languageabilities.html.

Maclean, Calum I. 1956–1957. "Hebridean Traditions." *Gwerin* 1, 21–33.

Maclean, Lachlan. 1837. *Adhamh agus Eubh, no, Craobh Sheanchais nan Gàèl.* Edinburgh: Maclachlan and Stewart.

MacLeod, Angus, ed. 1952. *The Songs of Duncan Ban Macintyre.* Edinburgh: Oliver & Boyd for the Scottish Gaelic Texts Society.

Macleod, Donald. 2004. "Ciall and its Calvinists." In "Colloquium: Susan Parman's Scottish Crofters: A Historical Ethnography of a Celtic Village," *Journal of Scottish Historical Studies* 24 (2), 172–175.

MacLeod, John. 1996. "If Gaelic is lost, tomorrow's Highlanders will be strangers to their own art and culture." *Daily Mail*, 15 August.

MacLeod, Murdo. 1966. "Gaelic in Highland Education." *Transactions of the Gaelic Society of Inverness* 43(1960–1963), 305–25.

MacNeill, Morag. 1991. *Everyday Gaelic.* Glasgow: Gairm.

MacPhàdruig, Mìcheil. 1998. "Diombach mu Bharail nan Gàidheal/Despairing of Native Speakers." *Cothrom* 16 (Summer), 14–15.

Mallon, Margaret. 1999. "Girls say thanks but no thanks." *Daily Record*, 6 February, 7.

Martin, Laura. 1986. "'Eskimo Words for Snow': A Case Study in the Genesis and Decay of an Anthropological Example." *American Anthropologist* 88, 418–423.

McCrone, David. 1991. "Politics and Society in Modern Scotland." In *Regions, Nations and European Integration: Remaking the Celtic Periphery*, ed. Graham Day and Gareth Rees, 89–102. Cardiff: University of Wales Press.

McCrone, David, Angela Morris, and Richard Kiely. 1995. *Scotland—the Brand: The Making of Scottish Heritage*. Edinburgh: Edinburgh University Press.

McDonald, Maryon. 1989. *"We Are Not French!": Language, Culture, and Identity in Brittany*. London: Routledge.

McEwan-Fujita, Emily. 2001. "Negotiating Gaelic in the New Scottish Parliament." Presentation to Harvard Celtic Colloquium, Cambridge, MA.

McEwan-Fujita, Emily. 2003. "Gaelic in Scotland, Scotland in Europe: Minority Language Revitalization in the Age of Neoliberalism." PhD diss., Dept. of Anthropology, University of Chicago.

McEwan-Fujita, Emily. 2005. "Neoliberalism and minority language planning in the Highlands and Islands of Scotland." *International Journal of the Sociology of Language* 171, 155–71.

McEwan-Fujita, Emily. 2006. "'Gaelic doomed as speakers die out'? The public discourse of Gaelic language death in Scotland." In *Revitalising Gaelic in Scotland: Policy, Planning and Public Discourse*, ed. Wilson McLeod, 279–293. Edinburgh: Dunedin Academic Press.

McEwan-Fujita, Emily. 2008. "'9 to 5' Gaelic: Speakers, Context, and Ideology of an Emerging Minority Language Register." In *Sustaining Linguistic Diversity: Endangered and Minority Languages and Language Varieties*, ed. Kendall A. King, Natalie Schilling-Estes, Lyn Fogle, Jia Jackie Lou and Barbara Soukup, 81–93. Washington, DC: Georgetown University Press.

McEwan-Fujita, Emily. 2010a. "Ideology, affect and socialization in language shift and revitalization: The experiences of adults learning Gaelic in the Western Isles of Scotland." *Language in Society* 39 (1), 27–64

McEwan-Fujita, Emily. 2010b. "Ideologies and experiences of literacy in interactions between adult Gaelic learners and first-language Gaelic speakers in Scotland." *Scottish Gaelic Studies* 26, 87–114.

McEwan-Fujita, Emily. 2010c. "Sociolinguistic Ethnography of Gaelic Communities." In *The Edinburgh Companion to the Gaelic Language*, ed. Moray Watson and Michelle Macleod, 172–217. Edinburgh: Edinburgh University Press.

McEwan-Fujita, Emily. 2013. "Gaelic revitalization efforts in Nova Scotia: Reversing language shift in the 21st century." In *Celts in the Americas*, ed. Michael Newton, 160–186, Sydney, NS: Cape Breton University Press.

McEwan-Fujita, Emily. 2015. "Anti-Gaelic Bingo." Gaelic.co. 20 February. https://gaelic.co/anti-gaelic-bingo/.

McEwan-Fujita, Emily. 2018. "Anti-Gaelic Bingo Revisited." Gaelic.co. 15 June. https://gaelic.co/anti-gaelic-bingo-revisited/.

McIntosh, Janet. 2009. "Stance and Distance: Social Boundaries, Self-lamination, and Metalinguistic Anxiety in White Kenyan Narratives about the African Occult." In *Stance: Sociolinguistic perspectives*, ed. Alexandra Jaffe, 72–91. Oxford: Oxford University Press.

McKechnie, Alexander. 1934. *Introduction to Gaelic Scotland*. Edinburgh: Blackie & Son.

McKibben, Sarah E. 1997. "Lamenting the Language: On the Metaphor of Dying Irish." MPhil thesis, University College Dublin.

McKibben, Sarah E. 2000. "Born to Die and to Live on: Terminal Metaphors in the Life of Irish." *The Irish Review* 26, 89–99.

McLeod, Wilson. 1996. "Official status for Gaelic: prospects and problems." MSc thesis, Department of Celtic, University of Edinburgh.

McLeod, Wilson. 2002. "Language planning as regional development? The growth of the Gaelic economy." *Scottish Affairs* 38, 51–72.

McNeil, Robert. 2000. "Gaelic Flavours a Peculiarly Scottish Debate." *The Scotsman*, 3 March, 1.

McNicol, Rev. Donald. 1779. *Remarks on Dr. Samuel Johnson's Journey to the Hebrides; in Which are Contained, Observations on the Antiquities, Language, Genius, and Manners of the Highlanders of Scotland*. London: Printed for T. Cadell.

Meek, Donald E. 1990. "Language and style in the Scottish Gaelic Bible (1767–1807)." *Scottish Language* 9, 1–16.

Meek, Donald E. 1996. "Saints and Scarecrows: The Churches and Gaelic Culture in the Highlands since 1560." *Scottish Bulletin of Evangelical Theology* 14, 3–22.

Meek, Donald E. 2000. *The Quest for Celtic Christianity*. Edinburgh: Handsel Press Ltd.

Meek, Donald E. 2001. "The Language of Heaven? The Highland Churches, Culture Shift and the Erosion of Gaelic Identity in the Twentieth Century." In *Religion and National Identity: Wales and Scotland c. 1700-2000*, ed. Robert Pope. Cardiff: University of Wales Press.

Mendick, Robert. 2000. "Gaelic Doomed as Speakers Die Out." *The Independent on Sunday*, 16 July.

Menter a Busnes. n.d. Accessed 2 Novmeber 2002. http://www.menterabusnes.co.uk/.

Mertz, Elizabeth. 1982a. "'No Burden to Carry': Cape Breton Pragmatics and Metapragmatics (Nova Scotia)." PhD diss., Dept. of Anthropology, Duke University.

Mertz, Elizabeth. 1982b. "Pragmatic and Semantic Change: A Cape Breton System of Personal Names." *Semiotica* 44 (1/2), 55–74.

Mertz, Elizabeth. 1989. "Sociolinguistic Creativity: Cape Breton Gaelic's Linguistic 'tip.'" In *Investigating Obsolescence: Studies in Language Contraction and Death*, ed. Nancy C. Dorian, 103–16. Cambridge: Cambridge University Press.

Mertz, Elizabeth. 1993. "Learning What to Ask: Metapragmatic Factors and Methodological Reification." In *Reflexive Language: Reported Speech and Metapragmatics*, ed. John Lucy, 159–174. Cambridge: Cambridge University Press.

Messing, Jacqueline. 2007. "Multiple Ideologies and Competing Discourses: Language Shift in Tlaxcala, Mexico." *Language in Society* 36, 555–77.

Mewett, Peter G. 1982a. "Associational Categories and the Social Location of Relationships in a Lewis Crofting Community." In *Belonging: Identity and Social Organisation in British Rural Cultures*, ed. Anthony P. Cohen, 101–130. Manchester: Manchester University Press.

Mewett, Peter G. 1982b. "Exiles, Nicknames, Social Identities and the Production of Local Consciousness in a Lewis Crofting Community." In *Belonging: Identity and Social Organisation in British Rural Cultures*, ed. Anthony P. Cohen, 222–246. Manchester: Manchester University Press.

Miller, Hugh. 1838. *The Mountain Minstrel, or Poems and Songs, in English, by Evan M'Coll.* Inverness Courier, 10 October.

Milligan, Lindsay. 2010. "The Role of Gaelic (Learners) Education in Reversing Language Shift for Gaelic in Scotland." Ph.D. thesis. Dept. of Celtic, Aberdeen University.

Milroy, James and Lesley Milroy. 1999. *Authority in Language: Investigating Standard English*, 3rd edition. New York: Routledge.

Milroy, Lesley. 2000. "Britain and the United States: Two nations Divided by the Same Language (and Different Language Ideologies)." *Journal of Linguistic Anthropology* 10, 56–89.

M'Intyre, Donald, of Kincardine. 1866. *On the Antiquity of the Gaelic Language Showing the Identity of the Present Vernacular of the Highlands with the Gaelic of Ancient Times; A Supplementary Essay*. Edinburgh: W. P. Nimmo.

M'Nish, Neil. 1828. *The True Method of Preserving the Gaelic Language; or, How to Retrieve the Decaying Honour and Prosperity of the Highlands, and Islands of Scotland*. Edinburgh: George A. Douglass.

Moffat, Alistair. 1995. "Dreams and Deconstructions/Dòchas Agus Dì-chruthachadh: The Sabhal Mòr Lecture 1995." Glasgow: Scottish Television.

Moore, Robert E. 1998. "'The People Are Here Now': The Contemporary Culture of an Ancestral Language: Studies in Obsolescent Kiksht (Wasco-Wishram Dialect of Upper Chinookan)." PhD diss., University of Chicago.

Moore, Robert E. 1999. "Endangered." *Journal of Linguistic Anthropology* 9, 65–68.

Morrison, Margaret. 1996. "My family left behind the old back-breaking work of croft life. If the language now dies too, then so be it." *Daily Mail*, 15 August.

Morrison, Marion F. 2006. "A' Chiad Ghinealach – the First Generation: A survey of Gaelic-medium education in the Western Isles." In *Revitalising Gaelic in Scotland: Policy, Planning and Public Discourse*, ed. Wilson McLeod, 139–154. Edinburgh: Dunedin Academic Press.

Müller, Martina. 2006. "Language use, langauge attitudes and Gaelic writing ability among secondary pupils in the Isle of Skye." In *Revitalising Gaelic in Scotland: Policy, Planning and Public Discourse*, ed. Wilson McLeod, 119–138. Edinburgh: Dunedin Academic Press.

Munro, Gillian, and Iain Mac an Tàilleir, eds. 2010. *Gaelic Communities Today: Coimhearsnachd na Gàidhlig An-diugh*. Edinburgh: Dunedin Academic Press.

Munro, Gillian, Iain Taylor, Tim Armstrong. 2011. "Gaelic in Shawbost: Language Attitudes and Abilities in Shawbost." Sleat: Sabhal Mòr Ostaig.

Murray, John. 1989. "Gaelic Education and the Gaelic community." In *Gaelic and Scotland / Alba agus a' Ghàidhlig*, ed. William Gillies, 56–63 Edinburgh: Edinburgh University Press.

Murray, John, and Catherine Morrison. 1984. *Bilingual Primary Education in the Western Isles Scotland*. Stornoway: Acair.

Nance, Claire. 2013. "Phonetic Variation, Sound Change, and Identity in Scottish Gaelic." PhD thesis, University of Glasgow.

Nance, Claire. 2014. "Phonetic variation in Scottish Gaelic laterals." *Journal of Phonetics*, 47, 1-17.

National Literacy Trust. n.d. "Scotland: Overview of Scottish Policy on Literacy and Education." Accessed 14 June 2010. http://www.literacytrust.org.uk/policy/regional/scotland.

Nelde, Peter H., Miquell Strubell, and Glyn Williams. 1996. *Euromosaic: The Production and Reproduction of the Minority Language Groups of the EU*. Luxembourg: Office for Official Publications of the European Communities.

Nettle, Daniel, and Suzanne Romaine. 2000. *Vanishing Voices: The Extinction of the World's Languages*. Oxford: Oxford University Press.

Newcombe, Lynda Pritchard. 2002. "'A Tough Hill to Climb Alone' – Welsh Learners Speak." *Hong Kong Journal of Applied Linguistics* 7 (2), 39-56.

Newcombe, Lynda Pritchard. 2002. "'A Tough Hill to Climb Alone' – Welsh Learners Speak." *Hong Kong Journal of Applied Linguistics* 7 (2), 39-56.

Newcombe, Lynda Pritchard. 2007. *Social Context and Fluency in L2 Learners: The Case of Wales*. Clevedon, UK: Multilingual Matters.

"News." 2000. *Anthropology Today* 16 (5), 31.

"Newsnight Scotland." 2000. Segment on the Macpherson Report with Gordon Brewer interviewing Allan Brown, John Alec Macpherson, and Mike Russell. BBC Scotland, 7 September.

Newton, Michael. 2000. *A Handbook of the Scottish Gaelic World*. Dublin: Four Courts Press.

Newton, Michael. 2005. "'This Could Have Been Mine': Scottish Gaelic Learners in North America." *e-Keltoi: Journal of Interdisciplinary Celtic Studies* 1, 1-37. http://www4.uwm.edu/celtic/ekeltoi/volumes/vol1/1_1/newton_1_1.pdf.

Newton, Michael. 2009. *Warriors of the Word: The World of the Scottish Highlanders*. Edinburgh: Birlinn.

Nonaka, Angela. 2004. "Sign Languages—The Forgotten Endangered Languages: Lessons on the Importance of Remembering." *Language in Society* 33, 737-67.

Ó Baoill, Colm. 1979. *Eachann Bacach and Other Maclean Poets*. Edinburgh: The Scottish Academic Press for the Scottish Gaelic Texts Society.

Ó Baoill, Colm. 2010. "A History of Gaelic to 1800." In *The Edinburgh Companion to the Gaelic Language*, ed. Moray Watson and Michelle Macleod, 1-21. Edinburgh: Edinburgh University Press.

Ochs, E., and Schieffelin, B. B. 1984. "Language acquisition and socialization: three developmental stories and their implications." In *Culture Theory: Essays on Mind, Self, and Emotion*, ed. R. A. Shweder and R. A. LeVine, 276–320, Cambridge, UK.

Ochs, Elinor. 1990. "Indexicality and Socialization." In *Cultural psychology*, ed. James W. Stigler, Richard A. Shweder, and Gilbert Herdt, 287–308. Cambridge: Cambridge University Press.

Ochs, Elinor. 1996. "Linguistic Resources for Socializing Humanity." In *Rethinking Linguistic Relativity*, ed. John Gumperz and Steven C. Levinson, 407–437. Cambridge: Cambridge University Press.

Ochs, Elinor, and Bambi B. Schieffelin. 1989. "Language Has a Heart." *Text* 9, 7–25.

Ó Giollagáin, Conchúr. 2011. "Irish in the Gaeltacht: Problems and Prospects." Keynote address at Maintaining and Revitalising Minority Languages in their "Heartlands" conference, Sabhal Mòr Ostaig, Scotland, September.

O'Hanlon, Fiona. 2012. "Lost in transition? Celtic language revitalization in Scotland and Wales: the primary to secondary school stage." Ph.D. thesis, Dept. of Celtic, University of Edinburgh.

O Hianlaidh, Ailig. 1999. "Gràin a' chànain se gràin cinnidh" [Hatred of the language is ethnic hatred], *The Scotsman*, 1 September.

Oliver, James. 2002. "Young People and Gaelic in Scotland: Identity Dynamics in a European Region." Ph.D. thesis, University of Sheffield.

Oliver, James. 2010. "The Predicament: Planning for Culture, Communities and Identities." In *Gaelic Communities Today: Coimhearsnachd na Gàidhlig An-diugh*, ed. Gillian Munro and Iain Mac an Tàilleir, 73–86. Edinburgh: Dunedin Academic Press.

Oxford English Dictionary Online. 1989. Oxford: Oxford University Press.

Oxford, Rebecca L. 2011. *Teaching and Researching: Language Learning Strategies*. Upper Saddle River, NJ: Pearson Education Limited.

Paredes, Américo, and Richard Bauman. 1972. *Toward New Perspectives in Folklore*. Austin: Published for the American Folklore Society by University of Texas Press.

Parman, Susan. 1972. "Sociocultural Change in a Scottish Crofting Township." PhD diss., Dept. of Anthropology, Rice University.

Parman, Susan. 1990. *Scottish Crofters: A Historical Ethnography of a Celtic Village*. Fort Worth: Holt, Rinehart and Winston, Inc.

Parman, Susan. 1993. "The Future of European Boundaries: A Case Study." In *Cultural Change and the New Europe: Perspectives on the European*

Community, ed. Thomas M. Wilson and M. Estellie Smith, 189–202. Boulder: Westview Press.

Parman, Susan. 2005. *Scottish Crofters: A Historical Ethnography of a Celtic Village*, 2nd ed. Fort Worth: Holt, Rinehart and Winston, Inc.

Paterson, John M. 1964. *The Gaels Have a Word for It! A Modern Gaelic Vocabulary of 2000 Words*. Glasgow: Dionnasg Gaidhlig na h-Alba [The Gaelic League of Scotland].

Paterson, John M. 1997 [1952]. *"Gaelic Made Easy": A Guide to Gaelic for Beginners: Part 1, Comprising 10 Lessons in Gaelic*. Glasgow: Gairm Publications.

Pollock, Irene. 2006. "The Acquisition of Literacy in Gaelic-medium Primary Classrooms in Scotland." Ph.D. thesis, University of Edinburgh.

Price, Adam, Caitríona Ó Torna, and Allan Wynne Jones. 1997. *The Diversity Dividend: Language, Culture and Economy in an Integrated Europe*. Brussels: European Bureau for Lesser Used Languages.

Pullum, Geoffrey K., 1991. "The Great Eskimo Vocabulary Hoax." In *The Great Eskimo Vocabulary Hoax and Other Irreverent Essays on the Study of Language*, ed. Geoffrey K. Pullum, 159–171. University of Chicago Press.

Rae, Chris. 1997. "My Observations on Gaelic TV in Scotland." 13 August. Accessed 2 February 2001. http://www.chrisrae.com/gaelictv.html.

"Rampant Scotland Newsletter." 2003. http://www.RampantScotland.com/letter.htm. Issue 309, 15 March.

Raymond, Joan. 1998. "Say What? Preserving Endangered Languages," *Newsweek* (US edition), 14.

Reyhner, Jon. 1999. "Introduction." In *Revitalizing Indigenous Languages*, ed. Jon Reyhner et al., v–xx. Flagstaff, AZ: Northern Arizona University. Accessed 1 May 2003. http://jan.ucc.nau.edu/~jar/RIL_Intro.html.

Robertson, John. 1997. "The Enlightenment above National Context: Political Economy in Eighteenth-century Scotland and Naples." *The Historical Journal* 40, 667–697.

Rogerson, Robert J., and Amanda Gloyer. 1995. "Gaelic Cultural Revival or Language Decline?" *Scottish Geographical Magazine* 111(1):46–53.

Romaine, Suzanne. 2006. "Planning for the survival of linguistic diversity." *Language Policy* 5 (4), 443–75.

Sabban, Annette. 1984. "Investigations into the syntax of Hebridean English." *Scottish Language* 3, 5–32.

Said, Edward W. 1978. *Orientalism*. New York: Vintage Books.

Sasse, Hans-Jürgen. 1992. "Theory of Language Death." In *Language Death: Factual and Theoretical Explorations with Special Reference to East Africa*, ed. Matthias Brenzinger, 7–30. Berlin: Mouton de Gruyter.

Schegloff, Emanuel A. 2007. *Sequence Organization in Interaction: A Primer in Conversation Analysis I*. Cambridge: Cambridge University Press.

Schieffelin, Bambi, Kathryn A. Woolard, and Paul Kroskrity, eds. 1998. *Language Ideologies: Practice and Theory*. New York: Oxford University Press.

"Scotland the Brand." n.d. Accessed 9 March 2003. http://www.scotlandthebrand.co.uk/.

Scottish Executive Enterprise and Lifelong Learning Department. 2001. "Adult Literacy and Numeracy in Scotland (2001)." Edinburgh: Scottish Executive. Accessed 23 February 2008. http://www.scotland.gov.uk/Resource/Doc/158952/0043191.pdf.

Searight, H. FF., C. M. A. Bathurts, and R. O. Noone. 1944. "A Contribution to the Anthropology of the Outer Hebrides." *Journal of the Royal Anthropological Institute* LXXIV:25–32.

Shaw, John. 1997. "The Ethnography of Speaking and Verbal Taxonomies: Some Applications to Gaelic." In *Celtic Connections. Proceedings of the 10th International Congress of Celtic Studies*, ed. Ronald Black, William Gillies and Roibeard Ó Maolalaigh, 308–23. East Linton: Tuckwell Press.

Shaw, John. 2003. "Gaelic Cultural Maintenance and the Contribution of Ethnography," *Scotia: Interdisciplinary Journal of Scottish Studies* 27, 34–48.

Shaw, Margaret Fay. 1999 [1977]. *Folksongs and Folklore of South Uist*. Edinburgh: Birlinn.

Shaw, William. 1972 [1778]. *An Analysis of the Gaelic Language*. Menston: Scolar Press.

Shields, Bob. 1999. "Get Us up the Isle: £711,000 EU grant to put the brides back into Hebrides." *Daily Record*, 6 February, 7.

Silverstein, Michael. 1976. "Shifters, Linguistic Categories, and Cultural Description." In *Meaning in Anthropology*, ed. Keith H. Basso and Henry A. Selby, 11–55. Albuquerque: University of New Mexico Press for School of American Research.

Silverstein, Michael. 1977. "The Limits of Awareness." Sociolinguistic Working Paper 84, Austin, TX: Southwest Educational Development Lab.

Silverstein, Michael. 1979. "Language Structure and Linguistic Ideology." In *The Elements: A Parasession on Linguistic Units and Levels*, ed. Paul R. Clyne, William F. Hanks and Carol L. Hofbauer, 193–247. Chicago: Chicago Linguistic Society.

Silverstein, Michael. 1985. "Language and the Culture of Gender: At the Intersection of Structure, Usage, and Ideology." In *Semiotic Mediation: Sociocultural and Psychological Perspectives*, ed. Elizabeth Mertz and Richard J. Parmentier, 219–259. Orlando: Academic Press, Inc.

Silverstein, Michael. 1987. *Monoglot "Standard" in America*. Chicago: Center for Psychosocial Studies.

Silverstein, Michael. 1996. "Monoglot 'Standard' in America." In *The Matrix of Language*, ed. Donald Brenneis and R. K. S. Macaulay, 284–306. Boulder: Westview Press.

Silverstein, Michael. 2003. "Indexical Order and the Dialectics of Sociolinguistic Life." *Language and Communication* 23, 193–229.

Sinclair, John. 1804. *Observations on the Propriety of Preserving the Dress, the Language, the Poetry, the Music, and the Customs, of the Ancient Inhabitants of Scotland: Addressed to the Highland Societies of London and of Scotland*. London: The Highland Society, W. Bulmer and Co.

Smakman, Dick and Cassie Smith-Christmas. 2008. "Gaelic Language Erosion and Revitalization on the Isle of Skye, Scotland." In *Proceedings XIIth conference of the Foundation for Endangered Languages*, ed. Tjeerd de Graaf, Nicholas Ostler & Reinier Salverda, 115–122. Leeuwarden: Fryske Akademy.

Smith, Angela. 1999. "STEP 1999: Evaluation of the Gaelic in the Community Scheme in the Western Isles and in Argyll and Bute." Comunn na Gàidhlig Placement Report. Stornoway: Comunn na Gàidhlig.

Smith, Christina A. 1948. *Mental Testing of Hebridean Children in Gaelic and English*. London: University of London Press, Ltd.

Smith-Christmas, Cassie. 2012. "I've lost it here *dè a bh' agam*: Language Shift, Maintenance, and Code-switching in a Bilingual Family." PhD thesis, University of Glasgow.

Smith-Christmas, Cassie and Dick Smakman. 2009. "Gaelic on Skye: Older speakers' identity in a language-shift situation." *International Journal of the Sociology of Language* 200, 27–47.

Smith, Maurice. 1994. *Paper Lions: The Scottish Press and National Identity*. Edinburgh: Polygon.

"Soft-Soaping the Gaels." 1992. *The Economist*, November 14, 70.

Sparling, Heather. 2003. "'Music is Language and Language is Music': Language Attitudes and Musical Choices in Cape Breton, Nova Scotia," *Ethnologies* 25 (2). Accessed 25 February 2008. http://www.erudit.org/revue/ethno/2003/v25/n2/008052ar.html.

Spolsky, Bernard. 2009. "Language Beliefs and the Management of Endangered Languages." Paper presented in the ELAP Workshop on Beliefs and Ideology in Endangered Languages, The Hans Rausing Endangered Languages Project, School for Oriental and African Studies, London, February.

Sproull, Alan. 1996. "Regional Economic Development and Minority Language Use: The Case of Gaelic Scotland." *International Journal of the Sociology of Language* 121, 93–117.

Sproull, Alan and Brian Ashcroft. 1993. *The Economics of Gaelic Language Development*. Glasgow Caledonian University.

Sproull, Alan, and Douglas Chalmers. 1998. *The Demand for Gaelic Artistic and Cultural Products and Services: Patterns and Impacts*. Department of Economics, Glasgow Caledonian University.

Statistics Canada. 2007. "Population by mother tongue, by province and territory (2006 Census): (Newfoundland and Labrador, Nova Scotia, Prince Edward Island)." Accessed 1 June 2011. http://www.statcan.gc.ca/tables-tableaux/sum-som/l01/cst01/demo11a-eng.htm.

Strand, Paul, and Basil Davidson. 1954. *Tir a' Mhurain*. New York: Aperture.

Street, Brian and Niko Besnier. 1994. "Aspects of Literacy." In *Companion Encyclopedia of Anthropology: Humanity, Culture, and Social Life*, ed. Tim Ingold, 527–62. London: Routledge.

Street, Brian V. 1995. *Social Literacies: Critical Approaches to Literacy Development, Ethnography, and Education*. Reading, MA: Routledge.

Street, R.L. and Howard Giles. 1982. "Speech Accommodation Theory: A Social Cognitive Approach to Language and Speech Behaviour." In *Social Cognition and Communication*, ed. M. Roloff and C. R. Berger, 193–226. Beverly Hills, CA: Sage.

Strubell, Miquell. 2001. "Catalan a Decade Later." In *Can Threatened Languages be Saved? Reversing Language Shift, Revisited: A 21st Century Perspective*, ed. J. A. Fishman, 260–83, Clevedon, UK: Multilingual Matters.

Stubbs, Michael. 1980. *Language and Literacy: The Sociolinguistics of Reading and Writing*. London: Routledge.

Stubbs, Michael. 1986. "A Matter of Prolonged Fieldwork: Notes towards a Modal Grammar of English." *Applied Linguistics* 7, 1–25.

Thompson, Frank. 1992. *History of An Comunn Gàidhealach: The First Hundred (1891–1991). Centenary of An Comunn Gàidhealach*. Inverness: An Comunn Gàidhealach.

Thomson, Derick S. 1951. *The Gaelic Sources of Macpherson's 'Ossian'*. Edinburgh and London: Oliver and Boyd for the University of Aberdeen.

Thomson, Derick S. 1964–66. "The Role of the Writer in a Minority Culture," *Transactions of the Gaelic Society of Inverness* 44, 246–271.

Thomson, Derick S. 1979. "Gaelic: Its Range of Uses." In *Languages of Scotland*, ed. A. J. Aitken and Tom McArthur, 14–25. Edinburgh: W & R Chambers.

Thomson, Derick S. 1984. *Why Gaelic Matters*. Edinburgh: The Saltire Society.

Thomson, Derick S. 1989. "Gaelic Publishing." *Scottish Language* 8, 34–41.

Thomson, Derick S. 1994a. "Attitudes to Linguistic Change in Gaelic Scotland." In *The Changing Voices of Europe: Social and Political Changes and Their Linguistic Repercussions, Past, Present and Future*, ed. M. Mair Parry, Winifred V. Davies and Rosalind A. M. Temple, 227–235. Cardiff: University of Wales Press, with Modern Humanities Research Association.

Thomson, Derick S. 1994b. "Gaelic. General Survey." In *The companion to Gaelic Scotland*, ed. Derick S. Thomson, 89–91. Glasgow: Gairm.

Thomson, Derick S., ed. 1996. *Alasdair Mac Mhaighstir Alasdair: Selected Poems*. Edinburgh: Scottish Academic Press Ltd. for the Scottish Gaelic Texts Society.

Thomson, Derick S. and Grimble, Ian, eds. 1968. *The Future of the Highlands*. London: Routledge & Kegan Paul.

Tovey, Hilary. 1988. "The State and the Irish Language: The Role of Bord na Gaeilge." *International Journal of the Sociology of Language* 70, 53–68.

Toynbee, Polly. 2000. "We can be English without falling into the racist trap." *The Guardian*, 12 January.

Trosset, Carol S. 1986. "The Social Identity of Welsh Learners." *Language in Society* 15, 165–92.

Tsitsipis, Lukas D. 1981. "Language Change and Language Death in Albanian Speech Communities in Greece: A Sociolinguistic Study." Ph.D. diss., University of Wisconsin-Madison.

Tsitsipis, Lukas D. 1998. *A Linguistic Anthropology of Praxis and Language Shift: Arvanítika (Albanian) and Greek in Contact*. Oxford: Clarendon Press.

UNESCO Institute for Statistics. n.d. "National Literacy Rates for Youths (15–24) and Adults (15+)." Accessed 14 June 2010. http://stats.uis.unesco.org/unesco/TableViewer/tableView.aspx?ReportId=210.

Urban, Greg. 2001. *Metaculture: How Culture Moves through the World*. Minneapolis, MN: University of Minnesota Press.

Ure, Jean. 1982. "Introduction: Approaches to the Study of Register Range." *International Journal of the Sociology of Language* 35, 5–23.

Urla, Jacqueline. 1993. "Cultural Politics in an Age of Statistics: Numbers, Nations, and the Making of Basque Identity." *American Ethnologist* 20 (4), 818–843.

Vakhtin, Nikolai. 2002. "Language Death Prognosis: A Critique of Judgment." *SKY Journal of Linguistics* 15, 239–250.

Vallee, F. G. 1954. "Social Structure and Organisation in a Hebridean Community. A Study of Social Change." PhD thesis, Dept. of Anthropology, London School of Economics.

Vathjunker, Sonja. 1992/93. "Review of An Stòr-Dàta Briathrachais Gàidhlig—The Gaelic Terminology Database, Vol. I." *Scottish Language* 11/12, 181–182.

Walker, Andrew Lockhart. 1998. "Chan ann tro Osmosas" [It's not through Osmosis], Letter to the editor. *Cothrom* 17 (Autumn), 35.

Walker, David. 1999. "Speak Easy: Behind the Prominence of Any Official Language is the Political Dominance of a Nation, as the French Government Shows Us on Bastille Day." *The Guardian*, 14 July.

Walker, Maud. 1973. "Social Constraints, Individuals, and Social Decisions in a Scottish Rural Community." PhD diss., University of Illinois at Urbana-Champaign.

Watson, Moray. 2009. Personal communication. E-mail, 3 August.

Weinreich, Uriel. 1953. *Languages in Contact: Findings and Problems*. New York: Linguistic Circle of New York.

Wenger, Etienne. 1998. *Communities of Practice*. Cambridge: Cambridge University Press.

Wenger, Etienne. 2006. "Communities of practice: A brief introduction." Accessed 11 November 2011. http://www.ewenger.com/theory/index.htm.

Wentworth, Roy G. 2005. *Rannsachadh air Fòn-eòlas Dualchainnt Ghàidhlig Gheàrrloch, Siorrachd Rois*. Dublin: Dublin Institute for Advanced Studies.

Whisnant, David E. 1983. *All that is Native & Fine: The Politics of Culture in an American Region*. Chapel Hill: University of North Carolina Press.

Wilce, James M. 2009. *Language and Emotion*. Cambridge, UK: Cambridge University Press.

Williams, Glyn, and Delyth Morris. 2000. *Language Planning and Language Use: Welsh in a Global Age*. Cardiff: University of Wales.

Williams, Tim. 1999. "Barbarous Brogues No More." *The Scotsman*, 3 June, 17.

Will, Vanessa K. A. 2012. "Why Kenny Can't *Can*: The Language Socialization Experiences of Gaelic-Medium Educated Children in Scotland." PhD diss., Depts. of Anthropology and Linguistics, University of Michigan.

Withers, Charles. 1984. *Gaelic in Scotland 1698–1981: The Geographical History of a Language*. Edinburgh: John Donald.

Withers, Charles W. J. 1988. *Gaelic Scotland: The Transformation of a Culture Region*. London: Routledge.

Wolff, Hans. 1959. "Intelligibility and Inter-ethnic Attitudes." *Anthropological Linguistics* 1, 34–41.

Womack, Peter. 1989. *Improvement and Romance. Constructing the Myth of the Highlands*. Houndmills, Basingstoke, Hampshire: Macmillan.

"Women's Rock: A chance to meet the Casanovas of the crofts." 1999. *The Times*, 5 February.

Woolard, Kathryn A. 1989. *Double Talk: Bilingualism and the Politics of Ethnicity in Catalonia*. Stanford, CA: Stanford University Press.

Woolard, Kathryn A. 1992. Language Ideology: Issues and Approaches. *Pragmatics* 2, 235–249.

Woolard, Kathryn A. and Bambi B. Schieffelin. 1994. "Language Ideology." *Annual Review of Anthropology* 23: 55–82.

Wuethrich, Bernice. 2000a. "Learning the World's Languages – Before They Vanish." *Science* 288 (5469), 1156–9.

Wuethrich, Bernice. 2000b. "Peering Into the Past, With Words." *Science* 288 (5469), 1158.

Index

100,000 speakers   100–111

additive bilingualism. *See* bilingualism as positive
adult learners
   Corsican   207
   Gaelic   26, 30, 36, 194, 238–241, 276, 299, 305, 311, 317, 322–324, 328, 329–330
      and Gaelic literacy   245–247, 252–258, 259
      and mentors   235–238
      socialized not to speak it   212–223; 223–234
      in Uist   199-201, 207–212
   Welsh   207, 241, 325
advocacy, by researchers   25
affect, affective. *See also* emotion
   definition   203
   domain and   9
   emotion versus   203
   language ideology and   201–204
   language learning and   331
   language shift and   294
   mismatch of   212, 221, 223
   negative   126–127, 129, 146, 207–208, 214–218, 220, 223, 228, 234, 235, 242, 245–246, 247, 256–257, 259, 260, 295, 323–324, 326, 332
   orientation   205–206, 213, 221, 222, 237, 262, 295
   positive   xiii, 125, 128, 233, 235–238, 242, 257, 259, 277, 295, 318, 326, 331
   socialization of   212, 223–234
   stance   116, 125–126, 128, 204, 206–207, 214–218, 219–223, 225, 228–229, 230, 232–235, 239, 257
alcohol   15, 40, 50, 54, 87
ancient language (trope)   32, 61, 76, 89, 104, 120, 125, 127, 129–132

An Comunn Gàidhealach   270, 271, 275, 279
animal, animal-like (trope)   67, 76–77, 78, 79–81, 117, 128–129
anthropology of emotion   203. *See also* emotion
Anthropology Today   103, 110
Anti-Gaelic Bingo   iv, xiv
anti-Gaelic rhetoric   170, 174
Antigonish   24, 309
Antigonish County   297, 308
anxiety   92, 207
Apple Macintosh computer   276, 283
Archaeologia Brittanica   118–119, 126. *See also* Lhuyd, Edward
archaeology   45, 119
Argyll & Bute   183, 184, 317
Australia   61, 69, 93
Australian indigenous languages   98

banks, banking   145, 186, 226–227
barbarous language (trope)   67, 78–81, 90, 119, 121, 129
Basque   145, 212
BBC Scotland   68, 72–74, 76, 85
Beaton, Reverend John   119, 131, 146
Benbecula   44, 45, 47, 55
Berneray   210, 242
best speakerhood   248, 250. *See also* literate speakerhood, ideology of
Bible, Gaelic   123, 146, 190, 262, 267
Bilingual Education Project   22, 252
bilingualism   145, 318. *See also* Gaelic-English bilingualism
   as linguistic lag   71
   and linguistic tip   18, 205
   as negative   87–89, 275–276
   as parallel monolingualisms   214, 265
   passive (receptive)   191, 194, 218, 324
   as positive   64, 125, 138–139
bilingual signs, Gaelic-English   72, 88–89, 94, 176

bird sounds (trope). *See* animal, animal-like
Blair, Tony   31, 153, 166, 174, 175, 177, 195
Bord na Gaeilge   144
Bòrd na Gàidhlig   138, 323
borrowing   10, 273, 280
Boswell, James   123
boundaries
   disciplinary   4, 33–35
   ethnic   31, 65, 76, 92, 114
   sociolinguistic   11, 15–16, 223–224, 229–230, 234, 238–240, 244, 323, 329
Bowmore   316, 327
Bràighe, Am   311
branding   155–156, 175
Breton language   37, 38, 101, 105
British Broadcasting Corporation. *See* BBC Scotland
Broadcasting Act 1990   158
broadsheet newspapers. *See* newspapers, broadsheet
brogue (trope)   90
Brora   10, 13, 18, 40
Brown, Allan   62–64, 74, 81, 83, 84, 86, 88, 90, 164, 176
Bun is Barr   305, 307, 308
by-naming. *See* nicknaming

California Master-Apprentice program   266, 305
Campbell, Robert   126
Canada
   census. *See* census, Canada
   emigration to   77
   French in   265, 309
   Nova Scotia. *See* Nova Scotia
   sociolinguistic ethnography of Gaelic   5, 19–20
Canadian-American Gael, The   311
Cape Breton   5, 9, 11, 15, 18, 19–20, 24, 38, 288, 289, 297, 308, 310, 312, 314
Careful Gaelic. *See* Gaelic language, registers & varieties of
Carloway   8–9, 9–10, 12, 15, 21, 39, 40, 225, 226, 243

Carmina Gadelica   47, 129
Castaway 2000   53–54
Casual Gaelic. *See* Gaelic language, registers & varieties of
Catalan   224, 244
Catawba Sioux   98
Catholic   6, 19, 24, 35, 310
cèilidh, cèilidh house   39, 47, 251
Celtic languages   84, 104, 105, 118, 119, 288. *See also* Irish, Manx, Breton, Welsh
Celtic studies   4, 36, 162
census
   Canada   288–289, 310
   Scotland   17, 111, 115–116, 179, 182, 206, 209, 210, 242, 252–253, 259–261, 262, 282, 324
   Scottish media use of   52–53, 62
   statistics, problems of   114, 194, 265, 266
Chewin' the Fat   85
childcare   22–23, 163, 183, 185, 189, 191, 299–302, 322
children
   and bilingualism   71, 88, 139
   birth order   19
   cessation of intergenerational transmission to   287–288, 289
   described by media   50, 61–62, 99, 101, 105, 106, 111, 114
   and EGIDS scale   292–296, 300–305, 306
   future success of   xiii, 214
   in Gaelic medium education   26–27, 320
   intergenerational transmission of Gaelic and   307, 311
   linguistic socialization of   19, 35, 41, 202, 205, 295, 308, 313, 322
   mockery of   16
   and nicknaming   39. *See also* nicknaming
   of learners   213, 219, 222–223, 323
   of native speakers   213, 220, 221, 223
   parents choosing English   xiii, 19, 20, 64, 168, 169
   research on   16–17
   socializing adults   296

Church Gaelic. *See* Gaelic language, registers & varieties of
Classical Gaelic. *See* Gaelic language, registers & varieties of
class, social   65, 69, 118, 173, 268–269
 classless   22
 and literacy   264
 middle class, Gaelic   76, 173, 267, 268
Clì Gàidhlig   201
CNAG. *See* Comunn na Gàidhlig
codeswitching, Gaelic-English   10–12, 39, 142, 225, 231, 265, 273–274, 276
 and mockery of Gaelic   83, 84, 86
 and indexicality   205
colour terminology   14
Comataidh Craoladh Gàidhlig   271
Comataidh Telebhisean Gàidhlig   271
Comhairle nan Eilean Siar   56, 184, 192
Comhairle nan Sgoiltean Àraich   271
Commission for Racial Equality   75
commodification, commodity
 of culture   154
 of Gaelic   31, 125, 140–145, 156, 161
 of the past   154, 174
Commonwealth   77, 210, 254
Communities, Culture and Heritage, Dept. of   305, 308
communities of practice   25–26, 27, 296, 300, 305, 328–331
 definition   296
community. *See also* communities of practice; crofting
 constituted through research   51
 definition in language revitalization   296
 definition as voluntary groups   183, 190, 192, 195
 egalitarian ideology in   269
 geographically-bounded Gaelic communities   4–20
 new Gaelic   20–33
 revitalization based in   315–332
 unexamined conceptions of   189–190, 193
 complaint tradition   156, 163–174

Comunn na Gàidhlig   31, 43–44, 52, 62, 89, 93, 138–145, 157–162, 164, 165, 175, 177, 182–185, 268, 270–275, 276, 278–283
confidence   17, 143, 152, 188, 194, 208, 219, 222, 234, 235, 236, 256, 258, 273, 301, 318, 326. *See also* morale
 self-confidence   159
consciousness, Gaelic   30, 136, 298
contempt, ideology of   68, 84, 92, 207, 256; definition   78
contestation   21, 33, 294
continuity
 of denigrating discourses   79, 80
 of language and culture   31, 70, 326, 330
 in language shift   202, 289, 319
 in research on Gaelic   4, 34–35
copious, copiousness (trope)   125, 132–135
Cornish   98
corpus planning   183, 187, 280
Corsican   xi, 25, 207–208
Courtesy Rule   12, 225. *See also* etiquette of accommodation
Coxon, Phillip   50
crofting   3, 5, 6, 8, 12, 16, 18, 20, 21–22, 27, 30, 31, 39, 40, 41, 45, 50, 56, 70, 225, 226, 237
cròileagan. *See* playgroup, Gaelic
cultural inferiority complex   69
Cùrsa Comais   28–29

Daily Mail, The   57, 165, 170, 171, 282
Daily Record, The   93
dance of disclosure   217, 229
death metaphor   96, 97, 99, 127, 128, 132. *See also* discourses of death; dying (trope); language death; living organism (trope)
decline (trope)   21, 52–53, 64, 101, 110, 111, 128, 167, 170, 182, 208, 288
deficit (trope)   78, 81–84, 135
deixis   165, 170–171, 174
demesne extension   8, 38

denigration. *See* discourses of death and denigration
development discourse, English and Gaelic   185–188, 192–193
dialect   10, 32, 37, 38, 70, 81, 84, 98, 101, 119, 231, 238, 249, 272–273, 280, 281, 282, 299, 315–327
dialogicality   66
dictionary, dictionaries   14, 26, 39, 82, 83, 94, 118–119, 120–121, 122, 137, 211, 248, 249, 252, 257, 273–274, 277, 281
diglossia   185
disagreement   22, 25. *See also* contestation
discourses of death & denigration   72, 75, 91, 96–99, 117, 145
  definition   65–66
  descriptions   77–91
discourses of revitalization & redemption   72, 75, 91, 116–118, 121, 124, 145
  definition   66
distancing (trope)   65, 75–77, 79, 87, 221–222, 228
domains
  critique of concept   8–9, 322
  definition   7
  of English use   7–9, 16
  of Gaelic use   7–8, 11, 33, 38, 185–186, 260, 270, 273, 275, 278, 282
  intergenerational transmission and   319
  loss of   152, 267
Dormant (EGIDS)   292, 293, 295, 297, 298
double-voiced discourse   172
Dunbar, William   79, 128, 129
Dùthchas Project   54–55, 57
dying (trope)   61, 63, 76, 77, 83, 96, 97, 98, 99, 112, 128, 132, 146, 163, 168

Earse, Erse, Ersche   79, 121, 122
East Sutherland Gaelic   10, 15, 18–19, 40, 98, 225, 236, 249–250, 273, 310

EBLUL. *See* European Bureau for Lesser-Used Languages
economic development, regional   17, 22, 31, 51, 54–55, 89, 140–144, 151–152, 155, 158–163, 169, 175, 180–181, 182–185, 255. *See also* Objective One
economics of language   143, 195. *See also* Grin, François; Sproull, Alan; Chalmers, Douglas
  and Gaelic development   43
  and revitalization   331
Economist, The   76, 99, 146, 165, 166, 171, 172, 174, 177
Edinburgh   28, 72, 85, 88, 92, 124, 164
education. *See also* Bilingual Education Project; Gaelic medium education (GME)
  academic field of   3
  Breton medium   38
  as a domain of language use   8, 10
  fragmentation of funding and policy in   24
  parents choosing Gaelic medium or not   23, 64
  and registers of Gaelic   32
  role in language shift   17
  secondary, role in Western Isles Gaelic language shift   16–17
  secondary, Sixth Year Studies   51
  tertiary, tenure-track academic positions in   41
EGIDS. *See* Expanded Graded Intergenerational Disruption Scale
Egypt, in Scottish pseudo-history   130
elites   310
Embo   10, 13, 18, 40, 249, 250
emigration   22, 77, 287, 288, 295
emotion   xiii, 202, 203, 327, 331–332. *See also* affect
  affect versus   203
  anthropology of   203, 206–207
  as an attribute of Gaelic   67, 81
  barrier to language revitalization   30, 109, 239–240, 256–257, 322, 323
  codeswitching and   11

endangered dialects 321. *See also* East Sutherland Gaelic; Islay Gaelic; endangered languages
Endangered Language Fund 99
endangered languages
   academic research on 99–103
   academic warnings about loss of 32, 100–103
   academic writing for general public about 97–98
   application of research to Nova Scotia Gaelic 287–314
   intergenerational transmission of 321
   journalism about 105–113
   science journalism about 104
endogamy 39
English
   answering in English 215, 216, 227, 232, 246
   borrowing from 10, 133, 136, 280
   calque on 279
   domains of use. *See* domains
   "English to strangers, Gaelic to locals". *See* Courtesy Rule
   habitual use in Gaelic immersion 29
   as language of Scotland 70
   official language 100
   shift from Gaelic to 5, 7, 14–20, 151–152, 206, 208, 288, 311. *See also* language shift
   in tertiary education 29
English language, registers & varieties of
   American 47
   East Sutherland English 38
   Hebridean English 272, denigration of 81
   Highland English 38–39, 272
   Island English (Lewis) 10
   Received Pronunciation (RP) 38
   Scottish English 81, 88, 117
   Standard English 10
   Scots. *See* Scots language
enterprise culture 180. *See also* Local Enterprise Companies; neoliberalism
Eriskay 44, 210, 242–243
Erse. *See* Earse, Erse, Ersche

"Eskimo words for snow" (trope) 135, 147
essentialism 31, 136
ethic of accommodation 12, 16. *See also* etiquette of accommodation
ethnicity, Gaelic 25, 65, 68–71, 72–75, 92, 268–269, 318, 325–327
ethnographic fieldwork, difficulty of 35
Ethnologue 290, 292, 313
etiquette of accommodation. *See also* linguistic accommodation
   Catalan 224
   definition 224
   Gaelic 30, 199–200, 224–234, 265, 323–324
   Hungarian and German 224
   Welsh 224, 244
European Bureau for Lesser-Used Languages 144–145, 176
European Commission 176, 184, 190
European Regional Development Fund 163, 183, 191
European Structural Funds 181, 183, 184, 194
European Union 6, 54–55, 144, 155, 163, 176, 183, 194, 272
Expanded Graded Intergenerational Disruption Scale (EGIDS) 290–295. *See also* Nova Scotia Gaelic EGIDS; Revitalization EGIDS
experts, expertise
   in language planning 192, 327
   linguists as 95, 100, 104–113
   in reported speech 172–174
   socializing novices 202–203, 204–205, 228, 233, 296, 331. *See also* language socialization
Extinct (EGIDS stage) 292–294, 297–299
extinct, extinction (trope) 61, 89, 91, 102, 107, 145, 165, 173
Eyak 98

fancy 22–23
fank 40, 44, 56
Féis an Eilein 311, 314
fluency xiii, 212, 257, 309, 311, 323

INDEX   369

folklore 4, 24, 44, 45, 46–49, 56, 129, 225, 250, 311
formal schooling 251, 253–254. *See also* education; literacy
Fraser of Allander Institute 141
French 81, 100, 146, 209, 232, 275, 288, 309, 327

"Gael farce" (trope) 86, 94
Gaelic
  compared to English 52, 63, 78–91, 132–135
  economy. *See* Gaelic economy, the
  ethnic identity. *See* identity, Gaelic ethnolinguistic
  goods and services. *See* Gaelic goods and services
  learning infrastructure 212, 323
  literacy. *See* literacy, Gaelic
  music 24, 50, 94, 134, 136, 161, 162, 176, 190, 299, 300, 311
  orthography. *See* orthography, Gaelic
  placenames. *See* placenames, Gaelic
  playgroup. *See* playgroup, Gaelic
  preschool. *See* preschool, Gaelic
  revitalization. *See* language revitalization
  song 24, 94, 124, 134, 146, 250, 262, 298
Gaelic Broadcasting Committee. *See* Comataidh Craoladh Gàidhlig
Gaelic College, The 24, 311, 314
Gaelic economy, the 31, 140–145, 157–163, 165, 174, 321
Gaelic-English bilingualism 124, 138–139
Gaelic-English bilinguals 9, 12, 85, 135, 174, 182, 185, 187, 188, 190, 193, 199, 209, 224, 225, 226, 227, 228, 238, 244, 246–247, 257, 260, 264, 268, 272, 273, 281, 330
Gaelic-English contact 17, 67
Gaelic goods and services 140, 142, 157, 175
"Gaelic granny" 213

Gaelic in the Community Scheme (Sgeama Gàidhlig 's a' Choimhearsnachd) 162–163, 182–185, 189–192
Gaelic language, registers & varieties of
  business Gaelic 187
  Careful Gaelic 10, 38
  Casual Gaelic 9, 38
  Church Gaelic 10
  Classical Gaelic 123, 127, 146
  development Gaelic 187. *See also* development discourse
  everyday Gaelic 187
  learners' Gaelic 244, 329
  "new Gaelic" 133, 275
  news-speak 187, 267
  professional Gaelic 33, 267–270, 278–282
  SMO Gaelic 281
  textbook Gaelic 10
  "tinker Gaelic" 9
Gaelic (Learners) Education 320
Gaelic mafia (trope) 173–174
Gaelic medium education (GME) 26–28, 30, 64, 72, 94, 111, 139, 157, 161, 163, 175, 176, 252, 265, 272, 315, 320, 321, 328. *See also* education
Gaelic medium unit 72, 99
Gaelic office 269–283
  English-language context of 270, 274–275
Gaelic Playgroup Association. *See* Comhairle nan Sgoiltean Àraich
Gaelic Society of London 124
Gaelic Television Committee. *See* Comataidh Telebhisean Gàidhlig
Gàidhlig aig Baile 305, 307, 308
Garden of Eden (trope) 131
German 37, 222, 224, 275, 288
GIDS. *See* Graded Intergenerational Disruption Scale; *See also* Expanded Graded Intergenerational Disruption Scale
Glasgow 27, 31, 41, 61, 68, 69, 72, 90, 92, 94, 139, 155, 239, 271, 320

Glasgow Caledonian University 53, 141
Glasgow Herald, The. See *Herald, The*
Glasgow University. *See* University of Glasgow
globalization 90, 96, 175
glocalization 326
GME. *See* Gaelic medium education (GME)
Golspie 10, 13, 18
governmentality
  definition 181
  and Gaelic revitalization 181
  surveys as 50
Graded Intergenerational Disruption Scale (GIDS) 287, 289–291. *See also* Expanded Graded Intergenerational Disruption Scale (EGIDS); Nova Scotia Gaelic EGIDS; Revitalization EGIDS
Great Depression 20
greetings, Gaelic
  evaluation of 231
  greeting card 273
  hallo 280
  madainn mhath 283
  routine 11
  telephone 278–281
  weather 231–232, 280–281
Grimsay 210, 242
Grin, François 143, 195
Guardian, The xiv, 76, 114

Hale, Kenneth 100, 102–103
Halifax 289, 297, 305, 313, 314
Harris 6, 13, 14, 16–17, 46, 48, 54, 92
Harris Tweed 6
heartland xiii, 318
  Cape Breton as 297
  definition 325
  heartlandism 31
  role in RLS 325–327
Herald, The 173
heritage
  centres 161
  cultural 191
  family 27

Gaelic as Scotland's 137
  language 293, 297–298, 309
  learner 313
  natural 57
  organizations 161
  and Thatcherism 153–155, 174–175
Highland Clearances 54, 251
Highland English 272. *See also* Highlands and Islands Enterprise (HIE)
Highlanders
  denigration & stereotypes of 66, 79, 116–117
  ethnolinguistic identity of 53
  language of 122, 134, 135
  racist criticism of 93
  as soldiers 147
Highlands and Islands 51
Highlands and Islands Development Board (HIDB) 22, 31, 38, 157, 158–159, 180, 182
Highlands and Islands Enterprise (HIE) 31, 141, 159, 180–181, 194
Highlands and Islands Objective One Partnership Programme (HIPP) 163, 183, 184, 189
Highland Society of London 124
Highland Society of Scotland 121, 124
hippies 24, 310
history and philosophy of science 95
home-family-neighbourhood-community nexus 291, 295, 307, 308, 320. *See also* GIDS
hospitality 12, 49–50, 230
humour
  about Gaelic 78, 83, 85–87, 94, 146, 171–172
  in Gaelic 11–12, 43, 133–135
Hungarian 37, 224
hybridity 31

Ibrox Stadium 62, 92
identity
  community 19
  confidence and 326

contextual   27, 265
Gaelic in Scottish   72–75, 136–138
heritage   293, 297, 298
local   5, 22
negotiation of   27
Gaelic learners'   29, 207
role of language in   31, 53
Scottish   72
theory of   21, 36, 205
ideological-affective. *See also* affect;
ideological-emotional barriers to
language revitalization
complex   139, 228
discourse   242
mismatch   223
stance   225
ideological-emotional barriers to
language revitalization   297, 312.
See also affect; ideological-affective
ideologies of language   65, 203
definition   203, 247–248
indexicality and   66
language shift and   203, 208, 235
nationalist   25, 71, 110–111, 124,
136–139, 177, 208, 214, 232, 327
idiolect (trope)   63, 84
Île ga Bruidhinn   315–332
immersion   296, 307, 311, 314, 315,
325–326
immigrants   39, 287, 311
imperialism   51
incomers   10, 22, 152, 224, 233, 234,
239, 269
Independent, The and *Independent on
Sunday, The*   99, 103, 105–111
indexicality, indexical, indexed   66,
77, 137, 152, 203, 215, 216, 225, 235,
242
definition   204–205
Innu-aimun   324
Innuttut   324
intensive care unit (trope)   99
intergenerational transmission   156,
202, 206, 294, 321
definition, expanded   295–296
Nova Scotia   11, 287–288, 307–309
prioritization of   28, 319–322
Shawbost   319

intertextuality   83, 94
Inverness   31, 46, 72, 86, 139, 160, 251,
271, 272, 275, 278–279, 283
Inverness Courier   134
Ionad Chaluim Chille Île   316, 318
Irish language   25, 84, 97, 105,
107, 108, 119, 122, 144, 146, 175,
263–264, 288–289
and death metaphor   127
Islay   81, 315–318, 332
Islay Gaelic   315–332

Jacobite   69, 124
Jock (trope)   171–172
Johnson, Samuel   121–123, 132, 146
Johnstone Report   139
joking. *See* humour

kill, murder (trope)   98–99
kinship, Gaelic   6, 12–14, 39
Krauss, Michael   100–107

Labrador   324
language as behaviour   12
language attitudes   16, 244
language as behaviour   3, 7, 8, 11–13,
36–38, 97, 99, 112, 114, 126, 140,
156, 175, 185, 194, 201–207,
223–228
language choice   7, 9, 29, 228, 271
choosing English-medium education   64, 168
choosing Gaelic-medium education   64
and neoliberalism   169
language-culture complex   110, 169,
325–326
language death. *See also* language
obsolescence; *See also* language
shift; *See also* discourses of death
and denigration
Gaelic-Arvanítika Model of   40
metaphors of   96–99
not a preferred term   95
poetics of   170
scientistic discourse of   100–111
language and emotion   203. *See
also* emotion

language ideology. *See* ideologies of language
language object. *See* objectification
language obsolescence 97, 99, 113. *See also* language death; language shift
   definition 95
language planning 3, 25, 27, 31, 33, 35, 61, 72, 76, 124, 140, 144–145, 156–157, 161–162, 175, 179, 182, 185, 189–192, 223, 260, 268, 270, 319, 322
language revitalization xi, xiii, 4, 43, 52–53, 65, 72, 124, 125, 126, 140, 143, 159, 163, 165, 201, 239, 241, 271, 282, 289, 312. *See also* reversing language shift (RLS)
   definition xi, 289, 319
   ethnographic perspective 267–268
   language socialization and 202
   literacy and 260, 262
   metaculture and 115
   nationalism and 137
   new Gaelic communities 20–33
   proposal for community-based 315–332
   Revitalization EGIDS 292–294
language shift 34, 35, 36, 53, 89, 92, 112, 151, 152, 162, 187, 191, 192, 208, 212–234, 239, 252, 324, 327
   affect and ideology as components of 201–204, 239, 331–332
   cultural retreat model of 17
   definition 95, 202, 318
   erasing social causes of 91, 165–166, 168–169, 174, 175
   Gàidhealtachd model of 17, 151
   gender and 40
   indexicality and 203, 205
   language socialization and 201
   negative affect and 207, 256
   uneven process of 205–206
language socialization 41, 257
   definition 201–202
   expert-novice relationships 296, 308
   family context and 212–223
   ideologies and emotions in 331
   language shift and 204–206
   literacy and 246–247
   local context and 223–234
   mentors and 237
language worker 267, 269, 275, 278
last speaker (trope) 97, 98
learner. *See* adult learner
LEC. *See* Local Enterprise Company
legitimate peripheral participation (LPP) 328–332. *See also* communities of practice
Lewis 6, 10, 13, 14, 16, 18, 37, 38, 40, 41, 45, 90, 208, 225, 226, 242, 245, 315, 319, 320
lexicon, Gaelic
   development discourse 188–189
   evaluations of 275
   register and 32–33
   verbal art and 250
Lhuyd, Edward 118–120, 123, 126–127, 130–132
linguistic accommodation 12, 16, 30, 190, 192, 220, 224–229, 233–235, 243–244, 265, 323
linguistic anthropology xi, xiv, 3, 43, 203, 287, 288, 325, 331
linguistic lag as an ethnic marker 70–71
linguistic "tip" 18–19, 206, 313
literacy. *See also* non-literacy
   English literacy 76, 136, 247–249, 253–256, 258
   Gaelic literacy 10, 26, 35, 87, 188, 192, 238, 244, 245–247, 251–253, 256–265, 273–274, 283, 312, 332
literate speakerhood, ideology of 244, 249, 250, 257–258. *See also* literacy
   definition 246–247
   impacting language revitalization 259–264
living organism (trope) 97, 98–99, 125, 126–128
loan-word 82, 85, 91, 125, 133, 136, 273–274
local enterprise companies (LECs) 142, 159, 169, 181, 183, 194

local language, Gaelic as a 20, 323
Lowlanders
　mocking Highlanders 66–67, 94, 116–117, 126

Mabou 11, 19, 288
MacGregor, Alasdair Alpin 49–50
MacIntyre, Duncan Ban 124, 131, 134–135
Maclean, Reverend John 118–120, 128–129
MacMhaighstir Alasdair, Alasdair 120, 124, 126, 131
Macpherson, James 121–124, 132, 134
Macpherson, John Alick 62, 64, 76, 128, 138, 140, 164, 167–168, 170
Maighstir Seathan. See Maclean, Reverend John
Major, John 153, 177
Manx 84, 98
Margaree 314
Master-Apprentice program. See California Master-Apprentice program
matched guise 4, 16
Max Planck Institute for Evolutionary Anthropology 105
Max Planck Institute for Psycholinguistics 104–108
measurable outcomes 181, 190–191, 190–192
media coverage of Gaelic 25, 32, 52–56, 61–92, 95–113, 125–145, 156, 163–176, 310
men 9, 37, 40, 130, 322 *and passim*
Menter a Busnes 144
metaculture 115–145
　definition 115
metaphor xiii, 77–84, 96–99, 117, 126–129, 140–145, 156, 292, 332
metapragmatic
　beliefs 23
　discourse 115, 127, 168
　filter 20, 203
　theme 125
　views, definition 19

methodologies 4, 9, 36, 262
middle class, Gaelic. See class, Gaelic social
misrepresentation 52–55
mock Gaelic 85–86, 94. See also humour
mock Spanish 85, 94
Mòd, the. See Royal National Mòd
moladh. See panegyric poetry, Gaelic
monolingualism, ideology of 87–89
　definition 139–140
morale 17, 147, 152, 245. See also confidence
Moribund (EGIDS stage) 100, 293, 299
mother tongue 214, 288–289, 291, 295
motivation
　for learning Gaelic 29, 212, 223–224, 236, 268, 326, 330
　for research 49, 52
Mull 119–120
mutual intelligibility 244

naming 12–14, 70. See also nicknaming
　institutional 92
National Gaelic Arts Project. See Pròiseact nan Ealan
National Heritage Act 1983 154
nationalism, Scottish. See ideologies of language, nationalist
nationalist ideologies of language. See ideologies of language, nationalist
National Trust for Scotland 154
Native American languages 93. See also Eyak, Catawba Sioux, Navajo, Tlingit, Wappo
native speakers 21, 29–30, 35, 98, 133, 186, 201, 213, 214, 237, 240, 241, 244, 245–247, 272, 280, 311, 325, 329
natural (trope) 32, 67, 76–77, 79–81, 93, 125
Navajo 101. See also Native American languages
negative affect. See affect, negative

neighbourhood   8, 18, 289, 290–291, 295, 307–308, 318, 320–323
neoliberalism
   definition   153, 179–180
   and Gaelic development   31–32, 56, 140, 156, 163–169, 174–176, 182–193, 321
   in Scotland   140, 142, 153–156, 180–182
neutralistic stance   63, 68, 168
"new Gaelic". *See* Gaelic language, varieties & registers of
New Labour   153, 155, 166, 174–175, 180, 195
"Newsnight Scotland"   61–64, 65, 68–69, 73, 74–75, 78, 83, 84, 89, 90, 128, 132, 137–138, 140, 156, 164–166, 168–169, 170, 176
newspapers
   broadsheet   75–76, 85, 93
   tabloid   57, 72, 75–76, 80, 86, 90, 93, 165, 169, 170, 282
new speakers   318, 326–327
nicknaming   12–14, 39
non-literacy   256, 258. *See also* literacy
North Shore   11, 19, 24, 288, 307
North Uist   44–45, 47–48, 50, 54–55, 57, 184, 209, 210, 242, 272
Nova Scotia   15, 18, 19, 24, 39, 139, 266, 287–312
Nova Scotia Gaelic EGIDS   297–309
novice
   definition   202–203
   in language socialization   204, 296, 302, 312, 331

objectification   51, 76–79, 96
Objective One   184, 189, 191–192. *See also* Highland and Islands Objective One Partership Programme (HIPP)
   definition   194–195
obscenities   72–73, 93
100,000 speakers   100–111
oral tradition   4, 39, 46–48, 250, 287, 312
orthography, Gaelic   86, 122–123

Ossian   121, 122, 123–124, 132, 134
othering, the Other   76, 85
outmigration   16. *See also* emigration
outsiders   11, 24–25, 223, 269, 326

panegyric poetry, Gaelic   118, 120, 124, 129–131, 134–135, 146
parallel monolingualisms. *See* bilingualism as parallel monolingualisms
Parliament, Scottish. *See* Scottish Parliament
Parliament, UK. *See* UK Parliament
pastoral   97, 99
past, the   48, 71, 77, 78, 89–91, 104–105, 129–132, 133, 153–154, 174, 264, 326
patois   63, 74, 84
patronymic   12–13
peasant (trope)   69–70, 226, 268, 282
Pedersen, Roy   159–163, 176
personation, in Irish verbal art   263
Pictou County   297
placename, Gaelic   92
playgroup, Gaelic (*cròileagan*)   23, 184, 189
poetics of statistics   111, 170
politeness   12, 224–225, 243, 246. *See also* etiquette of accommodation
positive affect. *See* affect, positive
poverty   18, 61, 69, 152, 270
power   8, 17, 22, 33–34, 56, 114, 152, 173, 204, 205, 249, 327
Presbyterian   6, 7, 10, 19, 35, 39, 40, 199
prescriptive   25, 248
preschool, Gaelic   161, 179, 301
Press and Journal, The   75
Press Complaints Commission   74–75
press release   52–53, 139, 143, 274
prior ideological clarification   23
professional Gaelic. *See* Gaelic language, registers & varieties of
professional Gaels   267–270, 282. *See also* language workers
Pròiseact nan Ealan   157, 271
Protestant   24, 267, 310
pushiness   23, 234

quasi-NGOs 51

racism 73, 74, 94
Radio nan Gàidheal 271, 274, 282–283
Reawakened (EGIDS scale) 295, 300
received pronunciation (RP) English. *See* English language, registers & varieties of
receptive bilinguals 324. *See also* bilingualism, passive (receptive)
redemptive discourse. *See* discourses of revitalization and redemption
Re-established (EGIDS scale) 294–295, 301
regional economic development. *See* economic development, regional
register 255. *See also* Gaelic language, registers & varieties of
  definition 267
  formation 267
Reintroduced (EGIDS scale) 295, 299, 300
remoteness, construction of 52, 53–54, 55–56, 76
research ethics 34, 48–49
research fatigue 34, 49
reversing language shift (RLS). *See also* Graded Intergenerational Disruption Scale (GIDS)
  adult Gaelic learners and 30
  definition 289, 319
  economic development and 160, 192
  "heartlands" and 325–327
  in Nova Scotia 287–313
  practical challenges 322–325
  theoretical challenges 320–322
Revitalization EGIDS 294–295. *See also* Expanded Graded Intergenerational Disruption Scale (EGIDS); Nova Scotia Gaelic EGIDS; *See also* Nova Scotia Gaelic EGIDS
Revitalized (EGIDS scale) 295, 301, 302

Royal Mail 275
Royal National Mòd 86–87, 169–170, 275
Russell, Mike 62–64, 76, 88, 137, 164, 168–169

Sabhal Mòr Ostaig 28–29, 237, 243, 269, 272, 273, 277, 280, 281–282, 307, 325
Safe (EGIDS) 292–293
safe (Krauss) 100–102
schooled literacy 249, 252, 254, 256–257, 260, 264, 265
Science 103–108
scientistic discourse. *See* language death, scientistic discourse of
Scotland the Brand 155
Scots language 92, 117, 136
Scotsman, The 73, 85, 92, 106–108, 282
Scottish census. *See* census, Scotland
Scottish Council for Research in Education 16
Scottish English. *See* English language, registers & varieties of
Scottish Geographical Magazine 52
Scottish identity. *See* identity, Scottish
Scottish nationalism. *See* ideologies of language, nationalist
Scottish National Party 62, 136, 137
Scottish Natural Heritage 154, 167
Scottish Parliament, Gaelic debate in
  72, 83, 88, 94, 137, 146
Scottish Television 72
Scottish Tourist Board 154, 155
semantic re-calibration 14
semi-speakers 191, 194, 236, 273
  definition 19
shame 30, 123, 207, 208, 218, 229, 233, 235, 244, 256–258. *See also* affect, negative
Shawbost report 319, 321, 325, 327
Shell Corporation 195
SIL International 290, 313
Skye 6, 14, 21, 22, 27, 28, 38, 39, 40, 44, 57, 74, 99, 142, 159, 237, 269, 272, 273, 281, 320

sloinneadh. *See* patronymic
social Darwinism, linguistic 109, 165
  as a discourse of death 89–91
Society in Scotland for Propagating Christian Knowledge 120, 121
sociolinguistic boundaries 224, 228, 229, 234, 238–240, 323, 329
sociolinguistic mentor 235–238, 240, 317
  definition 235
Sorbian 30–31
Spanish. *See* mock Spanish
Sproull, Alan 43, 141–143, 145
stance, affective. *See* affective stance
standard language, ideology of 66, 81–84, 91, 94, 146, 185–186, 188, 249, 281
  definition 125
  and Samuel Johnson 122–123
"Star Trek: The Next Generation" 72
statistics. *See* census
stereotypes 32, 48, 52, 55, 66–67, 71, 92, 244
  formation of 66
St. Francis Xavier University 310, 314
Stòr-Data Briathrachais Gàidhlig, An 277. *See also* dictionary, dictionaries
Stornoway 17, 18, 46, 54, 233, 242, 271, 272
Strathclyde University 45, 52, 141, 243
subtractive bilingualism 139. *See also* bilingualism as negative
Sunday Mail, The 86, 93, 165, 169, 170
Sunday Times, The 62, 74, 76, 86, 93
surveys 8, 9, 16, 26, 30, 44, 56, 143, 201, 245, 288, 311, 319, 320, 322–323, 327
  problems with 3, 37, 38

tabloid newspapers. *See* newspapers, tabloid
taigh-cèilidh. *See* cèilidh, cèilidh house
Taransay 54, 57
tartan, tartanism 70, 311
tertiary education 29, 161, 328

teuchter (trope) 69, 92
Thatcherism 31, 152–155, 157–158, 174–175, 180, 321
Thatcher, Margaret 140, 153, 165–166, 179
Times Higher Education 52
"tip". *See* linguistic tip
Tlingit 256
Tobar an Dualchais 56
Total Immersion Plus (TIP) 266, 305
tourism 129, 154, 155, 175, 181, 318
  cultural 161, 162
train-spotting (trope) 169, 177
transcription conventions 243

Ubykh 98
Údarás na Gaeltachta 144
Uist 52, 54–55, 209, 210
UK Government 137, 157, 163, 177, 180, 194, 195
UK Parliament 154, 277
Ùlpan 266, 315, 317, 323, 329
understanders 202, 316, 324. *See also* receptive bilinguals
UNESCO 262, 263, 290–291
Union of 1707 69
University College of Cape Breton 314
University of Aberdeen 243
University of Edinburgh 48, 159, 243
University of Glasgow 45, 119, 243
University of the Highlands and Islands 28
Urdu 73, 138
"us" (trope) 171. *See also* deixis; "we"

Veljanovski, Cento 158
village 8, 9, 10, 13–14, 15–16, 18, 22, 25, 33, 202, 224, 249, 270, 275, 289, 296, 318
Visit Scotland. *See* Scottish Tourist Board

Wales 45, 57, 72, 92, 118, 144–145, 154, 166, 183, 192, 213, 243
Wappo 98
"we" (trope) 77, 137. *See also* deixis; "us"

Welsh   37, 90, 94, 105, 118, 122, 144, 158, 166, 169, 175, 193, 201, 207, 213, 224, 241, 244, 288, 313, 325, 326
Western Isles (na h-Eileanan Siar)   xiv, 16, 30, 31, 41, 44, 46, 50, 53, 110, 159, 182–183, 185, 187, 188, 191, 199, 209, 212, 228, 252, 257
Western Isles Council. *See* Comhairle nan Eilean Siar
West Highland Free Press   74, 75
White Paper on Broadcasting   157
Wodrow, Reverend Robert   119
women   15, 17, 22, 37, 40, 45, 50, 55, 118, 210, 322
Wordsworth, Dorothy   128
world language   263, 327

A' co-cheangal leughdairean
ri cànan is cultar na Gàidhlig
air feadh an t-saoghail

Airson tuilleadh leabhraichean, tadhailibh air

bradanpress.com

*Connecting readers worldwide
with Gaelic language and culture*

For more titles, visit

bradanpress.com

www.ingramcontent.com/pod-product-compliance
Lightning Source LLC
Chambersburg PA
CBHW071949070526
44583CB00015B/1123